With very best wishes,

[illegible]

CRAFT GUILDS IN THE EARLY MODERN LOW COUNTRIES

Craft Guilds in the Early Modern Low Countries

Work, Power, and Representation

Edited by

MAARTEN PRAK, CATHARINA LIS,
JAN LUCASSEN, AND HUGO SOLY

ASHGATE

Published by
Ashgate Publishing Limited
Gower House
Croft Road
Aldershot
Hampshire GU11 3HR
England

Ashgate Publishing Company
Suite 420
101 Cherry Street
Burlington, VT 05401–4405
USA

Ashgate website: http://www.ashgate.com

British Library Cataloguing in Publication Data
Craft guilds in the early modern Low Countries : work, power and representation
1. Guilds – Netherlands – History 2. Guilds – Belgium – History
3. Netherlands – Economic conditions 4. Belgium – Economic conditions
5. Netherlands – Social conditions 6. Belgium – Social conditions
7. Netherlands – History 8. Belgium – History
I.Prak, Maarten Roy, 1955–
338.6'32'09492

ISBN–10: 0 7546 5339 0

Library of Congress Cataloging-in-Publication Data
Craft guilds in the early modern low countries : work, power and representation / edited by Maarten Prak ... [et al.].
p. cm.
Includes bibliographical references and index.
ISBN 0–7546–5339–0 (alk. paper)
1. Guilds – Benelux countries – History.
I. Prak, Maarten Roy, 1955–

HD6473.B425P73 2006
338.6'32094920903–dc22 2005031652

ISBN 0 7546 5339 0

Printed and bound in Great Britain by Antony Rowe Ltd, Chippenham, Wiltshire

Table of contents

List of tables, figures and maps

Tables

Figures

Maps

About the authors

Sandra Bos has a PhD from the Vrije Universiteit Amsterdam and is currently working for the United Nations in Nairobi, Kenya

Johan Dambruyne has a PhD from the Universiteit Gent, and now works as a researcher at the Heritage Unit and Municipal Archives in Malines

Harald Deceulaer has a PhD from the Vrije Universiteit Brussel and works at the Algemeen Rijksarchief in Brussels

Bert De Munck is lecturer in the History Department at the Universiteit Antwerpen

Catharina Lis is Professor of History at the Vrije Universiteit Brussel

Piet Lourens is researcher at the Internationaal Instituut voor Sociale Geschiedenis, Amsterdam

Jan Lucassen is senior researcher at the Internationaal Instituut voor Sociale Geschiedenis, Amsterdam, and professor of Social History at the Vrije Universiteit Amsterdam

Bibi Panhuysen has a PhD from the Universiteit Utrecht and is currently coordinator at Imagine IC, an organization for immigrants and their cultures

Maarten Prak is Professor of Social and Economic History at the Universiteit Utrecht

Hugo Soly is Professor of History at the Vrije Universiteit Brussel

Alfons K.L. Thijs is emeritus Professor of History at the Universiteit Antwerpen

Preface

This book is the result of a project that began about ten years ago. In the early 1990s, the editors, for a variety of reasons, became independently interested in craft guilds and their historical evolution. In 1995 we decided to join forces and submitted a research proposal to the *Vlaams-Nederlands Comité* (VNC), a joint committee of the Dutch and Flemish National Research Councils, NWO and FWO. We received a grant that allowed us to appoint two junior researchers who would both write a PhD-thesis on tailors and the clothing industry, in the Northern and Southern Netherlands respectively. Bibi Panhuysen and Harald Deceulaer duly produced their books, which were published in 2000 and 2001. Equally important, the project funding also allowed us, the two PhD-students, and some other colleagues to meet several times a year over a four-year period, for intensive discussions on our topic. We fondly remember the contributions made to those discussions by Sandra Bos, Johan Dambruyne, Karel Davids, Ritske Mud, Eric Palmen, Erwin Steegen, Marianne Vanbellingen, Karin Van Honacker, Bart Willems, and especially Marc Jacobs, as well as the lively meals we shared afterwards. We are grateful to the Internationaal Instituut voor Sociale Geschiedenis in Amsterdam, the Vrije Universiteit Brussel and the Universiteit Utrecht for supporting the research of the other members of the team.

The books by Bibi Panhuysen and Harald Deceulaer were the direct outcome of the VNC-project, but obviously our efforts produced many other results, which were published in numerous articles, as well as two Dutch-language volumes edited by Catharina Lis and Hugo Soly. Their titles will be found in the bibliography of this book. It seemed to us, however, that the project should be properly terminated with a coherent volume, in English, that brought all our results together. This is the book now in front of you.

This book took far longer to produce than we initially expected. In the process, we incurred many debts. We are grateful, first of all, to our authors, who patiently awaited the publication of their work. Three anonymous reviewers made valuable suggestions for improving the manuscript when the book was reviewed for publication. We want to thank Chris Gordon for translating chapter 2, and Lee Mitzman for translating most of the rest of the book. The English of chapter 3 and the Conclusion was edited by Phyllis Albert Mitzman. Giota Bekiaraki provided much-needed editorial assistance. The Dutch National Research Council NWO financed the translation. Bert Heesen efficiently prepared the manuscript for publication; his work was financially supported by Utrecht University. Last but not least, we are grateful to our editors at Ashgate, Thomas Gray, Anne Keirby and Celia Hoare, (etc) who, by accepting the book for publication, have helped make our work accessible to the many fellow-historians who share our interest in, and enthusiasm for the history of craft guilds.

Finally a short note on geography: the Low Countries, by which we mean the territory more or less covered by present-day Belgium and the Netherlands, were for a short time (between 1543 and 1572, and again between 1815 and 1830) united as one country. For most of the period treated by this book, however, they went their separate ways. Because 'Belgium' and 'the Netherlands' were only introduced in the nineteenth century, we have variously used Southern, Spanish (until 1713) and Austrian (from 1713) Netherlands for the territory that is now Belgium, and Northern Netherlands or Dutch Republic for what is now the Netherlands. The word 'Dutch' refers in this book exclusively to the Northern Netherlands. Whenever 'Low Countries' is used, we mean to refer to all of the Netherlands, North and South combined.

Maarten Prak, Catharina Lis, Jan Lucassen, Hugo Soly
April 2005

Chapter 1

Craft guilds in comparative perspective: the Northern and Southern Netherlands, a survey

Catharina Lis and Hugo Soly

Few institutions have been so omnipresent as craft guilds in the lives of such a multitude of city dwellers in so many European countries during the late Middle Ages and early modern period — and even well into the nineteenth century in Germany. These institutions operated as local forces in military, religious, economic, social, political, and cultural circles. Admittedly, they lost some ground after 1500: the guild-based militias gradually made way for professional armies, and direct or indirect participation by master artisans in local politics was curtailed in many cities. Nonetheless, craft guilds nearly everywhere continued to have several functions simultaneous. It is precisely their longevity and their tendency to assert their influence in so many fields that makes them so difficult to comprehend. Over the past two centuries, craft guilds have surfaced repeatedly on the research agenda, leaving fundamental questions unanswered time and again. More accurately, divergent and often conflicting explanations have been provided for their emergence and their centuries of existence. These discrepancies arise largely from the different ways that such organizations are defined.

Max Weber considered monopolizing local industrial production to be the central issue: 'A guild is an organization of craft workers specialized in accordance with the type of occupation. It functions through undertaking two things, namely, internal regulation of work and monopolization against outsiders. It achieves its objective if everyone joins the guild who practices the craft in the location in question.'[1] While universal membership was undoubtedly of decisive importance for specific groups of producers in certain periods, the economic scope of guilds was far broader. In many cases craft guilds tried to control and organize the local market, based on moral criteria indicating what was socially acceptable, and what was not.[2] Nor were craft guilds exclusively or even primarily occupational associations. Some have argued that in cities where these organizations were involved in political decision-making, membership had little or nothing to do with professional activities but was in fact a vehicle

---

1 Weber, 1961, p. 110.

2 See the pertinent remarks by Maurice Aymard, quoted in Haupt, 2002, pp. 12-13.

toward obtaining positions of power. Some craft guilds thus served mainly as political lobbies that protected the interests of citizens.[3] The socio-cultural and ideological dimensions of urban corporatism were also considerable. Craft guilds often started out as religious confraternities. Even when devotional practices later no longer proved to be their main *raison d'être*, they remained primordial in Catholic countries.[4] Regardless of the religious context, two socio-cultural elements were consistently placed high on the agenda for most craft guilds: mutual aid and sociability. During the pre-industrial period, membership of a craft guild was one of the primary channels for the 'middling sort of people' to acquire and realize social and cultural capital as well as economic capital, obviously with varying degrees of success but always within a context of collective practices conducive to the formation of a group identity.[5]

The dominant functions of craft guilds at a certain stage do not automatically explain their origins or survival. The progressive trend among guild-based organizations during the eighteenth century of operating as insurance providers (see below), for example, was not the reason behind their establishment in previous centuries. An additional complication is that different craft guilds in the same city might adopt widely discrepant economic, social, political, and cultural positions. The multiform nature of these institutions may be considered from a deterministic as well as from a voluntaristic perspective: either as institutions that conformed to a historical dynamic modulated by balances of power over which they had little or no control or as institutions constructed and transformed by powerful, goal-oriented actors in keeping with their changing needs and ambitions. The intertwinement of politico-institutional, socio-economic, and cultural-ideological dimensions suggests that views of craft guilds are by definition influenced by the world views of historians and by contemporary standards and values. This is all the more true, because the craft guilds declined during the transition to the capitalist society to which researchers pertain. As a result, observations about such organizations are in fact always current.

1. Historiographic traditions and revisionism

This chapter is not intended as a comprehensive historiographic account covering the political-ideological positions (which are rarely formulated explicitly) of the authors concerned.[6] Until well into the twentieth century, however, ideas about craft guilds centred around two contradictory perceptions that historians have come increasingly to reject. On the one hand, craft guilds have conjured up images of 'a world we have

---

3 In his contribution to this volume, Maarten Prak argues that the origins and further development of craft-guilds owed as much to politics as to economic developments. See also Prak, 1999, pp. 22-7, 317-20.

4 Farr, 2000, pp. 258-9.

5 See the interesting comments in Barry, 1994, pp. 1-27 and 84-112.

6 Black, 1984; Oexle, 1982, pp. 1-44; Mozzarelli, 1988; Lambrechts, 1994, pp. 143-55; Bainbridge, 1996, pp. 1-21; Crossick, 1996, pp. 105-38; Ehmer, 1998, pp. 19-35.

lost' since the mid-nineteenth century. Even though the authors concerned differ on many issues, they all observe that these institutions were characteristic of an era in which elites and the 'middling sort of people' shared an ideological commitment toward the local community. Small-scale production and dedication to quality curtailed competition between members of the same guild and enabled them to act unanimously both to protect their own privileges and in matters that concerned the local community as a whole. Even though master artisans were not always politically influential in all communities, they were in a position to speak out and to manifest themselves as the backbone of urban society. Some historians — including Henri Pirenne — have even argued that craft guilds provided the foundations for 'urban democracies' in the Low Countries during the thirteenth and fourteenth centuries.[7] A history of guild-based organizations has been written from this perspective featuring heroes and martyrs and specific *lieux de mémoire*, especially the Battle of the Golden Spurs at Kortrijk (1302)[8] and the execution of Frans Anneessens in Brussels (1718),[9] about Flanders and Brabant. These historians have invoked cultural and ideological ideals and values that they considered all but abandoned during their own era: security, solidarity, honour, respectability, and, to some authors, uncontested religiosity. The historiographic tradition of nostalgic reflection about craft guilds remains interesting because of the effort to demonstrate that alternatives to modernity and capitalism were conceivable and possible. As such, these works may be read as a critique of modern society.

Another historiographic tradition burdens the craft guilds with all the sins of Israel. Critics justify this accusation by arguing that the craft guilds were not future-oriented and could therefore not be part of modernity, or that they impeded economic progress and consequently the rise of capitalism. While such reservations were already expressed in the context of mercantilism and the Enlightenment, they grew much harsher during the nineteenth and early twentieth centuries and came to cover all aspects of the corporative system, at least with respect to the early modern period. Henri Pirenne and other historians were in fact inclined to label craft guilds as positive forces until the mid-fourteenth century or even until around 1400. After that point, however, these organizations declined in their view and became prototypes of economic exclusivism, social conservatism, political particularism, and ideological bigotry.[10] Whenever fundamental changes endangered their positions, artisans — masters and journeymen alike — were said to cling to their traditional rights. In other words, in their rare appearances as actors, they seemed to be cast in the wrong play and failed to influence the course of history constructively. All they could do was block innovations, or rather contain them. Such positions are formulated primarily by economic historians that focus on cities where major export industries were guild-based during

---

7 Pirenne, 1910.

8 Tollebeek, 2002, pp. 194-239; Tollebeek and Verschaffel, 2002, pp. 183-205.

9 Wertheim Gijse-Weenink, 1984, pp. 408-34.

10 Pirenne, 1922, pp. 436-8; 1919, p. 427; Prevenier, 1986; *Archives et Bibliothèques de Belgique*, special issue 28, pp. 48-9.

the late Middle Ages and the early modern period, as was the case in Flanders and Brabant.[11] In studies about regions where craft guilds were formed rather late or were less economically influential, these institutions are rarely taken seriously. In their recent synthesis of economic history of the (Northern) Netherlands between 1500 and 1815, Jan de Vries and Ad van der Woude mention them only in passing, suggesting that guild-based institutions had no part in what they label as the first stage of modern economic growth.[12]

Obviously, some historians have adopted more qualified positions. Back in 1962, for example, the Belgian medieval historian Raymond Van Uytven mentioned that the political influence of craft guilds in the larger Flemish cities during the fourteenth century was by no means a democratic revolution; the most affluent master artisans were in fact in charge.[13] In several publications from the 1960s and 70s his colleague Jean-Pierre Sosson distinguished standard from practice and ideal from reality as far as the economic and social positions of master artisans were concerned in towns in Brabant and Flanders during the late Middle Ages: major differences existed both between and within corporative organizations, relations between the officials and the other members could be rigidly hierarchical, and a small group of affluent masters often monopolized the most lucrative commissions.[14] Nearly half a century ago, Jan Craeybeckx demonstrated with respect to the early modern period that corporative organization of production in the textile centres of the Spanish (and later: Austrian) Netherlands was perfectly compatible with the rise of capitalism.[15]

Since the 1980s, however, the traditional views have been so radically contested that the trend may rightly be described as revisionist.[16] This is especially true for perceptions of the economic aspects of urban corporatism. Historians are increasingly coming to believe that dichotomies such as privileged versus competitive, monopolistic versus market-oriented, rigid versus flexible, or regulated versus liberal do not accurately convey the role of craft guilds during the late Middle Ages and the early modern period. All revisionists would agree with Josef Ehmer's conclusion about the craft guilds in Central Europe: 'Concepts such as *altes Handwerk* (old handicraft) and craft mode of production acquire a new meaning when markets, competition, social inequality, flexibility and individualism are viewed as their characteristics rather than as their antitheses'[17] Craft guilds have in fact ceased to be regarded as obstacles to economic growth. Some authors have observed that these institutions often signifi-

---

11 Van der Wee, 1988, p. 324.

12 de Vries and van der Woude, 1997, passim, esp. pp. 162-3.

13 Van Uytven, 1962, pp. 373-409; Boone, 1994a, pp. 1-8.

14 Sosson, 1962, pp. 225-58, 1966, pp. 457-78, and 1977. See also 1990, pp. 339-48.

15 Craeybeckx, 1962, pp. 413-68.

16 Mackenney, 1987; Kaplan, 1988, pp. 453-78, and 2001; Sonenscher, 1989; Lis and Soly, 1994c, pp. 365-90, and 1997c, pp. 228-38; Prak, 1994, pp. 10-33; Crossick, 1997; DuPlessis, 1997, pp. 127-34; Farr, 1997 and 2000b; Ehmer, 1998, pp. 35-77; Reininghaus, 2000b), pp. 1-19; Haupt, 2002.

17 Ehmer, 1998, p. 77.

cantly reduced transaction costs and promoted all kinds of innovation thanks to the apprenticeship system.[18] Others argue that urban corporatism and the free market were not only compatible but reinforced one another as well.

While such revisionism undoubtedly offers new prospects, it also raises new questions. After all, asserting that craft guilds easily adapted to changing conditions, especially to market imperatives (i.e. by emphasizing their flexibility) entails the risk of reverting to the other extreme: if these institutions were always or nearly always functional with respect to their surroundings, if they were comparable to chameleons, then they are being deprived of all substance. Flexibility would then mean that anything was possible in such an institutional context, and the urban craft economy was simply a 'freewheeling affair'.[19] This perspective simply does not *explain* why apparently similar institutions could serve so many different purposes in one and the same time period, or why their existence seems to have had very different effects in some cases than in others.

We believe that studies of craft guilds should take three factors at once into account. First, like other institutions, craft guilds should be situated in a broader context, which means considering the specific characteristics of the urban economy, society, politics, and culture where they operated, as well as the relationship between the local powers and the central government in many cases. Second, craft guilds were established in a wide variety of sectors that each had very specific characteristics: brewers were not weavers, builders were not transport workers, tailors were not surgeons. Last but not least, many groups of actors were in a position to influence the way that such institutions operated, whether directly or indirectly; some were part of the guild system, others were not. All, however, had their own interests and objectives, which often differed enormously and were at times incompatible. Clearly, balances of power in the 'capitals' of the Duchy of Brabant, for example, where privileged craft guilds were important political lobbies, were entirely different from those in many French cities, where a great many craft guilds were established in the seventeenth century for tax purposes.[20] The outcome of initiatives to found new craft guilds or of efforts to transform established organizations did not depend exclusively on the political balances of power. Economic interests and social positions often came into play as well. The more affluent producers, their poorer colleagues, and journeymen were not necessarily on the same side, and merchant entrepreneurs – depending on their involvement in the sector – might urge the municipal authorities either to prohibit certain groups of producers from teaming up or, conversely, to compel them to incorporate.[21]

---

18 Epstein, 1998, pp. 684-713.

19 The expression comes from Farr, 1997, pp. 25, 50-1.

20 Coornaert, 1968, pp. 125-46.

21 Thijs, 1987b, pp. 191-200.

2. A comparative perspective

Comparative research is perhaps the most appropriate strategy for shedding light on this issue, which is precisely the aim of the following contributions. All concern the Low Countries and focus on the early modern period. Why the Low Countries? In a nutshell: because of the combination of unity and diversity. In the sixteenth century political unity was obviously very real, since the Northern and the Southern Netherlands constituted the 'Seventeen Provinces' at the time; only after 1585, following the 'fall' of Antwerp, were the North and the South again separated from one another. Both areas, however, were very similar in economic terms, both before and after 1585.[22] They had a very advanced system of agriculture, were highly urbanized, were hubs of international trade, and had major industrial centres. Understandably, therefore, guilds were established in both areas, albeit earlier in the South than in the North.[23] This brings us to the differences, which make the Low Countries interesting from a comparative perspective.

Admittedly, craft guilds in the Southern Netherlands followed a different course of development and acquired a different significance in many respects from the ones in the Northern Netherlands. The differences became apparent in both politics and the economy from the Middle Ages onward. During the sixteenth century tendencies toward convergence arose. After the Revolt, however, the North and the South continued along entirely different courses. The social, religious, and cultural functions of urban corporatism were no exception. The early modern period is therefore the main focus of this volume, although the Middle Ages has been deliberately included in most of the contributions; various changes can be understood only by looking back to the fourteenth and fifteenth centuries or even further.[24]

Two factors complicate comparing the North with the South. On the one hand, the provinces in each of the two areas often differed with respect to the balances of power that prevailed and their institutional foundations, as well as in terms of their urbanization rate and economic development. These provincial differences may be assumed to have affected urban corporatism and to have manifested themselves in both the prevalence and the nature of craft guilds. On the other hand, the differences between North and South were anything but static between 1600 and 1800. While in the seventeenth century the Spanish Netherlands was by no means an economic backwater, the Republic was the hub of the expanding world economy. In the eighteenth century, however, urban trades stagnated or even declined in the Republic, whereas the ones in the Austrian Netherlands expanded considerably after 1750. The authors of the fol-

---

22 van Zanden, 1993, pp. 357-67.

23 On the origin of craft guilds in Flanders and Brabant, see Wyffels, 1951.

24 For a European perspective, see Epstein, 1991. On the medieval craft guilds in the Low Countries, see Wyffels, 1951; Sosson,1984, pp. 79-90 and 1990; Nicholas, 1992, *passim*; Prevenier and Boone, 1993, pp. 33-42; Boone, 1994a; Goudriaan, 1996, pp. 21-63; Blockmans, 1999, pp. 51-63.

lowing contributions address provincial and chronological variations wherever possible but obviously do not cover each aspect in the same depth.

This is not the first time that comparative research is used to shed light on variations in urban corporatism. The *Zunftlandschaften* (guild regions) concept devised by Wilfried Reininghaus identifies areas comprising several cities with corporative organizations that had similar institutional characteristics. Reininghaus presents four examples of historical-comparative guild research in Germany, including some performed as far back as the second half of the nineteenth century. In his study about the mobility of *Gesellenverbände* (journeymen associations), Georg Schanz, who studied under Gustav Schmoller, described various geographic patterns back in 1876. Schmoller himself used this method in 1898 to distinguish regional variations in the guild policy in the German territories during the seventeenth and eighteenth centuries and attributed great significance to the measures of the Prussian state. Third, Karl Bücher and other German historians have explored the *Handwerkerverbünde*, which were collaborative arrangements between corporative organizations established in various parts of the Holy Roman Empire from the late Middle Ages onward. Fourth, the designations used for craft guilds in different parts of Central Europe have been identified. Despite the many attempts at regional comparisons, however, this method was not applied systematically in German guild research until recently, as Reininghaus rightly notes.[25]

Despite the wealth of research in recent years on urban corporatism in the Low Countries during the early modern period,[26] too much data is lacking to present a comprehensive picture that covers all details. Some aspects are just starting to be explored, and others will hopefully be reviewed in the future. The contributors to this volume are aware of the shortcomings but believe that embarking on a regional-comparative perspective at this stage is useful to encourage additional research. In the second chapter we examine where, when, and in which sectors craft guilds appeared in the Northern and Southern Netherlands to trace several similarities and differences. In the following chapters six major facets concerning the operations of corporative organizations in both areas are examined: their political foundations, their impact on production of and trade in export goods, their significance for local artisans who worked largely or exclusively for the local market, their role as mutual benefit institutions, their religious rituals, and finally the relationship between corporative capital and social representation.

---

25 Reininghaus, 2000a.

26 Much of this research has been conducted as part of a collective project involving the International Institute of Social History in Amsterdam (Piet Lourens and Jan Lucassen), the Instituut voor Geschiedenis at Utrecht University (Maarten Prak), and the Centre for the Study of Preindustrial Production Processes and Labour Relations at the Vrije Universiteit Brussel (Catharina Lis and Hugo Soly).

3. Prevalence, distribution, and intensity

Conveying urban corporatism in quantitative terms is difficult, even for apparently simple matters, such as the number of craft guilds and their distribution during a specific period or the numbers of master artisans, journeymen, and apprentices in a certain place. In addition to the frequent gaps in the source material, interpreting the data raises all kinds of problems that often lack straightforward solutions. The sources that survived and the existing monographs do not always distinguish craft guilds from alternative types of organizations, such as *neringen*, to which all persons involved in manufacturing a certain product automatically belonged in Leiden and some towns in the Republic. Strictly speaking, this system was not an actual membership system, where members were free to join or withdraw.[27] On the other hand, craft guilds in one town might incorporate several different occupational groups that would have been organized separately in other places. This was often the case in the South. In Louvain, for example, the guild of smiths comprised 12 occupations in the second half of the eighteenth century,[28] while at the end of the Ancien Régime in the small town of Lier, the mercers' guild encompassed no fewer than 45 occupations, of which most had nothing to do with retail trade.[29]

Although Piet Lourens, Jan Lucassen and Bert De Munck acknowledge these problems, they have nonetheless attempted to calculate the prevalence and distribution of craft guilds in the various provinces of the Low Countries.[30] Despite the shortcomings mentioned above, their quantitative analysis leads to several interesting observations. First, corporatism was an urban phenomenon in both the North and the South. Craft guilds were also established in semi-urban settlements or even in typically rural localities, especially on the islands of Zeeland and in the peripheral areas of the Republic during the eighteenth century. Quantitatively, however, none of them could hold a candle to the guilds in the cities.[31] Second, the number of craft guilds appears to have been linked to urbanization. In centres with fewer than 500 inhabitants, corporative organizations were rarely established, while new ones were generally founded in towns experiencing strong demographic growth; demographic decline, on the other hand, was rarely cause to abolish such institutions. Moreover, craft guilds seldom appeared in localities not officially designated as towns, regardless of their population size. This prohibited the rise of craft guilds in, for example, Lokeren in the County of Flanders (the current province of East Flanders), which had about 10,000 inhabitants at the end of the Ancien Régime but remained technically a village.[32] Another factor was that when towns were founded, establishing craft guilds might be explicitly

---

27 Posthumus, 1937.

28 Van Buyten, 1989, p. 61.

29 Van den Broeck, 1993, pp. 55-6.

30 Bert De Munck, Piet Lourens and Jan Lucassen, in this volume.

31 Zeiler, 1994, pp. 91-106; Mastboom, 1994, pp. 57-75.

32 Van Houtte 1920, pp. 18-19.

prohibited. This happened in Charleroi (in the current province of Hainaut), which originated as a fortress city in 1666 but evolved into a major industrial centre during the eighteenth century.[33] Third, there was an upper limit, in that few cities in the Low Countries ever had more than 60 craft guilds. The ratio of craft guilds to citizens consistently fluctuated between 1:1,500 and 1:1,000 in all places, except for the sparsely populated and little urbanized Duchy of Luxembourg, where the ratio hovered around 1:250 from the sixteenth century onward.

Diachronic analysis reveals more than similarities between North and South. The three authors mentioned have selected four random points in time according to the available material and general processes that might influence urban corporatism: *c.* 1400, *c.* 1560, *c.* 1670, and *c.* 1780. This gives rise to a third observation, which is that the timing of the incorporations varied considerably between the two areas. Between 1100 and 1400 more craft guilds were established in the County of Flanders and the Duchy of Brabant than anywhere else in the Low Countries. The figures were lowest in the North during this early stage. Even the ones reported for the counties of Holland and Zeeland are modest. The high rates in Flanders and Brabant are understandable, as these regions experienced both urbanization and strong industrial growth, especially in cloth production, a sector noted for its specialization and division of labour. During this period Bruges became the primary trading centre in Northwest Europe, while Ghent became not only the leading textile manufacturing centre in the Low Countries but also the largest European city north of Paris.

Between 1400 and 1560 two changes took place. On the one hand, the Northern Netherlands caught up, especially in Holland and Zeeland, undoubtedly due to the urban expansion in these regions: the number of craft guilds soared and was in fact higher than anywhere else in the Low Countries. On the other hand, a shift in the economic centre of gravity from Flanders to Brabant, where Antwerp evolved into the 'metropolis of the West', coincided with an increase in the number of craft guilds in that province.

After 1560 no more substantial changes occurred in the South, at least not in quantitative terms: corporative organizations continued to be established, and existing institutions were split up, especially in the County of Flanders, but such cases were not very numerous. While the stagnating or even declining degree of urbanization was certainly one of the reasons, other factors must have played a role as well, since the revived urban expansion after the mid-eighteenth century did not instigate a new wave of incorporations.

In the North the trends were entirely different. Urban corporatism thrived in the seventeenth and eighteenth centuries as never before. Lourens and Lucassen have calculated that between 1560 and 1670 nearly as many new craft guilds were established as during all previous centuries combined, with the highest concentrations in Holland

33 *Caroloregium Valde Concelebratur, MDCLXVI-MCMLXVI. Bilan de trois siècles d'histoire locale* (Charleroi, 1966); Hasquin, 1971.

and (in a somewhat lesser measure) Zeeland. The link between economic growth and urbanization is obvious: by 1675 the share of the population living in centres with at least 2,500 inhabitants had increased to 42 per cent and even amounted to 61 per cent in the province of Holland.[34] Urban corporatism was undoubtedly highly compatible with the exceptional economic prosperity in the Republic during its Golden Age, which most historians describe as an acceleration in the rise of merchant capitalism.[35] This does not automatically imply a causal relationship between the rising number of craft guilds and the growth of the urban export trades. Many of these trades were not organized in guilds during the seventeenth century (see below). In fact, several new craft guilds appeared during the eighteenth century, especially in Holland, although most urban trades declined, and the percentage of city dwellers decreased.

The quantitative data gathered and presented by De Munck, Lourens and Lucassen thus demonstrate that understanding the history of urban corporatism in the Low Countries requires considering urbanization and economic development. At the same time, however, they make clear that these factors do not explain all differences between North and South with respect to the numbers of new craft guilds in different periods.

4. Balances of power

The high numbers of craft guilds in many regions of the Low Countries should not make us forget that the corporative organizations formed in the North rarely had formal political power. Their counterparts in the South, on the other hand, operated as political lobbies in many cities from the late Middle Ages onward. In the County of Flanders and the Prince-Bishopric of Liège, master craftsmen had perpetual room to manoeuvre in the thirteenth and fourteenth centuries, because various groups with interests that diverged or even conflicted vied for political power (in one case the king of France, the count of Flanders, the aristocracy, and the urban patriciate and in the other case the bishop, the chapter of Saint Lambert, the aristocracy, and the patriciate of Liège) and enabled them to form changing coalitions. In the Prince-Bishopric the craft guilds emerged as victors from an extended and violent struggle in 1384.[36] During the 1360s the power in Flanders was divided: henceforth the deans of the guilds, including those of the wool weavers, participated in political decision-making in Bruges, Ghent, and Ypres, as well as in quite a few smaller towns.[37] In the Duchy of Brabant

---

[34] de Vries and van der Woude, 1997, p. 61.

[35] van Zanden, 1993; Davids and Noordegraaf, 1994; Davids and Lucassen, 1995. Note that de Vries and van der Woude, 1997, pp. 690-3, reject the merchant capitalism concept. They recommend assessing the economic history of the Dutch Republic in modern terms. See the critical remarks of Van der Wee, 1999, pp. 461-9.

[36] Hansotte, 1950, pp. 1-34; Kupper, 1991, pp. 54-64; Xhayet, 1990, pp. 361-78.

[37] Blockmans, 1978, pp. 72-81; Boone, 1990, and 2002, pp. 27-49; Stabel, 1995, pp. 144-6, 203-4, 222-6; Nicholas, 1992, pp. 242-6.

towns were less advanced during this period, and the social middle classes had less political room to manoeuvre. Ultimately, however, the craft guilds in Antwerp, Brussels, Louvain, and 's-Hertogenbosch acquired immense political influence: no new taxes were passed without their consent.[38]

In the first half of the sixteenth century the power of the craft guilds was curtailed in some towns in the Habsburg Netherlands. The most dramatic case was Ghent, where Emperor Charles V revoked their privileges in 1540.[39] In most towns where corporative organizations had spoken out during the late Middle Ages, however, they continued to act as political lobbies during the early modern period. In our view, their ongoing influence was attributable to two factors. On the one hand, the interests of the urban elites often diverged from those of the central government in the seventeenth and eighteenth centuries, especially with respect to the political balance of power, leaving room for the guilds to participate in local politics. On the other hand, the central government was reluctant to enter a confrontation with organizations that derived their power from strong constitutional foundations in some provinces, especially in Brabant.[40] In the Prince-Bishopric of Liège the international balances of power long favoured the craft guilds, which generally had the French kings and the United Provinces behind them. When the international context changed radically, however, the prince-bishop discontinued the political influence of the *grignoux* in 1684.[41] In the Austrian Netherlands no efforts were made to curtail urban corporatism until the 1780s. Emperor Joseph II had no intention of abolishing the craft guilds, but he did try to keep them under official supervision. Precisely because his measures upset the precarious balance that had existed for centuries between the State and the local powers, they were a major factor instigating the outbreak of the Brabant Revolution in 1789.[42] Only once France annexed the Austrian Netherlands and the Prince-Bishopric of Liège in 1795 were craft guilds abolished in all 'Belgian' departments.

Not all corporative organizations in the towns of the Habsburg Netherlands were involved in local political decision-making to the same degree. In Antwerp during the early modern period only 24 to 26 'privileged' guilds were represented on the *Brede Raad* (General Council), which supervised the financial and tax policy of the city government; 35 guilds had no direct say.[43] Specifically, organizations such as those of the silk weavers, with over 250 members, had no vote, while others with fewer than ten members did.[44] Membership of certain craft guilds may therefore be assumed to have been motivated less by economic concerns than by political ambitions.

The 'democratic' aspect of urban corporatism in the Spanish/Austrian Netherlands merits qualification for three other reasons. First, men dominated the corporative

---

38 Jacobs, 2000, pp. 558-624.

39 Decavele and Van Peteghem,1989, pp. 107-13.

40 Van Dievoet, 2000, pp. 19-31 and 97-132.

41 Hansotte, 1987, pp. 253-5, 258-62, 271-2.

42 Heirwegh, 1989, pp. 365-8; Lis and Soly, 2002, pp. 177-8, 180.

43 Boumans, 1965, pp. 38-40.

44 Thijs, 1987b, pp. 215-16.

sphere, even more in the South than in the North (see below). Second, in most craft guilds only the masters had voting rights. Journeymen were thus rarely represented on corporation boards. Third, the board tended to comprise a small minority of affluent masters, who primarily protected the interests of their own group and circumvented the 'ordinary' members wherever possible.[45] Whether this situation changed between the late Middle Ages and the end of the Ancien Régime remains unclear. At any rate, fragmentary data suggest that the progression was not linear. In Ghent, for example, during the second half of the seventeenth century relatively more master masons and master stonecutters served on the boards of their respective organizations than during the preceding and subsequent periods.[46]

All the same, craft guilds in many towns in the Southern Netherlands were politically influential. This was the case primarily and especially in local affairs but also in provincial ones in some regions, which explains why the central government kept a close watch over all matters concerning urban corporatism. The deans of the craft guilds were aware of their position amid the political forces, especially in the Duchy of Brabant, as apparent from the numerous and often extended collective actions they organized against the central authorities in Brussels, Antwerp, and Louvain, the three regional 'capitals', in the seventeenth and eighteenth centuries.[47]

In the Northern Netherlands the situation was entirely different, as Maarten Prak demonstrates.[48] Overall, craft guilds had little political influence there during the late Middle Ages. Three zones were identifiable.

The first was the western provinces, where craft guilds hardly managed to obtain real political power anywhere. In Dordrecht, the oldest town in Holland, guild deans participated in the annual election of the mayors. This was exceptional, though, as in the other towns of Holland corporative organizations did not achieve political emancipation, nor did they do so in Friesland. In Zeeland the craft guilds were politically influential only in the provincial capital of Middelburg and in Zierikzee and lost what little say they had during the first quarter of the sixteenth century. The second zone consisted of the eastern provinces, where the situation varied more. In the cities of Utrecht and Groningen craft guilds were directly and forcefully involved in local politics but were excluded from any exercise of power in the 1520s. In Arnhem, Zutphen, and most other cities in the Duchy of Gelderland, which did not join the Burgundian-Habsburg Netherlands until 1543, on the other hand, corporative organizations expanded their influence in the course of the fifteenth century and retained their position of power after 1543. Finally, the third zone comprised 's-Hertogenbosch and a few other towns in the northern part of the Duchy of Brabant: in the fifteenth and sixteenth centuries craft guilds were the Third Member of the local administration there, although they lost their representation after the conquest by the Republic in 1629.

---

45 Thijs, 1987b, pp. 211-14; Van Honacker, 1996, pp. 209-24; Van Elsacker, 2000, pp. 135-6.

46 Dambruyne, 1994, pp. 77-8.

47 Van Honacker, 1994b and 2000, pp. 37-68.

48 Prak, in this volume. See also Prak, 2000.

Craft guilds in the Northern Netherlands had so little political influence during the late Middle Ages and the sixteenth century in part because urbanization and industrial development occurred later there and never advanced as far as they did in the South. In our view, however, the power constellation was a more serious problem for corporative organizations in the North: they rarely had real opportunities to manoeuvre. In the few cities where they obtained a say in local politics, they generally owed their success to a standoff between various forces, which enabled them to form coalitions. The dramatic increase in the power of the craft guilds in medium-sized cities and most small towns in Gelderland was not purely coincidental: they had the support of the duke, who could use all possible military and financial assistance in his struggle against the Habsburgs.

The establishment of the Republic of the Seven United Provinces did not increase the political leeway of the craft guilds. In fact, while their counterparts in the South continued to operate in the field of tension between central government and urban elites in the seventeenth and eighteenth centuries, corporative organizations in the North rarely had any recourse other than to the municipal authorities (i.e. the local potentates), the *regents*. Only when various elite-groups vied for power, did they manage in some cases to tip the scales in their favour. One such case occurred in Groningen during the 1640s, when the local elite became entangled in several conflicts with the regional gentry, and in Deventer (in the province of Overijssel) during the early 1780s, when the *regents* sought to dismiss the influence of the stadtholder. Such crises, however, were exceptional. They were invariably short-lived and were largely limited to the eastern provinces.

In Amsterdam and the other cities of Holland, which were the hub of the Republic, craft guilds surged in quantitative terms during the Golden Age,[49] although they acquired no political power there. Worse still, in Dordrecht, the only town in Holland where they had ever participated in the (indirect) elections of the mayors, their role in politics was purely symbolic. This did not mean that the craft guilds were completely silenced. They had alternative channels at their disposal to influence the policy of the urban authorities, especially through petitions, which were a frequently-used pressure tactic, as Prak has demonstrated earlier. During the eighteenth century craft guilds were indeed the largest group of petitioners in Amsterdam and probably in many other cities as well.[50] Their counterparts in the South, however, appear to have been far more active on that front. In the second half of the eighteenth century the city fathers of Antwerp received far more petitions from corporative organizations than their peers in Amsterdam: an average of seventeen a year compared with eight a year.[51] The discrepancy is particularly remarkable, since not only did Amsterdam have two to three times as many master artisans, but craft guilds in Antwerp had recourse to other means

49 For Amsterdam, see Lourens and Lucassen, 1998, pp. 121-62.

50 van Nierop, 1997, pp. 286-7.

51 Calculations based on Prak, 1996, pp. 190-1, 258-9.

of action as well — they were in a position to initiate legal proceedings[52] and could manifest opposition in the General Council.[53]

The lack of in-depth studies precludes systematic comparison of the rhetoric of the craft guilds in the Republic with that in the Spanish and Austrian Netherlands. It would seem, however, that there were as many similarities as there were differences. One parallel was that they manifested themselves as the backbone of urban society in both areas. The most noticeable difference was the emphasis in the discourses in the South on *collective, legal rights*, meaning that the arguments had little or no bearing on either of the two spheres that together constituted the discourse of guilds in the North, especially the social status of *individual* guild brothers. Master artisans there presented themselves as citizens who owned their homes and their means of production, paid taxes, and performed various duties for the urban community as a whole.[54] Their counterparts in the South consistently emphasized privileges, entitlements, and areas of authority and in Brabant the constitutional foundation of their rights.[55]

William Speck has very rightly observed 'that paradoxically in monarchical England municipal affairs tended to be more popularly based than they were in the Dutch Republic'.[56] All the evidence available indicates that the Spanish and Austrian Netherlands, governed by 'absolutist sovereigns' and 'enlightened despots', had far more in common with England than with the United Provinces in this respect. In fact, far broader segments of the urban population participated in local politics in the Southern Netherlands than in the North, both before and after 1585. This was essentially attributable to the very different power constellations, which enabled craft guilds in the South to retain continuous room to manoeuvre.

5. Corporatism, 'small commodity production' and capitalism

The lack of opportunities to achieve direct and effective input in political decision-making was not the only element that distinguished craft guilds in the North from many corporative organizations in the South. Other differences concerned economic and social aspects, both before and after the Revolt and the subsequent separation. This seems surprising at first. After all, various urban trades thrived in both areas, albeit somewhat earlier in the South than in the North, and many of those trades were

52 In the Spanish and Austrian Netherlands craft guilds were very frequently involved in court litigation. See Deceulaer, 1994 and Van Honacker, 1994a, pp. 193-5. This practice was exceptional in the Republic. Only in Friesland do corporative organizations appear to have resorted to litigation, at least in the eighteenth century: Mud, 1995.

53 On legal actions, see Deceulaer, 1994, pp. 137-77. On guild opposition in the General Council, see Soly, 1970, pp. 197-205, and Van Honacker, 1994b, passim.

54 Prak, 1996, p. 269.

55 Van Honacker, 1994b, pp. 113-23; Deceulaer, 1994, pp. 141-2, 151-2, 158-9; Van Elsacker, 2000, pp. 129-63.

56 Speck, 1995, p. 185.

major sources of local employment. The global context in which merchant-entrepreneurs, master artisans, and journeymen operated, however, merits consideration. This requires distinguishing between export-oriented trades and sectors that supplied goods for the local market on the one hand and between manufacturing and trade (and all related activities, especially transport) on the other hand.

Production for export markets was obviously not always clearly distinct from production for the local market. No universal criteria applied in this context. In most small towns brewers exclusively or primarily supplied local residents, although even in a small centre such as Lier (in the Duchy of Brabant), for example, a growing share of the beer production was exported in the eighteenth century.[57] Tailors tended to work for fellow citizens and in several cases for inhabitants of the surrounding countryside as well. In some cases, however, master artisans sold standardized garments on international markets; the manufactures of the Antwerp cloak makers were even sold outside the Low Countries in the early seventeenth century.[58]

Some labour-intensive urban trades, however, were export-oriented *as a rule*. This held true in the first place for textile manufacturing, in the late Middle Ages and during the early modern period, in the South and in the North alike. This raises the questions as to what share of the production process was guild-based at which stages, and what were the economic and social ramifications? Which actors were in charge? Could master artisans launch entrepreneurial initiatives, or were they largely dependent on merchants? And last but not least, how did corporatism relate to capitalism in both parts of the Low Countries? While too many gaps remain to provide satisfactory answers, we may be able to shed some light on the issue.[59]

As far as the urban export trades in the United Provinces were concerned, the decision-making power nearly always rested with the local authorities. Everywhere that production was organized in *neringen* (which entailed automatic membership), city officials were in control: they regulated production and supervised enforcement. While they tended to follow the recommendations of the producers, this group nearly always included merchant entrepreneurs, which meant that the intrinsic industrial importance did not necessarily prevail. These systems dominated in the textile industry in Leiden and in many other urban export trades. If producers of certain export goods nonetheless formed corporations (which they did in some instances), then local authorities generally entrusted quality control to the guild officials. Guild officials, however, were appointed by the local authorities and had very limited jurisdiction; in all important matters they had to comply with the demands from the town-hall. Moreover, most *neringen* and craft guilds that entered the export business accepted merchants as members.

Some historians have argued that the urban authorities in the Republic were largely intent upon supporting small, independent producers in the export trades, and that policies were similar in the Southern Netherlands and in Southern Germany during

57 Aerts, 1996, pp. 210-26.

58 Deceulaer, 1998, pp. 403-17, and 2000, pp. 133-49.

59 The following paragraphs are based on Lis and Soly, in this volume.

the early modern period. This would suggest that 'small commodity production'[60] remained dominant in an economically significant part of Western Europe until the end of the Ancien Régime.[61] Many municipal authorities in the Republic did in fact take measures that enabled small producers in export trades to preserve their economic independence. But does this mean that their policy was essentially aimed at protecting small commodity production? That remains to be seen. In some cases the local authorities seemed to merely encourage the rise or continued expansion of an export trade. In other cases the 'support policy' served the interests of the merchants, because measures that prevented producers from expanding their operations or gaining access to the markets complicated or even blocked the rise of large industrial entrepreneurs. The available data suggest that producers in labour-intensive export trades had little or no difficulty circumventing the restrictions on company size. The frequent prohibitions on engaging in commercial activities, however, severely curtailed their opportunities to accumulate capital. In other words: the practice among municipal authorities of promoting 'equality among producers' in fact benefited the parties in control of the export trades, i.e. the wholesalers. Because of the absolute preponderance of mercantile capital and the absence or structural weakness of craft guilds in the export trades, industrial entrepreneurship nearly always finished second in the United Provinces. Even when it became obvious during the eighteenth century that focusing on import substitution would yield major economic improvement, the States General continued to favour the interests of the wholesalers in disproportionate measure.[62]

In the Southern Netherlands the relationship between corporatism and capitalism was far more complex. Most urban export trades were guild based. Except for spinning,[63] nearly all operations in the Flemish wool industry were performed within guilds from the thirteenth and fourteenth centuries onward. The same applied later on for weaving and finishing linens and silks, provided that these activities were located in towns and cities. Master artisans also figured prominently in the manufacturing of fabrics consisting of a mixture of cotton and linen, which thrived during the eighteenth century.

Master artisans producing export goods in the South had more opportunities to accumulate capital than did their peers in the North for two reasons. First, they were allowed to sub-contract and could thus set up networks of centrally-run small and medium-sized workshops.[64] While this method of organizing industrial production,

---

60 DuPlessis and Howell, 1982, pp. 49-84.

61 Davids, 1996, pp. 95-119.

62 Klein, 1989, pp. 202, 205, 209.

63 In all branches of the textile industry, spinning remained outside the corporative framework. The same held true for most preparatory operations in silk manufacturing. These tasks were performed primarily by women. Nor did the thousands of young girls and adult women who made lace in the towns of Brabant during the seventeenth and eighteenth centuries belong to corporative organizations.

64 On this form of industrial organization, see Lis and Soly (forthcoming).

which enabled the most affluent masters to achieve economies of scale, was certainly not unknown in the North, the evidence indicates that sub-contracting was less common in the export trades there. Second, master artisans involved in such trades in the Southern Netherlands were nearly always allowed to become commercially active as well, which was indispensable for turning a substantial profit. In our view, both factors combined explain why the vicissitudes of the urban export trades in the Southern Netherlands did not depend entirely on the logic of circulating capital. On the contrary, the subsequent cycles of product innovation between the twelfth century and the end of the Ancien Régime there were essentially 'driven' by large master artisans who became capitalist entrepreneurs.[65] Their success in this endeavour is largely attributable to the fact that in many cities corporatism soon became a political factor that both the local elites and the agents of the state needed to take into account. Wherever urban manufacturers lacked such structural room to manoeuvre, as was the case in the Northern Netherlands and Northern Italy,[66] the export trades were dominated by mercantile capital.

6. The backbone of the corporative world

The corporative 'boom' in seventeenth-century Holland thus involved more than catching up with Flanders and Brabant. After all, craft guilds remained rare in the export trades in the Republic. Commercial expansion was obviously related to incorporation among woodcutters, shipbuilders, rope makers, sail makers, coopers, and especially several groups of transport workers. Far more craft guilds in the Republic were specialized in freight transport than in the Spanish and Austrian Netherlands, which indicates that trade and distribution were more significant there. Despite the exceptional economic importance of transport in Holland, members of the organizations concerned were unable to act as lobbies. While the shipping guilds remained highly influential in politics in the South after 1585 (not only in Antwerp, Brussels, and Ghent but in many smaller towns as well),[67] they were basically extensions of the local authorities in the North.

The spectacular increase in the number of craft guilds between 1560 and 1670 paralleled the equally spectacular growth of the urban population, which of course coincided with a rise in local demand for goods and services. The mere increase in the number of urban dwellers in the Dutch Republic from 300,000 in 1525 to 815,000 in 1675 meant that several thousand new homes needed to be built each year, that demand for bread and other food products soared to unprecedented levels, and so on.[68] Corporative organizations were viable and useful only if enough members of the same

---

65 See the brilliant analysis by Van der Wee, 1988; also Lis and Soly, 1997c, pp. 219-24.

66 Ibidem.

67 Heirwegh, 1981, pp. 468-557.

68 de Vries and van der Woude, 1997, p. 61.

trade lived in a city to cover the cost of such an organization,[69] and the demographic expansion in many small centres brought about precisely that. While the craft guilds in the North that primarily served the local population might be expected to have had much in common with their counterparts in the South, any conclusions on this subject should be reached with caution, given the lack of in-depth studies at this time and the various possible interpretations of the data.

It is unclear, for example, whether the massive public works projects and the boom in residential construction in the Republic during the seventeenth century provided master masons and carpenters with the same opportunities to accumulate capital as was the case in the large cities of Flanders and Brabant both before and after 1585: in late-medieval Bruges,[70] in sixteenth-century Antwerp,[71] and in Ghent during the second half of the eighteenth century[72] capitalist production relations prevailed in the building trades. Except for the brewing industry, where growth coincided with scale expansion and concentration in several cities of the Low Countries during the early modern period,[73] the victualling trades have yet to be covered in sufficient depth by economic historians for similarities and differences to be identified. We know that butchers had powerful corporations in the Southern Netherlands by the fourteenth and fifteenth centuries; Jan Breydel of Bruges, one of the 'heroes' of 1302, was a master butcher. We also know that — unlike in the North — they made their trade hereditary in many towns there.[74] We have very little data, however, about their economic activities. This is also the case for the bakers, although the socio-political and in many cases also the tax-related significance of breadbaking and all related activities in the pre-industrial towns and cities would be difficult to overestimate.[75] In nearly all urban centres of the Low Countries, the bakers became incorporated at some point, and their organizations and operations were consistently supervised very closely by the local authorities in all places.

Some authors have argued that bakers and other producers that served the local market in Holland were in fact supported by the municipal authorities and were thus able to earn high profits. This income policy for the urban middle class is believed to have been the result of enlightened self-interest. On the one hand, bread, and other daily consumer items generated a large share of the tax revenues, and on the other hand the government's expenditures on interest to service the state debt accounted for the main source of income of the *regents*. As a result, the *regents* had an increasing interest in sustaining a stable base for assessing taxes.[76] This hypothesis, however, is

---

69 Lourens and Lucassen, 1997, pp. 44 and 46; Epstein, 1998, p. 689 n. 14.

70 Sosson, 1997, pp. 167-201.

71 Soly, 1977, and 1976.

72 Dambruyne, 1994, pp. 79-91.

73 Soly, 1968, pp. 337-92, 1166-1204; Unger, 1995, pp. 261-92, and 2001, pp. 179-82; Yntema, 1995, pp. 185-201.

74 Van Werveke, 1942, pp. 5-26.

75 Kaplan, 1996.

76 van Zanden, 1985, pp. 317-18, 321, and 1993b, pp. 148-56; Prak, 1988, pp. 148-54.

based on little empirical data at this time, and moreover raises the question as to why the bakers in Holland, despite their higher profit margins, were not on average better off than their counterparts in Flanders, where assize of the bread was intended to keep food prices low.[77]

At any rate, considering only the guilds of which the manufactures were rarely or never subject to tax assessments, all the data indicate that the economic and social characteristics of such organizations did not differ fundamentally between the North and the South. Everywhere, such master artisans cared deeply about compulsory membership, perpetuation of the local monopoly, rigid compliance with regulations intended to ensure equal access to means of production as well as labour, meticulous quality control, ongoing supervision of the labour market to prevent journeymen from becoming independent producers, and, last but not least, the right to conduct visits or house searches to track down and prosecute those who violated corporative regulations. In summary, their ideal was working according to the rules. This meant carefully circumscribing their own turf and distinguishing between 'us' and 'them', i.e. the 'others', the 'outsiders'. Both the struggles between craft guilds over their respective 'boundaries' and the actions of some organizations to make certain groups of outsiders taxable, or incorporate them, should be situated in this context.

It is crucial to bear in mind that the majority of guilds in most towns in the Low Countries pertained to this category. Little wonder, therefore, that they have largely determined public impressions. One of the consequences is that corporative circles are often seen as a middle ground or third class: they were neither wage workers nor capitalists but a world of small, independent entrepreneurs who were more or less equal and had limited but nonetheless real opportunities for upward social mobility. This impression is accurate in that socio-economic relations between master artisans who served the local market tended to be less hierarchical for this reason than they were in other sectors (see below). Such masters, however, were not necessarily a majority. In many towns in Flanders and Brabant far larger numbers of producers were engaged in guild-based export trades in several periods.

Comparing the clothing trades in the Northern and Southern Netherlands in the seventeenth and eighteenth centuries demonstrates that the differences between both parts of the Low Countries were less significant than the ones between small centres and large cities. The quantitative data gathered by Harald Deceulaer and Bibi Panhuysen reveal that the number of master tailors per thousand residents in small centres is easy to capture in lower and upper limits.[78] In large cities, where they served an affluent and fashionable clientele and in some cases the export trade as well, however, matters were more complicated. All proportions considered, the clothing sectors in Brussels and The Hague resembled the one in Paris more than those in small centres

---

77 Compare de Vries and van der Woude, 1997, pp. 672-3, with Lootens, 1971, and Gilté, 1996.

78 Deceulaer and Panhuysen, in this volume. See also Deceulaer, 2001, and Panhuysen, 2000.

in the Low Countries.[79] In each of these three large cities the more affluent tailors could expand the scale of their business by increasing the number of journeymen per workshop, by subcontracting to poorer colleagues, or by gaining control of related occupations: in short, by adapting corporative regulations to suit their interests.

As for women's labour in the clothing sector, the North differed from the South. In the United Provinces seamstresses were often incorporated in any of several different ways, ranging from founding their own corporation (i.e. self-regulation) through submitting entirely to the rules imposed by the tailors' guild. In the Spanish and Austrian Netherlands, on the other hand, seamstresses remained outside the corporate framework, with the sole exception of Mons (in the Province of Hainaut), where women who sewed black clothes formed a guild together with the tailors.[80] This was probably attributable to a combination of factors, such as differences in the demand for labour, a different supply of labour, and a different institutional context. The factor or factors that tipped the balance, however, remain unclear.

The case of the clothing sector was not universally applicable. Although little research thus far has addressed the role of women in guild-based trades in the Low Countries, males undoubtedly predominated in the institutional world of the guilds in the North and South alike, as they did everywhere else in Europe as well.[81] While this was already the case in the late Middle Ages, access to many incorporated trades became more difficult and sometimes even impossible for women during the early modern period. Toward the eighteenth century, women were admitted to only a very small number of craft guilds anymore; their official role in corporative circles was largely restricted to sectors such as the garment trades, food-processing, and above all retail.[82] This definitely did not mean that labour by women was marginal in skilled workshop trades. Wives of master artisans were generally entitled to work for their husbands, at their workshop and under their privilege, as were their daughters. Many craft guilds continued to allow widows to run a workshop, albeit subject to certain conditions. Last but not least, indications exist of quite a few semi-legal courses of action to circumvent the corporative prohibitions on women's labour.[83] North and South are believed to have differed little or not at all in this respect.

7. Mutual aid

The corporative world was by no means one of social equals. Variations abounded, not only between cities but also between and within guilds: members of the same occupation might be far more affluent on average in one city than in another. In all cities

---

79 On the clothing trades in Paris, see Roche, 1994.

80 Heirwegh, 1983, pp. 298, 300, 305.

81 Farr, 1988, pp. 37-41, 107-13.

82 Deneweth, 1987; Thijs, 1987b, pp. 174-82; Daems, 1988; Van Buyten, 1989, pp. 86-8.

83 Vastesaeger, 1998.

members of some guilds tended to be richer or poorer than those of other guilds, and distribution of wealth within individual trades varied enormously.[84] Although systematic, in-depth research on disparities of wealth in the corporative world in the Low Countries has not yet been forthcoming, some general patterns are identifiable.

The overwhelming majority of all those involved in guild-based and labour-intensive export trades were either poor masters or journeymen with no other prospect than performing wage labour for the rest of their lives. In both the late Middle Ages and the early modern period, journeymen weavers could register as masters relatively easily, as the admission fee tended to be low, even for non-masters' sons, and looms did not cost very much. Few master weavers, however, pertained to the social middle class; most struggled to make ends meet. Among the 800 master silk weavers in Antwerp in 1584-5, only fifty owned property, and even they were assessed in the lowest tax bracket.[85] In textile trades where raw materials were relatively inexpensive the same situation prevailed: in 1748 only one third of the master linen weavers in Bruges earned a taxable income, and all but three were assessed in the lowest bracket.[86] Most journeymen in labour-intensive export trades requiring major investments in fixed capital obviously had little or no incentive to become masters. In the early modern period, most journeymen hatters, for example, opted to remain wage workers. Because of their key role in the production process and the expansion of hat manufacturing, they earned high wages, and they understood that advancing to master status would not improve their situation. After all, the widening gap between large and small firms drove increasing numbers of masters to the periphery of the hatting industry, where they worked as subcontractors or repaired hats.[87]

In the construction industry relations between master artisans tended to be rigidly hierarchical. This was the case in large and medium-sized towns, where public works projects were conducted over extended periods, and residential construction thrived. These situations were conducive to scale expansion and concentration. Under these circumstances, master status rarely offered secure prospects. On the contrary, several masters became proletarianized and were dependent on more affluent colleagues, who became capitalist entrepreneurs. It is thus far from coincidental that at the end of Antwerp's Golden Age over 80 per cent of all master masons and master carpenters lacked sufficient personal assets to pay taxes.[88]

The craft guilds that served the local market comprised a broad range of social profiles, as the distribution of wealth in Bruges in 1748 demonstrates. Master bakers appeared both in the highest tax bracket (about 3 per cent of the total) and in the group exempted from taxes due to indigence (nearly 7 per cent of the total); most, however,

---

84 The same can be said about the corporative world in other parts of Europe from the fifteenth to the eighteenth centuries. See Farr, 1988, pp. 113-28.

85 Thijs, 1987b, pp. 189-201, 219-36.

86 Denolf, 1981, p. 119, and 1983b, p. 115.

87 Lis en Soly, 1994d, pp. 19-20.

88 Van Roey, 1963, pp. 39-40.

belonged to the upper middle class. The overwhelming majority of the master tailors, on the other hand, pertained to the lower echelons of Bruges society: 16 out of 127 were listed as poor, and the rest were in the lowest two tax brackets.[89] In Antwerp at the end of the Ancien Régime master tailors were also socially homogeneous and fairly poor; guild officials reported that over half the members were unable to pay even their annual dues.[90] The income tax of 1742 reveals that wealthy tailors were few and far between in the towns of Holland; most masters belonged to the lower middle class.[91]

The distribution of wealth among craft guilds engaged in small-scale production tended to be somewhere between that of the bakers' and that of the tailors' guilds.[92] Their social profile thus corresponded largely to what passed for the corporative ideal. In practice, this meant a clustering in the lower middle rank: men of modest means who realized that they were perpetually at risk of losing their economic independence; an extended period of being disabled from work could even reduce them to beggars, unless they received mutual aid.

Many corporative organizations in the Low Countries established their own social plans, which were nearly always intended for 'full' members (i.e. masters). Sometimes provisions for corporative charity were available to journeymen as well, but they were exceptions to the rule. In the course of the late Middle Ages and the sixteenth century in nearly every large city and medium-sized town in the Southern Netherlands, especially in Flanders and Brabant, craft guilds opened hospices (*godshuizen*), where elderly members found shelter. Antwerp had six such institutions, and Ghent even had nine. At the time these homes opened, the guilds involved had large memberships and were thriving. Some institutions housed over 20 elderly people, although in most cases the number of beneficiaries varied from six to 12. These residents were not necessarily indigent or infirm. Some guild-hospices were accessible only to masters with property, which they were required to surrender upon entering the institution.[93] In the Northern Netherlands very few guilds opened homes for the elderly.[94]

The *bussen* or guild boxes, which protected masters and their family members from financial risks, were of far greater social significance. Sandra Bos has investigated these mutual aid funds, which operated increasingly as real insurance funds in the Republic. She argues that many guilds in the North adapted their pattern of expenditure to the 'new religion' by the late sixteenth century, which, combined with an economic upswing, was particularly conducive to the establishment of mutual aid

89 Denolf, 1981, p. 120.

90 Deceulaer, 2001, pp. 102-3.

91 Panhuysen, 2000, pp. 172-4.

92 For Brabant and Flanders, see especially Van Roey, 1963, 1968, pp. 239-57; Degryse, 1974, pp. 136-45; De Belder, 1974, and 1976, pp. 258-79; Denolf, 1981a. For Holland, see Oldewelt, 1952, pp. 167-248, and de Vries and van der Woude, 1997, pp. 571-81.

93 Huys, 1926; Païs-Minne, 1975, pp. 188-9; Dambruyne, 1997 pp. 161, 192-4; Eeraerts, 1997.

94 Bos, 1998, p. 45.

systems. While no exact figures are available, about 250 craft guilds appear to have had a *bus*, which is rather impressive for a total of approximately 1,300 corporative or semi-corporative organizations.[95] After all, sound financial operations required a great many members in a position to pay both a substantial admission fee and annual dues, and a favourable age composition (i.e. a regular supply of new members). Nearly all guild boxes were based on compulsory membership. The members were thus collectively responsible for the risk of each individual member. The most common provisions were funeral aid and sickness benefits; some *bussen* also provided retirement pensions, not merely to the members themselves but often to their widows as well. Expansion and monetarization of the social services packages coincided with capital growth within the funds. Especially in Amsterdam, guilds expanded their capital considerably through investments in bonds and used the interest for the benefit of the members.

What about mutual aid in labour-intensive trades that existed largely outside the corporative framework? The Leiden municipal authorities did not authorize establishment and expansion of mutual aid organizations until increasing numbers of textile workers could no longer make ends meet, and public poor relief services were on the verge of collapse. In fact, only in the final quarter of the seventeenth century, when proletarianization and impoverishment became widespread, did voluntary boxes become numerous. At first these mutual aid organizations were trade-related. Over time, however, other groups were admitted as well. Many journeymen's boxes are believed to have emerged during periods of increasing economic and social hardship, as did the boxes for textile workers in Leiden. Bos has registered about 200 such boxes. Some were formed by skilled, well-paid workers with powerful shop-floor organizations, such as the journeymen hatters and the journeymen cloth shearers, whose boxes doubled as strike funds.[96] Most, however, operated exclusively as mutual aid funds and peaked during the late seventeenth and early eighteenth centuries.[97]

The dearth of research on trade-related assistance in the cities and towns of the Southern Netherlands during the late Middle Ages and the early modern period makes comparisons hazardous.[98] No conclusion is possible as yet as to whether proportionately more guild boxes arose here than in the Republic. Fragmentary data suggest, however, that corporative assistance in towns in Brabant and Flanders tended to be informal, and that the related expenditures often remained integrated within the general guild fund. Wherever separate boxes existed, membership was usually compulsory.

---

95 See the computations of De Munck, Lourens and Lucassen in this volume.

96 Dekker, 1990, pp. 397-400, 409-10, and 1992, pp. 137-9, 141-4.

97 Bos, in this volume, and 1998; Timmer, 1913.

98 Aside from Huys' study from 1926, which contains information about guild boxes in Antwerp, Bruges, Brussels, and Louvain, the only research available is Willem's 1995, which focuses on the social provisions of nine craft guilds in eighteenth-century Ghent. Data may, however, be gleaned from several (often unpublished) monographs about individual craft guilds.

They were not necessarily focused on poor relief in the true sense of the word. The 'poor box' of the mercers' guild in Louvain, for example, was in fact like a true insurance fund around 1700. All members, rich and poor alike, were free to dip into its contents; even the dean of the guild requested and received a disbursement on several occasions.[99] Disregarding the investments in guild-hospitals, little doubt remains that guild funds in the Republic on average spent more on social security than their counterparts in the Spanish and Austrian Netherlands.[100] Part of the reason was that the ones in the Spanish and Austrian Netherlands had entirely different expenses: upkeep of their own guildhall, social-cultural activities, litigation — all matters on which the guilds in the North spent little or nothing by virtue of their minimal autonomy. On the other hand, public assistance may conceivably have been far more substantial in the South than in the North during the early modern period.[101] If corporative solidarity was not forthcoming, municipal poor relief was always an option. Both in Louvain in the mid-sixteenth century and in Antwerp at the end of the Ancien Régime, the lists of indigent reflected large numbers of male and female heads of households engaged in labour-intensive trades.[102]

Like in the North, journeymen's boxes were formed in the South, although even less information is available on them than on the boxes of the masters. The cloth dressers and hatters are known to have set up mutual funds by 1608 and to have started using them as strike funds soon afterwards.[103] In the course of the seventeenth and eighteenth centuries journeymen hatters even organized an entire network of related *gemene bussen* (common boxes), which had close links with comparable organizations abroad, especially in France. These common boxes, which operated as syndicates, as is apparent from their frequent collective actions (that were nearly always successful), enabled journeymen to regulate labour in the hatting industry in the Southern Netherlands: they forced entrepreneurs to hire only their own members and to consult them about the distribution of tasks within the firms.[104] The associations of journeymen carpenters and masons established in several large and medium-sized cities in the eighteenth centuries formed boxes as well and used them both as mutual funds and as strike funds, especially in the 1770s and 80s.[105] In Bruges the two groups also

---

99 Van Buyten, 1989, pp. 85-6.

100 See the calculations of Johan Dambruyne, in this volume.

101 Lindert's calculations, 1998, pp. 101-40, suggest that in the Netherlands a larger percentage of the gross national product was allocated toward poor relief than in Belgium. The data available are not directly comparable, however, as the author himself indicates. This is particularly true for the period considered here, as the figures are from 1792 (the Netherlands) and 1833 (Belgium), respectively. At any rate, far more in-depth research is required on the South to shed light on the seventeenth and eighteenth centuries.

102 Cuvelier, 1940, pp. 48-55, 101-15; Païs-Minne, 1952, pp. 179-83; Lis, 1986, pp. 120-1, 187-8.

103 Huys, 1926, pp. 116-19; Thijs, 1987b, pp. 410-14.

104 Lis and Soly, 1994d. For a European perspective, see Lis and Soly, 1994a.

105 Heirwegh, 1981, pp. 558-646; Absolon, 1994, pp. 172-80, and Schoonjans, 1996, pp. 124-9.

opened their own *godshuizen*.[106] In some cities journeymen with less socio-economic prestige, such as tailors and shoemakers, formed associations as well.[107] While some of these groups started mutual aid funds, they often continued to operate as religious confraternities or social associations.

8. Religious rituals and representation strategies

Just as analysing craft guilds exclusively in formal-institutional terms would be a mistake, they should not be studied from a rigidly political, economic, or social perspective either. Joining a corporation was one way to obtain security in a highly uncertain world,[108] where bonds of fraternity and friendship could have a deeper emotional and spiritual significance in addition to their material consequences. Like in other West-European countries during the late Middle Ages, both master artisans and journeymen in the Low Countries formed confraternities that accepted only fellow tradesmen and were dedicated to adoration of their respective patron saints. Sometimes craft guilds were preceded by religious associations, and some craft confraternities coexisted with guilds. In most cases, however, the religious activities took shape within the corporation. Alfons Thijs demonstrates how abundant these activities were, and how much they were appreciated by master artisans.[109] In the second half of the fifteenth century guilds began to erect altars for their patron saints, generally in an existing church, but frequently also at a chapel constructed specifically for that purpose at their own expense. In honour of their patron saint,[110] they organized annual celebrations comprising a mass, which all members were required to attend subject to heavy fines, followed by a banquet to reaffirm their collective identity, mutual solidarity, and internal hierarchy. Craft guilds marched in all large processions held in their town. They would appear in full regalia, decked out in their specific liveries and bearing their coats of arms, as well as their corporation's banners, blazons, and torches. In Ghent these guilds and their coats of arms were such an impressive spectacle in the *Auweet* (the Night Watch procession held during the Mid-Lent Fair) that Duke Philip the Good turned out to watch them in 1431 and 1444, as did Philip the Fair and Margaretha of York in 1500.[111] In 1520 Albert Dürer, the most acclaimed artist of his day, depicted his admiration for the splendour of the Antwerp guilds in their procession for the Feast of the Assumption.[112]

---

[106] Huys, 1926, p. 106.

[107] Goetstouwers, 1908, pp. 228-30; Deceulaer, 2001, pp. 303-11.

[108] Lis and Vanthemsche, 1995, pp. 37-43; van Leeuwen, 2000, pp. 104-14, 419-22.

[109] Thijs, in this volume.

[110] On the patron saints of the craft guilds in the Southern Netherlands, see Heirwegh and Van Belle, 1991.

[111] Arnade, 1996, pp. 61-2.

[112] Goris and Marlier 1970, pp. 61-2; Hewak and Hugue 1993, pp. 19-20.

The victory of the Counter Reformation enhanced the significance of the religious element in the Spanish Netherlands. The municipal authorities ordered that craft guild altars severely damaged or even destroyed during the Iconoclastic Fury of 1566 be restored, and most guilds allocated considerable sums toward the repairs. The most powerful and wealthiest corporations even commissioned works from famous painters, such as Peter Paul Rubens and Maarten de Vos.[113] The revival of corporative devotion was by no means exclusively a religious phenomenon, as Thijs rightly emphasizes. Precious and artistic altars had a high 'user value': in addition to indicating that the members concerned were law-abiding and had a clear sense of orthodoxy, such altars enhanced their prestige by distinguishing them collectively from other occupational groups and were featured as a visual extension of corporative privilege.[114] Participation in processions and other religious parades may be considered from the same perspective. Precisely because both the religious and the secular authorities attributed still greater value to such rituals after 1585 than they had previously, craft guilds focused more than ever on the order of precedence in the parades. The Brussels *Ommeganck* of 1615 conveys this practice: the painter depicted the 46 corporative organizations in the right sequence, each with the exact number of participants — presumably all masters — totalling 4,654 figures.[115]

There are indications suggesting that the religious importance of the guilds gradually dwindled in the Southern Netherlands after 1650, that is to say their devotional practices appear to have served increasingly to distinguish them from the 'others', especially from the politically mute unskilled masses, probably in keeping with the trend toward proletarianization. While printed pennants, blazons, and sacrificial prints already figured among the corporative repertoire in the sixteenth century,[116] such visual materials became wildly popular after 1650.[117] They had an immense communicative value. In their ostentatious public displays of images of their patron saint amid his attributes, often surrounded by their own instruments and products, craftsmen conveyed more than the religious dimension of their work, including skill and quality as key concepts. They also manifested themselves as respectable citizens and members of an exclusive organization and thus as entirely different from all those who were unaffiliated with a particular corps. Similar concerns increasingly led groups of journeymen to request the local authorities for permission to establish confraternities from the late seventeenth century onward. In a period of declining standards of living they hoped that such a religious organization would distinguish them from unregulated labour. Although members of these fraternities were sometimes involved in collective actions,[118] such bodies were dedicated primarily to religious and cultural aspects,

---

113 Baudouin, 1972, pp. 45-91.

114 Verleysen, 2001, pp. 159-66.

115 Des Marez, 1904, p. 105 n. 2; De Peuter, 1999, pp. 90 and 373 n. 5.

116 Van der Stock, 1998.

117 Thijs, 1997, pp. 213-41.

118 Craeybeckx, 1957, p. 306.

associated with the quest for social distinction on the one hand and autonomy on the other hand. The journeymen involved emphasized the individuality of their fraternity compared with the masters, either by choosing a different patron saint or by holding their celebrations at a different chapel or church.[119]

In the Northern Netherlands the situation was obviously entirely different in the seventeenth and eighteenth centuries. The institution of the Dutch Reformed Church as the 'public Church', which was unknown elsewhere in Europe, was introduced there in all seven provinces and in the so-called Generality Lands.[120] As a result, the Calvinists had a monopoly on public religious services. Compared with the Spanish and Austrian Netherlands, however, where only Roman Catholics were free to organize religious services and had full citizenship until Joseph II introduced civil tolerance in 1781,[121] the United Provinces were a paragon of religious pluriformity. The supreme prevalence of Calvinists in public religious matters did not withhold people of different beliefs in a great many cities from observing their own religious practices, provided they acted with discretion. This held true both for Protestant 'dissenters' (e.g. Anabaptists and Lutherans) and for Roman Catholics and Jews. The tolerance was not universal, however, and was moreover very relative. It differed between the Western and Eastern provinces on the one hand and between Christians and Jews on the other hand.

Except in Utrecht, where Roman Catholics suffered discrimination from 1655 onward, all Christians in the Western part of the Republic were generally eligible to become citizens, which was an essential prerequisite for joining a corporation. In the Eastern part, on the other hand, non-Calvinists were usually excluded from citizenship and consequently ineligible to join guilds or at the very least had to overcome numerous obstacles: that applied to the Anabaptists and the Lutherans until the mid-seventeenth century and to the Roman Catholics through to the end of the eighteenth century. This discriminatory legislation was in effect in places such as Arnhem, Deventer, Groningen, Nijmegen, and Zutphen and was rigidly enforced.[122]

Regulations for Jewish families were very regionally diverse as well: widespread settlement prohibitions in the Eastern provinces and general eligibility for citizenship in the Western provinces, albeit subject to restrictions. Jews were rarely allowed to engage in guild-based occupations. This was also the case in Amsterdam, where they were the most numerous. Only the guilds for booksellers, brokers, and surgeons sometimes admitted Jews. The overwhelming majority of Jews in Amsterdam therefore sold food products and second-hand goods on the one hand or worked in trades that

119 Thijs, 1994, pp. 240-51.

120 In these peripheral areas, which by 1648 comprised nearly a third of the Republic, the States General was the formal sovereign.

121 Crahay, 1982.

122 Lourens and Lucassen, 2000, pp. 18-19. Also Panhuysen, 2000, pp. 51, 83-6; Prak, 2002.

were not guild-based, such as silk spinning, diamond finishing, tobacco manufacturing, and sugar production on the other.[123]

There is little doubt that the discrimination against non-Calvinists in the Eastern part of the Republic arose largely from economic motives and was intended primarily to protect local craftsmen and shopkeepers.[124] We attribute the willingness of many municipal authorities to impose and enforce prohibitions or restrictions to a combination of two factors: on the one hand, as noted, this zone already had a tradition of guild representation that enabled members of such organizations to influence decision-making, and on the other hand, the orientation of most craft guilds toward the local market meant that everything that might affect the livelihood of small, independent producers was taken very seriously indeed.

The status of the Dutch Reformed Church as the 'public church' ruled out erecting altars, participating in processions, and other manifestations of 'papal superstitions' throughout the United Provinces. Nonetheless, traces of old rituals lingered for a long time. Some were even perpetuated, albeit in somewhat modified versions. Many corporations, for example, retained the name of their patron saint and even continued to feature his likeness on all kinds of corporative objects. After the Revolt some corporations in the North maintained their own crypt in a church and expected all members to attend the funeral of one of their peers.[125] Over time, however, these ceremonies lost their significance in terms of both social and symbolic capital.

Aside from religious rituals, cultural differences between the guilds in both parts of the Low Countries were equally pronounced, as Johan Dambruyne demonstrates.[126] In the late Middle Ages and the sixteenth century guildhalls were built in all large and medium-sized towns in the Southern Netherlands. Though intended primarily as meeting areas, they were used for festivities as well. Their symbolic purpose often exceeded their user value considerably. These generally monumental stone edifices, with façades featuring illustrious and appealing ornamentation, sent a direct and continuous signal to the entire urban community of the power of the corporations involved. When Charles V confiscated the guildhalls in Ghent following the Revolt in 1539, he seized symbolic capital in addition to considerable economic capital. Corporative organizations in the Northern Netherlands rarely invested in guildhalls precisely because so few of them were truly autonomous. The corporative 'heyday' in the seventeenth century did not lead to frenzied construction. Around 1798 very few guilds in the Republic had their own accommodations, and those that did usually occupied very humble rented premises. In the Spanish and Austrian Netherlands, on the other

[123] van Dillen, 1940, pp. 561-616; van Eeghen, 1965, pp. 17, 31, 66-8, 92, 111-12; Fuks-Mansfeld, Hilversum, 1989, pp. 80-2; Lucassen, 1994, pp. 32-47; Israel, 1995b, pp. 102-11, 141-3; Panhuysen, 2000, pp. 13, 80-3, 271.

[124] Israel, 1995a, p. 1025.

[125] Van Leeuwen, 2000, pp. 104-10, and Bos, 1998, pp. 66-8, 161-4, 189-91.

[126] Dambruyne, in this volume. Dambruyne, 1994, pp. 151-211, and 2002, pp. 83-173.

hand, most corporations continued to spend money, often in very large sums indeed, on building, restoring, decorating, and maintaining their guildhall. Immediately after the *Grand Place* was razed to the ground in 1695, 16 Brussels corporations started rebuilding their guildhalls and spared no expense to make their buildings appear still more prestigious:[127] the aim was to reaffirm their political power in the centre of the capital. Their ability to wield their influence effectively became clear in 1698 and especially in 1699, a year of successive collective actions with pronounced political overtones.[128]

From the final quarter of the seventeenth century, many craft guilds in the Southern Netherlands started to purchase more precious objects. This trend increased toward the end of the Ancien Régime. Some investments were intended to add lustre to the corporation's participation in processions and other parades; this was especially true for the silver ceremonial breast plates and silver torch shields.[129] Did this growing interest in external appearances arise from the construction of a corporative idiom, in which respectability was the underlying principle? This seems plausible. After all, in a period when the risk of downward social mobility was very real, master artisans may well have been inclined to attribute still greater importance to prestige and honour. Other corporate purchases served to make the meeting room in the guild hall appear more luxurious: furniture, paintings, and ornaments made of precious metals. This trend coincided with the rise of consumer culture among the urban middle class in Western Europe,[130] although other factors may have come into play as well. The new luxury items may have been intended and perceived as markers of social hierarchy both to the outside world and within the corporation. The practice, in the second half of the eighteenth century, among deans and other board members of some craft guilds of having themselves immortalized in group portraits during the late eighteenth century is probably no coincidence.[131] After all, relations between the masters became more hierarchical, as may be inferred from the increasingly frequent reproaches from 'ordinary' members regarding the 'greed' and 'wastefulness' of the officials.[132]

The combination of political and religious factors explains why the craft guilds in the Republic did not devise the same representation strategies as their counterparts in the Spanish and Austrians Netherlands. The available data suggest, however, that the corporations in the North invested far less in generating symbolic capital than would have been within their means, and that they also spent far less on meals and festivities. Why? Was the influence of the Dutch Reformed Church decisive even in this area? Or were the master artisans more inclined to join other networks of sociability, such

[127] Culot, 1992; Goedleven, 1993.

[128] Van Honacker, 1994b, p. 113.

[129] Vermeersch, 1988, pp. 23-33.

[130] Berg and Clifford, 1999.

[131] Vermeersch, 1988, pp. 16-19.

[132] Van Houtte, 1920, pp. 67-8; Goetstouwers,1908, pp. 44-7, 248-50; Heirwegh, 1981, pp. 133-4, 635; Thijs, 1987b, p. 209.

as civic militias (*schutterijen*),[133] membership of which provided far greater prestige, and neighbourhood associations?[134]

9. North and South: two trajectories of development

The Low Countries were by no means the only region of pre-industrial Europe where urbanization was closely related to incorporation. The greatest concentrations of craft guilds were in the 'central belt', which was the arc of large and small towns from Northern Italy, across Switzerland and Southern Germany, to the Rhineland and the Low Countries, including Northern France, and from there to London and the Midlands.[135] In all those regions, in addition to the increased demand for goods and services due to growth of the urban population, commerce was conducive to the development of export trades. At three points during the period under consideration, some parts of the Low Countries were in the exceptional position of being at the vanguard both in international trade and in industrial development. Each time, cities with an abundance of craft guilds were pivotal: Bruges and Ghent in the thirteenth and fourteenth centuries, Antwerp in the sixteenth century, and Amsterdam in the seventeenth century.

This by no means suggests that the corporative world was homogeneous. The situation was the same in the Low Countries as in other parts of Europe: nothing that could be described as a 'guild system' ever existed in the sense of a universal system of institutions with specific essential features and functions. As a general category, the guild system is no more and no less than an ideal construction of which the foundations were laid in the eighteenth century by political economists who believed that craft guilds inhibited social development, and to which the adherents of a new ideological movement (corporatism) added still other dimensions during the final quarter of the nineteenth century and the interwar years.

Researchers should not become obsessed with the common elements among craft guilds in certain periods, regions, or sectors. Careful examination often reveals that these elements were purely formal. The only fundamental common feature among craft guilds, considered here to be associations of fellow tradesmen required to join the organization, was that each one had a local privilege and thus acquired a legal status, although with vast differences among them. Variations in space and time on the one hand and differences between craft guilds within a single geographic and chronological context on the other hand therefore merit far greater consideration. Comparative research is indispensable for explaining these variations.

---

[133] Knevel, 1994. See also the special issue of *Tijdschrift voor Sociale Geschiedenis*, 26 (1997), no. 1.

[134] Roodenburg, 1992; Dorren, 1998.

[135] On the 'central belt' or 'urban belt', see Davids and Lucassen, 1995, pp. 11-18.

Comparing the Northern and the Southern Netherlands has revealed for the time being that explicit differences existed, especially in politics and religion but also in economic, social, and cultural respects. The divergent manifestations of urban corporatism are best described in the context of the defining actors. After all, these organizations were constructed, transformed, or dissolved in a dynamic interplay of forces between different groups of actors who each had their own objectives, aspirations, and strategies. Local and regional balances of power were the main factors that determined whether the urban producers might form associations, as well as the applicable conditions and procedures. The party that issued the production regulations, the party in charge of quality control, and the party that supervised the labour market: everything was the outcome of negotiations and struggle, in which the positions of the different actors were not predetermined. Exploring only the local scene will not yield the complete picture: the trilateral relationship between master artisans, local elites, and the central government determined the strong political representation of many guilds in Flanders and Brabant. Where they lacked structural room to manoeuvre, such as in Holland and Zeeland, guilds never had much political clout. What is crucial here is that coalitions emerged in the Southern Netherlands along various lines, whereas this was rarely possible in the most urbanized and economically significant section of the Northern Netherlands before 1585 and was virtually out of the question afterwards.

All the data suggest a close link between the measure of political autonomy and the institutional opportunities for master artisans to become entrepreneurs. In the export trades, striking differences thus emerged between North and South, both before and after the Revolt, and had far-reaching consequences for long-term industrial developments in both parts of the Low Countries. Craft guilds that served the local market, on the other hand, were very similar in all regions. The actors were comparable and consisted primarily of small masters who were economically independent. During the early modern period they appeared as the 'backbone' of urban society. It would seem that their self-image needs to be taken seriously, even literally. Without at least their tacit cooperation, political stability and social peace proved impossible to maintain. It may be assumed, however, that they were unable to sustain the same measure of sociability everywhere. After 1585 the deeply religious context became a factor. This was both because the craft guilds in the Republic had to abandon the representation strategies they had applied for centuries, while their counterparts in the Spanish Netherlands honed them, and because achieving a social impact was easier. While all kinds of corporative sociability were easier and often more rational to maintain in a Roman Catholic setting, social spending allocations were more likely to be emphasized in the North. One of the implications was that while the official abolition of the craft guilds deeply affected the societal structure in the South,[136] it enabled them to transform into thriving insurance funds that operated for extended periods in the North.[137]

[136] No in-depth research has been performed yet on the extent to which and the ways that master artisans in the Southern Netherlands accumulated economic, social, and symbolic capital after 1795.

[137] van Genabeek, 1999.

Chapter 2

The establishment and distribution of craft guilds in the Low Countries, 1000-1800

Bert De Munck, Piet Lourens and Jan Lucassen

1. Introduction

Underlying every geographical comparison of the craft guilds is a quantitative dimension. According to a now popular view, craft guilds were primarily an 'empty' organizational framework concealing a range of functions and used for different purposes by various groups of actors, both within and outside the guilds. In the historical debate, 'flexibility' has replaced the legal rigidity and conservatism that historians have previously attributed to guilds for a very long time. This view of guilds as 'flexible institutions' might easily lead one to conclude that a quantitative analysis of guilds has little, if any analytical value — certainly not if we want to make comparisons over a long time-span and across a large geographical area. This is not the case, however, for two reasons which are directly related to the definition of 'craft guilds' used in this book. First, these organizations were officially recognized. As a result, under the Old Regime a craft guild could not simply be set up or dissolved; nor could its statutes be easily amended. On the contrary, as a rule a guild — once established — led a resilient institutional existence. Secondly, a craft guild is defined here primarily as an economic organization of fellow tradesmen whose purpose was to defend their shared interests. Whatever other functions craft guilds might have had (and there could be many: religious, military, insurance, and so on), the enforcement of an economic monopoly by fellow tradesmen was a prerequisite for inclusion in our analysis.[1]

---

[1] For questions of definition, see section 1 of the appendix. It is important to note that most guilds were primarily associations of masters. As will be apparent from what follows, there were guilds that accepted journeymen, guilds that included only journeymen in sectors which had no masters (peat-porters or heavers for example), and journeymen associations that operated alongside masters' guilds in the same sector. All these organizations, though not the journeymen associations in the South nor the *neringen* in the North, are included in the data presented later. *Neringen* were organizations established by an urban government and charged with regulating and controlling a particular branch of the export industry. Unlike guilds, they had no formal membership but included all persons working in a specific

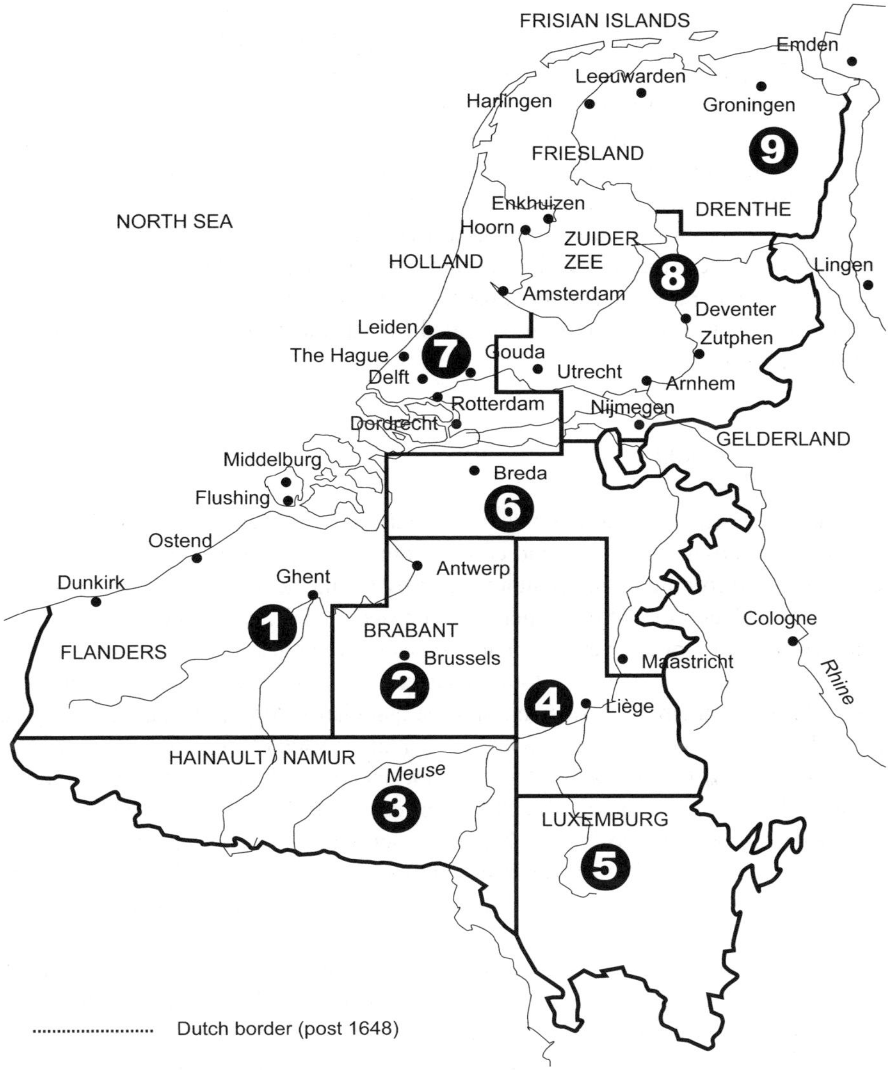

Map 2.1 *The Low Countries in the late sixteenth centrury (divided into nine sub-regions)*

key: numbers to the regions in table 2.1

sector of production. See Karel Davids, (unpublished paper), p. 6. In the case of the Southern Netherlands, we occasionally come across umbrella organizations comprising several *letten*, or chapters. Each of these umbrella organizations is included just once in our totals for craft guilds.

Put another way, an analysis of the incidence of craft guilds (as we have defined them) in the Low Countries by subregion (see map 2.1) and subperiod or for a cross section of years, can provide a good basis for a further study of their specific functions later in this book. However, we will not be limiting ourselves to just a series of bare facts. We will also be endeavouring to point out similarities and differences, principally concerning the relationship between the foundation and existence of craft guilds on the one hand and demographic, economic and political-institutional developments on the other. One way of doing this is to track as many craft guilds as possible in the Low Countries from the early eleventh century until the abolition of the guilds eight hundred years later. For this purpose, datasets for Belgium and Luxembourg and for the Netherlands have been compiled, and, as much as possible, analysed in a consistent fashion.

2. The earliest guilds

The earliest reference to an organization of fellow tradesmen in the Low Countries is almost a thousand years old and comes from Tiel, now in the Dutch province of Gelderland. According to an account written by the monk Alpertus of Metz between 1021 and 1024, an association of merchants existed in Tiel. Apart from having a social function (drinking-bouts were popular), the association also played a role in providing credit and in mediating in trade disputes.[2] Soon afterwards, Tiel ceased to be a significant commercial settlement, and the association too disappeared. It is quite possible that associations of fellow tradesmen had existed even earlier in the Roman cities of the Low Countries, but they are not documented for this period — unlike those in the South and southeast of the Empire;[3] nor, then, do we have any evidence regarding the possible continuity between such early associations and their later medieval counterparts. We are on firmer ground when we look at the cities founded from the eleventh century onwards. The earliest extant texts we have relate to cities in the extreme northwest of present-day France — governed at that time by the counts of Flanders and Hainault. There, associations of tradesmen developed into permanent organizations, officially recognized by the government, and whose aim it was to secure and defend a monopoly against the claims of fellow citizens and competitors from elsewhere. We know from a charter possibly drawn up around 1067 that the city of Valenciennes in Hainault had an organization of cloth merchants; a similar document dating from 1072-1083 has survived for Sint Omaars in Artois.[4] Other larger urban agglomerations, almost all of which lay south of the line between Maastricht and

---

2 Oexle 1989; Verhulst 1999, p. 123.

3 Wyffels, 1951, pp. 16 and 33.

4 Verhulst 1999, pp. 123-4.

Antwerp at that time (the main exception being Utrecht), might also have had such organizations, but no written documentation has survived.[5]

The early development of craft guilds in the southwestern Low Countries continued in later centuries. By 1267 Louvain had 25 craft guilds, Bruges had 52 by around then. Ypres had just as many by the beginning of the fifteenth century, and Ghent had at least 25 by 1400.[6] Craft guilds emerged early on in the smaller cities of the southwest too. Nieuwpoort had at least five by 1400, and no fewer than 14 by 1500. Given that Nieuwpoort's population was no more than 5,000, this is far from insignificant. Proximity to the sea was not the only factor however. The craft system in Ostend, for example, did not develop fully until the seventeenth century. In fact, the nature of the local industry seems to have been more important. Bruges, Ypres and Ghent were key centres of the cloth industry, and often it was in this sector that the first corporative system of regulation was established, with the setting up of a 'cloth guild' for example. In other cities too, the cloth industry was the first to organize on a corporative basis. In Sint Truiden an organization of fullers and shearers is said to have existed in 1237 (though it might originally have been a religious confraternity), and a cloth guild was set up in the relatively small town of Lier as early as 1275. The question remains though to what extent weavers and fullers operated independently of the merchants, and thus to what extent the craft guilds were autonomous. For example in Diest, where a drapers' guild was founded in 1316, it is unclear whether at that time weavers had an organization which was independent of the merchants.[7] There were other organizations alongside the textile sector, even at this early time, and not just in the coastal towns of Flanders. Tailors, brewers and smiths are also frequently mentioned.

Once a corporative organization had been set up in a particular city, it was not unusual for others to follow soon after. Furthermore, with urban expansion and the emergence of urban centres towards the North and east the system of craft guilds also spread to those regions. Apart from the case of Tiel, already mentioned, the earliest data we have relating to the North are for Dordrecht. It was there in 1200 that the St Pontiaans (or cloth merchants') guild received its first charter. There are other early examples: the Deventer cloth merchants' guild dates from 1249 (followed by the tailors'

---

5 Van Uytven 1981, p. 210, mentions the following early attempts at collective manifestations of urban tradesmen; they are, in chronological order, the servants at the abbey of Sint Truiden (mid-eleventh century), the brewers of Hoei (1068), bakers, brewers, cobblers and others in Sint Truiden (1112), religious confraternities of tailors, coiners and cloth shearers in Atrecht (pre-1150), the fraternity of Sint Eloy in Béthune (1188), and the fraternity of the millers of Dowaai (1198). For the mediaeval history of the guilds in the Southern Netherlands, Wyffels, 1951, remains indispensable.

6 In addition to the databases referred to throughout this chapter, reference is made to Wyffels, 1951; Van Uytven, 1980a, pp. 203-4; Warnkoenig and Gheldof, 1851, pp. 52, 132-55 and 196-221; Petit, 1975, p. 18.

7 This question has been studied extensively in the literature, for Louvain, Bruges, Liège and Diest for example. See Verhavert, 1940, ch. 1; Van De Velde, 1909, p. 6; Van Werveke, 1943, pp. 18-19; Hansotte,1950, p. 13; Van Der Eycken, 1980, pp. 109-10.

guild in 1282), the Maastricht tanners' guild was founded in 1264 (followed by the weavers' guild in 1276), while Middelburg's merchant fraternity dates from 1271. We also know that several guilds existed in Utrecht in 1267 and 1274, though no evidence of either their number or their names has survived.[8] One obvious precondition for establishing a guild was a certain critical mass in terms of population; otherwise there would have been too few fellow artisans to sustain a guild. One or two artisans would not be inclined to set up a craft guild, since they could regulate their professional relationship more simply. According to our data, towns with fewer than 500 inhabitants tended not to have any craft guilds, and they were also rare in towns with fewer than 1,000 inhabitants. Guilds were more likely to be set up in towns whose populations exceeded this (only slightly more likely in smaller cities, but much more so in larger ones), and guilds did generally exist in such towns.[9]

The more or less simultaneous development of towns and craft guilds meant that craft guilds also acquired political power. Verhulst assumes that this was true even before the end of the eleventh century, and he is certainly able to demonstrate the validity of his assumption for Atrecht in 1111 and Doornik in 1188. Here, too, we find the oldest surviving documentation relating to the southwest of the Low Countries.[10] In the second half of the thirteenth century the success of the guilds in securing political power created an opposition of interests between craft guilds and the urban patriciate in many southern towns, and occasionally in the North (namely Utrecht, which was governed by the aldermen of the guilds from 1274 to 1276). By then the phenomenon of the craft guild was already widespread, particularly in the South. It was only much later that they became widespread in the North. The greater incidence of the guilds in the South compared with the North prior to 1400 is evident in table 2.1. Over 40 per cent of all the craft guilds we know of in the South were founded before 1400; the corresponding figure for the North was barely 8 per cent. In Flanders, Hainault and Namur, and in Liège the pattern had largely been set by 1400, and this is apparent from the number of guilds founded in the two centuries before 1400 and in the century thereafter. In this respect, Brabant (and also Luxemburg) clearly belong to a later phase, but nonetheless they had developed much further than the North.

---

8 For the spread and growth of cities in the Early and High Middle Ages see Van Uytven 1982.

9 Lourens and Lucassen, 1997. This observation is principally based on northern material since we have little data on southern cities with fewer than 2500 inhabitants (see appendix). We have no reason to suppose that the South was fundamentally any different from the North in this respect.

10 Verhulst, 1999, pp. 124-5.

Table 2.1 *Number of new craft guilds in the larger cities of the Low Countries (cities with 2,500 inhabitants and over in 1784)*

Southern Netherlands	Date of foundation							
	1100-1399	1400-1559	1560-1669	1670-1784	Unknown	Total	Disappeared prior to 1784	% disappeared
1 West and East Flanders	149	86	43	40	>95	413	>95	23
2 Brabant and Antwerp	129	120	24	19	>64	356	>90	25.3
3 Hainault and Namur	62	30	16	13	>4	125	>6	4.8
4 Liège and Belgian Limburg	75	6	0	2	>4	87	>5	5.7
5 Luxemburg	6	8	13	9	16	52	1	1.9
Subtotal	421	250	96	83	>183	1033	>197	19.1
%	40.8	24.2	9.3	8.0	17.7	100		
Northern Netherlands								
6 North Brabant and Dutch Limburg	31	87	56	31	3	208	60	28.8
7 Holland and Zeeland	41	272	324	138	1	776	160	20.6
8 Overijssel, Gelderland and Utrecht	33	85	121	24	0	263	49	18.6
9 Groningen, Friesland and Drenthe	4	34	60	29	0	127	27	21.3
Subtotal	109	478	561	222	4	1374	296	21.5
%	7.9	34.8	40.8	16.2	0.3	100		

Key:

- Current administrative and political boundaries.
- For the South the population in 1784 was used, for the North the population in 1795 (see section 1 of the appendix below).
- IISH guilds dataset on 6 April 2003 for the guilds in the North (60 guilds founded after 1784 are excluded); VUB (PIPA) guilds dataset on 26 May 2003 for the guilds in the South (33 guilds founded after 1784 are excluded).

The difference between the Southern Netherlands and the Northern Netherlands can be seen in the graph contrasting the data in figure 2.1 for Flanders and the South with those for Holland and Zeeland and the North as a whole. One can reasonably argue then that in the case of Flanders economic prosperity and the establishment of guilds coincided. Later, this same pattern became evident in other provinces too.

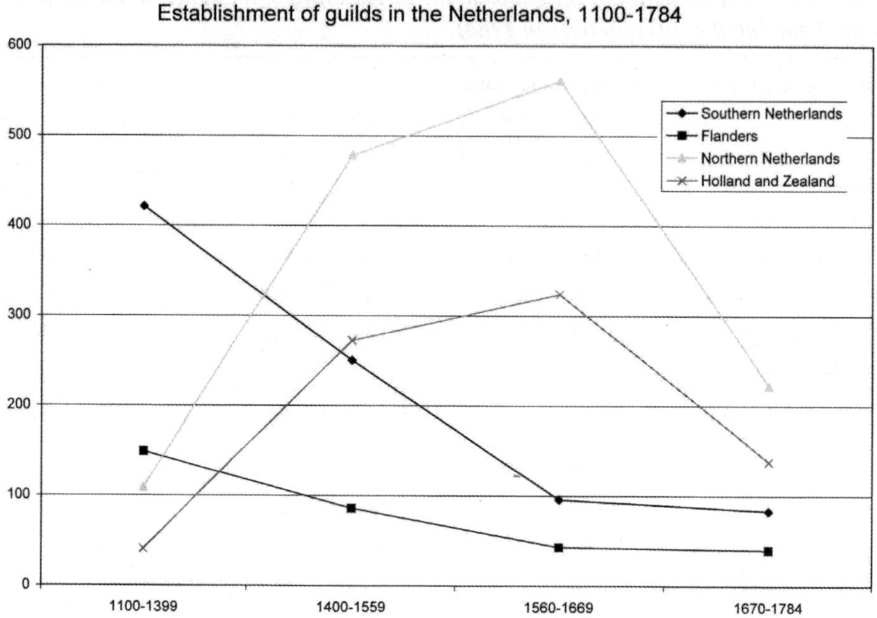

Figure 2.1 *Number of new craft guilds in the larger cities of the Southern Netherlands (Flanders in particular) and the Northern Netherlands (Holland and Zeeland in particular)*

3. The guilds in the late Middle Ages

Not surprisingly, there were a number of economic and demographic preconditions for the establishment of craft guilds. But to what extent was the opposite true? Was there — beyond a certain threshold of say 1,000 inhabitants — a fixed relationship between the number of inhabitants and the number of guilds? For the period around 1400 we have sufficient population data to consider the extent to which the guild system had penetrated various regions of the Low Countries (see table 2.2).

The close relationship between urbanization and the presence of guilds around 1400 is immediately apparent from table 2.2. Following on from what we suggested earlier concerning the emergence of cities, urbanization had — in all respects — progressed much further in the southwest than in the East and North. Furthermore, a town had to be easily accessible, particularly by water. With the exception of a town like Liège, on the river Meuse, there were scarcely any large cities (by the standards of the Middle Ages) more than 100 kilometres from the coast. Moreover, it was within these key cities that the density of guilds was highest, though — and this is our second conclusion — in the very largest cities this density was capped, due largely to political factors. Where specific guilds had secured political power, they were no

Table 2.2 *Number of inhabitants per guild c. 1400, 1560, 1670, and 1784 in cities with 2,500 or more inhabitants in 1784*

Southern Netherlands				
	1400	1560	1670	1784
1 West and East Flanders	814	552	503	513
2 Brabant and Antwerp	669	814	789	810
3 Hainault and Namur	875	688	481	558
4 Liège and Belgian Limburg	558	677	969	1061
5 Luxemburg	550	262	*c.* 260	274
Subtotal	728	668	*c.* 620	648
Northern Netherlands				
6 North Brabant and Limburg	1191	569	442	456
7 Holland and Zeeland	1083	561	1099	800
8 Overijssel, Gelderland and Utrecht	585	801	466	510
9 Groningen, Friesland and Drenthe	1250	656	645	607
Subtotal	967	617	824	680

Key: see table 2.1. Since there are fewer dates of dissolution known for the South than for the North, the total number of guilds we know to have disappeared prior to 1784 in the South is divided by three and the result deducted from the figures in columns two to four in order to ensure that the figures for 1560, 1670, and 1784 approximate as reliably as possible to the actual number of organizations (very occasionally, where the literature is unequivocal on this point, craft guilds known to have already disappeared were deducted from the relevant figure before 1400). The craft guilds whose date of foundation is unknown were added, in proportion to the number whose date of foundation is known. Finally, the number of inhabitants in Luxemburg in *c.* 1670 is estimated at 10,000.

Table 2.3 *Establishment of craft guilds in the Low Countries, by sector and period*

Southern Netherlands		Agriculture and fishing	Food	Industry	Building	Trade	Trans-port	Services	Total
<1400	N	9	56	228	32	64	12	16	417
	%	2.2	13.4	54.7	7.7	15.3	2.9	3.8	100
1400-1559	N	2	24	140	21	33	8	22	250
	%	0.8	9.6	56.0	8.4	13.2	3.2	8.8	100
1560-1669	N	0	10	54	6	18	1	7	96
	%	0	10.4	56.3	6.3	18.8	1.0	7.3	100
1670-1784	N	2	7	41	7	10	3	13	83
	%	2.4	8.4	49.4	8.4	12.0	3.6	15.7	100
1100-1784	N	13	97	463	66	125	24	58	846
	%	**1.5**	**11.5**	**54.7**	**7.8**	**14.8**	**2.8**	**6.9**	**100**

Key: See table 2.1. There are another four guilds whose sector is unknown. Adding these, plus the 183 guilds whose date of establishment is unknown, yields a total of 1033.

Southern Netherlands		Agriculture and fishing	Food	Industry	Building	Trade	Trans-port	Services	Total
<1400	N	3	19	63	10	24	9	4	132
	%	2.3	14.4	47.7	7.6	18.2	6.8	3.0	100
1400-1559	N	10	58	233	59	56	37	46	499
	%	2.0	11.6	46.7	11.8	11.2	7.4	9.2	100
1560-1669	N	12	50	242	46	64	63	87	564
	%	2.1	8.9	42.9	8.2	11.3	11.2	15.4	100
1670-1784	N	5	32	66	19	29	33	34	218
	%	2.3	14.7	30.3	8.7	13.3	15.1	15.6	100
1100-1784	N	30	159	604	134	173	142	171	1413
	%	**2.1**	**11.3**	**42.7**	**9.5**	**12.2**	**10.0**	**12.1**	**100**

Key: IISH dataset on 6 April 2003. Categorized according to Statistics Netherlands' Standard Industrial Classification (Agriculture 01, Fishing 03, Food 20-21, Industry 22-39, Building 51-53, Transport 72-74; the remaining codes are included with services). For one guild we do not know when it was established, 21 guilds were established after 1784.

longer inclined to admit new organizations, and certainly not by splitting up existing guilds. Ghent, for example, had many more inhabitants than Bruges, but only a few more craft guilds. Similarly, Ghent and Ypres had the same number of guilds, even though Ghent was over five times the size of Ypres.

The specific geographical distribution of guilds was also related to the development of the most important industry during this period — the textile industry. We can explain this in terms of the industry's two main raw materials — wool and linen. While the woollen industry was a typically urban phenomenon, the linen industry flourished largely in rural areas, and it matured only fully later on. As a result, the rise of the woollen industry was accompanied by the early establishment of what were initially general cloth guilds, and later of separate guilds for weavers, fullers and other specialist occupations in the industry. It was only later that guilds of linen workers too were founded in most large and medium-sized cities (they remained general linen guilds, and, unlike the wool guilds, did not give way to more specialist guilds within the industry). Bruges and Ghent had linen weavers' guilds as early as the thirteenth century, but in most other cities it was not until the first half of the fifteenth century that such guilds appeared — thus once the cloth industry had begun to decline in the Southern Netherlands. In general, the woollen industry produced for the quality market, while the linen industry targeted cheaper market segments.[11]

In the Northern Netherlands the late onset of urbanization is just one explanation of why the guilds took much longer to take root there. Provincial politics, particularly in Holland and Gelderland, certainly played a role too in impeding the establishment of guilds. By the time these cities began to flourish, the political authorities were already well informed about the guild revolts in the much older cities of Flanders and Brabant (and, as we have seen, in Utrecht too), particularly in the second half of the thirteenth century, but also of those later too in Flanders, Doornik and Namur as a consequence of the Battle of the Spurs in 1302.[12] In Liège the guilds had already secured substantial political power by then. In Utrecht (1304) and in several cities in Brabant (Louvain 1378, Brussels 1421, Antwerp 1445) this took longer.[13] These revolts apparently deterred the Count of Holland and the Duke of Gelderland. In Holland, Dordrecht was the only city to have institutionalized the political power of the guilds by 1367, and its guilds continued to wield political power until they were abolished. Blok's claim that the Northern Netherlands had no autonomous guilds in general is still correct.

---

[11] That no textile guilds were established in Ronse despite the importance to the city's economic prosperity of the local woollen and linen industry can perhaps be explained by the rural character of that industry. See Declercq, 1979, pp. 17-35. A number of other occupations — the tailors, hosiers and shoemakers, tanners, curriers and saddlers — did form associations, though not until the sixteenth century. It was only in *c.* 1708 that a weavers' guild was founded.

[12] Wyffels 1951; see too Van Houtte,1964, p. 98.

[13] For Utrecht see de Bruin 2000, pp. 107-10, 115, 129-32, 192, 229.

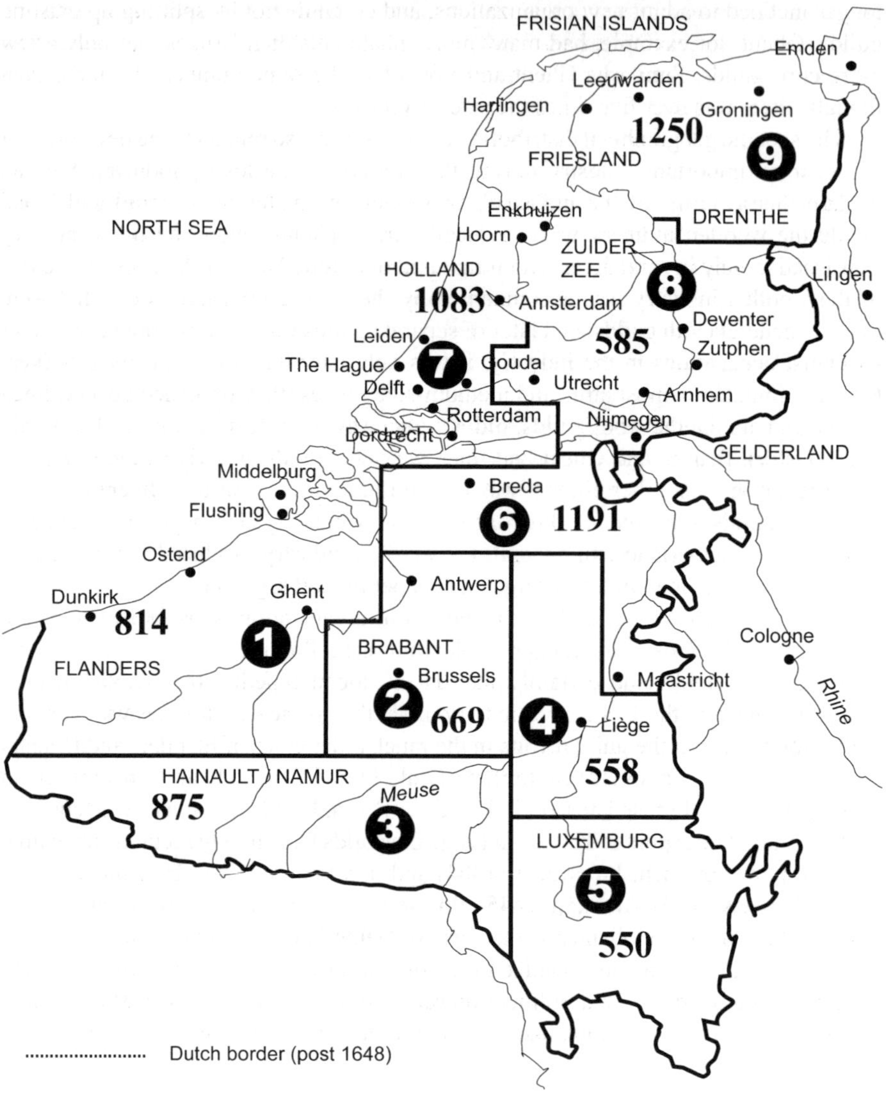

Map 2.2. *Inhabitants per guild c. 1400*

But guilds did play an important role in sounding out the opinions of artisans during politically troubled times, as subsequent centuries were to prove.[14]

Turning now to developments in the various sectors of the medieval urban economy, it is apparent that by 1400 the guilds had fully matured. While at first only merchants

---

[14] See also the useful summary in Van Uytven, 1982 on the political role of the guilds in the Middle Ages, particularly in the South, but sometimes in the North too, especially in Utrecht.

and woollen workers had guilds, within a few centuries a whole range of occupations had become organized, particularly in industry. In the Southern Netherlands industry was somewhat more important than in the North, but transport in the Northern Netherlands was relatively more important than in the South. The distribution of guilds across the various sectors was fairly stable and after 1400 most new guilds probably resulted from existing guilds being split up. The North was somewhat more dynamic than the South — the result largely of the great expansion in services in the North from the end of the sixteenth century.

Before concluding this section on developments in the Middle Ages, we would like to touch on the formal labour relations within the craft guilds. As noted earlier, the organizations discussed here generally included only masters. Occasionally, there were separate associations of journeymen and apprentices. In the case of the Southern Netherlands little research has been carried out into these associations, with the exception of the unusually active journeymen hatters.[15] The journeymen associations we know of from the fifteenth and sixteenth centuries seem initially to have been organized principally for religious purposes. However, they also served to express a collective identity, and their underlying objective might well have been to defend social and economic interests.[16] Whatever the case, it is clear that here too a critical mass was necessary before associations of journeymen could be formed. Quite where that threshold lay is less clear, but in most of the examples mentioned above there must have been dozens if not hundreds of journeymen.

Despite extensive research into journeymen associations in the Northern Netherlands, few have been identified, particularly for the earlier period. In total, we know of only 20 journeymen associates in the Northern Netherlands, and only six of these predate the Reformation.[17]

4. The guilds on the eve of the Dutch Revolt

On the eve of the Dutch Revolt, the guild system was more widespread than ever before, not only in the Southern Netherlands but also in the Northern Netherlands, with Groningen, Friesland and Drenthe in the extreme northeast having the lowest

---

15 Des Marez, 1901, pp. 44-6; Des Marez, 1909, pp. 137-243; Des Marez, 1911, vol. 2, pp. 209-13; Lis and Soly, 1994d.

16 Thijs, 1994, pp. 231-81.

17 These were the journeymen brewers' of Gouda and Kampen (1404 and 1450 respectively), the journeymen shoemakers' of Zierikzee and Sluis (1425 and 1545 respectively) and the tailors' journeymen of Middelburg and Sluis (1430 and 1545 respectively). The concentration in the southwest was remarkable. This changed after the Reformation, when nine were founded in Groningen in the northeast, along with two others in Leiden and one in 's-Hertogenbosch. See Timmer, 1913; Bos, 1998. These authors calculated a slightly higher number of organizations than we did. However, they included organizations that we regard as merely funds for providing relief to members.

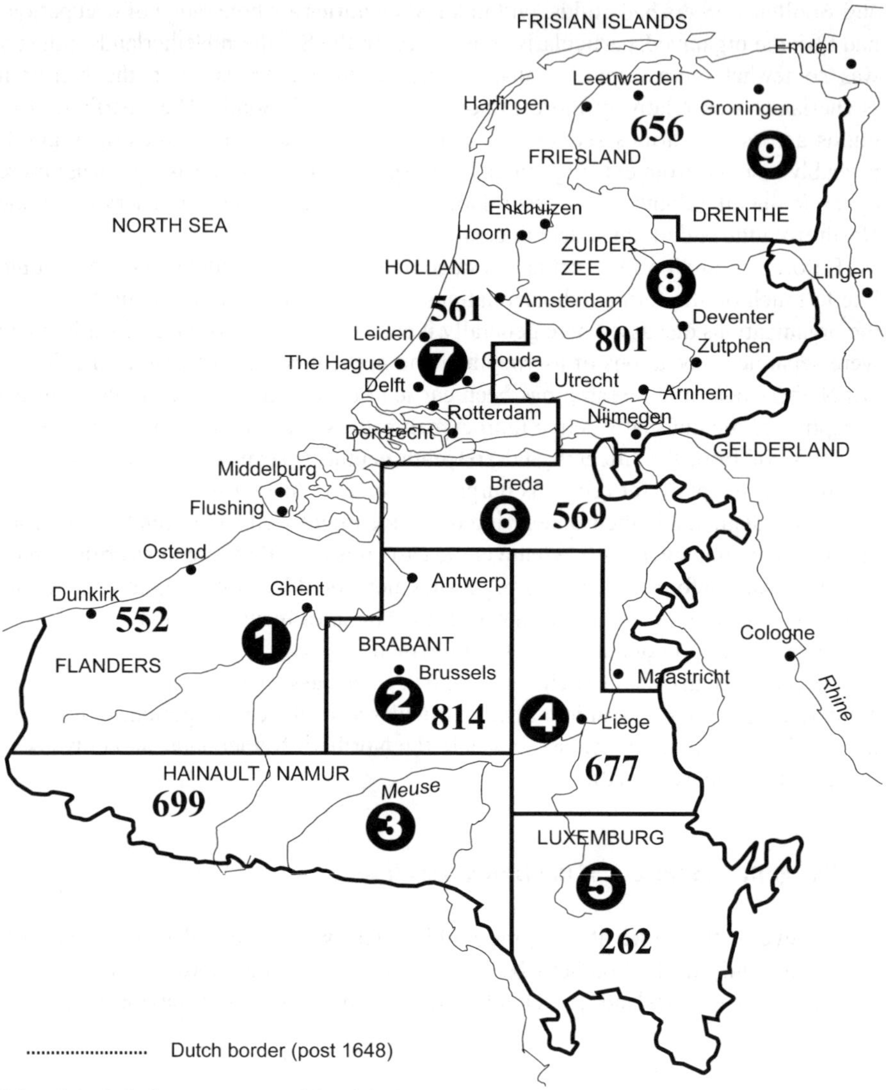

Map 2.3. *Inhabitants per guild c. 1560*

number of guilds (see table 2.1). Although the political power of the guilds in some cities being subjugated by central government, and the effect this had on standardizing the guilds, they remained primarily urban organizations — with all the variegation this implied.

Centralized government, which was at the peak of its power at this time, rarely imposed general measures in relation to the guilds. One exception were the regulations imposed on goldsmiths and silversmiths; this reflected the centralization of mintage under the Burgundians, which had been underway for over a century. The quality of the precious metals supplied to the mints had to be safeguarded, and so in 1489 uniform quality standards were set for gold and silver. Goldsmiths and silversmiths played an important role here, which is why in 1503 Philip the Fair subjected their profession to national regulation, although the implementation of the regulations was delegated to provincial and local bodies.[18]

In several towns, such as Utrecht (in 1528), Charles V, ruler of the Habsburg Netherlands, brought to an end the political power of the craft guilds once and for all. As a result, the political restrictions on their number were lifted, and they were able to develop more in response to the dictates of the economy. In the Southern Netherlands political developments took a different course, though this observation is largely based on the case of Ghent, where Charles V — having dealt first with Utrecht — drastically curtailed the political independence of the craft guilds in the Caroline Concession of 1540.[19] The same tendency could be seen in the prince-bishopric of Liège, where restrictions were imposed on the total number of craft guilds per city. In Hasselt, Sint Truiden, Tongeren and Liège, craftsmen seem to have had little freedom to set up new craft guilds. Perhaps potential new groups were forced to join existing guilds, which might explain why the bricklayers and carpenters of Tongeren joined the smiths' guild and why, within existing guilds, separate occupational fraternities continued to be established well into the eighteenth century.[20]

There were now scarcely any larger cities without guilds. Nonetheless, despite the greater degree of homogeneity, the Northern and Southern Netherlands remained distinct from one another. For a long time the South was far more developed in terms of urbanization, and it was thus the region with the most craft guilds. There were exceptions to this pattern, but these can be explained by local circumstances. Lokeren is an example of a city with no craft guilds. Further south, Verviers and Charleroi were also conspicuous. These towns had all developed only late on and so were free 'of all medieval tradition', as has been remarked for Charleroi.[21] In Verviers, the most important industry was the woollen industry, but Verviers was really nothing more than the centre of an extensive industrial region, which actually fell under the joint jurisdiction of Liège and Brussels. The boundary between town and countryside was thus less well-defined, and moreover industry emerged quite late on. In 1563 the original market town Verviers had as few as 750 families — no more than 4,000 inhabitants — while the development of its civic institutions was still in full swing. It

18 Van Gelder and Hoc, 1960.

19 Van Werveke, 1947, pp. 51-2, 70 et seq.

20 In Liège, for example, the surgeons, barbers and wigmakers at the beginning of the sixteenth century, the minstrels and cooks in 1526, lawyers in 1555, schoolmasters in 1627, playing-card manufacturers in 1669, and the College of Sint Lucas (an association of physicians) in 1699; in Tongeren the musicians established a fraternity in 1750. See Hansotte, 1987, p. 272.

21 Hasquin, 1971, pp. 67-75.

was not until 1651 that Verviers became a chartered town (a 'bonne ville').[22]

Whatever the case, the density of guilds, which in the larger cities of the South had been double that in the North, began to converge (see table 2.2). In most provinces one could expect to find one craft guild per 500 to 750 inhabitants. This convergence was least evident in the northeast, but there too the tendency was unmistakable. The background to this convergence was undoubtedly the pattern of population development and urbanization in the Northern Netherlands. The population of the larger cities in the southernmost provinces fell slightly, while it doubled in Brabant, tripled in Holland and Zeeland, and quadrupled in Utrecht, Gelderland and Overijssel. The population of the main cities in the three northern provinces actually increased fivefold.

However, as we noted earlier, the incidence of guilds was determined not just by the level of population growth. At the same time, the density of guilds fell unexpectedly in the Belgian parts of the Duchy of Brabant. Closer study reveals this to have been wholly the result of events in Antwerp and Brussels; excluding Brussels and Antwerp, the density for Brabant was one guild per 430 inhabitants. In both large cities, however, the population grew so rapidly that institutional developments failed to keep pace. Brussels's population doubled from 1400 to 1560, while Antwerp's increased almost tenfold. New craft guilds emerged in both Brabantine cities, but at a much slower rate. Moreover, it was not only in low-density areas that the relationship between population growth and corporatism began to diverge; the same was true of those locations with a high density of guilds. In fact, generally speaking the highest proportion of craft guilds per population was in the small and smaller cities (as for earlier periods, we include here cities with fewer than 2,500 inhabitants). Small cities with relatively many guilds were largely a feature of the Dutch provinces of North Brabant (Helmond, Eindhoven and Bergen op Zoom) and Zeeland (Middelburg, Goes, Hulst, Veere, Zierikzee — one guild per 145 inhabitants, and Sluis — one guild per 100 inhabitants). In Belgium, a similar average can be found for Waremme in the prince-bishopric of Liège, with ten craft guilds per 1,000 inhabitants. Nor was this at all exceptional. Deinze in Flanders had one craft guild per 300 inhabitants. Herk-de-stad and Maaseik in Liège both had one craft guild per 330-400 inhabitants. Bilzen (Liège), 's Gravenbrakel (Hainault) and Nieuwpoort (Flanders) had one guild per 400-430 inhabitants.[23] Durbuy in Luxemburg, which is said to have had nine craft guilds for no more than 500 inhabitants, had the highest density, at one per 55 inhabitants. To understand the factors behind these remarkable figures, one could examine the local history of these towns in more detail, and, more specifically, their population histories and the rise and decline of their craft guilds. It is not inconceivable that these guilds were founded in more fertile demographic times, and that as populations declined

---

22 Mathieu, 1946, pp. 33 and 37.

23 If we are to believe Van Houtte, 1920, p. 18, who based his conclusions on the inquiry of 1738, Ninove in Flanders had one craft guild per 73 inhabitants. One would have to examine this case in more detail before being able to confirm this however. Perhaps these workers were actually grouped into fewer guilds.

they atrophied, becoming empty shells, continuing to exist in name but functionally redundant. The large number of craft guilds in a city like Bruges too can be attributed to the city's growth in the late Middle Ages and the continued existence of these guilds once Bruges had begun to decline.[24]

In several large cities of the Southern Netherlands the 'composite character' of many craft guilds also played a role. Peter Stabel has argued that in the sixteenth century Kortrijk and Oudenaarde, for example, were characterized by fairly general groupings of artisans. These groups then split into independent guilds. For Oudenaarde Stabel identified fifty occupational groups subsumed within twelve more general organizations. The drapers' guild included even some occupational groups with their own governing body.[25] As a result, Oudenaarde was one of the few Flemish cities where the number of craft guilds rose markedly after the fifteenth century. Their number seems to have peaked in the sixteenth century, when the city apparently had 'fifty corporations', in which 'all occupations' were represented.[26] The reverse also occurred, however. Leuven apparently had at least forty craft guilds in 1360 and 1378;[27] by 1784 only 25 were still in existence. Even before 1450 many guilds seem to have amalgamated, perhaps for political, economic and demographic reasons. The same occurred in Tongeren, where the number of craft guilds declined from fourteen in 1400 to twelve in 1467.[28]

Despite the tendency towards greater uniformity between south and north under the influence of demographic and political developments, remarkable differences persisted in the relationship between the city and its environment, differences that actually became sharper during this period. Traditionally, the interests of the town and country were opposed, and the guilds played a crucial role in this, since one of their principal objectives was to ward off competition from rural areas, where subsistence costs (and thus wages) were lower — largely because of the absence of urban excises.

Some cities managed to completely subdue the surrounding countryside. Early examples include the cities of Flanders, Zeeland and Groningen. Following the Flemish example — though in this case with the permission of the Count — Zeeland's woollen industry east of the river Scheldt was concentrated in Zierikzee in 1305, and its woollen industry west of the Scheldt moved to Middelburg in 1351. The city of Groningen too succeeded in subduing the countryside.[29] However, in the late Middle Ages and the early modern period the North and south diverged in this respect. For

---

24 The generally late rise of the craft guilds in Dendermonde — whose population at the start of the fourteenth century had been 9000, but which declined later to less than half that number — again confirms that population size was not the only factor determining directly the number of guilds: Stabel, 1995, p. 21.

25 Stabel, 1995, pp. 224-5.

26 De Jaegher, 1973, p. 212.

27 Cuvelier, 1935, p. 257.

28 Helsen, Moermans, Severijns and Vandeplas, 1988, pp. 61-2.

29 Henderikx, 2001, p. 92; Unger, 1931, p. 19.

a while the North continued its exclusionist policies in relation to the countryside, while the southern cities changed their policy on this point. In 1531 Holland's cities succeeded in persuading the government in Brussels to grant them permission to take steps to regulate competition from rural industry. Utrecht and Friesland took similar initiatives, though with less success. Whatever the effect,[30] not only was such a policy much less likely in the South, competition from the countryside actually increased. This reflected two essential differences between north and south. First and foremost, in the South the nobility and the church wielded much greater political power, and their economic interests were tied more to the countryside than to the city.[31] After the Dutch Revolt, this difference in political constellation became even more pronounced, not only because the nobility and the monasteries lost power, especially in the coastal provinces of the North, but also because northern cities succeeded in annexing more and more of the surrounding seigneuries (*ambachtsheerlijkheden*). Individual cities thus increased their power over the adjacent countryside. Secondly, and this factor is probably related to the first, the breach between large master and small master began to widen in the southern guilds, with large masters not only subcontracting work to fellow citizens (journeymen, but also small masters), but also putting out work to the countryside.[32] In some cases this led to villages dominated by cottage industry expanding, and outgrowing many cities in terms of population. Examples include such textile centres as Hondschoote (now in France) and Sint Niklaas in Flanders and Duffel in Brabant, which, despite having thousands of inhabitants, never acquired the status of a city in the early modern period.

In the North, it was not until the seventeenth century that a city like Tilburg experienced the same development. Despite having 8,500 inhabitants by 1795, this large 'township' remained a village in legal terms. This seemed to mark a new phase in the relationship between town and country, with the latter already having succeeded in achieving economic though not legal emancipation. This was true not only in the North, but also in the South.[33]

---

30 De Vries and van der Woude 1997, pp. 274, 508-9, believe the effect was limited. The basis for their conclusion is not entirely clear.

31 See the unpublished PhD-thesis by Michael Limberger, which goes into some detail about the countryside around Antwerp *c*. 1450-1650.

32 Lis and Soly, 1994c.

33 In the South it was not until the end of the seventeenth century that the cities took formal steps in order to gain control over certain rural industries. See Dickschen, 1995.

5. The guilds in the North and South in the seventeenth century

The Dutch Revolt against Spain certainly led to divergent economic and demographic developments, but also to cultural dissemination, when, for example, many southern guild members fled to the North and introduced southern institutions and customs. Posthumus noted that the neringen — which were characteristic of Leiden and other key cities such as Haarlem and Delft — and the associated clothmakers' halls were introduced first in Leiden, in imitation of Norwich. In Norwich they were set up by immigrants from the Southern Netherlands, created out of nothing as it were, since at that time they existed neither in the Southern Netherlands nor in England. Also, the custom among craft guilds in the Northern Netherlands of using attendance tokens was actually introduced by immigrants from the South. With the help of these so-called 'guild tokens', the guild could monitor the compulsory attendance of members at funerals and other events.[34]

The guild system remained dominant in both regions, but in the seventeenth century its greatest expansion was in the North. In the South, the guilds seem to have stagnated rather than expanded. Even where — perhaps because — the population declined markedly due to war and emigration, corporative structures remained intact. In Antwerp, whose population declined from over 100,000 to under 50,000 between 1567 and 1591 (after which it recovered to over 70,000 in the mid-seventeenth century), the guilds continued to function very much as they had before. Some disappeared, and some amalgamated, but such changes were few and far between. Earlier, we pointed to the high density of guilds in Sluis — a result of the early dependence of this small town on Bruges. The mother city forced Sluis to retain separate control of all its industries authorized to have a guild of their own in Bruges. The decline in the number of inhabitants did not cause a rapid dissolution of the guilds, but another factor in addition to this institutional sluggishness was the fact that Sluis became a regional centre, and as a garrison town it was keen to check competition from soldiers billeted in the town who hoped to carry on a trade too. In short, one could not simply abolish existing institutions, certainly not when they also had institutional power. Karin Van Honacker has demonstrated this for Brussels, which had guilds with one or two deacon-deputies to represent hundreds of members, but also craft guilds providing political representation for just a handful of masters.[35]

---

[34] Following Minard 1879, this seems mainly to have been an Antwerp custom of the 1540s (although the 'discovery' should perhaps be attributed to Bruges, since the earliest example there dates from 1532. It was introduced to the North by immigrants from the Southern Netherlands, first in Zeeland (especially Middelburg) and then in other regions, and even in a few German cities along the border.

[35] Van Honacker, 1994, pp. 185-6.

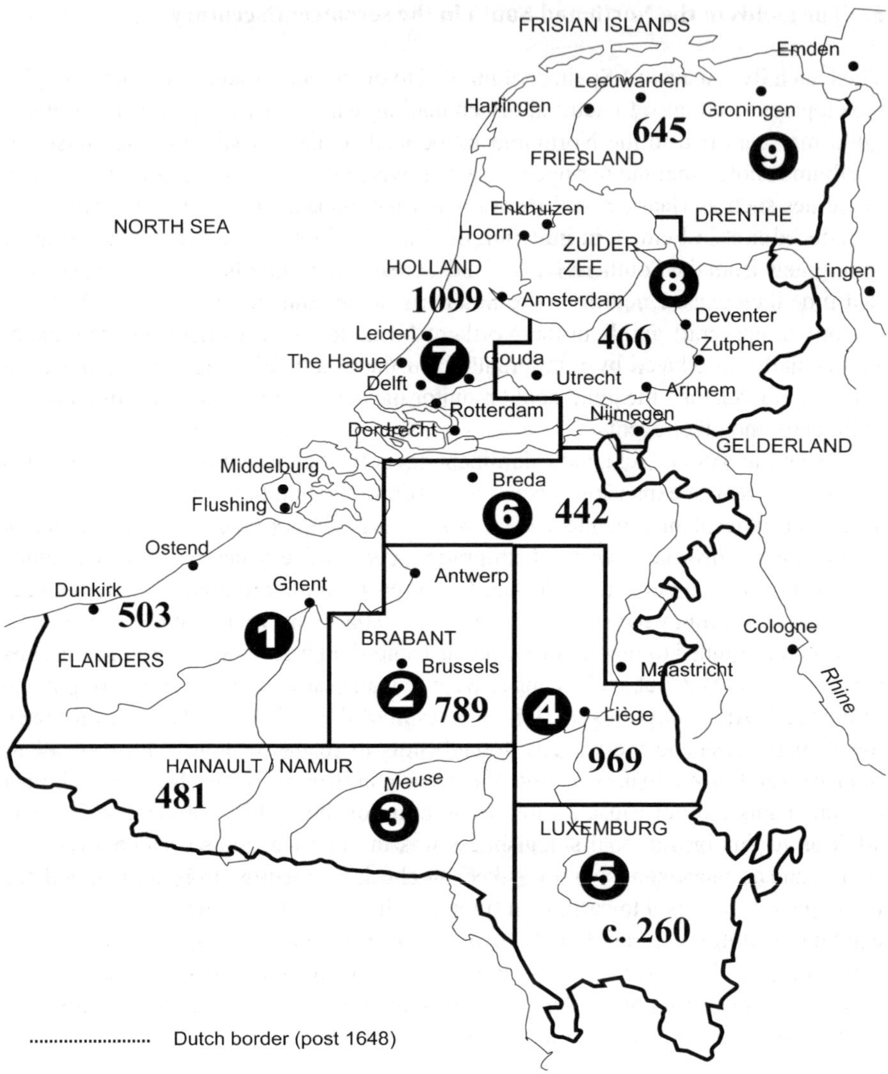

Map 2.4. *Inhabitants per guild c. 1670*

In the North the Reformation had major consequences for how the guilds functioned.[36] It was extremely rare for guilds to be abolished on account of their traditional Catholic character. However, with the abolition of the 'papal superstitions' some public celebrations — in the form of annual or more frequent processions — lapsed. In a number of Holland's cities, alternatives appeared in the form of gifts of church windows and psalm boards to Reformed churches, but such gifts quickly went out of fashion, and

36 See also the chapter by Alfons Thijs in this volume.

after the mid-seventeenth century they became extremely rare. On the other hand, the box system was given a strong impulse. In Amsterdam, for example, following the *Alteratie* of 1578 the city council directed that the income of the guilds could be used only to usefully assist their members. As a result, the insurance role of the guilds developed much more vigorously in the North than in the South.[37]

One should not forget that the Reformation had been only partially successful in the North.[38] In the West, Centre and East of the Low Countries, the population retained a mixed religious affiliation. In the South, Catholics were still in the majority, and it was only in most of Zeeland and on the islands of South Holland, as well as in the northeast, that large continuous areas emerged where the Reformed were numerically predominant. The consequences for the guild system differed widely from one region to another. In the West, guilds generally did not exclude individuals from membership on religious grounds. At most, there were a few guilds, in Rotterdam for example, which excluded the non-Reformed from holding office. In the Centre and East though, the Reformed did discriminate: against Catholics first and foremost, but also against Mennonites, Lutherans and other Protestant minorities.[39]

This religious discrimination was part and parcel of a general reluctance on the part of the cities of the provinces of Utrecht, Overijssel and especially Gelderland to accept immigrants. The right of citizenship there was hugely expensive — especially in relation to the level of wages — and the same was true of guild membership. The discrimination against the non-Reformed is perhaps less apparent than the reluctant (certainly compared with the coastal provinces) reception offered to newcomers, but it was real enough. In the city of Utrecht, for example, Catholics were excluded from the right of citizenship in 1655, with an exception being made in 1674 for Catholics from the province of Utrecht and in 1724 for those from elsewhere in the Republic. Catholics from abroad continued to be excluded from citizenship until 1795, unless they could prove they were 'useful' and 'necessary'. East of Utrecht, Jews and Catholics were denied the right of citizenship until 1795, as were Lutherans and Mennonites until the end of the seventeenth or early eighteenth centuries. In the Southern Netherlands the situation was essentially no different, though the roles were reversed, with non-Catholics excluded from citizenship. Naturally, the impossibility of becoming a citizen had direct consequences for guild membership, and in the East guilds could actually exclude resident Catholic citizens from becoming members too.

Religious developments in the Southern Netherlands were dictated by the Counter-Reformation and left the craft guilds more powerful. The unstable financial and political situation under Spanish rule meant that central government was unable to prevent a power vacuum, one that offered corporative civil society an opportunity to move centre stage.[40] In some cities, such as Antwerp, there was a degree of understanding

---

[37] See the chapter by Sandra Bos in this volume. See also van Leeuwen 2000.

[38] Bergsma, 1995.

[39] Lourens and Lucassen, 2000.

on this point between guild representatives and the local administrations in which they were represented.[41] By refusing to pay the levies imposed by Spain to defend the South, the guilds could make things very difficult for the central government.[42] It is no coincidence that in the region bordering on France there was a link between the guild system's quantitative and qualitative peak on the one hand and the Counter-Reformation and the peak of 'la civilisation hispano-tridentine' on the other.[43] Even under Joseph II, in the second half of the eighteenth century, local councils defended the craft guilds with fervour, though not everywhere.

In the prince-bishopric of Liège the opposite occurred. Until the sixteenth century the craft guilds were self-governing, and guild members elected their own representatives. In the course of the seventeenth and eighteenth centuries the civic authorities gradually deprived them of that autonomy. In the city of Liège, for example, the guilds lost much of their political influence in 1649, and the rest in 1684,[44] though they retained their professional and economic functions.[45] A similar development occurred in Hasselt in 1728.[46]

There is another possible link between the Counter-Reformation and the further institutional entrenchment of the guild system, namely the flourishing of the luxury trades in cities such as Antwerp and Brussels. One important stimulus to the expansion of these trades was the need to decorate or redecorate churches, monasteries and convents with the work of skilled artisans (altars, paintings, tapestries, silver, and so on), not just in Antwerp or the Southern Netherlands, but throughout the Spanish Empire, from Italy to South America via the Iberian peninsula, and even parts of Asia. A global religious export industry developed, based on the Southern Netherlands. The local nobility also provided a significant source of demand; the deteriorating economic situation prompted them to invest their money in status-enhancing luxuries. Wealthy citizens, too, furnished their interiors with examples of decorative craftsmanship: expensive paintings, statues, tapestries and show-pieces made from precious metals. Antwerp's diamond sector for example grew astonishingly, from 30-40 masters in 1582 (the year in which the guild was founded) to no fewer than 164 in 1618.[47] It is

---

40 Thijs, 1990, pp. 145-8; Deceulaer, 1994, pp. 155-6.

41 In Antwerp there were about 56 guilds in the early modern period. Around half of those sent delegates to the *Brede* or *Maandagse Raad*. The *Brede Raad* appointed the delegates who represented the third estate in the States of Brabant. Jacobs, 2000, p. 565.

42 Van Elsacker, 2000, pp. 129-63.

43 Guignet, 1990, p. 295.

44 Poncelet, 1900, p. 10.

45 Hansotte, 1987, pp. 270-2.

46 Bussels, 1960, p. 96. Doornik is an interesting exception: here the guild system was independent of local government and came under a 'chambre des arts et métiers', which comprised 72 deacons or subdeacons (elected by the guilds), and which was authorized to hear disputes relating to the guilds. See Guignet, 1990, pp. 310-12.

not surprising then that by the sixteenth century masterpieces tended to be required as a formal test of competence.[48]

Curiously, in the Northern Netherlands the unprecedented flourishing of the arts, organized in the guilds of St Luke, was unrelated or only indirectly related to religious developments there. The interiors of the Reformed churches were left sober, but there was a strong growth in demand for art from wealthy citizens. Naturally, this art might have strong religious or moral overtones (most obviously in the emblems), but it need not.[49]

Finally, local government could also put pressure on certain craft guilds, again out of a desire to regulate quality, but in this case linked to intellectual developments more generally. It was not unusual for instance for corporative associations in the medical sector to be brought under the supervision of a medical college, drastically restricting the autonomy of apothecaries and barber-surgeons. The university-educated physicians who sat in these colleges justified this intervention in terms of their superior learning and skills, and assumed that guild members were simply a menace to public health. Antwerp was the first city to establish a medical college, in the early seventeenth century.[50] The physicians reserved for themselves the right to prescribe medicines — effectively abolishing the monopoly of the apothecaries and barber-surgeons — and compelled guild members to study medical theory and sit examinations; as a result, guild members lost control over membership of their own organization.[51] There are indications that similar developments took place in the Northern Netherlands too.[52]

Earlier, we noted that both the Flemish cities of Bruges and Ghent in the late Middle Ages and Antwerp in Brabant in the sixteenth century had an extensive system of craft guilds. In these three cases, which cover the period from the fourteenth to the sixteenth centuries, craft guilds and economic prosperity went hand in hand. The same observation can be made on the basis of seventeenth-century data for cities in the Northern Netherlands, and Amsterdam in particular (see tables 2.1 and 2.2). It was not only the number of guilds that increased rapidly in times of economic prosperity; so too did the number of guild members, and thus the proportion of the urban population subject to guild regulations.[53] Amsterdam is the most notable case in point. At the end of the seventeenth century a quarter of all Amsterdam's employed males were guild members, and 60 per cent were subject to the regulations of the guilds as journeymen. Only 15 per cent of employed males were beyond this corporative system.[54] For the

47 Thijs, 1988, pp. 208 et seq.

48 De Munck, 2002, pp. 94-108, 363-95; De Munck, 2003, pp. 40-8, 116-18.

49 Bok, 1994; Prak 2003.

50 Brans, 1957, pp. 37-8.

51 De Munck, 2001, pp. 459-84.

52 Huisman, 1992, pp. 315-29, 360-9 and 396-403; Huisman, 1993, p. 121.

53 Lucassen, 2001, pp. 161-74, esp. 162-3.

Southern Netherlands Hubert Van Houtte has concluded that 'while no guild active in the first half of the eighteenth century reached the size of the large drapers' guilds of the late Middle Ages, the corporative system was, as a whole, much more developed'. Van Houtte assumes that the number of direct and indirect members working in industries geared to local markets rose until at least the mid-eighteenth century, and that to a large extent the cloth industry was replaced by a range of specialisms within the textile sector. One can conclude then that in the case of Bruges relatively more workers were organized on a corporative basis in the eighteenth than in the fourteenth century. In smaller cities too the number of masters, free journeymen and apprentices organized on a corporative basis is thought to have increased significantly during the early modern period — the result, according to Van Houtte, of an increase in the number of craft guilds.[55] On the other hand, the density of guilds fell in Brussels, and probably in Antwerp and Ghent too. For Brussels, Roger De Peuter has calculated that the number of masters, journeymen and apprentices as a percentage of the total active population fell from 42 per cent in 1615 to barely 26 per cent in 1738.[56] As a percentage of the total population the corresponding figure would be around 13 per cent, significantly less than the 22.3 per cent that Walter Prevenier calculated for fourteenth-century Ghent (in both cases including journeymen and apprentices) and considerably lower than our figure for Amsterdam.[57] Johan Dambruyne estimated the number of Ghent masters in the second half of the sixteenth century (1572-1584) at 4,000 — *c.* 9.5 per cent of the entire population of 42,000; including journeymen and apprentices gives a figure of less than half the working population.[58] Dambruyne assumes that the situation in 1738 was essentially no different, but in the case of Antwerp only 32.5 per cent of the active population worked within the context of a craft guild in that year.[59] Since almost a quarter of Antwerp's population was employed in the non-corporative organized lace industry, this can hardly surprise.

Did the influence of corporative organizations extend to the countryside? In the previous section we referred to the competition between urban and rural industry in Flanders and south Brabant. Examples can also be found from the seventeenth century, but, most remarkably, this expansion of urban industries into the countryside now began to appear elsewhere in the Netherlands too. In Leiden, for instance, woollen textile manufacturers, who were independent or largely free of guild regulation, began outsourcing work to places such as the village of Tilburg in Staats Brabant (the northern part of the Duchy of Brabant) and to Verviers in the prince-bishopric of

---

54 Lourens and Lucassen 1998, p. 145; cf. de Vries, Lourens, Lucassen and Nijboer, 2003.

55 Van Houtte, 1920, pp. 17-18.

56 De Peuter, 1979, pp. 116-29.

57 Prevenier, 1975, p. 277.

58 Assuming a ratio of masters to journeymen of 1:1.8 (based on the *ambachtsenquête* [guild inquiry] of 1738), this implies a total of 26.7%, with an active population of 48.5%. Dambruyne uses a figure of 55% for the sixteenth century. See Dambruyne, 2000, pp. 265 et seq.

59 De Munck, 2002, pp. 43 et seq.

Liège and other neighbouring villages, including Eupen.[60] Exceptionally, an attempt was made to set up craft guilds — for example in Charleroi by textile manufacturers who migrated there from Liège, and who in 1687 attempted, with the support of the central government, to institute a requirement to submit a 'masterpiece'. In Verviers, again in the second half of the seventeenth century, it was the local government that attempted to set up craft guilds, again without success. Nevertheless, with the exception of several large cities and some proto-industrial areas in the South, the general trend throughout most of the North and south was one of intensification of the guild system. In the second half of the seventeenth century, the proportion of guilds to inhabitants was greater than ever before in the larger cities. On the face of it Holland seems to have been an exception. However, the phenomenon we noted in Antwerp a century earlier was evident here too: while the population grew exponentially, the number of guilds did not. If we exclude Amsterdam, however, the density of guilds rose (slightly) in Holland compared with a century earlier, to one craft guild per 750 inhabitants in Holland and Zeeland.

We are thus in a position to distinguish three models of development. While mindful of our caveat in relation to Amsterdam, we could characterize the larger cities (which also grew rapidly in number) in the northern coastal provinces (Zeeland, Holland, Friesland and Groningen) as type one: unprecedented population growth coinciding with an even more rapid increase in the number of guilds. Contrasting with these were the provinces whose urban populations either stagnated or actually declined: Flanders, Brabant, Hainault, but also Dutch Brabant and Limburg, and in a sense Utrecht, Gelderland and Overijssel too, i.e. most of the Low Countries. One cause of this development was of course the sharp drop in population due to the military conflict (particularly in the East) and the emigration (especially from the South) of large numbers of urban craftsmen to the North around 1600. In this second type of city, the number of craft guilds continued to rise despite population decline, at least in the North, and so the density of guilds also rose. In the case of the Southern Netherlands the absolute number of guilds stagnated, despite the decrease in population size. During the period 1100 to 1784 at least 197 guilds disappeared in the Southern Netherlands.[61] If new craft guilds were set up in cities where the guild system had long since matured, the cause should be sought in the economic restructuring in the aftermath of the religious troubles. In Antwerp, for example, new guilds were founded in the increasingly important luxury trades (diamond and ruby cutters in 1582) and in the relatively new textile sectors (the camlet dyers in 1577). In Malines, associations by, for instance, the sawyers and manure collectors continued to be set up, as did groups of button makers, tanners and (later) wig makers (in 1756). The establishment

60 Van Houtte 1964, pp. 186, 238, probably based on Posthumus 1908-39, vol 3, chs 7-8; de Vries, Lucassen, Lourens and Nijboer, 2003, pp. 84-107; van Gurp, 2004.

61 Of these, we know of only 53 that amalgamated; the others — 14% of all the guilds in our dataset — simply ceased to exist. Perhaps some carried on in the face of a decline in membership, until they began to lead an almost virtual existence.

of groups of button makers and tanners can be attributed to growing specialization within the textile industry,[62] and the foundation of a wig makers' guild to changed patterns of consumption. In Nijvel too a wig makers' guild was set up, in 1735; in Brussels, a wig makers' fraternity had been set up as early as 1697. In a similar vein, a hatters' guild was founded in Dinant in 1705, and in Menen a guild for goldsmiths and silversmiths was established as late as 1716. Regardless of whether these new foundations reflected the reorientation towards luxury articles or the later rise of new fashions, the guild system and the urban authorities can hardly be regarded as having had conservative inclinations. By setting training and quality standards for example, corporative regulations allowed a dynamic response to new circumstances, and in Antwerp contributed to the subsequent continued expansion of the luxury trades.[63]

Finally, a third model is represented by the cities of Liège and Belgian Limburg. In the prince-bishopric, cities with a population in excess of 5,000 expanded rapidly, without the number of guilds keeping pace. Indeed, in cities such as Liège the number of guilds (which was politically determined) did not change after the late Middle Ages.

6. The guilds in the North and south in the eighteenth century

A divergent pattern set in during the eighteenth century, with economic growth in the South and economic stagnation in the North. Even sharper were the contrasts between the urban industries, which enjoyed renewed prosperity in the South while generally declining in the North. What significance did this have for the development of the guild system?

First, and most importantly, the growth of rural industry continued; in the North

[62] In Kortrijk for example the button makers and the tailors parted company in 1753. The wig makers' guilds apparently spread from the South to the North. We know of such guilds in Flushing (1740), Sluis (1745), The Hague (before 1748), Dordrecht (1750) and Leiden (1752).

[63] After 1750 the local and central governments sometimes pursued a conscious policy of amalgamating guilds in order to reduce the large number of law suits (and the corresponding mountains of debt). There are a number of examples: Antwerp's carpenters and cabinet makers merged in 1756; the same occurred in Bruges in 1762; in Bergen the mercers amalgamated with the drapers and a number of small retail professions in 1763; in Geraardsbergen the shoemakers merged with the *oudeschoenmakers* (who patched and then resold old shoes) in 1763; in Bruges the shoemakers and the *oudeschoenmakers* merged in 1769; in Ghent the curriers merged with the tanners and the carpenters with the cabinet makers in 1769, a number of specialist weavers groups merged in 1772, as did the turners and woodworkers in the same year; in Malines the saddlemakers and saddlers merged in 1775; in Doornik the tanners and curriers merged in 1778; and in Kortrijk the carpenters and the cabinetmakers did so in 1780. See Van Houtte, 1920, pp. 70-1 and 96.

this sometimes manifested itself in the establishment of rural guilds. We know of 92 craft guilds in 43 different villages, most of them set up at the end of the seventeenth and in the eighteenth century. In a very few cases, these villages were actually semi-urban settlements that had retained the legal status of a village, such as Meppel with its nine guilds, Oosterhout with seven, Zwartsluis with six and Roosendaal with five, distributed across different sectors. In places of economic development, interlocal traffic increased significantly. As a result, there were no fewer than 30 transport guilds, mostly of skippers, concentrated on the islands of Zeeland and South Holland. Fifteen rural textile guilds were of chief importance in relation to rural industry. They were concentrated in northern Limburg, North Brabant and the Achterhoek (eastern Netherlands), but also located as far away as Texel and Makkum.[64] Also noteworthy were several rural smiths' guilds in Limburg, including the county of Geleen.

For the South rural guilds are not well documented.[65] The prince-bishopric of Liège had several rural pedlars' fraternities. The mercers of Walcourt, for example, acquired a privilege in 1399 that permitted them to sell their wares between the rivers Sambre and Meuse; those of Ciney obtained a similar privilege in 1520. Though these 'circuits' were termed fraternities, and administered by 'un roi du tour', they conformed in every respect to our definition of guilds. In economic terms their statutes were similar, characterized principally by the right to exercise a monopoly.[66] They differed from genuine guilds in that they were not tied to a specific city, nor confined to its walled-in space.[67] Further, Heirwegh has suggested that in various parishes potters formed 'des corps de métiers', comparable with urban craft guilds. In the jurisdiction of Walhorn in Limburg, for example, a sort of potters' corporation had existed since 1619, in which up to fifteen ovens, employing as many as 300 workers, are thought to have operated.[68] Finally, one should also mention Nijvel's braziers. They had no rural guild, but their organization transcended the individual city — to such an extent in fact that the authorities of Charleroi complained in 1784 that the local braziers claimed to belong to the group of Namur braziers.[69] Perhaps they were the same group, with the braziers being semi-itinerant.

If we compare the figures for 1784 with those for a century earlier, the conclusion that, for the first time in five hundred years, very few new craft guilds were founded is inescapable (see table 2.1). In the South, this might have been true from as early as the seventeenth century, but in the North too the number of new foundations began to fall sharply. Those already in existence continued, sometimes with just a handful of members, but few were added. And yet this seemingly static picture in the South obscured a situation more dynamic than one might suppose: though the number of

---

64 Mastboom, 1994; Zeiler, 1994.

65 The *teuten* (groups of tinkers, pedlars, hawkers and such like) cannot be regarded as guilds since they were not recognized by the authorities. See the standard work by Mertens, 1995.

66 Gérard, 1935, p. 145.

67 Brouwers, 1910, 29, pp. 57-72.

68 Heirwegh, 1981, p. 166; Hasquin, 1971, pp. 69 et seq.

69 Goetstouwers, 1908, p. 181. Hasquin, 1971, p. 67, and Lourens and Lucassen, 2000, p. 30.

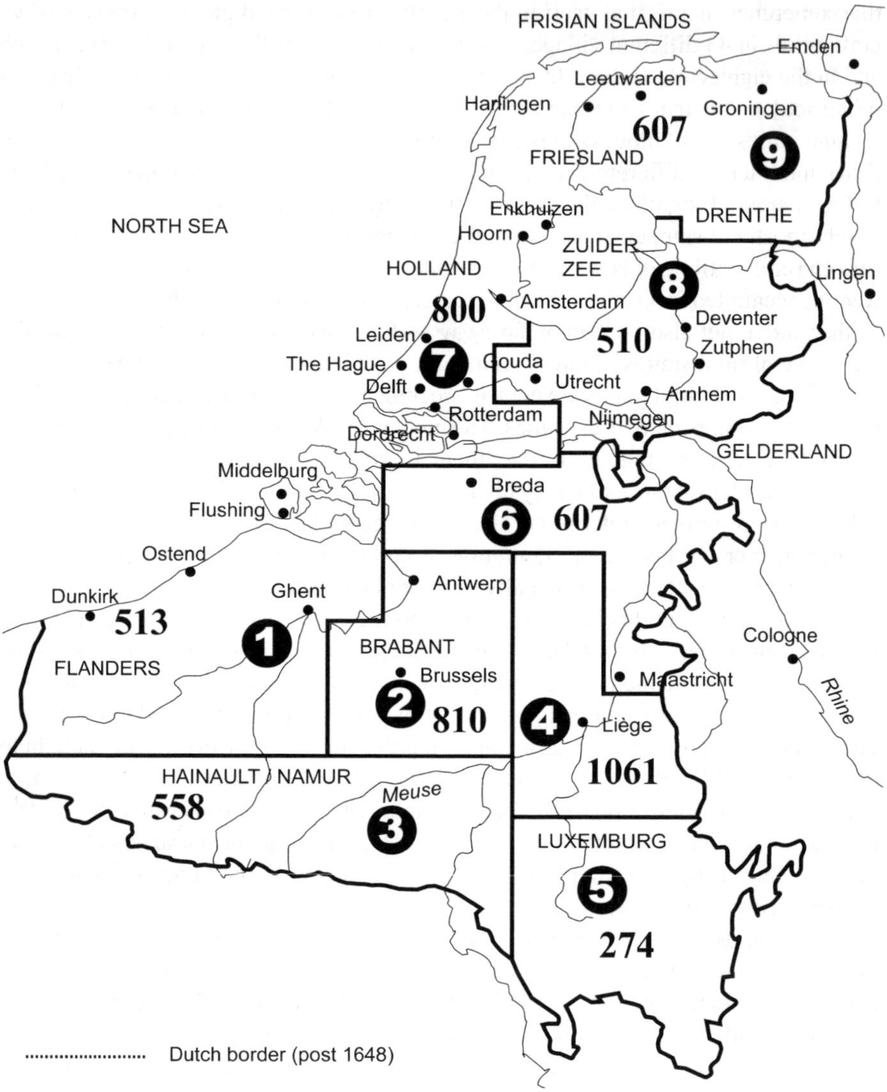

Map 2.5 *Inhabitants per guild c. 1784*

guilds remained more or less constant, within these guilds a marked differentiation occurred with the emergence of more or less autonomous chapters, the *letten* or *naties*. This phenomenon was not entirely unknown in the North, though the terminology was different, but it was much less developed there. Characteristic examples in the South included the smiths and the mercers, each having perhaps dozens of sub-organizations, each with their own monopoly. The building, leather and clothing sectors also had umbrella organizations, covering various groups. This partly explains why developments in the eighteenth century seem to have been limited, since we did not register for the South the dissolution or creation of new *letten* or *naties*. Generally speaking, one can conclude that composite craft guilds were more frequent in smaller centres, with fewer craftsmen per occupation or sector. A typical example is Geraardsbergen, where the twelve registered craft guilds actually comprised fifty sub-associations.

Alongside the new foundations in corporative 'late developers' such as Echternach, and the wig makers and button makers mentioned earlier — to which Nijvel's button makers can be added, founded in 1704 as a branch of the mercers — it is notable that most of the organizations founded in the eighteenth century can be considered civic bodies, especially in Ostend, where in 1734 the sack heavers' and barrowmen's guilds were founded, and in 1783 the 'new barrowmen'. We can tentatively hypothesize that these new foundations owed much to local politics, a hypothesis supported by the fervent defence of this type of organization submitted by Nieuwpoort in its reply to the central government's inquiry of 1784.[70]

Given the close relationship we noted earlier between population growth and the number of organizations this stagnation in the establishment of guilds in the North comes as no surprise. On balance, the population of the Republic as a whole remained constant during the eighteenth century at *c.* 2 million. In the South, a different phenomenon occurred: many cities experienced population growth, but without organizational growth. There are two possible explanations. Perhaps the tendency we noted in the seventeenth century on a small scale in the prince-bishopric of Liège spread to the Austrian Netherlands as a whole — more specifically in the form of institutional or political rigidity (as in the city of Liège) or a new sort of entrepreneurship (as in Verviers and Eupen). Or perhaps it was simply a question of the number of organizations being 'capped' above a certain population size (as in Antwerp in the sixteenth century and Amsterdam in the seventeenth century). This latter explanation seems unconvincing, however. The largest southern city in 1784 was Brussels, with just under 75,000 inhabitants. It had grown 10 per cent since 1670, a modest expansion compared with earlier boom towns, such as Antwerp, Leiden and Amsterdam.

All in all, economic factors must have been decisive for the lack of new foundations in those provinces that had previously seen a growth in the number of guilds. There are many examples: Wallonia, with Ath, Halle, Bergen, Namur and also Doornik in Hainault-Namur, but also Louvain, Turnhout and Nijvel in Brabant, and Kortrijk, Geraardsbergen and Ghent in Flanders. Liège and Verviers also seem to belong in this list, though earlier we noted an institutional rigidity in Liège which made it a special case. More generally, one can argue that in the Southern Netherlands it was principally the influence of the French physiocrats that put the guild system under so much pressure. Gradually, corporative regulations such as those on apprenticeship and the need to submit a masterpiece came to be regarded as 'barriers', and regulations on the means of production as 'abuse'. Increasingly, the virtues of the so-called free market were extolled, in the case of the Southern Netherlands, for example, by the Ostend wholesaler Willem Herries, who in 1783 argued that 'the guilds, with all their privi-

[70] Jacobs, 1997, pp. 243-92.

leges and rights, form an insurmountable barrier to the expansion of workshops and to any kind of industry. … These guilds are and will always be injurious in the utmost to the true good of the state that protects them. … All types of workshop and industry are inextricably linked to trade. That which stimulates the one must benefit the other and as long as the exclusivity of the guilds is maintained, one cannot reasonably hope to turn the country into a truly "trading" nation in general terms'.[71] In phrases such as these, economic motives were effortlessly linked to the public interest ('le bien publique'); as a result, the different positions taken by the protagonists of corporative regulation and those who supported *laissez faire* – positions that hardened in the eighteenth century, were often expressed in moral terms. The defenders of the guild system harked back not only to a mythical medieval past, but also to Christian ethics of the just price, good quality and 'the common good' ('le bien commun'), which they claimed were utterly incompatible with the free market and self-aggrandizement.[72]

In the North, in the meantime, very little of this was evident. Though the density of guilds generally declined again slowly during the eighteenth century (see table 2.2), it increased sharply in the coastal provinces of the North. The chief explanation for this must be the growing and successful insurance role of these guilds. Not only did this role expand markedly, in cities such as Amsterdam it also became professionalized. Increasingly, the guilds adopted a system of distributing the interest on the capital invested in bonds. In the South, there was no such development. At most, something similar can be found in the formal establishment of journeyman fraternities, a characteristically eighteenth-century phenomenon.[73] Alfons Thijs has argued that the deteriorating economic situation played a role in the establishment of these fraternities, since the consequences of this deterioration were a lower standard of living and increasing difficulty in becoming a master.[74] The deteriorating economic situation also led to the creation of poor relief boxes, including the boxes of Antwerp's

---

71 Quoted in Heirwegh, 1981, p. 110: 'les corps de métiers, avec tous leurs privilèges, et leurs droits, font une barrière insurmontable à l'agrandissement des manufactures et à toute espèce d'industrie. … Ces corporations sont et seront toujours nuisible dans le plus haut degré au vrai bien de l'Etat qui les protège. … Les manufactures et l'industrie de tous genres sont intimement liées avec le commerce. Tout ce qui encourage l'un, doit faire du bien à l'autre et tant que l'on maintiendra les corporations et métiers exclusifs … on ne peut raisonnablement espérer de rendre le pays en général vraiment commerçant').

72 Heirwegh· 1981, pp· 409 et seq.

73 In Antwerp the first to do so were the journeymen shoemakers (1686), followed by the silk-weavers (1698)· braiders (1722)· bakers (1727), linen weavers (1730)· tailors (1731), smiths (1737)· woodcutters (1761)· throwsters (before 1763), *oudeschoenmakers* (before 1764) and diamond workers (1778). In Louvain, the journeymen shoemakers set up a fraternity in 1708, as did the journeymen slaters in 1717.

74 Thijs, 1994, pp. 240-1.

journeymen hatters and clothmakers, both of which were officially recognized in 1608. Nor was it unusual for religious confraternities to transform themselves into boxes.[75] However, compared with the Northern Netherlands their insurance role remained relatively undeveloped.

7. The abolition of the craft guilds

With just a little exaggeration, the history of the craft guilds can also be regarded as the history of the opposition to them, though on balance the guilds seemed able to effortlessly resist all attacks on their existence for a long time. The earliest reference to a guild in the Low Countries — the merchant guild in Tiel — was written by an opponent. In this case it was the church, but, soon after, in some cities the secular authorities also regularly attempted to curtail or even abolish the guilds. There are many examples: Leiden around 1300 and 1400, Zwolle somewhat later.

In the early modern period the guilds seem to have been under political pressure in Ghent, Liège, Halle and elsewhere. In 1639 guild representatives in Halle, for example, protested at the refusal of the civic authorities to admit them to meetings at which decisions were taken on taxation and the billeting of troops — in contravention of the traditional prerogative of the guilds.[76] Individual craft guilds were occasionally threatened with abolition, as Antwerp's cloth dyers discovered in 1583. Their guild was 'thrown open' at the request of the merchants, who owned the cloth the craftsmen dyed, while the technical regulations were made more stringent. In 1608 the guild was restored, but soon afterwards, in 1623, the cloth merchants again petitioned for 'that same guild to be thrown open again in order to prevent all monopolies and all bad practices stemming from the use of inferior or false dyes'.[77] This time the merchants succeeded partially, and for a period of three years the guild was compelled to admit anyone, without requiring them to undertake a period of apprenticeship, though applicants were required to produce a 'masterpiece'.[78] Perhaps the dyers used their guild to keep prices high and quality low, thus safeguarding their profit margins at the merchants' expense. In Brussels, there was a similar conflict, as is evidenced by the ordinance of 3 February 1703 entitling the cloth merchants to dye cloths themselves or have them dyed by whomever they wished. The cause might also have been a shortage of dyers in the trade, for when the guild was later thrown open, its membership rose by just one.[79]

Evidently referring to several of these events, the De la Court brothers — sons of

---

75 Thijs, 1994, pp. 251-6. It is possible that the same phenomenon occurred in other cities too, but we have been unable to find documentary evidence.

76 Everaert, 1975, p. 153.

77 Prims, 1942, pp. 26-9.

78 Thijs, 1986, pp. 288-9.

79 Van Houtte, 1920, p. 78.

an Ypres immigrant in Leiden — noted their objections to the monopolistic tendencies of guilds in *Het Welvaren van Leiden* (Leiden's Prosperity, written between 1659 and 1662) and in subsequent works. Karel Davids has shown that at that stage their views did not reflect prevailing opinion, but also that there were other writers who in one way or another shared these views. A few isolated examples are known from 1690 and 1714, but such views became more prominent during the protest movements of the late 1740s, and in the 1770s they began to attract permanent and growing support. The debate was not primarily about whether to retain the guilds, but about how to reform them so as to obviate the deleterious consequences of monopoly formation, and so contribute to a recovery in prosperity. With the failure of the Patriot revolutionary movement in 1787, support for the guilds revived for a time. Nonetheless, the debates that ultimately led to the abolition of the guilds at the end of eighteenth century clearly had a powerful ancestry, and the arguments supporting and opposing the guilds were not simply imported from abroad.[80] Though the guilds in the province of Friesland were subjugated for several decades, this had a quite particular political background, as we have seen.

Outside the Republic, the initial debates on the virtues and shortcomings of guilds took place in a quite different context. There, in the late seventeenth and eighteenth centuries, modern cameralistic regimes led by powerful sovereigns ventured a successful attack on these urban institutions, as in Brandenburg and France. In the Southern Netherlands it was the Habsburg rulers Maria Theresa and Joseph II in particular who took the first step towards framing a national economic policy in which the role of urban government was restricted simply to implementation. After 1750, corporative regulations came under increasing pressure, but the degree to which the craft guilds and local and provincial political and legal institutions were so entwined, together with the large debts the craft guilds had built up, ensured that no real consideration was given to the idea of abolishing them once and for all, not even initially by Joseph II (and certainly not prior to 1787). Gradually though, the influence of French physiocratic ideas began to be felt more strongly in the Austrian Netherlands, in and around the central institutions of Brussels for instance, among individuals such as Patrice-François de Neny. They campaigned for greater *laissez faire* in domestic production and labour, and restrictions on access to work, to guild membership and on the use of technology and means of production increasingly became a source of indignation. Generally speaking, the monopoly of the craft guilds does not seem to have been an issue, though their monopoly had been eroded, in part by a policy of mandatory amalgamation, as occurred under Maria Theresa. Initially, the intention of the measures taken to address the guilds' so-called abuses seems actually to have been to strengthen or reorganize the guilds by implementing measures designed to restrict their debts. It was not until the last quarter of the eighteenth century, and more specifically after the accession of Joseph II, that drastic measures were put into effect, including the elimination on 9 February 1784 of all restrictions on the number of workers employed by a master and of all requirements relating to their qualification,

80 Lucassen, 1992; Davids, 2001.

thus effectively abolishing the status of free journeyman at a stroke.[81]

Nonetheless, the definitive abolition was prompted from outside, from revolutionary France.[82] The Law of 2-17 March 1791 swept away the guilds in France. That decision took on a major significance for the Low Countries when gradually, from 1794 onwards, it was overrun by the French and eventually annexed. On 10 November 1795 the law abolishing the guilds was extended to include the nine 'Départements réunies', i.e. the whole of present-day Belgium, Luxemburg, Zeeuws-Vlaanderen and Dutch Limburg. As a consequence, on 4 April 1796 (15 Germinal An IV) the authorities of the departments wrote to all their cantons and municipalities ordering them to wind up the guilds and, for this purpose, to complete a number of questionnaires relating to the guilds' assets. Not all local administrations were in any rush to implement these orders, but all the guilds disappeared sooner or later. By 1798 they had vanished everywhere in the South.

At the same time, a much more laborious attempt to abolish them began in the North. The north retained its independence until 1810, certainly as far as its internal affairs were concerned. Nonetheless, in many respects the Batavian Republic followed the example of its large French sister, and so article 53 of the Dutch Constitution (*Staatsregeling*) adopted on 23 April 1798, declared as one of its fundamental civil and political principles 'all Guilds, Corporations or Fraternities or *Neringen*, Trades or Factories to be dissolved'. Four days after the decree on the freedom of movement of 1 October 1798, the Executive Directory (*Uitvoerend Bewind*) demanded that all guilds be dissolved within eight days; implementation was entrusted to so-called provisional commissioners, a body required to be set up in every municipality where guilds existed. A subsequent announcement on 24 December 1798 declared that access to all occupations subject to the supervision of provisional commissioners was to be unrestricted, although teamsters and certain skippers who had purchased their office were not to be disadvantaged. The sack heavers, weighers and measurers, and goldsmiths and silversmiths also retained their organizations.

As a result of opposition from city governments, which felt constrained in their ability to operate an independent economic policy, and spurred on (not surprisingly) by the guilds themselves, attempts at abolition were not always as successful in the North as they had been in the South. Under the 1801 Constitution the guilds were revived, using a variety of names (*ambacht*, *handelsbedrijf*, *nering*) invented to obscure their similarity to guilds. This revival was confirmed in the 1808 Corporation Act. These organizations were employed to collect the tax on patents introduced in 1805, and permitted to exclude competition from outside and regulate quality standards. The incorporation of the Kingdom of Holland into the French Empire in the autumn of 1810 led to the guilds again being de jure abolished, but the government neglected to repeal the Corporation Act; nor did it settle the issue of the fate of the sometimes

---

81 Van Houtte, 1920, p. 97.

82 For what follows see Lourens and Lucassen 1994, pp. 56 et seq., and van Genabeek 1994. For the details see Wiskerke, 1938.

considerable guild funds. It also omitted to declare the French law on the abolition of the guilds operative in Holland. To regulate labour, the French law of 1803 introducing the *livret* came into effect on 1 January 1811.

As a result, once the Netherlands had regained its independence, after just three years, the guilds were revived in several towns. However, in 1818 the government of William I settled the matter once and for all, and their abolition was confirmed. Two years later, the guild funds were liquidated. But it was difficult to resist the habit of so many centuries, and the municipal associations of weighers, measurers, porters and transporters were almost indistinguishable from their traditional guilds. That was the case even after a Royal Decree of 1827 had abolished all monopolies relating to the loading, unloading and conveyance of merchandise. Even the 1880 Conveyance Act (*Wet op het Vervoer*) brought no immediate end to the surviving guild-like organizations in the Netherlands, though by the second half of the nineteenth century their number no longer exceeded more than a few dozen. In a parallel development, many guild funds continued to exist under other names, and a few survive even to this day. Clearly then, attempts to abolish guilds in the North encountered much greater resistance than in the South, where, after earlier more or less successful attempts to curtail certain specific privileges, they had been abolished once and for all in 1795.[83]

8. Conclusions

Our quantitative analysis of guild foundations in the Low Countries and the comparison between the Northern and Southern Netherlands yields a number of distinct patterns. We already knew that the guild system was primarily an urban phenomenon, and that rural guilds were rare. To a large extent then, the emergence of guilds also paralleled the rise of cities and the procurement of civic charters. This implies too that economic prosperity and the guild system went hand in hand, regardless of whether this prosperity is defined in terms of capitalism, mercantile capitalism or modernity. At the peak of their prosperity, Bruges, Ghent, Antwerp and Amsterdam show that the institutional component of the guild system was an integral factor in this prosperity. However, we should not forget that the guilds also played a role in the inevitable periods of decline later, largely by protecting the interests of their members.

In addition to urban prosperity and decline, other factors played a role in the creation and survival of craft guilds too. The economic structure of the city for instance. Cities with a strong cloth industry were the first to see an effective guild system develop, and within the cities themselves it was not unusual for the earliest guilds to be textile guilds. The size of the city also mattered. Not surprisingly, guilds were rare in cities of fewer than 500 inhabitants; with just a few masters in each profession, it was easier to make informal agreements. Once a city had over 1,000 inhabitants, sooner or later the likelihood of guilds being set up gradually increased. Finally, there was the influence

---

[83] Van Houtte, 1920, p. 114.

of the sea. With the exception of Liège, it was in the coastal provinces of the Low Countries that guilds first appeared; they spread to inland cities, particularly in the North, only gradually. However, proximity to the sea was not a sufficient condition, as is evidenced by the port of Ostend, where the guild system did not fully mature until the seventeenth century.

Initially, guilds developed in the North very much as they did in the South, in the sense that craft guilds gradually spread across the interior, beginning in the Southwest of Flanders and ending in the northeast of the Low Countries. Generally speaking, this diffusion occurred at the same rate as urbanization and the development of urban economic activity — i.e. more rapidly in the South than in the North. Moreover, in the South the guilds succeeded in becoming enmeshed within local political structures, unlike in the North (with the exception of Utrecht and Dordrecht). The history of this phenomenon is too complex to go into here, suffice it to say that the coincidence of certain developments in state formation and the socio-economic and institutional development of the guild system and the cities ensured a unique dynamic. In cities where craft guilds did not develop until after 1500, as a rule these guilds failed to secure comparable political power, probably because local and provincial governments were by then predisposed to be extremely suspicious of them.

On the eve of the Dutch Revolt, the pattern in the North and South was similar. By then, the guild system had fully matured in most large and medium-sized cities, and in some very small towns too. There were now scarcely any cities without craft guilds, and the density of these guilds was more or less the same: by and large, one guild for 550 to 800 inhabitants. Where there were fewer, as in Brabant, this can be attributed to the effect of a few large cities such as Antwerp and Brussels, where the number of new guilds failed to keep pace with the rapid population growth. There was also a sort of natural ceiling, while political mechanisms too could cause the number of guilds to be restricted at some point. In contrast, the density of guilds in Luxemburg, in the extreme southeast of the Low Countries, was significantly higher. There were even places averaging one guild for fewer than 100 inhabitants, though one would have to examine the pattern of population change and guild foundations there in more detail to adequately explain this phenomenon.

After the Dutch revolt, developments diverged. The economic and demographic centre shifted to the North, where increasing urbanization and the flourishing urban economy ensured that the number of guilds continued to grow. The guild system in the Northern Netherlands did not peak until Holland's 'Golden Age', a period in which urban institutions also succeeded in dominating the countryside more than ever before. In the South, rural competition was more vigorous, and the number of craft guilds no longer grew appreciably — though the guild system did not fossilize either. Economic restructuring ensured that some guilds disappeared while new ones were founded, and the combination of flexible systems of subcontracting on the one hand and corporative regulations on the other made the necessary changes possible. Only in the prince-bishopric of Liège do the guilds seem to have fossilized, though the cause might well have been political rather than economic. In the South only the cities in the prince-bishopric lost their political power completely.

In a sense, the qualitative differences between the North and South were actually more significant. In the Northern Netherlands the political success of the Reformation caused a reorientation towards social functions, such as care of the poor, elderly masters and widows of masters. In the South, not only did the Catholic religious and political functions of the guilds continue to be prominent, the regulation of quality also became more important, as did a desire for status and prestige, which owed something to the Counter-Reformation. To a degree this can perhaps be attributed to the reorientation of production towards luxury goods, which were also associated with quality and prestige. Perhaps this is why in the eighteenth century economic growth in the South no longer led to a growth in the number of guilds. Not only was that growth concentrated in smaller towns and rural areas, often it also involved completely different products and methods of production. Further, a growing suspicion of corporative institutions emanating from France gradually created an opposition between corporatism on the one hand and 'the free market' on the other. As a result, the eighteenth century turned out to be a one-hundred-year-long overture to their abolition.

The North, again, was different. Economic and demographic growth stagnated there in the course of the eighteenth century, but prior to 1770 the guilds, with a few exceptions, were not held responsible. Criticism, which became increasingly vociferous, largely took the form of proposals to improve the guilds rather than abolish them. At the same time, new industrial growth in rural areas seems sometimes to have been accompanied by the establishment of new guilds. It is more than likely that the reason their abolition was much more protracted in the North than in the South was the slow but steady increase in the strongly defensive character of the northern guilds, and the corresponding extension of their role as agencies of social insurance.

Appendix: the datasets

1. General points

All the quantitative conclusions in this chapter are based on two datasets — one for Belgium and Luxemborg, compiled by the Centre for Pre-Industrial Production Processes and Labour Relations (PIPA) at the Vrije Universiteit Brussels, and one for the Netherlands, compiled by the International Institute of Social History in Amsterdam. Both aim to locate as many of the guilds that existed in these countries (as defined by their current national borders) as possible and to include relevant basic details — the name of the guild, the city in which it operated, and either the date of its foundation or the date of the earliest recorded reference to the guild.[84] These two datasets include those organizations meeting at least the following four conditions. First, within a locality (and very occasionally for a larger administrative unit) a craft guild either united individuals solely on the basis of a profession (unlike, for example, the civic militias or neighbourhood guilds) or united various groups of this type. Secondly, a craft guild therefore had members (unlike, for example, the '*neringen*'[85] — urban institutions that merely drew up regulations for occupational groups), with rights and obligations, and these members could to a certain extent regulate the guild's own affairs. Thirdly, the objectives of a craft guild were primarily economic (in contrast to religious confraternities, whose objectives were largely — if not entirely — spiritual), and in particular to protect their members from external competition. Fourthly, a craft guild was officially recognized by the political authorities, generally the local civic administration. This recognition brought with it the authority to regulate guild membership. Sometimes, the guild was set up by the local administration and awarded a monopoly, on the basis of which it could determine how a profession should operate.

Although both datasets employ the same definitions and share the same objective, their origins are quite different — a reflection of the different source material available in the South and the North. In the South, thanks to the much more centralist rule of the Austrian Habsburgs in the eighteenth century, the results of several inquiries (*enquêtes*), relating either directly or indirectly to the craft guilds in all or several major provinces, have been preserved; the inquiry of 1784 is the most famous of these. In the North, nothing comparable took place at the local or national level, with the exception of a number of inquiries following the abolition of the guilds. These abolition inquiries are much better preserved in the North than in the South, where in principle they were also held — though less frequently due to the less complex history of their abolition. This explains why the Belgian-Luxemburg dataset is based on the

---

84 For the first publication on this see Lourens and Lucassen 1994. For questions of definition, see also the clear exposition by Wyffels, 1951. We do not agree with Wyffels on every point though.

85 These had few, if any, members. See de Vries, Lucassen, Lourens and Nijboer, 2003, p. 90. Our data exclude the *neringen*.

1784 inquiry and the Dutch dataset on the 1798 abolition inquiry. In both cases, the basic data are supplemented by other material as much as possible: for example, the very incomplete results of the inquiry in the South were supplemented by information from urban monographs and the publications listed in a recent bibliography on craft guilds during the ancien régime.[86] For the Netherlands, separate datasets of mutual funds were also constructed.[87]

Because craft guilds were almost exclusively local institutions and, moreover, tended to be in fairly sizeable cities, information on the population size of these cities was essential for interpreting and comparing our guild data. Population data for the Netherlands had already been collected at an earlier stage as part of this project.[88] For Belgium and Luxemburg our population data are based on several core studies, such as the study by Bruneel, Delporte and Petitjean on the Austrian Netherlands, by Hélin on the prince-bishopric of Liège, and Klep's study on the Duchy of Brabant.[89] We also drew on monographs and specialist publications on an ad hoc basis.[90] We aimed to collect data on the number of inhabitants for specific points in time (*c.* 1400, 1560, 1670 and 1784) for all three countries, and for all cities with populations in excess of 2,500 in around 1784. In many cases the demographic data are subject to relatively wide margins, except perhaps for those of 1784. This is because for certain periods all we have are indications, and these do not necessarily coincide with the dates we selected; as a result, in most cases we have been forced to rely on estimates and averages. Furthermore, different authors interpret the data differently, forcing us ultimately to use two different sorts of average — an average of two figures at different points in time, and an average of the data given by authors whose findings are contradictory. In a few instances it was necessary to rely on the number of taxable hearths, and multiply this by a factor of 4.5. Since much of our data cannot be regarded as accurate, our population figures were ultimately rounded off to the nearest 500.

2. The structure of the Belgian-Luxemburg dataset

The Belgian-Luxemburg dataset is based on the *ambachtsenquête* (guild inquiry) of 1784.[91] On 9 February 1784, at the initiative of the central government in Brussels, a large

---

86 Jacobs and Vanbellinghen, 1999.

87 Bos, 1998, 357-8; van Genabeek, 1999, 315-28.

88 Lourens and Lucassen, 1997b.

89 Bruneel, Delporte and Petitjean, 1996; Hélin, 1963, pp. 238-41; Klep, 1981.

90 See, *inter alia*, *Het stedelijk netwerk in België in historisch perspectief (1350-1850). Een statistische en dynamische benadering* [Handelingen van het 15de Internationaal Colloquium te Spa, 4-6 september 1990)] (Brussels, 1992); *Historiens et populations. Liber amicorum Étienne Hélin* (Louvain-la-Neuve, 1991), p. 199; Blondé, 1999; Dumont, 1994; Guignet, 1990, pp. 16-41; Duvosquel and Dierkens, 1991, pp. 429-64; Morsa, 1987; Prevenier, 1983.

91 The data from this inquiry were initially collected by Marc Jacobs. He has been able to use them in only a few preliminary studies. Jacobs, 1997, pp. 243-93. We would like to express

number of civic administrations were sent a questionnaire on the prevalence and functioning of craft guilds. Initially, the questionnaire was sent to 36 cities: Aalst, Aarlen, Aarschot, Antwerp, Ath, Bergen, Bruges, Brussels, Charleroi, Dendermonde, Diest, Diksmuide, Doornik, Echternach, Geraardsbergen, Ghent, Herentals, Ypres, Kortrijk, Louvain, Lier, Limbourg, Luxemburg, Malines, Menen, Namur, Nieuwpoort, Nijvel, Ostend, Oudenaarde, Roermond, Tienen, Turnhout, Veurne, Vilvoorde and Virton. Two and a half years later, on 6 September 1786, three other cities were added (Waver, Weert and Zichem). On the basis of what we know about the urban populations at that time, we can conclude that the larger cities were certainly included. However, it is odd that smaller towns such as Limburg and Zichem (both of which had only 1,300 inhabitants), Aarlen (2,100), Veurne (2,200), Echternach (2,300), Diksmuide, Vilvoorde, Charleroi and Herentals (all of which had *c.* 2,500 inhabitants) were also included, while some larger cities — Eupen (7,400 inhabitants), Halle (6,000), Soignies (3,200), Binche and Enghien (both with 3,000 inhabitants) — were apparently not deemed interesting enough. For these cities, we are therefore forced to rely on secondary sources.

In our case, there are three other problems associated with this inquiry: the cities in present-day Belgium and Luxemburg which lay outside the Austrian Netherlands and thus, by definition, could not be included in the inquiry; the cities that were included but did not reply, or whose reply can no longer be located; and the cities that replied but whose reply cannot meaningfully be used in our dataset. The first problem largely relates to those cities in the former prince-bishopric of Liège (most of which now lies in the Belgian provinces of Liège and Limburg), principally Liège itself, but also Verviers, Sint Truiden, Hasselt, Tongeren and a handful of small cities with fewer than 5,000 inhabitants. All our data on these cities are drawn from secondary sources. The second problem relates to the cities of Brussels, Doornik, Luxemburg, Ypres, Tienen, Vilvoorde and Aarschot (in decreasing size). These seven cities were included in the inquiry, and in several cases we also know that they actually responded, but no trace of their replies has been found. Here, too, we have to depend on secondary sources, but even so our data remain incomplete. Then there is the third problem. Of the 32 replies submitted and preserved, two are actually from cities in the present-day Netherlands (Roermond and Weert, formerly part of Austrian Upper Gelderland). These replies have been included in the Dutch dataset (see section 3 of the appendix). This leaves 30 replies, and these form the basis of the Belgian-Luxemburg dataset. Several of these replies, mostly from very small cities, were 'negative'. Insofar as we can tell from other data, these cities — in ascending size Zichem, Limbourg, Charleroi and Waver — reported correctly that no craft guilds had been established in their cities. There remain then 26 cities providing data on the presence of craft guilds in 1784.

our thanks to Marc Jacobs for his assistance in constructing this dataset. For the origins and implementation of the inquiry, and the location of the surviving data, see Heirwegh, 1981, pp. 437-66 and 763-776; Coppejans-Desmedt, 1971. Sporadic attempts have also been made to publish parts of the inquiry: Smekens, 1950; Maddens, 1989.

These cities were distributed across the provinces as follows: twelve in Flanders, eight in Brabant, three in Luxemburg, two in Hainault and one in Namur. Clearly, for the western cities the Belgian-Luxemburg dataset relies much more heavily on data from the 1784 inquiry and for the eastern cities much more heavily on secondary sources.

Even when cities did respond, in some cases little information could be extracted from the responses to the inquiry since the guilds themselves had no archives to allow them to specify with sufficient accuracy the date on which they were founded, or because all that have survived are the summaries sent to the central government (and now kept in the National Archives in Brussels). Given that the summary prepared by the civic administration did not always state the date on which a guild had been founded (and since, often, the local-level replies have been lost), we were forced in the case of the cities of Diest, Diksmuide, Herentals, Menen, Nieuwpoort, Oudenaarde and Veurne to rely on secondary sources for the most part. At best, only scattered fragments of the inquiry have been preserved in the local archives of these relatively small cities, and so far it has not proved possible to retrieve these fragments.[92] Often, secondary sources proved useful, but where that was not the case we were left empty-handed, as with Diksmuide and Veurne.

Ultimately, which cities were included in the dataset depended also on the size of their population around 1784. Cities with fewer than 2,500 inhabitants were excluded, as were places with over 2,500 inhabitants but without city charter (and thus, as a rule, no guilds). The territorial boundaries used were those of present-day Belgium and the Grand Duchy of Luxemburg. The generally minor cities in the small Duchy of Limbourg (Eupen, Hervé, Limbourg, Petit-Rechain, Grand-Rechain and Soiron) were excluded, as were Malmédy and Stavelot in the principality of Stavelot, and Bouillon in the principality of the same name. In total, dozens of craft guilds were therefore excluded in addition to those in the Duchy of Limbourg (see table 2.4).

The chief problem in constructing the dataset was the nature of the data retrieved, starting with the data in the inquiry. The first problem concerns the nature of the question on the establishment of guilds. Though it was clear from the instructions of the central government that the first question was in two parts ('by whom ... it was established and by whom its privileges were granted') ['par qui … (il) a été établi, et par qui ses privilèges ont été accordés'], some cities conflated these into one. As a result, it is not always clear whether the date given is the date of establishment or the date of the guild's earliest charter. Moreover, craft guilds were often unable to verify the date on which they had been established, and extremely vague answers such as 'from time immemorial' ('de temps immémorial') or 'of ancient times' ('du très vieux temps') were far from unusual. At best, the responses included the date of the earliest recorded reference to the guild, or, if not, the date of the earliest charter (kept in the guild's own archive) was noted elsewhere in the document. As a result, for 486 of the 1033 craft guilds in our dataset we must make do with the date of the earliest recorded reference.

---

92 Though the city archive of Lier was searched extensively, replies from only 9 of the 18 guilds could be located.

For 183 organizations, no date whatsoever could be identified. We do not always even have accurate figures on the total number of craft guilds in a particular city. Brussels is a case in point. Niklaas Maddens has argued that the Kortrijk inquiry for example was incomplete, and that several craft guilds had been omitted.[93] One consequence of using this date of 'earliest reference' in the dataset is that the results tend (on average) to report a later date than was actually the case, though our search of the secondary literature has confirmed that the dates of establishment that were given to the inquiry were fairly accurate and reliable. Earlier historians working on data from the inquiry have already pointed out that the local authorities sometimes checked the information recorded, even going to the trouble of consulting archives for this purpose.

As regards the disappearance of craft guilds, it is often difficult to determine when precisely they were dissolved or petered out. The inquiry itself merely indicates the number of guilds in 1784, but by then groups such as the fullers and saddlers had become inconsequential and their respective guilds no longer appear in the dataset. For the figures in table 2.1 we deducted the number of craft guilds in existence in 1784 from the total number of known craft guilds. We also tried to determine whether the guilds that had disappeared had been abolished or amalgamated with other guilds.[94] One remaining problem though is that over time many guilds split up or amalgamated. Many so-called guild foundations were actually amalgamations of existing organizations, or the result of guilds splitting off from larger combinations; there were also cases of smaller entities being absorbed by larger ones.[95] To correct for this problem we tried, where we could, to distinguish between a 'demerger' and an amalgamation, but it was not always possible to do so consistently. Often, in the case of amalgamated corporations the date on which the oldest of the guilds was founded was given, and only when completely new and autonomous guilds were founded were they added separately.

To avoid further problems, the so-called *officies*, or offices, which operated mostly in the transport sector and can be regarded as public services, were counted as corporations since they were also included in the inquiry and they come within our definition of guild. Some exceptions were made however. For Bruges, which had eight groups 'belonging to the city' ('appartenant à la ville'), and nine 'which belong to various private individuals, having been passed down from generation to generation' ('qui appartiennent héréditairement à differens particuliers'), only the last category was included (and combined within one group). In Ghent, where the so-called *lastbreken*[96] led to an exceptional situation (with no fewer than seventeen 'offices' in 1784), these

[93] Maddens, 1989, p. 103.

[94] A further problem here is that sometimes craft guilds continued to be registered, while in reality they were no longer active.

[95] In Ghent, for example, several amalgamations took place prior to 1400.

[96] Ghent's skippers had a monopoly on the ship-borne conveyance of merchandise along the rivers Leie and Scheldt.

'offices' were omitted.[97] The 'fish and herring counters' in Malines were also omitted, since they were appointed by the fishmongers and not by the city's magistrates. Also excluded, for similar reasons, were Malines bow haulers (employed to tow boats along the canals), who were apprenticed to the skippers. So too were Malines grain-measurers, who were appointed by the bakers and brewers. On the other hand, some so-called *confréries* or fraternities were included as guilds — in Ath for example, where economic craft guilds too were called *confrérie*.

Table 2.4 *Cities and villages with guilds, based on the 1784 inquiry and the secondary literature*

	≥2500 inhabitants	<2500 inhabitants	Total	Of which had guilds
Number of replies preserved, sufficient data	18	1	19	15*
Number of replies preserved, insufficient data	8	0	8	8
Number of questionnaires not replied to (inquiry perhaps not carried out)	3	0	3	3
Replies lost in recent times	3	0	3	3
Replies not sent, since retrieved	3	0	3	3
Questionnaires not replied to, not (or only partially) retrieved	1	0	1	1
Total number of replies requested	36	1	37†	33
Number of cities omitted	≥20	≥12	≥42‡	≥19
Total number of Austrian Netherlands cities	≥56	≥13	≥79	≥52
Other cities in present-day Belgium	≥14	≥14	≥31‡	≥17
Total number of cities in Belgium	≥70	≥27	≥110	≥69
Villages (omitted)				≥15
Total number of cities and villages				≥84

* Charleroi, Limbourg, Waver and Zichem reported no local craft guilds
† Excluding Weert and Roermond, which are in the present-day Netherlands
‡ For some cities we have no population data for around 1784

Finally, we should point out that lack of space prevents us from giving full details of all the primary and secondary sources used to construct the dataset. The data are available for inspection at the Centre for the Pre-Industrial Production Processes and Labour Relations (PIPA) at the Vrije Universiteit Brussels.

97 Lenders, 1990.

3. *The structure of the Dutch dataset*

The dataset for the Netherlands is based on sources relating to the abolition of the guilds in the Batavian Republic in 1798-1799 and in the departments of Nedermaas and Schelde set up earlier under French administration (1796). These sources listed a total of 1,143 craft guilds, as well as several boxes and organizations of which it is doubtful whether they actually had an economic function.[98] Based on these data, we have also tried to obtain supplementary information, largely by carrying out research in city archives. This research yielded a considerable number of additional craft guilds. Currently, our dataset includes 1,917 organizations that meet our definition in full, as well as 103 that require further investigation, 18 journeymen associations, ten organizations with a purely religious function and two with a purely political one, giving a total of 2,050 organizations. Though our research is ongoing, this total is hardly increasing at all now, while our knowledge of the organizations already included in the dataset is.

Compared with the South, research in the North faces two problems — both political and religious in nature. Since many more southern guilds had a political function, much more information on this type of organization has survived in government archives. Furthermore, the Reformation deprived us of evidence of continuities in the case of craft guilds that had religious functions prior to the Reformation and that lost them subsequently. Not only was a great deal of material on, for example, altars and fraternities lost during or after the Iconoclastic Fury (*Beeldenstorm*, 1566), interest in this field was also extremely limited until the late nineteenth century. Insofar as our data are meagre, this pertains most to guilds in the fifteenth and early sixteenth centuries.

Translated by Chris Gordon

---

[98] Lourens and Lucassen 1994, pp. 56-9, covers this extensively.

Chapter 3

Corporate politics in the Low Countries: guilds as institutions, 14th to 18th Centuries

Maarten Prak

Introduction

The origins and evolution of craft guilds were influenced as much by political developments as economic ones.[1] The recent revival of historical interest in the guilds has largely overlooked this very important fact and its implications. Rather, it has focused attention on the economic and social aspects of the guilds,[2] which is unfortunate. Craft guilds were primarily institutions established by the authorities. Despite the fact that artisans may have claimed (sometimes even demanded) the privileges of economic protection and restricted access to their trade, they needed official endorsement of their claims. Intervention by the authorities was also required to change the rules or to settle disputes within and between guilds. Moreover, guilds sometimes became involved in politics: they fought their way into local representative institutions, sometimes even to the very heart of local government. This made not only for a different system of government but for changes in the guilds themselves as well. Some guilds evolved into full-blown political institutions, with only nominal links to the world of crafts. Besides, as a well-organized section of early modern urban society, the artisans and shopkeepers that constituted the bulk of guild membership were a political force to be reckoned with: the authorities had to define their own positions with respect to this social class, which tended to regard itself as the backbone of society.

This last point was emphasized by Robert DuPlessis and Martha Howell in their influential *Past and Present* article (1982) on the nature of the economy of the early modern period. In this paper they claimed to have identified a 'third way' of production that combined exports with a small-scale industrial organization. Catharina Lis

1 I would like to thank Piet Lourens, my colleague Jan Luiten van Zanden, and my co-editors for their comments on the draft version of this text.

2 It is impossible to be exhaustive here, but see, for example Kaplan, 1979, pp. 17-77; Sonenscher, 1989; Farr, 1988 and Farr, 1997; Rosser, 1997; Epstein, 1998; Ehmer, 1998. Notable exceptions are DuPlessis and Howell, 1982 and Bossenga, 1991.

and Hugo Soly have expressed serious doubts about the actual existence of such a specific 'mode of production',[3] but that need not negate a different point made by Duplessis and Howell. They claimed that urban elites were willing to compromise with artisans in their communities, 'even in the face of the expressed interests of some among the dominant class ... to uphold order within the city and to perpetuate existing power relationships.' Moreover, the authors believed that elites and guild members shared an ideological commitment to the community, where 'everyone should have the opportunity to earn a living without the humblest being crushed and oppressed by the advance of the most powerful', as the authorities in Lille (northern France) expressed it.[4]

The subject, of course, is not entirely new. In the German-speaking parts of Europe in particular, the political role of guilds has been the subject of substantial literature,[5] raising issues such as the social status of the guilds' political representatives, a comparison of the real influence of the guilds with their constitutional positions, and their role in the wider community. These are all issues that bear directly on the tantalizing suggestions by DuPlessis and Howell. It is the purpose of this chapter to explore these issues in the context of the history of the guilds in the Low Countries.

As in the other chapters of this book, the present chapter focuses on the early modern period, especially the seventeenth and eighteenth centuries. But it is impossible to discuss guild politics in the Low Countries without mentioning the revolutionary changes in local politics during the Middle Ages. As will be argued in greater detail below, if guilds did not gain political influence in the Low Countries before 1500, they would never obtain it. In the second half of the chapter we will examine the broad patterns of guild politics in the Low Countries, as well as explore in depth the local intricacies of these politics in Brussels, Arnhem, and Amsterdam. These towns will be used as models to illustrate three distinct constitutional patterns.

1. Revolutionary guilds (14th to 15th centuries)

The crucial date in medieval guild politics in the Low Countries is 11 July 1302. On that fateful day an army of French aristocratic infantry was beaten back by Flemish artisans just outside the town of Kortrijk (Courtrai), in the County of Flanders. This conflict, known as the Battle of the Spurs, was the dramatic outcome of a broader conflict among the powerful Flemish towns, the count of Flanders, and the French king. Although the artisans' victory came as a surprise to contemporaries, it was in fact just one more stage in a struggle that had been going on for several decades at least. In many towns in the Low Countries, but especially in the South where urbanization was

3 Lis and Soly, 1997b, pp. 12-15.

4 Duplessis and Howell, 1982, pp. 76, 80.

5 See e.g. Bischof, 1926; Füglisterl, 1981; Deter, 1990, ch. viii; Schulz, 1994, pp. 1-20.

most advanced, artisans had been clamouring for a greater say in economic policies and public finances, against the rule of a closed circle of patrician families.[6]

The Battle of the Spurs was not the first political conflict in the Low Countries to involve artisan organizations, however. In 1294, for example, the guilds of the city of Utrecht had already managed to remove the merchant elite from power — at least temporarily. While the Battle of the Spurs reverberated throughout Europe, it had the most impact in the region where it actually took place. In the following years artisans made some inroads in government in many of the important towns throughout the Low Countries.[7] In Bruges, for example, a new constitution in 1304 gave the community nine out of thirteen seats on the local magistrate bench, while the lord (the count of Flanders) retained four. Of these nine community seats, at least seven were controlled by groups of trades, while one was reserved for the patriciate (*poorterij*) and one for brokers (which was most likely controlled by the patricians as well).[8] Nonetheless, this left a majority of seats in the hands of artisan organizations. In Ypres the magistrate was selected by an electoral college of one hundred individuals, including 15 representatives of the guilds.[9]

The city of Ghent was granted a new constitution in 1301. In this constitution, the count of Flanders and the urban community, represented by the outgoing magistrates, each appointed four electors, who would then elect the 26 new aldermen for the next year.[10] After 1302 the guilds were able to gain substantial influence in these elections, mainly at the cost of the count, whose role was marginalized in the new constitution that gradually came into being in the course of the fourteenth century. In its final shape, the magistrate of Ghent still consisted of 26 individuals, divided, as before 1302, into two benches of 13 each. The election process, however, had been thrown wide open. The politically privileged patriciate, or *poorterij*, helped elect six aldermen. The count also had a role in selecting these six. The deans of the weavers' guild (which was very important in this textile town) could appoint as many as ten aldermen, while another ten were appointed by the deans of the 53 'small' guilds.[11] Except for the period from 1453 to 1477, the regime of the Three Tiers ran the public affairs of Ghent until 1540.

The Duchy of Brabant experienced similar developments. In Louvain, from 1303 to 1305, artisan representatives ruled the town until the duke of Brabant helped the patricians to regain power.[12] In Brussels the revolution of 1303 was equally short-

6 Boone, 1994a, pp. 6-8.

7 Wyffels, 1951, pp. 24-31.

8 Dumolyn, 1997, pp. 105-7.

9 Blockmans, 1978, p. 78.

10 This, and the following information on Ghent's constitution, comes from Boone, 1990, and in a more condensed version: Boone, 1994b, pp. 21-46. For the 1301 constitution, see pages 35 and 32 respectively.

11 See schedules of election procedures in Boone, 1990, p. 47; and Boone, 1994b, p. 35.

12 Van Uytven, 1980a, p. 219.

lived and did not leave any trace.[13] Den Bosch (Bois-le-Duc) experienced a guild revolution in the winter of 1305-6, although the guilds were reconciled with the authorities shortly afterwards. The revolt nonetheless enabled the artisans to have some control over the imposition of new taxes in the town.[14] Mechelen (Malines), although a separate enclave within the duchy, was also swept up in the political tsunami during these years. In 1305 it won the right to appoint its own magistrate, which included representatives of the artisan organizations.[15] Antwerp, the other principal town in Brabant, underwent only a mild uprising, and its 1306 constitution confirmed a full return to patrician rule. Some smaller towns in Brabant — Tienen, Zoutleeuw, and Diest — also participated in the revolts; in Tienen and Zoutleeuw guilds were able to obtain direct influence in local government.[16]

In the northern parts of the Low Countries the impact of the guild revolutions was much less evident. The main exception to this was the bishop's see for this region, the city of Utrecht. Here the guilds had already forced their way into local government at least once before, and in 1304 the guilds were able to impose a new constitution: the guild ordinance of 1304. This ordinance, promulgated by the elders of the Utrecht guilds, determined that henceforth the Utrecht council would be sworn in by the elders of the guilds, and that the elders would also select the 24 members of the town council.[17] Other towns in the bishop's territories, such as Amersfoort, Rhenen, and Wijk-bij-Duurstede, also had a certain amount of burgher representation, but it was not as a result of guild agitation, nor did it compare with the direct control exercised by the guilds of the city of Utrecht.[18]

In the past these urban revolts have been called 'guild revolutions', but recent scholarship views this designation as misleading because the upheavals were not exclusively the work of the guilds.[19] True as that is, the history of the Low Countries provides some strong arguments in favour of the old label. Carlos Wyffels has argued that the guild system was at the root of the revolutions: while the guilds may not have caused these revolutions, in many ways the guilds themselves were established in the process. During the thirteenth century merchants and artisans had been organizing, but the cooperation had been informal and private. Most references allude to military organizations of artisans, usually divided by district rather than by occupation.[20] These organizations belong to what Wyffels has called the 'pre-corporate' phase. The Battle of the Spurs and its political aftermath helped to formally establish guilds in many

---

13 Wyffels, 1951, p. 29; Favresse, 1961, pp. 150-2.

14 van den Heuvel, 1946, pp. 21-2.

15 Marnef, 1987, p. 51.

16 Wyffels, 1951, pp. 30-1.

17 Overvoorde and Joosting, 1896-7; van der Sprenkel, 1923, pp. 111, 115-18; Vijlbrief, 1950, p. 27.

18 Maarschalkerweerd, 1997, pp. 279-81.

19 Isenmann, 1988, p. 191.

20 Wyffels, 1951, pp. 108, 111-15.

towns.[21] In Den Bosch, for example, the earliest set of rules for the local blacksmiths' guild dates from 1302. It was followed shortly thereafter by rules for the shoemakers' and tanners' guild.[22] Wyffels explains the transition from a geographical division to an occupational one by the fact that similar occupations were often located in the same area, or even the same street of a town.[23] Further explorations into the earliest history of the guilds will need to clarify these issues.

Political participation had another impact on the guild system. In some towns the constitutional inclusion of the guilds in town government restricted the establishment of any additional guilds. In Utrecht 21 guilds participated in the election of the town council. Between 1341, when their rights were confirmed, and 1528, when the guild regime was abolished, the number of guilds in Utrecht remained fixed at 21. Elsewhere a more flexible solution was found. In Brabant several towns developed an intermediate level of representation, the *Natiën*, or Nations, each encompassing several guilds. In Louvain the system was introduced in 1360. In Brussels the guilds were regrouped into nine Nations in 1421. In Antwerp there were three *hoofdgilden*, or 'main guilds', each including nine different guilds. In none of these towns is there an economic logic behind the combinations.[24] The political character of the Nation system, and indeed that of the guilds themselves, was expressed in the fact that in Den Bosch at least all citizens had to enrol in a Nation in 1494 if they were not of patrician stock. Previously, the town's constitution ordered new citizens to become members of a guild irrespective of their occupation.[25]

Nations may have been characteristic of Brabant,[26] but the problems they addressed were general. In Flanders other systems were in place specifically to balance representation from social groups with often very different, even contradictory interests, both among the guilds, and between guilds and elites. Urban constitutions should therefore be understood as compromise solutions, the outcome of struggles that the sources sometimes merely hint at.[27] One example was the very complex constitution of Ghent. It developed from a relatively straightforward constitution of 1301 (i.e. immediately before the Battle of the Spurs) onto which new elements were grafted as the balance

---

21 It would be an exaggeration, however, to consider 1302 as an absolute watershed; there were artisan guilds in the Low Countries, even in the northern parts, before 1302, as is demonstrated by Lourens and Lucassen, 1997, p. 44.

22 van den Heuvel, 1946, pp. 20, 31-2.

23 Wyffels, 1951, p. 116.

24. Compare the lists provided by Van Honacker, 1994b, pp. 632-7.

25 van den Heuvel, 1946, p. 306; id 1946, 66 (B31, art. 17), 338 (B95, art. 13). In many German towns, this development was taken one step further still, and some guilds evolved into, or were even created with the special purpose of, institutions of political representation: see Schulz, 1994. This did not happen in the Low Countries.

26 But not exclusively so; in Liège the guilds were grouped into 32 Nations: Van Uytven, 1982, p. 235.

27 Ibidem, 234.

of power in the city shifted from one group to another. This also helps explain why the Ghent fullers' guild was excluded from power, despite the significant numbers of masters and journeymen in that trade.[28]

The aftermath of the Battle of the Spurs was only the beginning of the guild revolutions. In several towns the old order was restored before the first decade of the fourteenth century was out. In Brussels, where this had happened as early as 1306, the guilds were able to re-impose their power from the second half of the century. In 1366 the guild deans were admitted as an advisory body, but only in 1421 were they written into the local constitution, through the Nations system introduced on that occasion.[29] In Louvain the guilds achieved a similar position in 1360, which was confirmed in the charters of 1378 and 1383. The latter was to remain Louvain's constitution until the end of the Old Regime.[30] In Den Bosch the guilds' influence was steadily increasing throughout most of the fourteenth century. In 1336 they received permission to help close the town's annual accounts; in effect granting them initial control of local finances. In 1388 they were included, along with the aldermen, councillors and 'good men', in a charter regulating the imposition of local excise duties. Then, in 1408, the guilds of Den Bosch staged a full-scale rebellion, which the duke of Brabant personally helped to suppress. The troubles led to a completely new constitution. Henceforth, Den Bosch was to be ruled by a three-tiered government consisting of aldermen and jurors, councillors (i.e. former aldermen), and the deans of the guilds. Initially, the guild deans were to be elected by the aldermen and jurors, but in 1419 the guilds won back the right to select their own representatives.[31]

Inclusion of the guilds in a town's constitution was a revolutionary act. It suggested political representation for broad sections of the population in local government. This choice for the guilds was not self-evident, however, and guilds in many towns may in fact have been established for political purposes. One possible alternative was that of town districts. In the feudal period towns were required to supply the lord with men and equipment. The Battle of the Spurs showed the potential effectiveness of urban militia units,[32] which were generally recruited by district. During the guild revolutions of the fourteenth century, the newly established guilds took control of this aspect of urban life as well.[33] Significantly, the towns where guilds became part of the government were also the towns where guilds became directly involved in military duties. Utrecht is a case in point. After the guilds took power in 1304, the Utrecht guilds made

---

28 Cf. Boone, 1990, p. 48.

29 Favresse, 1961, pp. 228-9, 248. Favresse (229) sets the date at 1423, but other authors seem to agree that it already happened two years earlier: Louant, 1935, p. 224; Van Honacker, 1994a, p. 183.

30 van Uytven, 1980, pp. 219-20.

31 van den Heuvel, 1946, pp. 269-87; Jacobs, 1986, pp. 51-2, 55; Schuttelaars, 1998, pp. 86-90.

32 See Blockmans, 1978, pp. 440-2.

33 Wyffels, 1951, pp. 113-16.

sure that any alternative popular institutions would be powerless. They dominated the civic defences of the city, for instance. The night watch, manned by the residents, was organized through the guilds.[34] The guilds were also responsible for maintenance and repair of the town walls, each guild being assigned a specific section.[35] In Louvain, too, the guilds were responsible for the community's defences.[36] The statutes of the blacksmiths' guild of Den Bosch, established in 1302, stipulated that members 'who are present and healthy, shall march out with their banners, and stay together under that banner', whenever the duke of Brabant required them to do so.[37]

In some towns such alternative organizations of the citizenry became the basis for political representation, and guilds were politically marginalized as a consequence. In the Hansa towns of Overijssel, for instance, districts became the key institutions. In Zwolle the Battle of the Spurs had little impact. Guilds emerged there in the course of the fourteenth century. During the fifteenth century the Zwolle guilds became involved in public affairs. They undertook missions abroad, together with members of the magistrate, and participated in developing the local statutes. During a brief interlude from 1415 to 1416 the guilds may even have formally participated in local government, but the sources are not very specific about this.[38] Apart from this episode, however, the *gemeenslieden* (Common Councillors), elected by district, were the only representatives of the community.

In the Duchy of Gelre, to the South of Overijssel, we find a similar pattern. The citizens of the town of Zutphen probably acquired the right to confirm the town's annual accounts in the early fifteenth century.[39] Later in the century certain bylaws were introduced with the explicit approval of the citizenry. In the closing decades of the century, their influence grew perceptibly, both through the *gezworen gemeente* (Sworn Council) and through the guilds. This development was related to the precarious military situation of the duke of Gelre, who was trying to fight off a Habsburg threat.[40] The guilds of Zutphen were crucial to the town's defences. The Duke also needed a great deal of money to maintain his armies. In the bargaining over financial aid, the citizens acquired additional constitutional leverage, both in the supervision of local accounts as well as in the overall political process. On several occasions the guilds were invited to participate, together with the town council, in regional meetings on military strategy, for example. In 1538, just after the accession of a new duke, the guilds of Zutphen staged a major rebellion that sought reform of local finances and of the guild system in Zutphen.[41] Charles V's conquest of Gelre in 1543, however, put

34 Overvoorde and Joosting, 1896-7, vol. I, n°65.

35 Ibid, vol. I n° 88.

36 Verhavert, 1940, p. 94.

37 van den Heuvel, 1946, p. 328.

38 Elte, 1930, pp. 375-6; Berkenvelder, 1989, p. 10.

39 van Schaïk, 1989, pp. 74-80; Frijhoff, 1988, pp. 40-55.

40 Meij, 1975, pp. 13-78.

41 Schimmelpenninick van der Oye, 1971, pp. 39-83.

an end to this process, and in fact reduced the powers of both the Sworn Council and the guild deans.

In the eastern part of the Low Countries we see the evolution of alternative structures of popular representation. In these structures the guilds played a role, but they were not represented directly in the local government, as in many southern towns. Compared to the situation in Holland, Zeeland, and Friesland, however, popular representation in the East seemed relatively strong. This was all but absent in the West, as we will see shortly.

2. Guild 'democracy' (14th to 16th centuries)

So far we have portrayed guild regimes, or the inclusion of guilds in local governments, as examples of popular politics. In the early twentieth century the famous Belgian historian Henri Pirenne went considerably further: he perceived the guild regimes in the southern Netherlands as 'democratic' alternatives to princely rule.[42] The inclusion of guild deans in local public institutions may well have broadened the political class in some towns. Characterizing them as 'democratic', however, suggests they had a popular character that the guild deans themselves all too often belied, as an analysis of their social standing reveals. Recent research demonstrates two qualifications to this view.

First, the election of deans in itself was not necessarily a democratic process. While it may have been so at the outset, with the passage of time other institutions, notably the local magistrate, started to gain influence. In Brussels the sworn councillors of the nine Nations were selected by the patricians.[43] In Den Bosch the departing deans were entitled to make a list of possible successors, but the final election was performed by the First Tier of the town's government, the aldermen and sworn councillors.[44] Such procedures may have helped to keep the group of guild governors relatively small. To be sure, there were variations among guilds in this respect. Nonetheless, statistics for sixteenth-century Ghent demonstrate a perhaps inevitable degree of exclusivity in all guilds. Of a total of 1,473 tailors, only 202, or 13.7 per cent, were ever appointed as either dean or juror of their guild. Almost twice that percentage held office in the brewers' guild, but only 10 per cent of the 1,950 members of the mercers' guild became officeholders.[45]

Another argument against using 'democracy' in the context of guild regimes is that the guild members who participated in politics were not chosen at random. Raymond Van Uytven's painstaking research on the town councillors for many towns in Flanders, Brabant, and other regions in the Southern Netherlands reveals that in the

---

42 Pirenne, 1910.

43 Favresse, 1961, p. 233.

44 van den Heuvel, 1946, p. 78 (B 36). Schuttelaars, 1998, p. 103 has not found evidence that the magistrate actually did elect the deans.

45 Dambruyne, 1998a, p. 55 (table 6).

fourteenth and fifteenth century the middle and lower classes were seriously under-represented in local government. In Malines, for example, a religious collection in 1370 demonstrates that the poorest 77 per cent were represented by just 2.4 per cent of the magistrates. The wealthiest 5 per cent, on the other hand, claimed as many as 56 per cent of the seats. In Louvain representation of the well-to-do was actually higher during the years the guilds were in charge of the town than it was during the years of 'aristocratic reaction'.[46] In Ghent in the sixteenth century a very similar picture emerges. In a forced loan of 1578, levied according to wealth, almost three times as many deans and jurors contributed as ordinary members, even though the latter were, of course, far more numerous.[47] For Den Bosch it has been established that in 1552 the guild deans were on average twice as rich as the general taxpayer and should be considered 'upper middle class'.[48]

This social selectiveness came about in various ways. Probably the guild members were often in awe of their well-to-do fellow members, and assumed that these would be more successful in defending the guild's interests. To hold office, moreover, was time consuming and unrewarding financially; most temporary offices did not pay a salary.[49] As time went on, quite a few towns introduced wealth requirements for all their major offices, thus disqualifying the poorer artisans almost automatically.[50]

Even granting that 'democracy' may be anachronistic in this context, the rates of participation in guild affairs proper do seem to confirm Pirenne's original thesis. Moreover, in modern societies the impact of democracy is not measured by the percentage of the population that actually sits in parliament. And it is a fact that the nature of the regime did have an impact on the opportunities of guildsmen to participate in local politics. After re-thinking and re-arranging his data, Van Uytven found that the degree of exclusiveness of local regimes varied with the size and economic structure of the various communities. In small regional centres in the southern Netherlands the elite's impact was very strong, but in the large, industrial towns such as Ghent, Bruges, and Kortrijk it was less in evidence; middle-sized towns, like Louvain, Malines, and Dordrecht, also occupied a middle ground in this respect. All of this led Van Uytven to conclude that the Flemish industrial centres, 'traditionally pictured as bulwarks of medieval democracy, remained far removed from popular government, or even proportional representation, but they were nonetheless the least plutocratic'.[51] W. Blockmans noted similar results for the years between 1400 and 1550, in his comparison of social mobility in the local councils of Ghent, Dordrecht, Rotterdam, and Zutphen. The rate of exclusivity coincided with the size of the towns under investigation. But at the same time there was a certain degree of correlation with the nature of the constitution.

---

46 Van Uytven, 1962, p. 384, p. 388 and passim.

47 Dambruyne, 1998a, p. 65 (table 16).

48 Blondé, 1987, pp. 13-14.

49 Van Uytven, 1962, p. 408.

50 Van Uytven, 1982, p. 237; Blockmans, 1987, pp. 255-6.

51 Van Uytven, 1962, pp. 399-400 (quote on 400).

In Ghent the guilds were directly involved in local government, and this resulted in a relatively high turnover of councillors. To a lesser degree this was also the case in Dordrecht, where the guilds exercised indirect influence. In Rotterdam and Zutphen, on the other hand, the guilds were excluded from political participation, and the elites maintained a very strong hold on the main offices.[52]

3. Guilds on the defensive (16th century)

During the fourteenth and fifteenth centuries the guilds had established themselves as the representatives of the popular civic community in the most urban parts of the Low Countries. In some towns, notably Utrecht, they had become the dominant force in local politics, while in other towns they were included in local government under a compromise constitution. In many parts of the Low Countries, on the other hand, there was no guild participation at all, and councillors, generally from elite families, claimed to represent all of the community.

In the sixteenth century such elite claims were further enhanced. In general, the sixteenth century, and especially the reign of Charles V (1515-1555), was a period of retrenchment as far as guild influence was concerned. Charles, to be sure, was never ruler of all of the Low Countries under a single title. His claims to sovereignty always rested on the personal combination of individual titles in Flanders, Brabant, Holland, and Zeeland.[53] At the outset substantial parts of the Low Countries were still outside the Habsburg grasp. For all practical purposes Friesland and Groningen were included in the Habsburg domain only in 1524, Utrecht and Overijssel in 1528, and Gelre in 1543. In Friesland the guilds' role had been negligible, and in the town of Groningen it was informal rather than constitutional.[54] Not so in Utrecht, however.

As we saw earlier, the guilds of Utrecht had overturned the local government and imposed a new constitution in the guild ordinance of 1304, almost immediately after the Battle of the Spurs. This ordinance, promulgated by the elders of the Utrecht guilds, determined that the council would be sworn in by the elders of the guilds, and that henceforth the elders would appoint the 24 members of the town council. In 1525, nonetheless, the guilds of Utrecht mounted a major rebellion to put an end to an impending financial crisis in the city.[55] This rebellion again coincided with simultaneous corporatist upsurges across Western Europe.[56] The guilds called on the help of the duke of Gelre, the linchpin of anti-Habsburg policies in the northern Low Countries.[57]

---

52 Blockmans, 1987, p. 256 and passim.

53 Soly, 2000.

54 Blok, 1894, p. 42. See also 'Introductie' in: *De Groningse gilden*, catalogue of the exhibition in the Groninger Museum voor Stad en Lande, 21 December 1966 - 22 January 1967.

55 van Kalveen, 1972, pp. 93-114; and van Kalveen, 1979, pp. 54-86.

56 Schilling, 1975, pp. 231-6.

57 Gelre's role is decribed in detail in Meij, 1960. For Utrecht's involvement, see van Kalveen, 1974.

In 1528, however, the Utrecht guilds experienced a dramatic turn. In that year the bishop-elect, Henry of Bavaria, decided to hand over his worldly powers to Charles V, who immediately proceeded to build an imposing fortress, the Vredenborch, to consolidate his newly-won city. He also imposed a new constitution on Utrecht. While in February the guilds had been called together to a general assembly to elect new members of the council, 'according to custom',[58] an ordinance dated the 31st of October of that same year expressly excluded the guilds from politics: 'From now on, no elders, nor general elders will be called upon in law or in council, and they will not deal with any issues other than those pertaining to their guild.'[59]

Instead, a permanent council was installed, whose members were appointed by the new ruler. On 14 August 1538 the council voted in favour of several 'general points' to be included in all the guild ordinances.[60] As it was, the blacksmiths' guild received its new ordinance that very same day. Most other guilds received new sets of rules within the next decade. Almost without exception, these new rules had similar introductions, comprising the first eight articles. Two of these articles dealt specifically with politics. The first stipulated that

> the deans will not occupy themselves with issues other than those related to their guilds, and they are not allowed to meet without consent of the provincial governor's representative, the sheriff, and the mayors of the city.

The second article required the presence of a representative of the authorities at all meetings of the guild and his signature under any communications by the guild. It also announced that the authorities would permit the meeting of only one guild on any particular day.[61] These clauses were taken directly from the ordinance of October 1528. It is highly significant that they were inserted in the ordinances of the twenty guilds that existed in 1528,[62] but were not applied to those established afterwards. Thus, the regulations of the guilds of the printers and bookbinders, of the button makers, of the glassmakers, the tobacco sellers, and the fuse makers, established in 1599, 1601, 1657, and 1627, respectively, omitted any reference to the possible political aspirations of these guilds.[63] When, however, the blacksmiths' guild received new regulations in 1636, the articles against political meetings were copied word for word in the

---

58 Overvoorde and Joosting, 1896-7, vol. 1, n° 186.

59 Ibidem, n° 187.

60 Ibidem, n° 7.

61 Overvoorde and Joosting, 1896-7, vol. 2, n° 30, articles 5-6.

62 Ibidem, pp. 18-19, 45, 60, 72, 80, 189, 224, 243, 261, 272, 290, 302, 314, 320, 364, 404-5, 438.

63 Schoute-Bosman, 1944, p. 27. See in Het Utrechts Archief, Stadsarchief II, 461, 'Gildeboeck', fol's 362, 373, 388ii, 403ii, 411i.

new rules.[64] This suggests that more than a century after its abolition the authorities still saw a potential danger in the guild's former constitutional position. The new guilds did not have the weight of history behind them and were therefore considered less threatening.

The suppression of the guild regime in Utrecht was far from unique. In southern Germany the constitutions of twenty-seven towns, including the very important commercial centre of Augsburg, were modified to minimize or completely exclude the guilds during the reign of Charles V. [65] In other parts of the Low Countries, too, popular representation was under pressure. In Zwolle, where the guilds were not directly involved in government, which was left to the *gemeenslieden* elected in the town's four districts, the combination of representative (*gemeensman*) and guild dean was expressly forbidden in 1530.[66] In Middelburg (Zeeland) in 1477 the guilds, together with the civic militias, had won the right to control the councillors. Thirteen guild deans, in cooperation with the councillors, also proposed candidates for the town's magistrate, i.e. the local government. But in 1518 the electors were released from the constraints imposed: they were no longer to be held accountable to guilds and militias. Henceforth, they would act 'without inducement or persuasion from anyone, directly or indirectly'.[67] In Ghent, in 1540, the guilds' political participation was seriously restricted after the introduction of a new constitution, the Concessio Carolina, imposed by Charles V.[68]

The Dutch Revolt against Charles' son, Philip II (which began in 1566), might have led to the guilds regaining their political power. The Calvinist Republic of Ghent (1577-1584) did restore the pre-1540 guild powers immediately.[69] This was an exception, however. In Malines, for example, the Calvinists who were in charge of the town from 1580 to 1585, scrupulously observed the 'ancient constitution' that allowed the guilds only a limited influence.[70] Elsewhere, other corporations tried to claim the role of the guilds. In Utrecht the civic militia had played a part in the siege of Vredenborch castle, the fortress built by Charles V to take control of the city. In the winter of 1576-77 rebel forces and the burghers of Utrecht managed to oust the Spanish garrison. Soon afterwards, the eight captains, or *hoplieden*, of the militias began to behave like popular Roman style tribunes, a parallel that was made quite explicit at the time. They claimed to be speaking on behalf of the community as a whole. In 1583 the militias proposed forming a common council, consisting of the eight militia

---

64 Het Utrechts Archief, Bewaarde archieven I, 96, Stukken betreffende het Eloyengasthuis.

65 *Kaiser Karl V. und die Zunftverfassung. Ausgewählte Aktenstücke zu den Verfassungsänderungen in den oberdeutschen Reichsstädten (1547-1556)*, ed. by E. Naujoks (Stuttgart 1985), 10 and passim.

66 Berkenvelder, 1989, p. 20.

67 Unger, 1923, pp. 70-73 (n° 48), pp. 414-16 (n° 425); quote on 71.

68 Dambruyne, 2002, pp. 534-5, 634.

69 Decavele, 1984, pp. 35-7.

70 Marnef, 1987, pp. 206-7, 217.

captains and representatives from the militia precincts. This was thwarted by the elite families — even though their position was at times extremely precarious, they ultimately prevailed.[71]

This was also true in Holland to an even greater degree. In the towns of Holland (except for Dordrecht) the guilds had been unable to gain a political foothold. As a consequence, unlike Utrecht, there was no precedent or tradition for legitimizing claims of political participation. During the Revolt, however, town governments had sought the advice and consent of broader sections of the population. Usually they consulted the civic militias, who were also directly involved in the town's defence.[72] William of Orange saw them as a means to overcome the resistance of the established elites. This is indeed what happened in Amsterdam, where the Catholic council was dismissed by the militias in 1578.[73] But after they became more firmly established, the new Calvinist elites (whose social profile was very similar to that of the old elites) responded in no uncertain terms. On 23 March 1581 the provincial States of Holland explicitly decided to forbid consultations with 'civic militias, guilds, or any others, as has been done by some towns from time to time', in matters relating to provincial issues.[74] This put an effective end to all official political involvement by these popular organizations.

While the backlash in Holland may have been more evident than in other parts of the Low Countries, the pattern was the same everywhere. Nowhere did the Revolt lead to entirely new constitutions in the towns. Although attempts were made to revive older constitutions, allowing a role for guilds or other popular institutions, they had no lasting impact. The effects, if any, were relegated to popular memory. During the seventeenth and eighteenth centuries the brief interlude of the Revolt was referred to in pamphlets as an example of possible political goals to strive for.[75]

4. Guilds and urban politics in the Low Countries: three patterns (seventeenth to eighteenth centuries)

In a recent essay Piet Lourens and Jan Lucassen show that the northern Netherlands was divided in two distinct 'guild-regions' along religious lines, to exclude large groups from the guilds.[76] In the Low Countries, as elsewhere, citizenship was a prerequisite for guild membership. The inclusion or exclusion of Roman Catholics, Lutherans, Jews, and other religious minorities from citizenship was thus directly related

[71] Kaplan, 1995, pp. 134-6.

[72] Grayson, 1980, pp. 35-63.

[73] Knevel, 1994, pp. 87-91; Prak, 1995, pp. 346-9.

[74] Quoted from the original resolution in Knevel, 1994, p. 89.

[75] For example in 1672, as is demonstrated in Geyl, 1971, pp. 113-15.

[76] Lourens and Lucassen, 2000, pp. 11-43; Blockmans, 1999, pp. 51-63.

to guild policies. As will be seen below, this pattern of inclusion or exclusion was part of the role the civic community played in local politics.[77]

In their paper Lourens and Lucassen postulated an east-west division in the northern Netherlands. In the West, corresponding roughly to the provinces of Holland, Zeeland, and Friesland, members of any religious group could gain citizenship (except for Jews). In the East only members and adherents of the Calvinist Dutch Reformed Church, the public and privileged church of the Republic, could be citizens.[78] This division coincides with those areas in which the guilds were excluded from political representation and those where they were allowed partial representation. But this division does not include the Southern Netherlands, the area where guilds had won full participation in local politics in many towns. The Southern Netherlands should therefore be included in our survey as a third region.

In the Spanish Netherlands (later Austrian Netherlands) the lines had been drawn in the Middle Ages, albeit with some revisions during the reign of Charles V, whose reform of the local constitution of Ghent, the Concessio Carolina, was never permanently reversed.[79] But in Bruges the medieval constitution remained in force. Even at the end of the eighteenth century the guild deans together with the six militia captains formed the Third Tier of a three-tiered town government. The three tiers of the Bruges government were entitled to discuss issues important to the whole of the community. Nine 'head' deans also each held a key to the chest that contained Bruges' town privileges.[80] Louvain's constitution of 1383, which had confirmed the division of authority between the elites and the guilds, remained in force until the end of the Old Regime.[81] In Malines the constitution was reformed in 1585, but half the aldermen were still appointed from the ranks of the guilds. Malines' General Council (*Brede Raad*) consisted of the magistrates, i.e. two mayors and 12 aldermen, and the deans of each of the fourteen guilds of the town.[82] In Brussels, as will be explained in greater detail below, the nine Nations preserved the strong position in local government that they had gained in the 14 century. Antwerp is considered an exception to the general rule of guild participation in Brabant. This is because the Antwerp guilds failed to win representation at the magistrate level, i.e. in the town's executive. However, in Antwerp's General Council, or *Brede Raad*, the guilds were well-represented as one of the Four Tiers, together with the magistrate, elder magistrates, and *poorterij*. Antwerp also had a 'Monday' Council (*Maandagse Raad*), which dealt with public finances, economic policies, poor relief, and even set wage levels for some trades. The Monday Council was composed of guild representatives and magistrates.[83] The influence of the guilds

---

77 Prak, 2002.

78 Lourens and Lucassen, 2000, p. 31.

79 Lenders, 1990, pp. 97-9.

80 Van den Berghe, 1972, pp. 3-6, p. 59. The same author doubts the real influence of the guild deans in a political regime that he pictures as dominated by the elites, p. 62.

81 Van Uytven, 1980a, p. 220.

82 Installé, 1982, 14.

83 Boumans, 1965, pp. 22-37.

may have been less in Antwerp than it was in other towns in Brabant,[84] but compared to the northern parts of the Low Countries it was extensive and significant.[85]

Parts of Brabant were conquered by the Dutch Republic[86] during the 1620s and 30s. These conquered territories, known as the Generality lands because they were under the authority of the States General, did not gain full provincial status after their inclusion in the Dutch state. In Breda the lords of the town, the Orange dynasty, appointed all major officials, but in Bergen-op-Zoom, Eindhoven, Helmond, and in the regional capital Den Bosch the guilds had traditionally constituted the Third Tier of local government. In Den Bosch guild representation was suppressed after the city had been conquered by the Republic in 1629. Den Bosch was one of the strongest fortresses in the Low Countries. To ensure its loyalty, the States General installed a Protestant council in this overwhelmingly Catholic city. But the representatives of the guilds were almost certainly Catholics. To prevent Catholic representation, the Third Tier was no longer invited to council meetings.[87] In the other three towns, however, the deans of the guilds remained active participants in local government throughout the seventeenth and eighteenth centuries.[88]

In Holland there was a completely different situation. There the selection of urban magistrates was almost exclusively the privilege of local elite families who monopolized the major offices. Only in Hoorn, a medium-sized town in the northern part of the province, were ordinary burghers included in the annual election of the town's four burgomasters, through a procedure that was otherwise carefully orchestrated by the local elites.[89] The one notable exception to the general rule of elite exclusiveness was the city of Dordrecht, Holland's oldest and initially most important town. In Dordt, as it was commonly known, the guild deans selected the eight members of a special electoral college, the *Goede Lieden van Achten* (Eight Good Men) who participated in the annual selection of the town's four burgomasters. For most of the seventeenth and eighteenth centuries the local elite was able to limit the role of the guild deans to symbolic participation. In times of political crisis, however, such as in the late 1640s and 50s, in 1672, and again in the 1780s, the guilds and their privileges became a rallying point for disenchanted Dordt burghers who wanted to reclaim their

---

84 This is the opinion of Marnef, 1996, p. 39.

85 Compare also Van Honacker, 1994b, pp. 137-62, 290-337.

86 The data for the Dutch Republic, unless stated otherwise, have been collected from an 18th-century description of all the towns and rural districts: *Tegenwoordige Staat der Nederlanden*, that went through several printings. I have consulted editions from 1741 (Gelderland, Zeeland), 1742-44 (Holland), 1751 (Generaliteitslanden), 1758 (Utrecht), 1787 (Friesland), 1794 (Groningen) and 1801 (Overijssel). Additional data were kindly provided by Piet Lourens, from the IISH database on guilds.

87 Prak, 1999, pp. 52-3.

88 On Bergen-op-Zoom, see de Mooij, 1998, pp. 86-8.

89 Kooijmans, 1985, p. 38, 49, 66.

'ancient rights'.[90] Thus, for example, it was claimed in 1784 that the guild deans represented the 'people' of Dordrecht, and the people consisted of the 'membership of all the guilds taken together'. The contribution of the guild deans in the annual election of Dordt's burgomasters was deemed vital for the 'liberty' of the town and its inhabitants.[91] In 1786 a committee representing the guilds and civic militias dismissed the town council as unconstitutional, following a meeting of all the guilds and militias which had authorized them to do so.[92] But Dordrecht was an exception in Holland: in none of the other 17 enfranchised towns of the province did the guilds have any official political capacity.

In Zeeland's provincial capital, Middelburg, as well as in the town of Zierikzee, the guilds had gained political influence for a short period of time. In Middelburg, in 1477, when the Burgundian dynasty faced a serious succession crisis,[93] the elite was forced to accept a new constitution that had been 'approved by the citizens and guilds'. They instructed the council to seek the approval of the deans of the Middelburg guilds in any decisions under consideration. In 1523 the guilds again attempted, together with the civic militias, to gain a foothold in the local council. They were rebuffed, however, and instead an electoral college, not directly linked to the guilds, was installed, to ensure proper selection of new council members.[94] In Zierikzee the presiding deans of the 12 guilds lost their political role in 1515.

In Friesland's eleven towns (some of them very tiny) local officials were co-opted by the men in power. In Dokkum councillors were elected by the four districts of the city, in the provincial capital of Leeuwarden the citizen militias were included, but none of the Frisian guilds could claim political participation.[95]

The situation was different further east. In all Dutch towns the executives, or magistrates, were changed each year, and the annual elections of magistrates potentially provided a political opportunity for guilds and other local representative institutions. However, in the western provinces, i.e. Holland, Zeeland, and Friesland, magistrates were elected by urban councils, institutions with a permanent membership. By the sixteenth century, membership in these councils became a prerequisite for election as magistrate, i.e. as alderman or burgomaster. In the eastern provinces such permanent councils were generally absent, and the annual election of the local magistrate might include broader sections of the population.[96]

---

90 Schotel, 1998, pp. 17-25, 29, 34.

91 *Voorstel aan Dordrechts burgery, en inzonderheid aan Dekenen van de onderscheiden Gilden aldaar, etc.* (Knuttel 20907), 8, 11.

92 Gemeentearchief Dordrecht, Bibliotheek: Hs 1831: Brief 2 Augustus 1786 aan Mr. Barthout van Slingelandt.

93 Blockmans, 1985.

94 Unger, 1930, pp. 4-5; and Unger, 1923.

95 Guibal, 1934, pp. 45-7; for Leeuwarden also Spanninga, 1999.

96 Gabriëls, 1985, p. 47.

This was the situation in the three major towns of Overijssel. The Overijssel town magistrates were elected by a Sworn Council, which was comprised of representatives from the town's districts. To some extent the Sworn Councils themselves evolved into permanent bodies, but they remained more representative of the common citizenry than the councils of Holland had ever been. The election of magistrates in the cities of Overijssel did not in any way involve the guilds, however.[97]

Neither in Groningen nor in Utrecht were guilds any longer directly involved in politics in the seventeenth and eighteenth centuries, but they had been very much so during the Middle Ages and into the sixteenth century. In Groningen the guilds remained a major force in local and provincial politics until the 1660s, albeit outside the constitutional channels. Groningen was a one-town province. It liked to compare itself to Venice because of its extended *contado*, or rural hinterland. This worked initially to the guilds' advantage, but ultimately it would prove their undoing. The guilds of Groningen never had any constitutional rights in municipal politics.[98] But because the region's gentry and the town's magistrates were regularly at odds, the gentry faction sought and cultivated guild support. During the 1520s Groningen was in dire straits financially, and the guilds staged a coup-d'état in 1526. In 1529 the guild rebellion was suppressed, and the guilds were reduced to their former situation of political impotence.[99] During the Dutch Revolt they made another bid for power, successfully so for some time, but ultimately they lost their power when the Sworn Council lost its rights of nomination in Groningen in 1601. On that occasion, however, it was explicitly stated that the magistrate should ask the opinions of the guild deans.[100] In the 1640s, when the Groningen magistrate and the regional gentry were continually at odds over national policy, the guilds once again became a powerful force in local and regional politics, although Groningen's economy lost much of its dynamic of the previous decades. Local conflicts came to a head in 1660-62 over negotiations between the Republic and Portugal, which involved the fate of Brazil and the Dutch West Indies Company, a major asset of the Groningen economy. A guild revolt in 1662, to some extent a repetition of a revolt five years before, was put down by government troops, forcing guild leaders to flee the country.[101]

In the province of Utrecht (and especially in the city of Utrecht) the guilds had a clear political impact. Despite the fact that little or no popular influence was allowed in the local constitutions in the four smaller towns of the province, Utrecht had a long and well-remembered history as a stronghold of guild power.[102] Even though the political influence of the Utrecht guilds was broken in 1528 by Charles V, that was not

97 As is shown for Zwolle by Streng, 1997, pp. 102-7; and for Deventer by Prak, 1994b, p. 62.

98 Wijnne, 1865, pp. 13-19.

99 Blok, 1904, pp. 185-94.

100 Formsma, 1976, pp. 237-8.

101 De Boer, 1893; Formsma, 1976, pp. 249-56; Huisman, 1992, pp. 342-6.

102 For a more extensive discussion of the guilds' role in Utrecht, see Prak, 2000, pp. 76-80.

the end of popular politics in Utrecht. Indeed, in 1610, the burghers of the city rose in arms against the council, a revolt that could be repressed only with great difficulty and the threat of armed intervention.[103] In 1610, however, the guilds were no longer at the heart of the burgher movement. As was noted earlier, they had been replaced by the civic militias. Among the demands presented by the rebellious burghers, they insisted that[104]

> by and from the eight militia companies every year the magistrates of this city will be chosen and approved by His Highness the Prince [of Orange], in conformity with the ancient liberties of the inhabitants, all in conformity with the resolution taken by the magistrate and the common guild members on St Agnes eve in the year 1341.

This resolution was, of course, none other than the one that confirmed the rule of the guilds in the city of Utrecht.[105]

During the 1780s Utrecht was again the heart of a radical movement, claiming a larger role for the community in politics.[106] In 1784 the shopkeepers' guild insisted that the Main Guilds, i.e. those that had participated in the election procedures before 1528, be reinstated in the new local constitution that was under discussion.[107] A printed petition circulating in Utrecht at that time demanded revival of an ordinance of 1455 that confirmed the Main Guilds as the representatives of the community and electoral bodies of the city. Significantly, however, the 1784 petition added that, where the 1455 ordinance stated 'guilds', 'all citizens' should now be substituted. Another petition simply claimed that the eight militia companies were to be designated as the electoral bodies, and denied the guilds any political role.[108] The shopkeepers' guild was the only one that participated in the debate. Nonetheless, after the Restoration in autumn 1787, the authorities were anxious to assure the loyalty of the guilds, and the deans were asked to swear an oath on the 'Constitution and Form of Government' of the province and the city.[109]

The only northern province where the guilds were routinely involved in the selection of local officials was Gelderland (Guelders). The last of the Dutch provinces to become integrated in the Netherlands state structure devised by the dukes of Burgundy and completed by Charles V, Gelre, or Gelderland, it was occupied by Charles'

---

103 Felix, 1919; Kaplan, 1995, pp. 240-4.

104 Felix, 1919.

105 Overvoorde and Joosting, 1896-7 , vol. 1, n° 111.

106 van Sas, 1987.

107 Het Utrechts Archief, Bewaarde archieven I, 59: Resolutions of the Shopkeepers' (Marslieden) guild, fol. 116v-117r, 21st May 1784; see also Stadsarchief II, 79: Submitted complaints related to the publication of 17th April, 1784

108 Het Utrecht Archief, Stadsarchief II, 79: Submitted complaints related to the publication of 17th April, 1784.

109 Het Utrechts Archief, Bewaarde archieven I, 3: resolutions of the woolmerchants' guild, 24th December 1788, pp. 60-1.

troops only in 1543, i.e. after the legislation introduced in other provinces against guild participation in political life. In most Gelderland towns, guilds did not traditionally have that role. These were all medium or small sized towns; Arnhem's approximately 6,000 inhabitants made it the largest and most important in the province. Several towns claimed a high degree of autonomy; at times they explicitly referred to the Imperial Free Cities as their (German) counterparts.[110] In Arnhem the guilds and burgher militias proposed one candidate for the magistrate, the Sworn Council a second. In Zutphen, Doesburg, and Lochem the guilds and militias met annually in the main church to elect new magistrates in what were in effect popular assemblies. In Harderwijk and Tiel the selection of the magistrate was the exclusive prerogative of the local guilds. Of Gelderland's 13 towns, only two or three elected their magistrates without any participation by the guilds.

We can draw several conclusions about guild representation in the Low Countries from this brief survey. First, the three zones we have distinguished stand out quite clearly. This is not to say that the division is absolute. The conquest of the northern part of Brabant by the Dutch in 1629 placed Den Bosch in a somewhat anomalous position. Likewise, Dordrecht's guilds had a role in local politics that made them unusual compared with their sister institutions in other towns of Holland.

In the South the guilds were active members of local government. In Brabant's main cities, Brussels, Antwerp, and Louvain, as well as in minor towns like Bergen-op-Zoom, guilds had a constitutional position in the political process of their community. Guild representation had been limited in Brabant by Charles V's decree, which transferred the selection of the guild deans (the people who sat on the town council) from the guilds themselves to the local authorities. Guild deans were sometimes politicians who were no longer involved in guild trade. But when all is said and done there is no denying that the guilds of these southern towns were directly involved in the political process. In the eastern provinces of the Dutch Republic, Groningen, Overijssel, and Gelderland, guild representation was embedded in a general pattern of citizen participation in electoral procedures. In Overijssel these procedures operated through the territorial representation of urban districts; in the towns of Gelderland guilds were generally involved as well, in some towns to the exclusion of other institutions. In Groningen a Sworn Council was at times involved in the selection of the magistrate. In the western parts of the country guild representation was unusual. In only a handful of towns did the guilds manage to break the local elite's stranglehold on the political process. Significantly, what guild representation there had been was suppressed in almost all of these towns in the 1520s as part of the backlash against guilds throughout the Low Countries.

The regional division of guild political roles in the Low Countries helps us distinguish various types. It tells us little, however, about the practicalities of guild politics, or what happened when they were absent. Apart from highlighting these various

[110] Compare Pethegem, 1988.

types, the following sections also probe more deeply into the relationships between guilds and local authorities.

5. The South: guilds in politics (Brussels)

Charles V made Brussels the seat of government for all the Low Countries in the first half of the sixteenth century. It retained that role following the secession of the northern territories during the Dutch Revolt. As the seat of government, the many bureaucrats and court officials in Brussels led to the predominance of luxury products in its economy.[111] During the seventeenth and eighteenth centuries Brussels grew from 50,000 to 75,000 inhabitants. In 1738 the 49 Brussels guilds had a total membership of 3,813 masters, as well as 3,883 journeymen, 542 apprentices, and 176 labourers.[112] Guild members were seriously over-represented in the food and building trades, and underrepresented in textiles.[113]

As in other Brabant towns, the guilds of Brussels had won the right of political representation through an intermediate institution, the Nine Nations, first established in 1421. The Nations were purely political institutions, and their number probably corresponded to the number of magistrate offices they were allowed to fill: one mayor, two receivers, and six councillors.[114] For all practical purposes the guilds remained the basic units of corporate organization, and their political aspirations were perhaps most vividly expressed in the guild houses, with their extravagant façades, lining the Great Market and facing the town hall. After the French bombardment in 1695, which caused extensive damage to the Great Market, the guilds rebuilt their houses, often at great expense.[115]

The composition of the Brussels Nations was at best partially determined by economic considerations.[116] Thus, the Nation of Our Lady included butchers and fishmongers, who were arguably in the same line of trade, but it also included goldsmiths, who most obviously were not. The Nation of St John harboured blacksmiths, brass founders, and knife-makers, but also painters and saddlers.[117] The Nation may have been a solution to the variations in size among various guilds. Giving each individual guild a single vote in the election procedure implied that the members of small guilds would receive a relatively greater share in local government than those from larger

---

111 The economy of Brussels in the eighteenth century is the subject of De Peuter, 1999, which has also provided the data for this paragraph.

112 De Peuter, 1999, p. 91; Van Honacker, 1994a, p. 184 and p. 224 counted 3,817 masters, 3,313-4,127 journeymen and 680 apprentices.

113 Compare tables 4.1 (p. 91) and 4.2 (95) in De Peuter, 1999.

114 Favresse, 1961, pp. 229-31.

115 Dambruyne, in this volume.

116 De Peuter, 1999, p. 55.

117 Van Honacker, 1994a, p. 223.

guilds. If this was indeed the rationale behind the initial combinations in 1421, it was only a temporary solution. Obviously, the size of guilds was to vary in the coming centuries, whereas the Nations' composition remained fixed in the constitution. In eighteenth-century Brussels the Nation of St Giles included 934 masters, the Nation of St Christopher as few as 135.[118]

There are indications that some guilds in the eighteenth century survived entirely as convenient vehicles for the politically ambitious. In 1738 the fullers' guild had only 14 members, none of them active in the trade. The guild was nonetheless entitled to send two deans to the meetings of the St Lawrence Nation. Three metal-working guilds in the St Nicholas Nation were so small they counted as few as two or three masters to each dean.[119] Unfortunately, we have no biographical data on the political representatives of the guilds, and it is thus impossible to determine what their social backgrounds were. Data from the neighbouring town of Malines, however, seem to suggest that there was a substantial difference between the representatives from the bourgeoisie and those from the guilds. Whereas the former were military men, lawyers, and even of noble descent, the aldermen recruited from guilds were like the circles they represented. This is not to suggest that they were average artisans or shopkeepers, because many of the politically active guildsmen came from a limited number of families, long established in Malines, and working in wealthy trades like brewing. But even some of the less wealthy trades, such as the bakers, managed to procure seats on the magistrate for their representatives.[120]

As far as Brussels is concerned, we can assume a similar social background for at least a part of the guild deans serving in the local government. This is supported by research into their political attitudes and their relations with broader sections of the population. In spite of the fact that the guilds, through the Nine Nations, could claim equal representation in the local executive, their position was in fact defensive, as the bourgeoisie held the upper hand. Several institutional mechanisms ensured this unequal distribution of power. First of all, the Nine Nations could present candidates for their magistrate seats, but the appointments were in the hands of the aldermen of the *poorterij*. Moreover, the *poorterij* appointed ten magistrates compared to the guilds' nine. In the Broad Council (*Wijde Raad*), the second tier of the Brussels government, the former magistrates from the bourgeoisie were members *ad vitam,* representatives of the Nations for just one year. Only the third tier of the government, the Nine Nations, was controlled by the guilds. And the magistrate appointed the deans of the guilds, i.e. the members of the Nine Nations. The guilds had no similar role in determining the composition of the bourgeois element in local government.[121]

---

[118] Ibidem, pp. 223-4.

[119] Ibidem, p. 185.

[120] Installé, 1982, 141-63, 170-5, and passim.

[121] The composition of the Brussel government in Van Honacker, 1994b, pp. 93-5; and Van Honacker, 1994a, pp. 181-3; De Peuter, 1999, pp. 57-8.

One of the privileges of the three tiers of the Brussels town government was to help set regional and, in effect, national policies. Like the other two 'capital' towns,[122] Louvain and Antwerp, Brussels commanded a vote in the States of Brabant, and its consent was needed to introduce new taxation, for example. Taxes, and the related issue of infringement on local privileges, were among the most contested in any early modern European polity. Brussels was no exception. But it is striking how time and again the third tier of the town government, i.e. the Nine Nations, refused to consent to taxes, opposed collection of certain contentious taxes, or protested against violations of their privileges when the bourgeoisie found them perfectly acceptable.[123] We see this in 1610, 1619, 1649, 1657, 1662, 1669, 1672, 1675, 1676, 1680-81, 1684, 1692, 1697, 1699, 1717-19, and finally 1747. The Nine Nations repeatedly refused to accept new taxation, and would remain in their meeting room in the town hall until their objections had been dealt with. The news of their protest spread, and crowds would gather in the Great Market square. The people would then apply pressure on the authorities to change their proposals, or accept a compromise in other areas. In several of the mass mobilizations the national government was compelled to bring in troops and apply force to restore order. This happened, for instance, in 1619, when thousands of troops were billeted on the Brussels population. In spite of a general pardon, six guild deans were banned indefinitely from the town. Even more striking, another general rising of the Brussels community in 1717-19 ended with the execution of Frans Anneesens, master slater and dean of his guild, who afterwards became a hero of liberal democracy in Belgium. The ease with which the Nine Nations seemed capable of mobilizing a mass following suggests that they were perceived as closely linked with the popular cause.

The Nations' opposition against government tax policies demonstrates both the strengths and weaknesses of guild political representation. Frequent refusals to vote new taxes, despite the bourgeoisie's acceptance, reliance on popular demonstrations, as well as violent suppression of guild-led opposition movements (with Frans Anneessens' death as dramatic apogee) strongly suggest that the guilds were most likely to operate from a minority position. The Brussels constitution, however, allowed the Nine Nations important means to conduct such an opposition policy. According to the 1421 constitution, taxes could be imposed only with the consent of the Nations. Attempts to bypass them would mean introduction of an additional fiscal burden (always unpopular) as well as violation of the constitution. As a result, resistance was vindicated from the very start. We cannot say that the very threat of political turmoil would have made the authorities reluctant to provoke the Nine Nations, but despite the fact that it was the weaker partner in local government, the guilds in Brussels were a force to reckon with.

---

[122] The fourth, Den Bosch, was lost to the Dutch Republic in 1629.

[123] The following lines are completely dependent upon Van Honacker, 1994b, chs 2 and 3. See also the same author's 1990a, pp. 299-312, 1990b, pp. 187-200, 1992, pp. 41-52.

6. The East: guilds on the constitutional margins (Arnhem)

By and large the great wave of artisan revolutions of the fourteenth century passed the northern parts of the Low Countries by. In Gelderland, however, the guilds had a second opportunity in the fifteenth century, thanks to the duchy's role in the anti-Habsburg struggle. Arnhem was one of the towns where guilds were granted political representation. In 1466, when Arnhem was conquered by the duke's troops, the ruling families fled, thus leaving a power vacuum. The guilds were summoned 'to elect a new council'.[124] Two years later their influence was rescinded when the patricians returned to power. In 1478, however, when the town was again overwhelmed by ducal forces, the 1466 arrangements were reinstituted. In 1487, moreover, they were confirmed by Maximilian of Austria. From then on six 'guild masters' were to represent the six Main Guilds in the government of Arnhem. The Main Guilds were in effect political organizations that included several trades. The guild masters were granted extensive powers by a document drawn up in January 1488. On issues of war and peace, sale of town property, and introduction of new taxation, the council needed the approval of the guild masters. Bylaws relating to guild trades could be introduced only by the council and guild masters together. If a citizen were sentenced to pay an extraordinary fine, the guild masters would join in the bench of justice. They were also to propose candidates from their midst who would be appointed as an extra paymaster of the town 'on behalf of the citizenry'.[125]

In the course of the sixteenth century the guild masters were first supplemented by 18 other representatives of the guilds, called *gemeente* (Common Council, or Community). By the end of the century, the *gemeenslieden* (Common Councillors) numbered 48, but they were no longer the representatives of the guilds:[126] they were supposed to speak on behalf of the whole community. Their powers overlapped those of the guild masters. By the early eighteenth century an elaborate treatise on the constitution of Arnhem claimed that ever since the late fifteenth century the town's government had rested in the hands of 'mayors, aldermen and council, the six guild masters, and the 18 elected citizens'. Indeed, no decisions could be taken in 'serious matters' by the council alone, but always needed the approval of the 'guild masters and common council from the people, who have represented the people'.[127] In fact, this influential treatise claimed that Arnhem was a 'free and sovereign town', and as such equal to any prince.[128] The government of Arnhem, it was claimed, had always been of a

---

124 Graswinckel, 1933, p. 94.

125 Verkerk, 1992, pp. 364-6.

126 Graswinckel, 1993, p. 95.

127 *Deductie van de regten ende privilegien der vrye stadt Arnhem, het collegie van de geswoore gemeente, gildens, borgerye ende ingesetenen van dien competerende; ofte apologie van de wettige regeringe, na de oude gronden van de vrye-stadt Arnhem* (Arnhem 1703) (Knuttel catalogue, 15037), pp. 10-11.

128 *Deductie*, p. 9; compare van Dixhoorn, 1997, ch. 5; also van Dixhoorn, 1999, pp. 25-54.

popular nature, i.e. one in which ultimately the people decided their own fate. It was, however, far from clear who 'the people' actually were. In the corporatist tradition the 1703 *Deductie* mentioned various overlapping categories. The title page lists common council, guilds, citizens, and inhabitants side by side. The argument is mainly built around the category of *burghers*, a highly ambivalent term in Dutch, which could refer to full citizens, the middle classes, members of the citizen militias, or simply the people in general.[129] The guild masters are presented as the original representatives of the burghers, but they had to come to an understanding with the Common Council. A ruling of 1547 had actually forbidden them from seeking the advice of the guilds before making up their minds on any single issue! In the seventeenth and eighteenth centuries the guild masters were no longer recruited from the guild membership — if that had ever been the case. Guilds had to seek the approval of the local government for the slightest change in their rules.[130]

In 1674, moreover, the towns of Gelderland were forced to accept new constitutional rules giving wide powers to the Orange *stadholders*, theoretically only governors but actually the informal heads of state of the Dutch Republic. More specifically, the *stadholders* were entitled to elect members of the ruling councils, whose mandate in the towns of Gelderland had to be renewed every year. In effect, common councils and guild masters, like those in Arnhem, were pushed aside. In the spring of 1702, however, stadholder William III died without male issue. Almost overnight the rulers of the towns of Gelderland had to deal with popular claims demanding full restoration of 'our ancient rights and privileges'. In Arnhem petitions articulating such claims, as well as demanding a comprehensive reform of common council 'to purge them from such persons as have been elected against the rights and privileges, and replace them with honourable and honest men' were signed at guild meetings by most or all members present.[131]

These petitions would be the beginning of years of political wrangling between the political elites and the population of Arnhem. 'Burgher representatives' pressured on the authorities on behalf of the population. The natural constituents of these representatives were the guilds and the civic militias, whose opinions they regularly solicited. Two-thirds of the representatives were recruited from either the guilds or the militias.[132] In January 1703 the burgher representatives dismissed Arnhem's town council and installed a completely new one more sympathetic to their views. The acts confirming the legality of this election were signed by the common council, as well as 72 citizens on behalf of the guilds and the civic militias.[133] In 1707, however, the radical reformers were out-manoeuvred. A new constitution was introduced that

[129] About these highly relevant meanings of the word 'burgher', see Prak, 1995.

[130] De Groot, 1939, p. 91.

[131] Gemeentearchief Arnhem, Oud archief, 1160: petitions from 1702-3.

[132] van Dixhoorn, 1999, appendix iii, table 4.

[133] van Dixhoorn, 1999, p. 48.

confirmed the Common Council as representatives of the burgher community and hence the second tier of Arnhem's government. But the guild masters were reduced to overseers of the guilds, i.e. 'to regulate the guilds, as in former times'.[134] Even though this did not quash the guilds completely — there was another outbreak of popular protest in 1711 — for the time being their political role had effectively come to an end.[135]

A new crisis provided new opportunities for guild politics. In 1747 the country was threatened with invasion by French troops, who actually crossed the border into the province of Zeeland. Since the death of William III the provinces of Holland and Zeeland had refused to appoint a successor. There was strong popular pressure on the ruling elites to correct this. In Gelderland the Prince of Orange had been made *stadholder* in 1722, but on a very restricted basis. Now a petition was circulated among the Arnhem guilds to demand full restoration of the prince's dignities and powers.[136] This attempt to engage the court in the struggle against local patrician families completely backfired. In 1750 the Prince of Orange was granted extensive rights of appointment that excluded popular consultations, let alone nomination of candidates by the Common Council. Only in the 1760s was the heavy hand of the court on local politics temporarily lifted, during the minority of William V.[137] On 6 May 1760 the Bakers and Brewers' guilds were invited by the council to meet the next day in the Great Church to help draw up a slate to elect a new alderman. In the following years several similar meetings took place, with the last one being recorded in the guild book of the bakers and brewers in October 1763.[138]

During the 1780s another wave of popular protest engulfed the country, this time taking it to the brink of revolution and civil war in the summer of 1787.[139] In December 1782 the Bakers and Brewers' guild of Arnhem started a fresh book to record for posterity the new attempts to restore the guild's former political rights. Members of the guild once again signed petitions, and burgher representatives were appointed, as in 1702. In September 1783 the representatives received an official instruction from the 'Bookkeepers, Guardians, Councillors, and other members of all the guilds, in the name and on behalf of the body of citizens of this town Arnhem, presently meeting together'.[140]

---

[134] Gemeentearchief Arnhem, Oud archief, 1152: Reglement over regeringen van de Stadt Arnhem, 22 December, 1707, clause 9.

[135] Pols, 1996, pp. 86-7.

[136] Gemeentearchief Arnhem, Oud archief, 1488, Brieven van het bakkers and Brouwers gilde, 15 December 1747.

[137] Gabriëls, 1990, p. 69, p. 79.

[138] Gemeentearchief Arnhem, Oud archief, 1478, Resoluties van het Bakkers en brouwers gilde, fols. 76v, 84r, 86r. See also Bibliotheek ADC 212, gedrukte stukken over het jachtrecht, 15 March 1784, bijlage Z1.

[139] For an outline of events: Schama, 1977, ch. 3.

[140] Gemeentearchief Arnhem, Oud archief, 1479: Memorie en Resolutieboek van het bakkers- en brouwersgilde ... 1782 en 1783, 26 September, 1783.

Thus, up to the very end of the eighteenth century the guilds of Arnhem were active in local politics. Remarkably, they were not simply promoting their own interests; rather they attempted to gain permanent influence on the election of members to the town council, and thus to acquire a say in the way the town was run. In these attempts the Arnhem guilds succeeded only intermittently at best. But did they fail altogether? It is difficult to establish the extent of their influence and whether it made a difference. In one area, however, we have an indication that they did make a difference.

Unlike the situation in Holland, where, apart from Jews, anyone who wanted to become a citizen could do so, and hence qualify for membership in a guild, many towns in the eastern regions of the Dutch Republic discriminated against non-Calvinists. This was an issue the guilds felt very keenly about. A petition from the Roman Catholic community in Arnhem in 1784 clearly shows active involvement by the local guilds. In 1737 Catholics had been made eligible for citizenship, but they were not allowed to join the guilds. In 1747 the guilds petitioned the town council to ask for a return to the 'old situation', i.e. complete exclusion of Catholics from Arnhem's citizen rights.[141] In the town of Deventer, just across the border in the neighbouring province of Overijssel, the guilds in the early 1780s supported the local elites in their attempts to curtail the influence of the *stadholder*. But when reform proposals were circulated that promised to open Deventer citizenship to non-Calvinist inhabitants, the guilds withdrew their support and changed sides to join the Orange party.[142] This points to a significant division within the Dutch Republic, and in the Low Countries as a whole. In the East, where local governments were dominated by the elites but the population was represented through the Common Councils, there was a marked tendency towards excluding anyone who was not Calvinist from the urban community, and more specifically from rights to citizenship.[143] In towns with a tradition of guild representation, such as those in the East, as well as Utrecht and Dordrecht, guilds maintained strong links with the church.[144] In the West, where merchant elites ruled without popular interference, such religious discrimination was almost completely unknown. In the South the guild-church relationship seems to have been even stronger than in the East. During the Dutch Revolt the Protestants had been removed almost completely. Guilds remained strongly committed to their role in the Roman Catholic Church, continuing to maintain their altars, participate in processions, and other rituals. Guilds went on pilgrimage together and used religious symbols extensively in their 'public relations'.[145] The religious policies of the guilds were closely related to their constitutional positions in the various regions of the Low Countries.

---

141 Gemeentearchief Arnhem, Bibliotheek: 117: Request en Remonstrantie ... op den naam van de Roomschkatolieke gemeente van Arnhem (Nijmegen, 1784).

142 te Brake, 1989, p. 95, pp. 100-5.

143 Prak, 2002; Lourens, Lucassen, 2000, pp. 18-19.

144 Compare for Utrecht: Prak, 2000, pp. 78-9; for Dordrecht Palmen, 1998, pp. 229-31.

145 Thijs, in this volume.

7. The West: guilds and popular politics in the absence of representation (Amsterdam)

The city of Amsterdam grew to over 200,000 inhabitants in the course of the seventeenth century. Yet it was still ruled by its four burgomasters and a council of 36, as in the days when the town had a population of 20,000. The council, or *vroedschap*, moreover, was co-optive, i.e. if there was a vacancy, the remaining members chose their new colleague.[146] As in other towns of Holland, the council claimed to be representative of the whole community, the absence of elections notwithstanding.[147] This raises questions about relations between guilds and the authorities there. Given the fact that guild monopolies and other privileges ultimately depended on local government sanction, some sort of relationship had to be established. Such relationships could be personal or institutional, or both. If it were shown, for example, that deans and other administrators of the guilds were members of the town council, or perhaps relatives of council members, that could suggest informal alternatives to the guild political representation in the southern Netherlands.[148]

In Amsterdam the administrators of the guilds were appointed annually by the burgomasters of the town.[149] Once every year each guild would propose a list of names, usually twice the number required, and the burgomasters would then appoint administrators from among them. This procedure, with its *dubbeltallen* (literally: double numbers), was very common in the Dutch Republic for corporate offices, not just within the guilds but in other areas as well. In many towns the aldermen, for instance, were appointed in a similar fashion. The procedure allowed the guilds a major say in the recruitment of their officers, but at the same time allowed the burgomasters some discretion as well. Under normal circumstances the burgomasters were supposed to choose the names in the top half of the list.[150]

In most years the officers of the Amsterdam guilds were approved both by the membership of the guild itself and by the local authorities. In some guilds the situation was rather straightforward: there would be a dean and two 'overmen'. Other guilds had much more complex administrative structures. This was particularly true of guilds that included several different trades. Thus the board of the sail and compass

---

146 For a socio-political history of the Amsterdam council during the Dutch Republic, see Elias, 1923.

147 Prak, 1994b, pp. 67-70.

148 Unfortunately, no serious work has been done so far on these issues in the Netherlands. Obviously, tracing such informal relationships is very time-consuming. For the time being, therefore, we have to content ourselves with a limited survey, of the situation in Amsterdam around the middle of the eighteenth century. See for a similar argument concerning church councils, Schilling, 1980.

149 On the guilds of Amsterdam, see van Eeghen, 1974²; Nusteling, 1985, ch. 7; Lourens and Lucassen, 1998, pp. 121-62. Buchner, 2004 was published after this chapter was finished.

150 See Gemeentearchief Amsterdam, archive 5028 (burgomasters), pp. 522-3.

makers' guild included representatives from the two quite distinct trades. Less obvious, the board of the shipwrights consisted of representatives from the old and the new quarters of town. The most complex situations existed among the blacksmiths and the woodworkers. The board of the blacksmiths' guild always included a fine-smith, a locksmith, and a gun maker, and in alternating years a blacksmith and a farrier, or a brazier, a knife maker, and a sword maker. On the board of the St Joseph's guild no less than ten different trades, all specialist branches of woodworking, were permanently represented.

We do not have any precise information about the way candidates were selected within the ranks of the guild membership. It is very likely that their names were proposed by the dean and 'overmen' themselves. This is suggested by the fact that members of the boards in the various guilds of Amsterdam were not truly representative of guild membership as a whole. In the first place, the number of individuals serving on the board was remarkably restricted. A check of the names of those appointed in ten of the fifty guilds in Amsterdam between 1736 and 1747[151] reveals that a total of 331 mandates were available to the ten guilds. Yet only 144 individuals were sworn into office. Thus, on average, every officer served 2.3 terms during the 12 years. Although most guilds were close to the average, some guilds were more democratic than others. Thus, the pastry bakers' guild had 15 different individuals appointed to 24 mandates. Among the millers and the shoe menders, on the other hand, members of the board served on average three terms during the 12 years. The pastry bakers were a medium-sized guild, with a membership whose income was in the middling range, but so were the millers. The shoe menders were generally poor, in contrast with the goldsmiths, whose board members also served long terms: 2.6 mandates on average during the years under scrutiny. In other words, a clear pattern does not emerge from these figures, except for the fact that the same individuals were regularly returned to the boards of their guilds.

The figures, moreover, only represent the tip of the iceberg: between 1736 and 1747 the tailors' guild of Amsterdam appointed 15 different individuals to 37 mandates altogether, or 2.5 mandates for each member of the board. However, a survey of the same board over a longer period, 1734 to 1794, demonstrates a much higher incidence of the same phenomenon. In these years a total of 300 mandates came up for appointment. In all, only 35 individuals were actually elected. Almost to a man they first served several terms as 'overman' before becoming dean of the guild, the most prestigious office. Given the fact that the guild had a membership of more than 600, these figures starkly illustrate the social exclusiveness of the board.[152]

This is further underscored by data on the personal fortunes of the board members. In 1742 all inhabitants of Amsterdam earning more than 600 guilders a year

---

151 *Ibidem*, 53. These guilds were selected to provide the widest possible range of variation in guilds, as to size, and branch. We investigated the board members of the guilds of the artists (St. Luke), corn-millers, wine merchants, biscuit-rusk-pastry makers, goldsmiths, shoemenders, linters, shipwrights, surgeons, tailors, and blacksmiths.

152 Panhuysen, 2000, p. 52.

were assessed for purposes of taxation. Eleven members and former members of the tailors' guild board were considered for inclusion in the register. In fact four were not, indicating that their income fell below the threshold. Another two were assessed at the minimum rate, while two supposedly earned 800 guilders and three at least 1,000. These figures compared very favourably with the guild as a whole. Only 15 per cent of the membership made the cut, a dismal 3 per cent was assessed at 1,000 guilders and over.[153]

This pattern is typical for the situation in other guilds as well. We have checked the names of all 121 board members of the 50 guilds in Amsterdam in 1742 against the tax register of that year.[154] Of these, 79, or two-thirds, could be identified. Although there may possibly be a confusion of identities in a handful of cases, it can safely be assumed that the majority of those absent from the register were simply too poor. This is confirmed by the fact that none of the board members was assessed in such relatively poor trades as peat carriers, wool knitters, wicker workers, and shoe menders. The members of the boards of the shopkeepers, saw millers, and wine merchants' guilds, on the other hand, were all assessed on an average of no less than 2,900 guilders annual income. The four members of the board of the brokers' guild were on average worth 7,000 guilders a year. One of them, a man called Johannes Bontekoning, was supposedly earning 16,000 a year, which put him just below the one hundred wealthiest inhabitants of Amsterdam.[155]

Potentially, therefore, some overseers of the Amsterdam guilds would have qualified to be elected on the Amsterdam municipal council, or *vroedschap*, a body of 36 whose influence extended far beyond the boundaries of the town itself. Wealth was a precondition for gaining entrance to that charmed circle of power brokers. More was needed, however, than mere riches. The right family connections were equally important. Thanks to the extensive genealogies of Amsterdam's ruling families, we can trace such connections and are able to establish that the overseers of the guilds in fact were completely deficient in this area.[156]

Only one dean in all 50 Amsterdam guilds in the mid-eighteenth century managed to obtain a seat on the town council, and this seems to have been owing to extraordinary circumstances.[157] In 1748 extended rioting forced the dismissal of 17 members of the council. Their replacements were selected partly on condition that they had no connection whatsoever with the discredited regime. No less than 12 merchants were

---

[153] Ibidem, 53.

[154] *Kohier van de Personeele Quotisatie te Amsterdam over het jaar 1742*, ed. by W.F.H. Oldewelt (Amsterdam 1945).

[155] Oldewelt, 1945, pp. 15-16 lists the 102 richest inhabitants of Amsterdam in 1742.

[156] Elias, 1963². I checked the names of all overseers who were assessed in the 1742 tax list against the index of Elias' book. Two names could be matched: the *fabrikeur* Aaron Noëll, whose name appears in a list of genealogies that Elias was unable to connect to the ruling families (p. 1037); the other, Michiel Bruyningh, is discussed in the text.

[157] Quite likely, guild deans were appointed to lesser offices in town (e.g. Nieuwenhuis, 1995, 87n10), but given the great number of these offices it is hard to be more precise about this.

appointed to the council, which had become dominated by rentiers during the previous half century.[158] One of the new members was Michiel Bruyningh, dean of the wine merchants' guild. Bruyningh had been assessed at 5,000 guilders in the 1742 tax register and was one of the great merchants of his day. In 1761 his wine cellars, containing over eighty varieties, were reputedly worth more than 200,000 guilders.[159] It is significant, however, that Bruyningh was a representative of one of the very few merchant guilds in Amsterdam, one that, moreover, was typically related to export trades. With Bruyningh the exception, it is clear that the Amsterdam guilds had to find other ways to exert influence on the policies of the municipal authorities.

To judge from the documents preserved in the Amsterdam archives, the most common line of communication between guilds and local authorities was through the petitions filed by the guilds. Hundreds of them survive, and quite likely many have been lost.[160] Many of the petitions request a change in guild regulations, usually because new circumstances demanded an adaptation. Thus, in 1786, 238 members from various guilds, all representing trades involved in the making of carriages (such as carpenters, saddle makers, wheelwrights, woodcutters, and others), masters as well as journeymen, complained about the imports of English carriages that undercut their livelihoods. The carpenters' guild, responsible for protecting the trade, was in fact powerless. New legislation was required to support the local trade.[161] Likewise, ten wallpaper painters, all members of St Luke's guild that organized the artists of Amsterdam, complained in 1754 that their trade was undercut by ready-made wallpaper imported from outside of town. They predicted[162]

> [t]hat the notorious consequence of this [development] will be, that more than three hundred journeymen, and their families, who have so far earned an honourable and decent livelihood, will become destitute and dependent on town and poor relief, or be forced, unable to find a decent job, to move abroad and thus deprive this town of a substantial advantage.

In these petitions, significantly, the guilds never claimed legal entitlement to government support. Instead, they tried to build a case based on the civic community that included both the authorities and themselves. The wallpaperers suggested that destitute members would become a financial liability. The carriage makers were of the opinion, that 'they were paying their scot and lot, and therefore were helping to carry the burdens of the town and their guilds'. Other guilds added that taxation in Amsterdam was substantially higher than in the countryside, or reminded the authorities of their contributions to the civic militias.[163] All of this, according to the wallpaperers, entitled

---

[158] Elias, 1923, pp. 215-16.

[159] Elias, 1963², vol. 2, p. 853.

[160] These petitons can be found in Gemeentearchief Amsterdam, archive 5061 (Judicial archives), n°s 684-725: petitions to the Aldermen; and 5028 (Burgomasters), pp. 515-19: petitions filed by the guilds. For the analysis of their contents, see Prak, 1996.

[161] Gemeentearchief Amsterdam, 5061, 723, n° 23.

[162] Gemeentearchief Amsterdam, 5061: 700, n°3, (1754).

[163] Gemeentearchief Amsterdam, 5061: 697, n° 1 (1751).

them to the 'advantages that are due to them as inhabitants of this town and members of their guilds ... with the exclusion of others, particularly aliens'.[164]

Because the guild members, both as individuals and collectively, contributed to the upkeep of the community, the authorities should support them and their trades. If such help was not forthcoming, they would be forced to move elsewhere, they claimed. This argument was part of the dichotomy between established members and outsiders perceived by the guild petitions,[165] but also reflected in Amsterdam's 'particularistic' policies, which sought to favour the town's economy over the interests of other towns.[166]

Indeed, it seems that these guild petitions were generally looked upon most favourably by the Amsterdam government. A survey of Amsterdam's local legislation — very important in the absence of any significant national legislation — reveals that it resulted largely from the initiative of those sections of the population directly involved. More than 40 per cent of petitions led to the introduction of a bylaw. Even more telling, many bylaws copied the text of the petition verbatim into the Amsterdam statute book. To be sure, guilds were the single most important group of petitioners in Amsterdam; almost half the petitions preserved from the eighteenth century were signed in the name of a guild.[167]

Social security arrangements for the Amsterdam guilds also suggest a high level of support from local authorities. The shipwrights' guild was allowed to claim significant amounts of money from ships entering port, as well as from the shipbuilding industry, to help poor members. Likewise, the peat carriers' guild of Amsterdam charged its customers, i.e. the merchants of Amsterdam, not simply for services provided by the guild's members, but also for poor relief provided by the guild.[168] Thus, in spite of political weaknesses, the Amsterdam guilds were capable of expressing their needs, and of putting some weight behind their petitions.

Conclusion

The three towns we have used as examples in this study, Brussels, Arnhem, and Amsterdam, illustrate distinctive patterns in the urban landscape of the Low Countries. In the constitutions of the South guilds remained established participants in political decisions. In the East they were included in a system of political representation that also included other corporate institutions. In the West the population was not formally represented in local politics, as the elites claimed to represent the entire community.

---

[164] Gemeentearchief Amsterdam, 5061: 723, n° 23 (1786). Compare 5061: 694, n° 46 (1747-8); 5061: 702, n° 9 (1756); 5061: 713, n° 1 (1770); 5061: 720, n° 6 (1778).

[165] Prak, 1996, pp. 272-6.

[166] Israel, 1979, pp. 41-6; Price, 1994.

[167] van Nierop, 1997, pp. 286-7.

[168] Bos, 1998, pp. 104-5, 126-7.

This geographical distribution also hints at the origins of political participation by guilds in the Low Countries. As we have seen, guild representation originated in the Middle Ages, specifically in the fourteenth century. In no town in the Low Countries did guilds gain representation in local political institutions after the middle of the fifteenth century. The pattern that emerged in the fourteenth and early fifteenth centuries was very similar to the economic geography of the Low Countries at that time. The southern and to a lesser extent eastern areas were economically more advanced than the coastal areas of the West. The emerging middle classes were able to wield political impact mainly in places that were most developed at the time of the 'guild revolutions'. This is illustrated in the example of Dordrecht, the only town where the guilds had political representation in the western region. Dordrecht happened to be the most developed town of that region during the Middle Ages.

In the first half of the sixteenth century the acceleration of state formation under Charles V resulted in a decline of guild political power in many towns. Remarkably, the Dutch Revolt in the second half of the century did not change the established pattern in any significant way. The Revolt instigated other major changes in the Dutch political structure, however, particularly as it provided an arena for local politics and politicians that had previously been unthinkable. Nonetheless, in most towns, especially in the West, local elites prevented the rise of political representation in their towns. Guilds could present petitions to the local councils, as could any other institution or individual, and these petitions could expect to get a favourable hearing. But it was the elites that made the decisions, not the guilds.

As a result, the three geographical zones remained constitutionally distinct in the seventeenth and eighteenth centuries. In the South we still find direct political representation by the guilds. In the East we find them involved in the elections of town officials. In the West the elites are firmly in control of the political institutions. It would be an error, however, to see these constitutional distinctions as the direct expression of social differences among the three regions. Although most research in this subject tends to concentrate on the earlier periods, there is little reason to believe that guild regimes provided significant political opportunities to the average artisan or shopkeeper in the Southern Netherlands. In most cases the political representatives of the guilds were at best recruited from the wealthier members of the guild; at worst, such representatives had no relationship whatsoever with the guild's trade. As a result the social contrasts between the three regimes are less pronounced than are the constitutional ones. Yet the constitutional differences do not reflect the totality of popular politics. As the discussion of Amsterdam politics has demonstrated, the guilds of that town, in spite of their complete lack of formal influence, had alternative means of conveying their needs and demands to the local government.

It may be helpful to return to the idea of constitutions as compromise. Marc Boone, in his detailed study of medieval guilds in Ghent, pointed out that their influence in government was not so much an expression of the dominance of one group over another, but was rather 'a mechanism for the regulation of conflict'.[169] It should be understood

---

[169] Boone, 1990, pp. 52-3; Blockmans, 1999, p. 60.

against the background of the overriding goal of both urban elites and guilds in the Low Countries, i.e. the preservation of political autonomy for their local community. That autonomy was predicated on at least a minimum of cooperation within the community itself. The social foundation of this cooperation was property; all three types of governments were designed to exclude the working classes from the political process. Economically, the elite-guild alliance was threatened by the potentially conflicting interests of commerce and industry, of large enterprise and small firms. But politically the two groups were united in their attempts to avoid interference by outsiders such as princes and their ministers.[170] Thus, we can observe a tendency to mitigate the constitutional extremes. In the South the guild deans, and indeed some guilds themselves, tended to become 'elitist'. In the West, despite the absence of formal guild influence and personal connections between council and guild community, the ruling classes were careful to placate the sensibilities of the guild members.

---

[170] Blockmans, 1988, pp. 145-54; Boone and Prak, 1995. This argument is further elaborated in Prak, 1999.

Chapter 4

Export industries, craft guilds and capitalist trajectories, 13th to 18th centuries

Catharina Lis and Hugo Soly

Research on export industries in early modern Europe has long focused on rural areas. This interest is understandable, as many economic historians have been convinced ever since the publications by Henri Pirenne[1] that from the late Middle Ages industrial growth was incompatible with corporative interventions and regulations,[2] i.e. with the context in which much of urban production occurred until the end of the Ancien Régime (and in some cases until well into the nineteenth century). This perspective will easily lead to descriptions of urban and rural types of manufacturing in terms of dichotomies, such as regulated versus unregulated, rigid versus flexible, monopolist versus market-oriented, medieval versus modern. In the 1970s and 80s adherents of proto-industrialization theories, following Franklin Mendels,[3] reinforced such views, by attributing the superiority of the rural export industries to wage differences as well: in search of labour less expensive than the reproduction costs, merchant capital targeted the countryside, with its growing reservoir of comparatively inexpensive labour.[4] Several authors readily submit that only the rural export industries achieved the dynamics necessary for structural economic change, thereby making the transition to modern types of manufacture.[5]

In recent years some of these perceptions have met with criticism and even rejection, which has led to a bridging of the 'gap' between urban and rural areas: often urban and rural industries proved to be complementary rather than competitive.[6] This does not mean that a new consensus has been achieved. Some argue that the urban export industries had much in common with their rural counterparts. James Farr, for example, perceives a dynamic urban 'craft-economy' between the fourteenth and

---

1 Pirenne, 1912, p. 427.

2 Van der Wee, 1988, pp. 324-5.

3 Mendels, 1972, pp. 241-61, and Mendels, 1984, pp. 977-1008.

4 Kriedte, 1977, pp. 58-60, 232-3.

5 van Zanden, 1993, pp. 16, 109.

6 Fujii, 1990, pp. 77-97; Sortor, 1993, pp. 1475-99; Stabel, 1995, pp. 138-41, 146-8, 176-89; Lis and Soly, 1997a.

eighteenth centuries, unrestrained or hardly restrained by regulations and involving many producers operating along the periphery of, or even outside the guild system. He believes that the normative sources fully distort an economic practice he describes as a 'freewheeling affair'.[7] Other historians bridge the gap through a converse rationale. Arguing that rural areas were far from a free zone for manufacture during the early modern period, they concur with the fundamental reservation that Emile Coornaert and N.W. Posthumus have expressed regarding Pirenne's position that export industries could not exist without regulations and hence had to be urban-based: textile production in Hondschoote was as much subject to rules and regulations and quality inspections as it was in any Flemish town.[8]

Considering these views in the context of the new interest in institutions[9] and 'conventions'[10] in economic studies reveals that economic historians have good reason to modify their research agenda. Studies of industrial production during the late Middle Ages and the early modern period should devote far more attention to regional economies (including urban industries),[11] transactions costs, and institutions, especially to organizations with regulatory and supervisory duties, such as craft guilds.

1. Questions

Jan de Vries and Ad van der Woude have argued that the spectacular economic growth of the Dutch Republic during the first half of the seventeenth century is impossible to understand without taking into account the institutional and organizational progress,[12] which substantially reduced the risks of trade in commodities and financial instruments such as company shares and government bonds. They devote remarkably little attention to industrial organizations, however, especially to craft guilds and other urban institutions responsible for inspecting the quality of export goods.[13] Piet Lourens and Jan Lucassen, on the contrary, who present a different theoretical frame of reference, emphasize the economic prominence of craft guilds: the rise of merchant capitalism in the United Provinces during the first half of the seventeenth century coincided with continuous increases in the number of guild-based industries.[14]

---

7 Farr, 1997, pp. 24-54, esp. 49-52.

8 Coornaert, 1930a and Coornaert, 1950, pp. 59-96; Posthumus, 1937, pp. 18-19.

9 See the fundamental reservations in North, 1981, North, 1990 and North, 1991, pp. 97-112; Hodgson 1988; Eggertsson, 1990; Cohen, 1996, pp. 60-84.

10 Compare *Revue Economique*, 1989, special issue: 'L'Economie des conventions', and Orléan, 1994.

11 See the important remarks by Pollard, 1991, pp. 29-56.

12 In this chapter we will also refer to the Dutch Republic or the United Provinces as the Northern Netherlands.

13 de Vries and van der Woude, 1997, pp. 149, 162-3, 671, 693, 695.

14 Lourens and Lucassen, 1994, pp. 44, 48-9, and Lourens and Lucassen, 1997a, pp. 52-3.

This revisionism is very promising but may also lead us astray. How can we explain the 'anomaly' that regions where transaction costs were low, such as the Northern Netherlands during the Republic, did not necessarily undergo early and rapid industrialization? Nor is it sheer coincidence that economic historians have far greater difficulty explaining the decline of the Republic in the eighteenth century than the seventeenth-century 'miracle'.[15] Karel Davids is aware of this problem and invokes the new institutional economists, who relate problem situations to 'path-dependency': if at a given point in history, a certain decision is taken, self-reinforcing mechanisms are activated that progressively complicate switching to alternatives. This would seem to hold true for the Northern Netherlands, where a new era of extended economic growth began only in the late nineteenth century in the wake of major institutional changes.[16]

Such an explanatory model nonetheless raises new questions. After all, what held true for the Northern Netherlands during the eighteenth century would appear to apply for other regions and periods as well, including Northern Italy during the sixteenth and seventeenth centuries, raising the question as to whether this pattern affects every region. Are all regions path dependent, and, if so, are tendencies toward institutional rigidity and all related social and economic aspects inevitable? Is Mancur Olson right in arguing that in every stable society with fixed borders all kinds of interest groups and networks will automatically emerge and eventually undermine the ability of such a society to accept new techniques and reallocate resources?[17]

Comparative analysis may help here. Between the twelfth century and the end of the Ancien Régime, the urban export industries in the Southern Netherlands were never undermined by 'force of habit', i.e. institutional rigidity. While various economic changes deeply affected certain industrial branches or centres, some groups of entrepreneurs always adapted to the new circumstances. Nowhere on the European continent did the factory system emerge as early as in the Southern Netherlands. Moreover, Belgium, the new state established in this area in 1830, has always been a world leader in per capita exports of industrial goods.[18]

Why did urban export industries in the Southern Netherlands experience continuous dynamics both during the late Middle Ages and in the early modern period? Were transaction costs lower there than in the North? Did different types of institutions arise, or did similar institutions acquire different economic significances? Which social groups gave rise to institutions that regulated industrial production and the labour market in the two regions? And what was their interest in perpetuating or transforming the existing arrangements? How diverse were the strategies for responding to changes

---

15 We are referring to the title of the collection of essays published by Davids and Lucassen, 1995.

16 Davids, 1995.

17 Olson, 1982, pp. 17-72.

18 Bairoch, 1994, pp. 627-9.

in external circumstances? The current state of historical research precludes a satisfactory answer to all these closely related questions. Nonetheless, striking differences are identifiable between the Northern and Southern Netherlands that shed light on the issue.

2. Industrial trajectories

Urban export industries arose far earlier in the South and have always been far more significant there than in the North. Before elaborating on this argument, we stress that distinguishing branches of industry that were export-oriented from ones that produced for the local market is not always easy or even possible. An additional complicating factor is that people practising the same occupation may have been active in different market segments. Moreover, shifts might occur in one direction or another over time. Rather than aiming at a comprehensive account here, we will focus on labour-intensive industries known to have been largely export-oriented during their heyday and will pay particular attention to textile manufacturing.

Regarding the late Middle Ages and the sixteenth century, it has recently been argued 'that developments in North and South were more parallel and exerted more mutual influence on one another than assumed in historiography about the textile industry thus far'.[19] We support this assertion only if 'parallel developments' refer to the economy, and if 'mutual influence' does not suggest that both areas were equally important in textile manufacturing. After all, the South was at the vanguard in both qualitative and quantitative respects and was overwhelmingly dominant throughout the period under consideration.

By the eleventh and twelfth centuries, technological innovations in cities in the County of Flanders led to production of textile goods of such high quality that they could be exported to all parts of the known world.[20] From the outset, the Flemish textile industry featured a broad range of manufactures: in addition to heavy, fancy, and expensive cloths, there were reasonably priced and coarse, generally lightly woven worsted fabrics and all kinds of mixed weaves.[21] The same held true for the urban draperies that emerged toward 1300 in the Duchy of Brabant and (to a lesser extent) in other parts of the Southern Netherlands.[22]

In the Northern Netherlands, however, the conditions for some industries to become supra-local operations were achieved only in the second half of the fourteenth

---

[19] Kaptein, 1998, p. 244.

[20] Pirenne, 1930, pp. 563-6; Eck, 1931, pp. 591-4; Van Werveke, 1951, pp. 7-25; Vaczy, 1960, pp. 3-26; Verhulst, 1972, pp. 281-322.

[21] Munro, 1994, p. 41.

[22] Van Uytven, 1976, pp. 85-97.

century.[23] Not only did textile production get under way later in the towns of the County of Holland, the most advanced region in the North, but it was in most cases far less export-oriented, which explains the relatively modest range of manufactures and production volumes.

In the mid-sixteenth century the value of industrial output in Holland was estimated at one fifth of that in Flanders and at only one twentieth of that in the Southern Netherlands (excluding the Principality of Liège) as a whole.[24] While these figures, which are based on tax data, could be somewhat distorted, calculations of cloth production indicate that the contrast was very pronounced indeed: around 1550 no more than 1 million ells of cloth were produced each year in the North,[25] compared with at least 3 million in the South,[26] with an additional 3.6 million ells of English cloth being finished in Antwerp. Annual production of what were known as light draperies, which had emerged only in the South, amounted to 2.6 million ells at the time and had more than doubled by 1560.[27] Recent research reveals that while linen weaving in Holland was indeed significant,[28] Flanders and Brabant indisputably set the trend in that field as well: between 1560 and 1564 annual production for export markets averaged 4.8 million ells.[29] Moreover, tapestry-weaving and the silk industry did not get off the ground in the North, whereas they expanded enormously in the South during the sixteenth century.[30]

Textile production in Flanders, Brabant, Hainault, and other parts of the Southern Netherlands was obviously not restricted to the cities. The available data suggest that rural cloth weaving originated in the thirteenth century or perhaps even earlier,[31] and rural textile manufacturing indisputably became more significant during the late Middle Ages and much of the sixteenth century.[32] Nonetheless, most cities remained major textile centres. As we shall explain below, some of these centres were more adept than others at adapting to the changing circumstances. In general, the successive cycles

---

23 Jansen, 1976, and Jansen, 1983, pp. 3-18; de Boer, 1978; Israel, 1995, pp. 12-16.

24 Brulez, 1970, p. 43 n.2.

25 The new figures in Kaptein, 1989, p. 136, confirm this estimate by Soly and Thijs, 1979, p. 40.

26 Soly and Thijs, 1979, p. 41, estimate annual production at 2,950,000 ells, but have not counted Dendermonde, Diksmuide, Kortrijk, Ronse, or Wervik, unlike Peter Stabel in 1997b, pp. 116-17, who notes that '[q]uantitative data about cloth weaving in Ronse, however, are unavailable'. Moreover, the figures presented by Stabel (pp. 126, 130, 145) reveal that the combined turnover of the four other centres cannot have exceeded 126,000 ells around 1550.

27 Soly and Thijs, 1979, p. 41.

28 Kaptein, 1998, pp. 200-34.

29 Blomme and Van der Wee, 1994, p. 87.

30 Soly and Thijs, 1979, pp. 42-3.

31 Thoen, 1988, p. 1013.

32 Coornaert, 1930a; Van Uytven, 1975, pp. 57-76; Soly and Thijs, 1979, pp. 40-3; Thoen, 1988, pp. 980-1020.

of product innovation and product differentiation prove that urban export industries in the Southern Netherlands exhibited remarkable dynamics and continuity.[33] This remained the case after the actual separation of North and South in 1585.

Holland's spectacular commercial expansion during the first half of the seventeenth century is known to have been a major impetus behind the urban export industries.[34] Craftsmen from the Southern (Spanish) Netherlands figured prominently here, as they introduced several new techniques and manufactures to the North.[35] Still, the industrial growth in the North was not to the disadvantage of cities in the South. The main trend in textile manufacturing was the relocation of *rural* production centres in Flanders to towns in Holland.[36] Most *urban* export industries in Brabant and Flanders continued to maintain their position during the first half of the seventeenth century. Once again, Antwerp, Brussels, Ghent, and Bruges adapted to the changing situation. Thanks to import substitution, enlarged product ranges, and artistic creativity, they devised a new and attractive selection of luxury commodities.[37]

Only from the last third of the seventeenth century did urban producers in Brabant and Flanders face increasing problems. On the one hand, domestic demand for quality goods declined because of the agrarian depression,[38] and on the other hand the export trade suffered deeply from the mercantilist policies of England and France, which raised import duties on luxury commodities.[39] Employment figures nonetheless suggest that the urban textile industries in the South, despite the adverse conditions, remained of considerable economic significance. While employment in all towns in the Spanish Netherlands around 1700 is impossible to quantify at this time, the total for Brussels, Antwerp, Ghent, and Bruges *alone* was approximately 45,000.[40] Over one third of these workers were lace-makers producing primarily for export. Still, the figure — which does not include textile workers in other towns of Brabant and Flanders or in towns in the Walloon provinces — is impressive compared with the grand total of 55,000 textile workers for the towns in the United Provinces.[41]

The difference in the role of urban manufacturing in the economies of North and South became apparent once again during the eighteenth century, when the industrial trajectories of the two areas diverged entirely. In the United Provinces nearly all urban

33 In Van der Wee, 1988 the 'product life-cycle' theory is applied to brilliant effect to analyse the origins and rise of urban industry in the Southern Netherlands from the twelfth century until the end of the Ancien Régime. See also Lis and Soly, 1997, pp. 219-21.

34 de Vries and van der Woude, 1997, pp. 335, 338; Israel, 1990, pp. 38-42.

35 Briels, 1985; Israel, 1995a, pp. 307-11.

36 de Vries and van der Woude, 1997, p. 292.

37 Craeybeckx, 1962, pp. 411-68; De Peuter, 1988, pp. 213-40; Vermaut, 1988, pp. 187-205; Thijs, 1993a.

38 Verhulst, 1990, pp. 153-4, 182-4.

39 Despretz-Van de Casteele, 1965, pp. 294-317.

40 Craeybeckx, 1976, pp. 21-43; Vermaut, 1974, p. 274; Thijs, 1987b, pp. 174-82; De Peuter, 1999, pp. 89-102.

41 Israel, 1990, p. 356.

export industries lapsed into serious decline. The main exceptions were sugar refineries, tobacco processing plants, and gin distilleries. These industries did not, however, substantially enrich the raw materials imported and moreover generated little employment and thus did not offset jobs lost in other branches.[42]

Most urban export trades in the Southern (Austrian) Netherlands, on the other hand, entered a period of rapid revival and perhaps even real growth after 1750, which continued until the late 1780s. Textile manufacturers readily seized the opportunities offered by the growing market for fashion wear and produced linen-cotton mixed fabrics. While other export industries thrived as well, the restructuring of urban textile manufacturing was responsible for the structural economic change in the long run: the steady rise in demand for cotton yarns paved the way toward rapid introduction of mule spinning machines in Ghent and Lier during the Napoleonic era.[43] In the Northern Netherlands the factory system did not become operational until decades later.

3. Craft guilds

Differences in the institutional context in which the urban export industries arose are similarly striking. Craft guilds, i.e. public organizations that grouped those who practised the same trade primarily for economic purposes, emerged far earlier in the South than in the North.[44] Moreover, these patterns were entirely different in the towns of Flanders and Brabant, both in the late Middle Ages and during the early modern period.

In the County of Flanders the Battle of the Golden Spurs put an end to what Carlos Wyffels has termed the 'pre-corporative stage'. In this period some groups of skilled craftsmen had a say in urban labour and industrial legislation, had an embryonic financial organization, and were allowed to convene meetings with a restricted number of participants, but were still totally controlled by the local authorities. Their emancipation in 1302 or shortly thereafter entitled them to elect their own governors, who also acted as trustees and judges in corporative matters.[45] Moreover, in both the large cities and the many small towns, the guild deans, including those of cloth weavers and other textile producers, participated in local political decision-making processes from the 1360s onward. Contrary to what is generally assumed, they appear to have used their participation in the town government to exercise real power, which meant that the more affluent masters acted as lobbies.[46] In the towns of the Duchy of Brabant the skilled craftsmen waged a more protracted struggle for self-government, but the

42 de Vries and van der Woude, 1997, pp. 296-347, 501.

43 Lis and Soly, 1990, pp. 105-13.

44 See the contribution by De Munck, Lourens and Lucassen, in this volume.

45 Wyffels, 1951.

46 Blockmans, 1978, pp. 72-87; Boone, 1990, pp. 28-33, 59-7; Boone, 1994b, pp. 26, 45-6; Boone, 1994a, pp. 6-15; Vandewalle, 1999, pp. 27-40.

pre-corporative stage was concluded there as well around the middle of the fifteenth century.[47] Nowhere did the guilds gain control of local governments. Nonetheless, they wielded political power from that point onward, since decisions on tax-related issues and matters with financial consequences for the entire urban community required the consent of a great number of corporative organizations almost everywhere.[48]

Admittedly, the power of the guilds was curtailed in the Southern Netherlands during the early modern period, and in some cases even radically, as happened in Ghent in 1540.[49] In most towns, however, guild-based organizations continued to operate as political lobbies until the end of the Ancien Régime. Since the central government had to observe the constitutional framework established in the late Middle Ages,[50] forcing the representatives of the state to negotiate with powerful provincial States, the guilds in some cities extended their political influence beyond their own locality. This was especially true in the Duchy of Brabant, where the third member of the States needed the consent of several guilds to approve a 'request' or proposal.[51]

Matters were quite different in the Northern Netherlands. Not only did craft guilds emerge far later there than in the South, as has already been noted, but most of those organizations never obtained formal political power. In a very few towns — including Dordrecht in Holland, Middelburg and Zierikzee in Zeeland, and Utrecht in the homonymous province — representatives of guild-based organizations served on the local council during the late Middle Ages. By the first half of the sixteenth century, they had been excluded from political participation nearly everywhere. The Dutch Revolt did not change the constitutional position of the craft guilds, as local elites blocked the rise of political representation within their city. Only in a few cities, mainly in the South and East of the United Provinces, did craft guilds influence the local decision-making process, as had been the case during the late Middle Ages.[52]

4. Guild and non guild-based export industries

Which export industries were organized in craft guilds? In the Southern Netherlands, most artisans who ran an urban workshop producing or processing woollen, linen, or silk textile belonged to a guild in the late Middle Ages and the early modern period. The textile industry encompassed a broad range of occupations, but spinning was not organized in guilds anywhere, and master artisans who entrusted other preparatory tasks, such as silk-winding, to many women, children, and elderly people generally managed to keep these low-paid home-workers outside the corporative framework.[53]

---

47 Wyffels, 1951, pp. 26-31.

48 Blockmans, 1983, pp. 79-80.

49 Decavele and Van Peteghem, 1989, pp. 107-13.

50 Boone and Prak, 1995, pp. 114, 120.

51 Van Honacker, 1994b.

52 Lucassen and Prak, 1998, pp. 69-74.

53 Thijs, 1987b, pp. 215-16, 274-6.

Nor did the large numbers of young girls and adult women who made lace in many towns in Brabant and Flanders during the seventeenth and especially the eighteenth centuries belong to a guild: after learning the trade at a school or convent, they would work from home to fill commissions received from a *factores*, who acted as an intermediary for a wholesaler.[54] Except for lacework, manufacturing semi-cotton fabrics and cotton prints were the only major branches of the urban textile industry in the Austrian Netherlands without a separate corporative organization; master linen weavers, however, were driving forces in introducing and producing mixed fabrics containing cotton.[55]

The guild-based urban export industries included beer brewing, which was of major economic significance in many towns in Brabant.[56] Except in Lokeren, which despite its population was never officially recognized as a city under the Ancien Régime and did not have guilds, hat-makers belonged to a local guild in all export centres of the Spanish/Austrian Netherlands.[57] In Antwerp, where the diamond trade thrived throughout the early modern period, all craftsmen involved in finishing gemstones belonged to a guild as well from 1582.[58]

In the Northern Netherlands the substantial increase in the number of craft guilds between 1560 and the end of the seventeenth century happened mainly in industries that did not produce for export markets.[59] The overwhelming majority of textile producers in the Republic operated outside guilds, whether they were employers or workers. Among the thousands of craftsmen working with the new draperies in Leiden, the chief textile centre in the Republic, only a very small minority belonged to a craft guild.[60] The same situation prevailed in seventeenth-century Amsterdam,[61] where small groups, such as cloth dressers and silk dyers, were organized in guilds, whereas the many wool-weavers or silk-weavers were not. Nor did linen bleachers in the Haarlem area, cloth weavers in Delft, or producers of serges and fustians in Gouda organize guilds.[62] Except in Rotterdam, cotton printing, which flourished after 1680 and

54 Van Laerhoven, 1971, pp. 173-90.

55 Thijs, 1987b, p. 149; Vermaut, 1988, pp. 170-3.

56 Aerts, 1996, pp. 109-15.

57 Lis and Soly, 1994d, pp. 18-19, 28.

58 Schlugleit, 1935; Kockelbergh, Vleeschdrager and Walgrave, 1992, pp. 61-97.

59 See the contribution of De Munck, Lourens and Lucassen.

60 Posthumus, 1908, pp. 363-5, and 1939, pp. 17-18, 865-7.

61 Barbour, 1950, p. 71. Piet Lourens and Jan Lucassen report in 1998 that the overwhelming majority of Amsterdam's active male population was involved with craft guilds in 1688, either directly as members (masters) or indirectly as journeymen. The figures presented by the two authors reveal, however, that (1) nearly half the total number of members worked in trade and transport, and (2) the most labour-intensive export industries were not organized in guilds. While they were not entirely unregulated, they cannot in our view be regarded as pseudo-guilds. See also Aten, 1999, p. 70.

62 Smit, 1989, pp. 15-30.

peaked around 1750, was not organized in guilds anywhere, despite the predominance of small enterprises in this industry in the North.[63] In the Austrian Netherlands, by contrast, a single large manufacturer held a monopoly for a quarter of a century.[64]

Craft guilds in export industries outside the textile sector, were also far less significant in the North than they were in the South. While shipwrights in Amsterdam and Rotterdam did belong to a guild, their job was to repair ships; new ships were built in the countryside and the Zaan area, where no craft guilds existed.[65] Breweries in many cities, including Amsterdam, were not guild-based either.[66] The same held true for the diamond industry, which surged in Amsterdam from 1600. Finally, other industries that were not guild-based included what were known as 'traffic industries' and closely linked with international trade, especially due to the role of the Republic as a staple market in European goods transit, both in Amsterdam and in the other port cities: tobacco spinning plants, sugar refineries, salt and soap works, whale oil refineries, and gin distilleries.[67] This was also true for most 'traffic industries' in the Southern Netherlands, but they were far less advanced there than in the North.

The absence of craft guilds did not necessarily mean that no type of organization existed. Some export industries in the Dutch Republic were organized in *neringen* (literally: trades), which enforced the production regulations issued by the municipal authorities but differed from craft guilds in that all persons involved in manufacturing a given product automatically belonged to the corresponding *nering*. Membership in the sense of having the right to join or withdraw did not apply. From the late sixteenth century, nearly the entire textile industry in Leiden was organized in *neringen*, which differed from one another with respect to the raw material used and the type of textile produced from this material.[68] Similar institutions inspected the quality of cloth in Delft, of serges and fustians in Gouda, and of various woollen and mixed fabrics in Haarlem.[69] Whether silk weaving and silk winding were *neringen* in Amsterdam is unclear, but both branches were supervised by boards of commissioners or superintendents appointed by the municipal authorities.[70] Other versions of such inspection bodies also existed in the export industries outside the textile sector, as the Amsterdam board of brewers exemplifies.[71]

Craft guilds and *neringen* had no real decision-making power in the United Provinces: the local authorities, who appointed the officials of both types of organizations,

---

63 Thijs, 1970, pp. 157-90.

64 Unger, 1978.

65 Yntema, 1994, pp. 118-31.

66 de Vries and van der Woude, 1997, p. 338.

67 Wiskerke, 1938, pp. 67-72; Barbour, 1950, p. 71. In Amsterdam, soap boilers were organized in a 'college', but this was a type of cartel. See Poelwijk, 1999, p. 428.

68 Posthumus, 1908, pp. 335-59.

69 Posthumus, 1937, pp. 28-30.

70 van Nierop, 1931, pp. 42, 45-6.

71 Yntema, 1994, pp. 122-3.

used them as instruments to protect economic and tax-related interests that did not necessarily top the agendas of the industrial entrepreneurs. Another major difference with respect to the Spanish, later Austrian Netherlands was that in the Republic craft guilds or *neringen* dedicated to export often admitted merchants. This happened both in many branches of the textile industry and in other export industries. When after lengthy requests the pipe makers in Gouda finally obtained permission to form an association in 1660, the municipal authorities stipulated that pipe vendors would participate in the guild as well.[72]

5. Quality control

Despite their differences in assessing the other purposes of guilds, all economic historians agree that the quality control that such institutions exercised deeply affected export industries in the late Middle Ages and the early modern period.[73] After all, quality concerns made consumers less willing to purchase manufactured goods, especially if direct contact with the producer was not an option.[74] Every export centre, no matter how small, therefore tried to obtain a local privilege or monopoly conducive to its own industrial niche and subjected the producers involved to regulations and inspections with a view toward standardization. International traders considered inspection systems set up or approved by public authorities essential, as such arrangements reduced transaction costs and thus increased trading profits.

In the Southern Netherlands the link between urban corporatism and quality control meant that most guilds were authorized at some point to inspect the workshops of their members and to penalize those violating official regulations on raw materials, size, colours, and the like. No reverse causal link existed, however, as quality control might occur outside the corporative framework as well. By the thirteenth century (and perhaps earlier), i.e. long before the official guilds were established, many municipal authorities in the County of Flanders set up inspectorates (*waarmerkdiensten*) to inspect the quality of woollen fabrics produced locally. While the organization and areas of authority of the labelling services varied from one city to the next, the local authorities were the chief initiators, not the producers. The duties of these *eswardeurs* or *waerdeins* generally extended beyond inspecting and labelling the finished products. They would also visit workshops and arbitrate in disputes between persons involved in the manufacture or trade of textile goods in some capacity.[75]

Inspectorates served the interests of the wholesalers, as did industrial regulations in general, as Alain Derville has rightly noted: ‘Far from impeding the activities of

---

72 Hulshof, 1997, p. 134.

73 See in this connection the useful comments by Munro, 1999, p. 55.

74 A critique of the arguments ordinarily raised appears in Ogilvie, 1997, pp. 343-57.

75 See the fundamental observations of Wyffels, 1951, pp. 59-85, and Vermaut, 1974, pp. 304-23.

merchants, drapery labels served them as powerful tools; merchants used the system of the urban authorities to relieve themselves of the burden of product inspections.'[76] Industrial regulations in the large Flemish cities were therefore not fundamentally different from the ones in rural export centres such as Hondschoote, where no guilds existed, and where the serge trade was 'a branch, and indeed the most prestigious one, of the urban administration', as Coornaert observed.[77]

In some cities the cloth industry continued to be supervised by officers appointed and paid by the magistrate during the late Middle Ages; this was especially true in Douai, where textile manufacturing was never organized in guilds.[78] In most drapery centres, however, the situation was more complex. While the emancipation of the guilds during the late Middle Ages definitely did not mark the end of the inspectorates, it did instigate a protracted struggle between producers and merchants for control of these institutions. The case of Bruges reveals that the ultimate winner mattered less to small master artisans, as they could never meet the criteria for becoming inspectors anyway.[79]

Little information is available about the performance of the inspectorates in the early modern period. They are certain to have continued operating in several cities, although some municipal authorities are also known to have set up new inspection bodies.[80] Their respective areas of authority and who was in control — producers or merchants — remain open questions. The available data suggest in any case that quality control was the responsibility of the guild officials in most guild-based export industries in the Habsburg Netherlands.

Whether the inspections were performed by municipal officials or by guild-based organizations, however, made no difference to economic efficiency: both systems appear to have functioned properly. At any rate, they did not lead to complaints related to current or future sales problems. As far as can be determined, industrial regulations were flexible everywhere, both in centres with inspectorates and without corporative organizations and in centres where guilds were influential.[81] This suggests that corporative organizations of most export industries in the Southern Netherlands did not mean that these institutions necessarily prevailed in quality control. Other institutions were equally capable of performing these duties. The spectacular growth of Leiden's textile industry during the first half of the seventeenth century makes overwhelmingly clear that inspections by municipal officials through *neringen* were every bit as effective as those organized by the producers themselves.[82]

---

76 Derville, 1972, p. 354.

77 Coornaert, 1930a, p. 94.

78 Espinas, 1923.

79 Vermaut, 1974, pp. 337-64.

80 Coornaert, 1930b, p. 65; Thijs, 1969, p. 65.

81 Sortor, 1993, pp. 1486-7, 1488-9, 1495, 1498.

82 Posthumus, 1908, pp. 39, 50, 71, 89, 152-9.

6. Institutions and entrepreneurial initiatives

Insufficient data are available about the actual organization of industrial production in the Northern Netherlands to compare and assess all relevant elements. The evidence suggests, however, that master artisans producing for the export markets in the South had more opportunities to realize profits through trade and industry alike than did their counterparts in the North.

Most export-oriented guilds in the County of Flanders, the Duchy of Brabant, the County of Hainault, and the other districts in the Southern Netherlands were formed at the initiative of the craftsmen themselves. The hegemony of the more affluent producers or at least the decisive nature of their votes is also beyond dispute, as the institutions concerned offered vast economic leeway. This is apparent from the fact that wealthy master artisans could nearly always resort to subcontracting and consistently had access to the market.

Concentration of production by guild members might at first appear to have been impossible. Producers of export goods were indeed subject to restrictions on business size, as were their colleagues working for the local market, although export producers generally had larger workshops than producers for local markets. Moreover, such restrictions were progressively relaxed during the early modern period. The bottom line, however, was that the articles of association and the regulations of most export-oriented guilds in the Southern Netherlands lacked prohibitions on subcontracting. This omission was definitely not an oversight, as subcontracting enabled the more affluent masters to set up 'dispersed manufactures', which were centrally-run networks of small and medium-sized workshops. The practice kept investments in fixed capital to a minimum, facilitated meeting market demand, and enabled entrepreneurs to pass most risks on to the direct producers. During periods of economic prosperity, merchants tended to order their goods from affluent master artisans to avert all kinds of management problems: small producers could provide no guarantees regarding delivery and lacked the solvency to compensate damages. During periods of economic stagnation or downturn, however, this advantage might not offset the surcharge that these guildsmen imposed on their customers — the merchants — above the wages they paid their subcontractors; these added costs might be cause for merchants to launch their own entrepreneurial initiatives by engaging in manufacture themselves to secure their trading profits.[83]

The studies by Jos Vermaut reveal that subcontracting enabled some cloth weavers in Bruges to become drapers as early as the thirteenth century, and that local cloth manufacturing there during the fourteenth and fifteenth centuries was largely controlled by wealthy master artisans who purchased wool from wholesalers, ran their own workshops, and had poorer colleagues (known as *conventers*) work for them.[84]

---

83 Lis and Soly, 1994c, pp. 370-1, 376-7.

84 Vermaut, 1974, pp. 480-9.

Subcontracting systems were not limited to the major export centres. In a small town such as Menen, increasing numbers of master cloth weavers became dependent on a few affluent colleagues during the late fifteenth and early sixteenth centuries, and this tendency towards concentration was greater still at the tapestry-weaving works in Oudenaarde.[85] During the first half of the sixteenth century the international firms that sold considerable quantities of English cloth in Antwerp preferred to have affluent master artisans finish them. Each of these drapers employed 15, 20, or more journeymen and subcontracted to 'humble' masters during peak periods.[86]

The flexible subcontracting system did more than raise physical labour productivity. In the long run, it reduced production costs as well: as the system branched out and provided work to ever-rising numbers of craftsmen, subcontractors were pressured in increasing measure to reduce their rates and even to accept journeymen's wages. Throughout the Middle Ages there were impoverished masters who earned no more than skilled workers. During the seventeenth and eighteenth centuries the degradation progressed and also changed in character: growing numbers of masters had to work from home for journeymen's wages and have their family members assist them. At the end of the Ancien Régime, 14 capitalist master silk weavers in Antwerp engaged in massive subcontracting, controlling the labour of 1,200 persons.[87] In the linen industry in Bruges the situation was no different: by 1768 most master craftsmen had effectively become wage workers, leading the municipal authorities to abolish the restriction on the number of looms; two decades later, capitalist linen weavers employed 30, 40, or even 50 journeymen.[88]

Equally important is that master artisans involved in export industries in the Southern Netherlands were nearly always entitled to engage in commercial enterprise, which greatly increased their means to accumulate capital. The data gathered by Alfons Thijs prove that affluent masters in various branches of Antwerp's textile industry worked their way up to become merchant entrepreneurs during the early modern period. The silk dyer Roeland Stappaert, who introduced a new technique during the final quarter of the sixteenth century, enabling him to become a major industrial operator and subcontract extensively, marketed his finished goods himself.[89] During the second half of the seventeenth century, capitalist blue-dyers, who employed 50, 60, or even 100 workers each, traded with Germany, the United Provinces, and especially the Iberian Peninsula, which was the largest market. Several master weavers also became merchant entrepreneurs. By 1614, 130 silk weavers protested against the 'monopolist practices' of affluent colleagues, including guild deans. They were not exaggerating, as some silk weavers had placed over 100 looms each in the workshops of impoverished masters and were extremely active in international trade

---

85 Stabel, 1997a.

86 Thijs, 1987b, pp. 219-24, 227-34.

87 Ibidem, pp. 242-3.

88 Vermaut, 1974, pp. 170-5, 264, 491-9.

89 Thijs, 1968, pp. 235-41.

as well. The linen weavers Jan van der Smissen and sons, who in the mid-eighteenth century had a combined total of about 100 looms in operation (mostly at the homes of subcontractors), opened a large bleaching works. In addition to bleaching their own manufactures, they received commissions for vast quantities of yarns and fabrics from other parties elsewhere in the Austrian Netherlands and France.[90] While little information is available at this time about guild-based export industries other than textile production, master artisans are known to have combined industrial production with commercial activities in those branches as well. In 1619, for example, the master tinsmith Daniël Dor obtained all the tin exported from England to the Spanish Netherlands, valued at 100,000 guilders, thus forcing all producers to purchase their raw materials from him.[91]

Which type of entrepreneur prevailed in which guild-based export industries in the Southern Netherlands during the late Middle Ages and the early modern period remains unclear. Affluent master artisans, however, disposed of a structural economic leeway, given their ability to subcontract and trade. Their effective use of these opportunities and the success of their strategies depended on many different factors: the nature and composition of the range of products that were offered, fluctuations in market demand, the structure of trade in raw materials and finished products, the relationship between industrial income and commercial profit, and, last but not least, the local social and political balance of power. These variables obviously changed over time. Master artisans and merchant entrepreneurs might therefore alternately gain the upper hand in one town or another, without a clear-cut underlying pattern. While the geographic, chronological, and industrial variations are impossible to list at this time, the essential point is that throughout the extended history of urban export industries in the Southern Netherlands there have been periods, places, and branches in which affluent master artisans developed their own dynamics.

The explanation lies in a combination of economic and political factors. The early emergence of export industries in several cities was obviously important, as it implied competition and encouraged creativity at the same time. Likewise, the political constellation enabled producers to associate and to become highly autonomous. This benefited the affluent master artisans in particular, both with respect to exercising their power and in economic terms; the ability of this group to launch entrepreneurial initiatives and exert political pressure was precisely what prevented merchant capital from prevailing. Nor were international firms in late-medieval Bruges and sixteenth-century Antwerp generally eager to invest in fixed capital, as they were involved in many economic sectors, due in part to the broad range of export industries in the two cities; wholesalers preferred to commission local guild members to coordinate part or all of production.[92] This practice not only benefited management of the workforce but also enabled wholesalers to pass most risks on to the producers.[93]

---

90 Thijs, 1987b, pp. 103-4, 105-6, 239-40, 246, 283.

91 Thijs, 1989, p. 140.

92 Thijs, 1987b, pp. 219-24, 227-34.

93 Lis and Soly, 1994c, p. 370.

Relations between wholesalers and affluent master artisans were obviously not consistently symbiotic in export industries everywhere. During periods of economic stagnation or decline, the vast divergence between the interests of both groups might render tensions inevitable. The most heated conflicts that arose under such circumstances, however, were between medium-sized firms specializing in a specific export item on the one hand and master craftsmen marketing their own finished product on the other hand, as the case of silk weavers in seventeenth-century Antwerp demonstrates. At first silk merchants did not object to the rise of a dynamic group of capitalist producers. They were reluctant to entrust their silk and often their silver thread as well to small master weavers, whose assets equalled less than one tenth of the value of the raw materials they were issued. Once the more affluent master craftsmen had accumulated sufficient capital through subcontracting to trade on their own, they became known as stiff competitors — especially given the decline in foreign demand. The merchants tried in vain to convince the municipal authorities to prohibit the master silk weavers from trading. Together with the poorer master craftsmen, however, they negotiated a proclamation by the municipal authorities drastically reducing the number of looms in each workshop. The measure prevented the large masters from concentrating the labour (and everything related in terms of productivity and rates of pay).[94] Similar instances of 'devil's pacts' between merchant entrepreneurs and small producers, in which the former used the latter to curtail the power of their rivals, have occurred in other branches of industry and eras as well.[95]

Fragmentary data indicate that whenever conflicts arose between affluent producers and merchant entrepreneurs, the small producers consistently supported the merchant entrepreneurs. The disinclination of guild officials to consider the interests of the ordinary members undoubtedly motivated the position of the small producers.[96] Far more importantly, however, the prominent master artisans in labour-intensive industries not only resisted proposals to restrict the conditions for admission (which would have protected their poorer colleagues) but moreover tried to pad their profits by reducing the rates of the subcontractors and even paying them journeymen's wages, which became an increasingly common practice in the seventeenth and eighteenth centuries.[97]

While the lack of in-depth studies makes conclusions about the nature of entrepreneurship in the United Provinces extremely difficult to reach, all available data suggest that urban producers of export goods there had greater difficulty devising strategies to accumulate capital. Contrary to what some authors have argued, subcontracting did occur in the urban export trades of the Northern Netherlands. Around 1500, for example, half the cloth produced in Leiden came from 50 to 100 of the 400 drapers there. The only possible explanation is that they subcontracted to less afflu-

---

94 Thijs, 1987b, pp. 238-41.

95 Soly, 1975, pp. 340-1.

96 Thijs, 1987b.

97 Lis and Soly, 1994c, pp. 376-80.

ent colleagues, since the number of cloths per workshop was restricted by a quota.[98] During the seventeenth century, subcontracting is known to have occurred in the silk industry in Amsterdam and Haarlem,[99] as well as in tick-weaving in Schiedam.[100] Presumably, however, the system was far less widespread in the North than in the South, undoubtedly due to the measures of city councils to protect the small producers, as Karel Davids argues,[101] noting that such measures also suited the interests of wholesalers, who controlled most export industries and had no interest in the rise of a competing group of capitalists.[102]

By the same token, public authorities in the Northern Netherlands often denied producers of export goods the right to engage in certain commercial activities. In the early fifteenth century, for example, drapers in Leiden were prohibited from entering the highly profitable wool trade.[103] In Amsterdam dyers were not allowed to become directly or indirectly involved in the silk trade in the seventeenth century. Curtailing the freedom of the industrial entrepreneurs seriously compromised the adaptive capacities of the industry as a whole: since dyers were not allowed to trade, they had little incentive to introduce new colour procedures; after all, the merchants might either refuse to support the initiative or skim off most of the profits.[104] Pipe makers in Gouda, united in a guild since 1660, were prohibited in 1686 from selling their manufactures themselves: they were to offer them on the weekly 'pipe market' arranged by the municipal authorities, and where middlemen purchased supplies, generally as instructed by wholesalers from Amsterdam.[105]

The magistrates maintained that the prohibitions ensured equality among producers. While this is conceivable, the policy severely restricted opportunities for producers to accumulate capital: trading profits were nearly always far higher than industrial ones. Such measures therefore merely strengthened the dominance of merchant capital, especially since municipal authorities rarely placed any obstacles in the paths of merchants interested in engaging in industrial activities; several export-oriented guilds were even obliged to admit merchants as members.[106] In the Southern Netherlands the opposite situation existed: in nearly all guild-based export industries, merchants were barred from direct involvement in production, unless they became masters in the relevant guild. Sometimes they received dispensation from the years of apprenticeship, but the data indicate that this was highly exceptional.

---

98 Ibidem, pp. 372-3.

99 van Nierop, 1930, p. 165, and 1931, pp. 114-15; Mulder, 1995, pp. 96-8.

100 Sneller, 1930, pp. 254-5, 257.

101 Davids, 1996, pp. 109-11.

102 Lis and Soly, 1997b, pp. 15-19.

103 Posthumus, 1908, pp. 111-13, 188-90, 233-4.

104 van Nierop, 1931, pp. 29-30, 130.

105 Duco 1981, pp. 192-3; Davids, 1996, pp. 102, 110.

106 Kaptein, 1998, p. 149.

7. Did local authorities support producers of export goods?

In what measure did local authorities support producers of export goods in both sections of the Low Countries? The question is difficult to answer, both because too many data are lacking, and because the measures taken by the municipal authorities may lead to various interpretations. Municipal magistrates in the South and the North alike are certain to have agreed to set up and maintain facilities to inspect, store, and sell finished products to attract individual artisans or merchant entrepreneurs introducing new manufactures or techniques. They offered free use of land and buildings, tax exemptions, and various subsidies and in some cases also mediated sales of finished products. The question, however, is whether these measures were ad hoc or concerned economic policy and, in the latter case, whether such policy was intended to 'provide security to small producers working for export markets'.[107]

The lack of adequate preliminary studies precludes determining whether municipal authorities in the Southern Netherlands were more inclined to grant economic benefits to craft guilds involved in local politics than to corporative organizations with no formal political power, or to master artisans than to entrepreneurs operating outside the guild system. Perhaps the problem should be stated differently, since the members of the export-oriented guilds were never a socially homogeneous group. The urban magistrate was thus forced to consider divergent and frequently conflicting interests. His support for specific industrial initiatives therefore depended on the answer to two closely related questions: (1) what was best for the urban economy, especially with respect to employment, and (2) what was most beneficial or least harmful to the social order and political stability? The available monographs indicate that the position of the municipal authorities was never predetermined in the event of conflicts. Sometimes the large master artisans lost out, while on other occasions the rulings were against the merchant entrepreneurs and the small producers.[108] Among the many factors determining the outcome were the membership of the city council, the structure of the industry concerned, its economic significance, the patterns of social relations, and the political balance of power. Nonetheless, wealthy master artisans producing for export markets often prevailed, at the expense of both their poorer colleagues and the merchants. Restrictions on corporate size remained in effect until the end of the Ancien Régime but became so lenient in many export-oriented trades during the seventeenth and eighteenth centuries that the more affluent masters could set up small manufactures. This happened both in various branches of the textile industry and in other guild-based sectors, such as hat making.[109]

Regardless of whether they were organized in guilds, urban producers of export commodities received tax breaks in Brabant and Flanders during the early modern period. Around 1550, the share of the so-called blue-dye excise duties did not exceed 0.3

---

[107] Davids, 1996, p. 100.

[108] Thijs, 1987b.

[109] Vermaut, 1974, pp. 493-7; Lis and Soly, 1994b, pp. 731-3.

per cent of the total corporate expenditure of the Antwerp cloth dyers, and these duties were abolished during the second quarter of the seventeenth century;[110] by the eighteenth century all other duties on production and sale of export commodities had been discontinued as well.[111] In Brussels most export industries were entirely tax exempt in the seventeenth and eighteenth centuries. This was the case both in textile manufacturing (except for the bleachers' duties, which were of little significance) and in production of glass, delftware, china, and metal wares; leather goods were subject to excise duties, albeit minimal ones.[112] Nor were local taxes a heavy burden on entrepreneurs in the export industries in sixteenth-century Ghent[113] or in eighteenth-century Louvain.[114] Moreover, the provincial States in the County of Flanders and the Duchy of Brabant never levied taxes of any significance on production or sale of export goods during the early modern period.[115]

Conceivably and in fact most probably, the policies of the urban elites in the Republic served to protect small producers working for the local market,[116] although this is unlikely to have been their chief objective with respect to the *export* industries. Major trading firms generally controlled such industries, regardless of their organizational structure. Some wholesalers engaged in direct industrial production, preferring to use the putting-out system. They were far more likely, however, to wield indirect control, as they were key operators in supplying raw materials and in selling finished products. 'Protection' for the small producers on the part of the municipal authorities accommodated wholesalers, provided that such measures complicated or even blocked the rise of a competing group of capitalists.[117] If industrial entrepreneurs became eager to form associations and were on the verge of turning into actual or potential competitors, wholesalers would fight tooth and nail against the establishment of a guild and would prevail, as the case of the Haarlem linen bleaching works demonstrates.[118] While the Haarlem magistrate took measures to protect the small master artisans in linen weaving and silk manufacturing from frontal attacks by merchant entrepreneurs, he generally acted in response to vehement protests. Far more importantly, no true encouragement policy intended to boost the economic strength of the small producers existed; both industries were controlled by large trading firms.[119]

---

110 Thijs, 1987b, pp. 82-3, 437-42.

111 Boumans, 1965, pp. 59-90.

112 De Peuter, 1999, pp. 60-1.

113 Dambruyne, 2001, pp. 187-289.

114 Van Buyten,1985, pp. 389-401. Van Buyten also argues that beer brewing was the exception to the rule: even though their production was largely intended for export, brewers paid high taxes (pp. 550-63). The unpublished MA-thesis by Swevers, 1999, indicates, however, that beer exports were still exempt from taxes in the 17th and early 18th centuries.

115 Bigwood, 1900, Annexe C; Zelck, 1988, p. 195.

116 Prak, 1988, pp. 149-58, and van Zanden, 1993b, pp. 134, 137-9.

117 Davids, 1995, pp. 10-15; Prak, 1996.

118 Regtdoorzee Greup-Roldanus, 1936, pp. 195-8, 244-51.

119 Mulder, 1995, pp. 61-3, 68, 96-8.

If the cases from the silk industry and linen bleaching are representative, then the tax policies of the municipal magistrates in Holland hardly favoured producers of export goods: at the end of the sixteenth and during the first half of the seventeenth centuries, taxes were raised for virtually every type of silk and silken fabric in Amsterdam,[120] and by 1650, taxes accounted for about 19 per cent of the total business-related expenses of the owner of a medium-sized bleaching works in Haarlem.[121] Even assuming that such cases were exceptional, and that the complaints from entrepreneurs in other urban export industries about their tax burden were highly exaggerated, the absence of similar complaints in Brabant and Flanders is remarkable.

8. Centralized economic policies

The central government of the Spanish and subsequently Austrian Netherlands often favoured the producers in disputes between (urban) industry and trade. The role of the political constellation in this process is unclear, especially that of powerful corporative organizations with supra-local influence in some counties. At any rate, the most important change was that after the fall of Antwerp in 1585 and the subsequent blockade of the Scheldt by the Dutch from Holland, wholesale trade ceased to be a driving force behind the urban economy. As industry, especially production of luxury commodities, grew more important, state representatives became increasingly inclined to grant requests from manufacturers, even at the expense of commercial interests. The changes were obviously minor and did not involve a radical shift of course, as the Antwerp wholesalers remained a powerful lobby that the central government needed to consider. Nonetheless, the trend was unmistakable.

By 1618, measures were taken to protect the silk manufacturers from foreign competition. Over the vehement objections from the Antwerp wholesalers, Archdukes Albert and Isabella prohibited imports of finished and dyed silk from all countries except Spain and Italy, which supplied mediocre quality; despite reprisals from France, the ordinance remained in effect.[122] Between 1650 and 1670, imports of woollen fabrics were repeatedly prohibited, and protectionist measures increased during the final quarter of the century, culminating in what was known as the Eternal Edict of 1699: a genuine system of import and export duties intended to boost domestic industries.[123] This economic policy instigated so many countermeasures from England and France that the Edict soon had to be repealed.[124] Article XXVI of the third Barrier Treaty (1715) even prohibited the government of the Austrian Netherlands from pursuing an autonomous customs policy, leaving the country vulnerable to economic exploitation

[120] van Nierop, 1930, pp. 30-1.

[121] Regtdoorzee Greup-Roldanus,1936, pp. 119-39, 251.

[122] Thijs, 1987b, p. 143.

[123] Despretz-Van de Casteele, 1965, pp. 294-317.

[124] De Schryver, 1965.

by the maritime potentates.[125] Only with the Treaty of Aix-la-Chapelle (1748) and the subsequent Franco-Austrian rapprochement was the government able to introduce gradual rises on both import duties on various finished products (especially textiles) and export duties on raw materials widely used by producers in the Austrian Netherlands.[126] These protectionist measures are known to have greatly enhanced the success of various urban export industries.[127]

In the Republic, however, the system of import and export duties was almost entirely tax-based. While this arrangement obviously benefited international trade, it made urban export industries very vulnerable after 1650-1670, when they faced increasing foreign competition on the one hand and protectionist measures imposed by various countries, including England, on the other hand. The few groups of producers that received some protection, such as export restrictions on certain raw materials or increases in import duties on certain finished products, were the exceptions to the rule. Moreover, the measures were often transitory and were very minor in nearly all cases. The rates of the Republic rarely exceeded 5 per cent, which was particularly low compared with the ones of other European countries. Enforcement was largely entrusted to the local authorities, moreover, a practice conducive to fraud, given the highly divergent interests of the different cities.[128]

The most important export industries of the Republic — in terms of both production value and employment figures — never received effective protection, as the interests of industrial entrepreneurs (and local merchants) were consistently subordinated to those of wholesalers, with Amsterdam firms generally prevailing. The same held true for Leiden's textile industry during the first half of the seventeenth century, when a new, dynamic group of entrepreneurs, known as the *reders* (and hailing from Flanders in many cases), managed to concentrate productive labour and thus become dominant in the local arena. Despite this victory, the *reders* were no match for the Amsterdam wholesalers, who controlled the main trading networks, just as they had done in the past. The impact of this situation on capital accumulated is apparent from the fortune of the Amsterdam cloth merchant Dirc Alewijn, who in 1631 possessed ten times as much capital as the wealthiest Leiden *reder*.[129] Only when commercial and industrial interests largely coincided, were the authorities willing to take protectionist measures. The success of the efforts by the owners of sugar refineries in Amsterdam in getting the municipal levies and customs duties adjusted in their favour during the second half of the seventeenth century was not entirely coincidental: after 1650 wholesalers purchased and opened increasing numbers of companies.[130] The wholesalers, however,

125 Huisman, 1902, pp. 59-82.

126 Van Houtte, 1920, pp. 308-9, 552-4.

127 Lis and Soly, 1987, pp. 19, 31-3; Coppejans-Desmedt, 1989, pp. 75-6.

128 't Hart, 1997, pp. 23, 25-6.

129 Posthumus, 1939, pp. 503, 527-8, 531-3, 544, 552-3, 562, 809, 820.

130 Nováky, 1997, pp. 480-1.

were interested exclusively in traffic industries, which doomed nearly all attempts by textile manufacturers to have protectionist measures imposed.

High export duties on wool would have enabled Leiden cloth manufacturers during the late seventeenth century to cope with rising competition from Liège, where foreign fabrics were subject to extremely high import duties. The measure proved impossible to enforce, however, due to resistance on the part of the Amsterdam wholesalers; even the argument in 1741 that banning wool exports was the only way that the Leiden industry might avert ruin went unheeded.[131] Ongoing complaints from Amsterdam and Haarlem silk manufacturers from the end of the seventeenth century onward regarding the 'disgraceful' policy of the Dutch East India Company (VOC), which they believed imported too few raw materials and far too many silk fabrics from Asia, did not lead to binding, protectionist measures; after 1750 VOC officials even started to sell English and French silk fabrics in India.[132] Demands from linen bleachers fell on deaf ears as well. In 1768, when they were in very serious trouble indeed and urged the States of Holland to ban imports of bleached linens from the Austrian Netherlands, the matter was tabled but never received serious consideration.[133]

The States of Holland and the States General thus continued to favour the interests of wholesalers in disproportionate measure throughout the eighteenth century.[134] The effects of this policy were not exclusively detrimental, as the example of fustian weaving in Twente during the second quarter of the eighteenth century demonstrates. The rise of this new branch of industry, however, was an unintended consequence of rate changes that were enormously harmful to the linen weavers, and the merchant entrepreneurs from Enschede bringing about the product innovation were far less dependent on Amsterdam wholesalers than their colleagues elsewhere.[135]

9. Concluding observations

Guilds did not intrinsically promote or impede the rise of export industries. The success or failure of such industries depended on which groups wielded economic and political control, their independence from other groups, and their ability to launch initiatives that would enable the entire industry to adapt to economic changes. The involvement of several groups with divergent and often conflicting interests in the production of export goods explains the gamut of transformations that such guilds underwent in the Southern Netherlands during the late Middle Ages and the early modern period. One constant factor, however, was the opportunity for master artisans working for international markets between the thirteenth century and the end of the

---

131 Posthumus, 1926, pp. 375-7.

132 de Jongste, 1984, pp. 22-32; Vogel, 1986, pp. 89-91; Mulder, 1995, pp. 102-3.

133 Regtdoorzee Greup-Roldanus, 1936, pp. 201, 251-2, 256-62, 274.

134 See the pertinent remarks by Klein, 1989, pp. 202-3, 209.

135 Trompetter, 1993, pp. 43-54, and Trompetter, 1997, pp. 55-75.

Ancien Régime to subcontract and engage in trade. This option enabled them to accumulate more capital and encouraged them to innovate production.

The emergence of this favourable institutional context, first in Flanders and later in Brabant, is attributable to a combination of economic, social, and political changes: the early rise and rapid growth of export-oriented textile industries in several large and medium-sized cities; the upward social mobility of local craftsmen coordinating industrial operations and consequently acting as entrepreneurs, thereby relieving foreign merchants of management problems;[136] and, last but not least, the changing local, regional, and international balances of power, which enabled groups of skilled craftsmen to establish formal guilds in which the more affluent producers were crucial and helped the political emancipation of these organizations.

Precisely because the wealthy master artisans usually wielded economic *and* institutional control, urban export industries acquired their own dynamics independent from the logic of circulating capital. After all, those involved in guild-based export industries and selling their own manufactures were primarily producers and therefore used their social capital and political influence to defend industrial interests. What mattered was less that the guilds in the Southern Netherlands enabled lower transaction costs, which benefited all producers and consumers, than that that they allowed some masters to increase organizational productivity, as only a small part of transaction costs burdened individual entrepreneurs.[137]

The ability of the more affluent masters to become economically independent by setting up subcontracting networks and their success in controlling the guilds was highly conducive towards introducing and distributing new manufactures. All available data indicate that the parties 'sustaining' the successive cycles of product innovation and product differentiation were wealthy master artisans rather than merchant-entrepreneurs. This was the case both for cycles driven by the manufacture of luxury commodities, such as those in the fourteenth century and the first half of the seventeenth century, and for those revolving around production of goods for mass consumption. In eighteenth-century Bruges, linen weavers were enormously successful with their *zingas* (striped and chequered linen fabrics in a special dark blue). Introduced around 1700 by a few members of the guild, the *zingas* were in great demand to make clothes for members of the lower social classes in Europe and slaves in the colonies; by 1770 a small minority of capitalist weavers controlled the entire industry.[138] In the mid-1720s the Antwerp master linen weaver Jan van der Smissen, who was mentioned above, initiated production of *siamois* (a specialty of Rouen) in the Austrian Netherlands. As a result, he achieved hegemony both in the industry and within the guild.[139] The introduction of these mixed linen and cotton fabrics and

---

136 Holbach, 1994, p. 68.

137 Davids, 1995, pp. 11-12; Van der Wee, 1995, pp. 277-8.

138 Vermaut, 1988, p. 197.

139 Thijs, 1987b, pp. 149-50.

similar manufactures increased domestic demand for cotton yarns and thus paved the way for the rise of factories in the early nineteenth century.[140]

Some merchants undoubtedly combined commercial activities with forays into the production process. Contrary to what Henri Pirenne and Hans Van Werveke have argued,[141] it would seem that the leading traders in thirteenth-century Flanders concentrated their efforts on international trade.[142] During the late Middle Ages merchant-entrepreneurs are known to have been active in the textile centres in Flanders and Brabant. The practice became more widespread during the first half of the sixteenth century, due in part to Antwerp's spectacular rise as a trade metropolis. In later periods merchants were also intensely active in various export industries. During the second half of the eighteenth century, textile wholesalers even laid the foundations for structural economic change: they understood that to continue increasing their trading profits they would need to become directly involved in cotton manufacturing and started investing in fixed capital to achieve both industrial and commercial hegemony.[143]

Nonetheless, merchant capitalism did not determine long-term changes in most urban export industries, as industrial interests were not systematically subordinated to commercial ones. This was primarily attributable to the early and continuous presence of affluent master artisans, who used the guilds' articles of association and regulations to prevent merchants from engaging in production directly. In addition to being able to organize and coordinate local production, these master artisans had the right to launch commercial activities. The shift of the commercial centre of gravity to the North after 1585 obviously boosted industrial entrepreneurship in the South. None of these factors would have independently enabled guilds to become the driving forces they were in many Southern export industries. It was their combined action that set the stage for the ongoing industrial dynamics, as the following example demonstrates. Like their colleagues in the Southern Netherlands, master silk weavers in most cities in Northern Italy had a production monopoly. Unlike the silk weavers in the Southern Netherlands, however, they were rarely allowed to market their products and thus had very limited means to accumulate capital. As a result, industrial interests were consistently subordinate to commercial ones, and silk weaving lapsed into an irreversible decline once the merchants no longer saw cause to invest in this industry.[144]

The lack of sufficient quantitative data seriously complicates generalizations about the organizational characteristics of the urban export trades and their economic implications in the Northern Netherlands. All the available evidence suggests, however, that the institutional context was hardly conducive to ongoing industrial growth. The explanation lies in a combination of two closely related factors.

---

140 Lis and Soly, 1990, pp. 109-12.

141 Pirenne 1909, p. 273, and 1922, pp. 67-8.

142 Derville, 1972, pp. 357-60; Märtins, 1976, pp. 104-6; Van Uytven, 1978, pp. 477-8; Holbach, 1994, pp. 59-61.

143 Lis and Soly, 1997a, p. 313.

144 Piergiovanni, 1993, pp. 544-52, 557-60.

First, many labour-intensive industries were not organized in guilds, both because these industries were far less important in Holland and Zeeland than in Flanders and Brabant during the late Middle Ages and the sixteenth century and because of the political balances of power, which blocked the rise of fairly autonomous craft guilds. One of the consequences was that producers of export goods in the North had far greater difficulty becoming true entrepreneurs than their counterparts in the South did, which in turn meant that they consistently lost out in conflicts of interest with merchants.[145] While the rapid industrial growth during the first half of the seventeenth century necessitated the establishment of institutions to monitor quality, *neringen* (in which membership was automatic) or municipal inspectorates could serve this purpose as well. The organizational form mattered little, as all were accountable to the public authorities, even in industrial regulations.

Second, the performance of the export trades in the Republic depended largely on the logic of circulating capital.[146] The emergence of the United Provinces during the first half of the seventeenth century as the largest staple market in the world thus far undoubtedly boosted production of export goods in the cities enormously. Wholesalers tended to be directly or indirectly in control, however, with the Amsterdam firms prevailing in virtually all industries. This held true not only for *trafieken*, which required investments in fixed capital, but also for labour-intensive branches, such as the wool industry in Leiden,[147] silk weaving and linen production in Haarlem,[148] and pipe manufacturing in Gouda.[149]

The subordinate role of industrial entrepreneurship in the Republic was apparent both from the organizational structure of the export industries and from the measures that local authorities took to encourage their expansion. As far as their organizational structure was concerned, craft guilds were established in export industries only if they served the interests of merchant capitalists. Second and more importantly, merchants welcomed municipal policies dedicated to protecting small producers, as such measures complicated the rise of a group of industrial entrepreneurs (i.e. of competing capitalists).

The overwhelming supremacy of merchant capital and the absence or structural weakness of craft guilds explain why large and medium-sized entrepreneurs involved exclusively or primarily in manufacturing were fewer in number and less financially affluent in Holland than they were in Brabant and Flanders.[150] The combination of the two factors explains why few export industries in the North adapted to the changes during the eighteenth century. On the one hand, progressively fewer industries were associated with the wholesale trade, which deterred the commercial elite still more from engaging in industrial production; the only expansion in overseas trade after

[145] Lis and Soly, 1997c, p. 232.

[146] Lesger and Noordegraaf, 1997, p. 14.

[147] Posthumus, 1939, pp. 121, 785-9, 809, 820.

[148] Mulder, 1995, pp. 67-8, 96-8.

[149] Duco, 1981, pp. 192-3.

[150] Lis and Soly, 1997c, p. 235.

1720 was in import and re-export of colonial wares, such as sugar, tea, coffee, cocoa, and tobacco.[151] On the other hand, manufacturers had little faith in an oligarchy that consistently favoured the interests of wholesalers in disproportionate measure and consequently rejected an economic policy focused on import substitution. The collapse of the Dutch overseas trading system and the associated industries had no serious consequences for the merchant capitalists and members of the political elite (who were becoming a single group); they found financial speculation to be a lucrative area of investment.[152] For most producers in export centres, however, de-industrialization implied social degradation.

Clearly, social relations of production, which were reflected in the organizational structure of the export industries, followed entirely different courses of development in the North and the South. While seventeenth-century Holland was undoubtedly the most advanced stage of merchant capitalism, the combination of politico-institutional and socio-economic changes in Flanders and Brabant paved the way for the rise of industrial capitalism from the thirteenth and fourteenth centuries onward.

---

[151] Israel, 1995a, p. 1001.

[152] de Vries and van der Woude, 1997, pp. 156-8; Arrighi, 1994, pp. 141-4, 156-8.

Chapter 5

Dressed to work: a gendered comparison of the tailoring trades in the Northern and Southern Netherlands, 16th to 18th centuries

Harald Deceulaer and Bibi Panhuysen

Introduction[1]

The predominant idea in the historical literature is that women were virtually excluded from craft guilds in early modern period towns and cities.[2] Only as widows were they sometimes able to carry on their husband's occupation. The retail trade and the garment industry were notable exceptions in this respect: in several towns women in these trades joined guilds as full members. In most European towns, the garment industry was the second-largest employer. Since the tailor's trade required little capital — owning scissors, needles, and thread was usually enough to make clothes — the industry was easy to enter and competition from women thus far from hypothetical. International literature frequently emphasizes the increase in the share of women in the garment industry between the eighteenth and nineteenth centuries.[3]

Although during the early modern period women accounted for over half the population of cities and towns, the members of most tailors' guilds were exclusively male. This raises the question as to the procedures for excluding women in practice. In what

---

1 We are grateful to Catharina Lis and Hugo Soly for their critique of a previous version. Abbreviations used: ARA: Algemeen Rijksarchief [General state archive], GA: Gildearchief [Guild archive], GAG: Gemeentearchief Gouda [Gouda municipal archive], GAHt: Gemeentearchief 's-Hertogenbosch ['s-Hertogenbosch municipal archive], GAH: Gemeentearchief Haarlem [Haarlem municipal archive], GAZ: Gemeentearchief Zutphen [Zutphen municipal archive], OA: Oud Archief [old archive], RAG: Rijksarchief Gelderland [Gelderland state archive], SAA: Stadsarchief Antwerpen [Antwerp city archive], SAG: Stadsarchief Gent [Ghent city archive], Secr.AZ: Secretariaat Algemene Zaken [General affairs secretariat].

2 This is the opinion of many authors; see e.g. Wiesner-Hanks, 2000, pp. 81-4.

3 Lis, 1986; Coffin, 1994, and by the same author, 1996. See also, Juratic and Pellegrin, 1994; Pellegrin, 1999; Crowston, 2001.

measure did men monopolize certain activities? Were women in fact prohibited from working by craft guilds? If so, were effective measures taken against those violating this regulation, or were they quietly tolerated? Were 'women' and 'craft guilds' regarded as two separate worlds, or did more complex connections exist?[4] In the event of such connections, were women peripheral operators or integral within male organizations, or did they establish organizations of their own?

This study is explicitly comparative: we compare the Northern and Southern Netherlands during the seventeenth and eighteenth centuries. Comparative research on different industries, cities, or countries is rare in recent studies on craft guilds. The non-linear, complex, ambivalent, dynamic, and multi-layered reality makes many historians hesitate to formulate more general statements and broad comparisons. Many guild studies are local and have a limited scope. Micro-historical studies are indispensable and have revealed important research results for export industries, as well as for the ones that served the local market.[5] Ultimately, however, historians face questions about similarities and differences in time and space and need to consider explanations for variations.[6]

A comparative perspective on the relationship between guilds and women in different regions may reveal the opportunities and limitations of these guilds with respect to intervening against women's labour. This enables us to place corporative organizations and rules in their chronological and spatial contexts and to explore the influence of demographic, economic, political, and cultural elements on the actions of groups and organizations. This issue thus relates closely to concepts such as power and control: in what measure could individuals or groups (i.e. craft guilds) enforce their 'will', even if they met with resistance, and in what measure could they restrict the options available to other persons or groups (i.e. women)?

The Low Countries provide an interesting context for examining this issue. In addition to being one of the most densely populated and economically progressive regions in Europe, several previous studies have demonstrated that women could work there or became involved in public causes without bringing dishonour upon themselves.[7] Nor was the legal status of women unfavourable in the Low Countries.[8] Studying the issue in two countries and thirty cities and towns quickly reveals the need to consider a plethora of elements and demonstrates that explanations of variations should be based

---

4 This is suggested by Crowston, 2001, pp. 10, 74-112, 217-55. Examples of this complex relationship between women and guilds are provided by Hafter, 2001, pp. 11-40.

5 Cerutti, 1990; Kaplan, 1996; Poni, 1991, An account appears in Farr, 1997.

6 Initial efforts appear in Lis and Soly, 1997c; Epstein et al., 1998; Ehmer, 1998; Schulz and Müller-Luckner, 1999; Farr, 2000.

7 Kloek, 1994, p. 14; Hufton, 1998, p. 70. A critique of applications of Mediterranean honour concepts to the Northern Netherlands appears in Egmond, 1994, pp. 7, 22. Honour is discussed extensively in studies about German towns. See Simon-Muscheid, 1998.

8 Gillissen, 1962, pp. 256-7; Bosch, 1962, p. 323.

on more than one factor. Nor should we present two 'national' models for two highly decentralized areas with vast local and regional differences. Comparative study of the policies of certain craft guilds toward women may, however, help identify the different interactions between labour markets, institutions, and organizations and unveil the factors that influence them.

From the last quarter of the seventeenth century, the garment industry in Western Europe underwent a gradual transformation, driven by the rise in consumption and the concurrent change in gender identities.[9] This rise in consumption was a challenge to the organization of production and distribution in the industry, to which the responses varied depending on the region. These divergent responses entailed major implications for the membership size of craft guilds in the garment industry, the relationship between guild-based and non guild-based labour, and gender relationships within the industry.

To establish an effective comparison in the limited space available in this article, we will focus mainly on quantitative data. This article arises from a more detailed comparative study of the garment industry in cities and towns in the Southern and Northern Netherlands.[10] In addition, research findings about the Low Countries are placed in an international context wherever possible, by comparing them to several other European centres. Using aggregate figures for an entire sector generates huge methodological problems with comparisons between cities. Accordingly, we have not covered the entire garment industry in this article and have excluded occupational groups such as hat makers, furriers, glove makers, embroiderers, and the like. Instead, we will compare the two largest groups in the industry wherever possible: tailors and seamstresses. Before presenting the figures for the respective shares of the two occupational groups, we will explain exactly what tailors and seamstresses did, what they produced, for whom they produced, and the implications of the rise in clothing consumption.

1. Garments and garment production in the 17th and 18th centuries: tailors, seamstresses, and the rise in consumption[11]

Tailors during the early modern period produced mainly for the local market from small workshops. Although the data reveal occasional traces of female members of tailors' guilds (primarily widows), tailors were male. Journeymen tailors were all male as well. Most of the clothes they made were special orders. Since clients usually paid for the fabrics themselves, the tailoring trade required little capital. Only when tailors were responsible for supplying the fabrics, did the trade become more capital

---

9 The rise in consumption is pivotal in a series of studies, including: McKendrick, Brewer, and Plumb, 1982; Brewer and Porter, 1992; Schuurman, de Vries and van der Woude, 1997.

10 Panhuysen, 2000; Deceulaer, 2001.

11 Based on Deceulaer, 2001, and Panhuysen, 2000.

intensive due to the extended terms of payment for clients. Early modern tailors were rarely affluent: most did not even earn enough to pay taxes. Although tailors usually made large outer garments, they mended clothes as well. During the sixteenth and seventeenth centuries they appear to have produced both men's and women's garments and became more specialized in France and the big cities of the Southern Netherlands during the late seventeenth and early eighteenth centuries. Tailors started to produce either for men or for women. Data indicating the share of men's or women's tailors are scarce, but figures for Brussels and Ghent in the second half of the eighteenth century reveal far fewer tailors for women than for men.[12] Most eighteenth-century tailors thus specialized in men's clothing, leaving production of women's clothes to a different group. While tailors in the Northern Netherlands were in fact capable of producing both men's and women's clothing, they too tended to concentrate on men's wear.

Tailors, however, were not the only ones offering their services. In the Northern Netherlands, woollen seamstresses cut and sewed women's and children's clothes, from jackets and skirts through negligees. Linen seamstresses produced more basic linens and underwear. Patch seamstresses, known as such because they were allowed to use only small quantities of fabric for mending clothes, mainly did clothing repairs.[13] Production costs of seamstresses tended to be lower than those of tailors. While seamstresses existed in the Southern Netherlands as well, the same terms indicating a certain division of labour did not. This may be the first sign of differences between North and South.

Recent studies about clothing, consumption, and material culture reflect growth in England, France, and the Netherlands from the late seventeenth century onward.[14] In the course of the eighteenth century, palpably cheaper fabrics started to be used, due to production and distribution changes in the textile industry. Increased use of less expensive mixed and cotton fabrics and the popularity of lighter wool fabrics enabled people to purchase more clothes for the same amount of money.[15] The simplification of fashionable clothes in the 1770s and '80s also required less fabric, helping to bring down the price of clothes.[16] Ready-made garments started to be sold more frequently on markets and in shops, and fashion awareness appears to have increased among

---

[12] A Brussels almanac lists 43 tailors, including 30 who produced men's wear and 13 specializing in women's clothes. Bruneel and Delporte, 1997, pp. 468-9. A comparable situation existed in Paris: Crowston, 2001, p. 75.

[13] Panhuysen, 2000, pp. 109-11, 177-8, 197-9.

[14] On England: McKendrick, Brewer and Plumb, 1982, pp. 34-99; Lemire, 1997. On France: Roche, 1989, p. 110. On the Netherlands: Van Rijckeghem, 1988, pp. 33-50; Deceulaer, 2001, and Panhuysen, 2000.

[15] Shammas, 1994; Ponsot, 1987, pp. 371-2. The thesis that prices for textiles were already declining in the 17th century has recently been criticized by Spufford, 2003, pp. 47-63.

[16] Crowston, 2001, p. 150.

broad segments of the population during the eighteenth century. Accelerating fashions increased demand for replacements, and durability became less of a consideration.

This trend was clearly gender-related. Throughout the eighteenth century, the basic parts of men's suits continued to be made primarily from heavier woollen fabrics in dark, neutral colours. Women started to wear lighter, more colourful clothes, and their wardrobe became more varied. People started to own more different types of outer wear, ranging from assorted mantles and jackets through dresses. Women also purchased countless fashion accessories, such as stylish caps and shawls and were responsible for most of the increase in consumption. Daniel Roche has observed that by the end of the eighteenth century in Paris, people from all social classes invested more time and money in women's clothes.[17] In Delft and Ghent around this time, the increase in garments was also far greater among women than among men.[18]

Exploring the backgrounds to this cultural evolution would exceed the scope of this chapter. The market for women's clothing is known, however, to have grown more than the one for men's garments. This unequal growth was a challenge to the industry in the different market segments. Who was able or authorized to latch on to this growing market? Did the market share increase among tailors organized in guilds, among skilled woollen seamstresses, or among workers that were not organized? Answering these questions will require numerical data.

2. Employment in the garment industry: a quantitative survey of the Netherlands and selected European centres

Comparing the numbers of men (tailors) and women (seamstresses) active in the garment industry is possible thanks to the 1796 census for various towns and cities in the Southern Netherlands. Our data for the Northern Netherlands come from several reports from guild members and the patent taxes of 1806. These sources from the Northern Netherlands for Leeuwarden (1749) and 's-Hertogenbosch (1775) are almost certain to be distorted due to under-registration of women.[19] We counted master and journeymen tailors together or — if such data were unavailable — extrapolated the total number, assuming that one master tailor employed one journeyman on average.[20] We assumed that seamstresses did not employ staff, which undoubtedly increased the under-registration of women. During the eighteenth century in Haarlem, for example, woollen seamstresses took on a great many apprentice girls.[21] Next, we

17 Roche, 1989, pp. 98, 111.

18 Wijsenbeek-Olthuis, 1987, p. 460; Van Rijckeghem, 1988, pp. 48-9.

19 The censuses for 's-Hertogenbosch and Leeuwarden list only heads of households. This under-registration merely confirms the argument in the comparison (see below).

20 The numbers of tailors (masters and journeymen) has been extrapolated for Gouda and Haarlem, as only the numbers of masters are known for these cities.

21 Panhuysen, 2000, p. 194.

calculated the ratio of tailors to seamstresses (based on a sum of 100 per cent). We selected both large cities and medium-sized and small towns and have listed the cities with the largest share of women at the top.

Even though women are almost certain to have been under-registered in several cities and towns in the Northern Netherlands, their numbers are almost systematically higher than those for the Southern Netherlands. The pattern comprises several regional and local differences. In the Northern Netherlands, women appear to have been more prevalent in the Western cities of Haarlem, Amsterdam, and Gouda and less prevalent in Friesland in the North, Zwolle in the East, and 's-Hertogenbosch in the South. In the Southern Netherlands, women's work in the garment industry appears to have been restricted largely to Antwerp and Brussels. Although seamstresses were primarily active in larger cities, no mechanical correlation exists between population size and numbers of seamstresses. Ghent, for example, had very few seamstresses, even though the city's population was larger than that of Antwerp. The populations of Oostende, Lokeren, and Aalst in the Southern Netherlands differed little from those of Zwolle, 's-Hertogenbosch, or Leeuwarden in the Northern Netherlands, although women substantially outnumbered men in the garment industry in the latter three cities.

The data in table 5.1 below obviously have various limitations. First, they are samples from a specific point in time. No reliable figures are available on women's labour in the Southern Netherlands from before the 1796 census. In addition to the data being limited for the Northern Netherlands, the figures for four cities are from 1806. The table does not reveal whether these relationships existed previously, when various cities in North and South started to digress, and how local trends related to other European centres.

Most censuses from the Ancien Régime reflect a patriarchal view of society and indicate only the occupation of the male head of the household. Data are therefore available for earlier periods for the number of tailors but not for the number of seamstresses. We nonetheless believe that information may be gleaned indirectly about the number of women in the industry, based on the number of men. Rather than disregarding the conventional censuses, tax assessment registers, or guild registers, we want to consider these sources from a different perspective. This will reveal a glimpse of a concealed world of women behind the 'male' figures. Our argument is based on the general practice of producing clothing for a local market and the absence of corporate concentration in the garment industry. We assume that garments were made by tailors or seamstresses. If the number of male tailors in a city was remarkably low, without any reason being apparent from the sources, the situation may have been attributable to a larger market share of — unregistered — seamstresses. Conversely, if the share of tailors was relatively high, and the city concerned was not known as a fashion centre, it would have appeared far less likely that many seamstresses worked there. Interpreting numbers of tailors is obviously possible only in relation to population size and will require extensive observations, preferably from different sources, to counteract all kinds of source-related distortions. Censuses being compared will of course need to have been conducted in somewhat similar manners as well. Censuses in which only

Table 5.1 *Tailors, seamstresses, and their ratio in cities and towns in the Northern and Southern Netherlands during the eighteenth century*[22]
(towns in the Northern Netherlands appear in italics)

City	Year	Population	Tailors	Seamstresses	Tailors/ seamstresses
Haarlem	1745	24,695	172	224	43/57
Haarlem	1775	22,000	180	357	34/66
Haarlem	1806	21,227	128	349	27/63
Gouda	1745	20,000	108	192	36/64
Brussels	1796	66,441	1,028	1,692	44/56
Amsterdam	1806	200,000	1,562	2,027	44/56
Antwerp	1796	50,700	846	805	51/49
Zwolle	1806	12,550	126	96	57/43
's-Hertogenbosch	1775	12,484	122	211	52/48
's-Hertogenbosch	1806	12,841	100	165	38/62
Leeuwarden	1749	12,000	64	61	51/49
Ninove	1796	2,800	28	16	63/37
Ghent	1796	55,000	568	315	64/36
Tielt	1796	8,500	50	20	71/9
Oostende	1796	10,000	102	29	77/23
Lokeren	1796	11,000	63	16	80/20
Eeklo	1796	5,827	43	10	81/19
Geraardsbergen	1796	5,948	94	16	86/14
Aalst	1796	10,927	88	9	88/12
Oudenaarde	1796	4,267	54	2	96/4

masters are counted naturally differ from the ones that also include journeymen. We compared the data by calculating the number of tailors per 1,000 inhabitants.

Except for 's-Hertogenbosch and Zutphen, the numbers of tailors are significantly lower in the Northern than in the Southern Netherlands. Data for the towns of Geel and Herentals in the Southern Netherlands were included from the census of 1755, in which only the heads of households were counted.

Accurate comparison of selected cities in the Northern and the Southern Netherlands also suggests a historical evolution. Between 1738 and 1796, the number of

[22] See table 5.2; Lourens and Lucassen, 1997b; GAL, St. Bibl. E 253.Manuscript of B. van Keulen, 'Quotisatie Leeuwarden 1749'; GAHt, OA, C 106, Blokboeken 1775.

Table 5.2 *Master and journeymen tailors in the Northern and Southern Netherlands in the eighteenth century*[23]

Southern Netherlands

City	Year	Population	Master Tailors	/1,000	Masters + Journeymen	/1,000
Brussels	1738	65/70,000	294	4.2/4.5	881	12.5/13.5
	1796	66,441			1,003	15.0
Antwerp	1738	60,000	350	5.8	737	12.3
	1796	50,700			846	16.7
Ghent	1738	44,226	226	5.1	470	10.6
	1796	55,161			568	10.3
Bruges	1784	31,319	246	7.9		
Malines	1739	19,284	121	6.3	292	15.1
Geel	1755	3,408	26	7.6		
Herentals	1755	2,439	19	7.8		
Geraardsbergen	1796	5,948			94	15.8
Oudenaarde	1796	4,267			54	12.7
Dendermonde	1796	5,028			62	12.3
St. Niklaas	1796	10,890			84	7.7
Aalst	1796	10,927			65	5.9

tailors (masters and journeymen) increased in Antwerp and Brussels. While we have only data about the masters for the Northern Netherlands, their numbers decreased in Haarlem, Gouda, ‘s-Hertogenbosch, and Amsterdam between 1750 and 1806. No corporate concentration appears to have occurred in the Northern Netherlands, as the available figures for numbers of journeymen are very similar between the North and the South. We have calculated 1.9 journeymen for each master for Brussels in 1738 and 1.7 journeymen for each master for Amsterdam in 1806.[24] In Zwolle and ‘s-Hertogenbosch, master tailors employed one journeyman each on average, and the rate

[23] Van Honacker, 1994a, p. 223; S.A.A., GA 4007, S.A.G., Reeks 156, 3, 8; Verbeemen, 1956, 79-86; Verbeemen, 1955, p. 146, 159; De Belder, 1974; Van den Berghe, 1972. Noordelijke Nederlanden: GAA, RA 5061, inv.nr. 639/3a; GAA, BA 5028, inv. nr. 718; GA'sG, OA b. nr. 376, inv. Nr. 78; GAH, GA, inv. nr. 62; Hulshof, 1996; GAHt, inv. nr. 1 and 24; van den Eerenbeemt, 1955, p. 123; RAG, bloknr. 0698. Collectie Schomaker, cas 71, fol. 10-18; GAZ, GA, inv. nr. 518 8 nov. 1748; Odink, 1965, p. 317.

[24] In Brussels there were 294 tailors and 587 journeymen tailors. Van Honacker, 1994a, p. 223. In 1806 in Amsterdam there were 1,016 journeymen and 546 masters, and in 1812, 1,041

Table 5.2 Continued

Northern Netherlands

City	Year	Population	Master Tailors	/1,000	Masters + journey-men	/1,000
Amsterdam	1750	220,000	>600	>2.7		
	1806	200,000	546	2.7	1,562	7.8
The Hague	1750	33,500	138	4.1		
Haarlem	1750	24,695	90	3.6		
	1790	21,227	83	3.9		
	1806	21,227	64	3.0		
Gouda	1745	20,000	54	2.7		
	1808	11,715	29	2.4		
's-Hertogenbosch	1752	20,000	112	5.6		
	1775	12,484	87	7.0		
	1806	12,841	44	3.4	100	7.8
Zutphen	1703	5,000	50	10		
	1748	Ca. 5,040	42	8.3		
Eibergen	1798	1,450	12	8.2		

was similar in Antwerp, Ghent, Namur, Luxembourg, and Ninove.[25] The discrepancies between the North and the South probably had several causes: the economic downturn in the last quarter of the eighteenth century in the North, the abolition of the guilds, a new registration system (patent registers), the decline in the population of cities, and the like.

Were the increase in the number of tailors in the three largest cities of the Southern Netherlands and the corresponding decline in several centres in the Northern Netherlands attributable to differences between the local economies? Whereas the second half of the eighteenth century is often regarded as a period of major economic growth in the Southern Netherlands, it is considered to have been one of stagnation or

booklets were issued to journeymen tailors working for 519 bosses, Amsterdam municipal mayors' archive 5028, inv.nr. 718. Accounts of the council committee about the abolition of the patent law; Secr. A.Z. 5181, inv.nr. 2022. Report from the Amsterdam guild funds for the national survey about support benefits from 1812 and Nieuw Stedelijk Bestuur [new municipal administration] 5033, inv.nr. 267, 1811/1347. Booklets issued to workers in the City of Amsterdam.

25 van den Eerenbeemt, 1955, p. 123; GAZw, AAZ01, inv. Nr. 4578; Deceulaer, 2001, p. 245.

decline in the Northern Netherlands.[26] Nonetheless, economic differences are unlikely to have been the main cause. First, economic growth alone reveals little about the distribution of wealth among the general population. Second, no linear relationship existed between income growth and the rise in garment consumption. Economists argue that conclusions regarding the effect of changes in income are possible only following empirical observations, not based on *a priori* models.[27] The need for caution is also apparent from the discrepancies between individual cities. While Zutphen and 's-Hertogenbosch had more tailors, no Dutch historian would argue that these cities had thriving economies during the eighteenth century. Nor would it be logical to suggest that medium-sized or small towns in the Southern Netherlands, such as Bruges, Malines, or Geel, were more affluent than Amsterdam or The Hague, merely because such towns had more tailors per 1,000 inhabitants. In fact, the market share of tailors appears to have been smaller in the North and larger in the South. All the available data indicate that women became more numerically dominant in the garment industry in the Northern Netherlands.

Before considering possible explanations for these differences in the Low Countries, let us consider the situation in German, French, and Italian cities. The data about the number of tailors per 1,000 inhabitants are more conducive to comparisons across time and space. We gathered 23 observations for 19 cities and towns, including small, medium-sized, and large ones. Like in the previous table, the population figure used was the one for the closest year available.[28] No data from England appear in the table 5.3, as no reliable figures were available for that country before the nineteenth century.[29]

---

[26] Van der Wee, 1988, pp. 307-81. Blondé, 1999, describes regional differences within Brabant. The most recent account of the economy in the Northern Netherlands appears in de Vries and van der Woude, 1997.

[27] Van Rompuy, 1991, p. 106; Harte, 1991, p. 291.

[28] For Augsburg we compared the number of tailors in 1720, 1788, and 1806 with the population figures from 1700 and 1800. We compared the figures for tailors in Berlin from 1786 with the number of inhabitants in 1798. The population for Paris was based on the figure from 1775.

[29] Comment from Pamela Sharpe and Iorwerth Prothero in May 1999.

Table 5.3 *Number of tailors in selected small and medium-sized towns and large cities in Germany, France, and Italy, 1495-1800.*[30]

Town	Year	Population	Master Tailors	/1000	Masters + Journey-men	/1000
Mainz	1541	6000	29	4.8		
Speyer	1558	7500	45	6		
Landau	1495	2550	33	13.2		
Augsburg	1720	21,000	167	7.9		
	1788	28,000	226	8.0		
	1806	28,000	191	6.8		
Berlin	1729	75,000	411	5.5	771	10.3
	1786	170,000	859	5.0	1619	9.2
Turin	1705	33,773	258	7.6		
Rouen	1775	74,000	271/274	3.6/3.7		
Paris	1779	750,000	1884	2.5	6884	9.1
	1788	750,000	2800	3.7	7800	10.4
Lyon	1789	100,000	443	4.4	843/943	8.4/9.4
Soest	1800	5581	42	7.5	57	10.2
Iserlohn	1800	4380	20	4.5	39	8.9
Hamm	1800	3362	35	10.4	48	14.4
Altena	1800	3064	16	5.2	22	7.1
Unna	1800	2451	32	13.0	36	14.6
Schwelm	1800	2253	26	11.5	39	17.3
Hagen	1800	1837	14	7.6	24	13
Kamen	1800	1572	25	15.9	25	15.9
Lüdenscheid	1800	1484	14	9.4	21	14.1
Pletenberg	1800	1213	9	7.4	10	8.2

[30] Wesoly, 1985, pp. 19, 26, 30, 397-401; Cerutti, 1988, p. 325; Franklin, 1987, p. 678; Garden 1970, p. 341; Safley, 1997, p. 232 ; Sonenscher, 1986, p. 80, Reininghaus, 1995, p. 579, 584; Schulz, 1993, pp. 12, 142; Population figures from de Vries, 1984.

This data tends to be closer to the figures for the Southern Netherlands, although the numbers of master tailors declined slightly in Augsburg and Berlin as well. Numbers of master tailors were remarkably low in French cities, as they were in the Northern Netherlands as well.[31] The low numbers of tailors in Paris and Lyon are somewhat surprising, as these cities were major fashion centres. 'Paris ... appears to have asserted the exclusive right ... to produce fashions not only in all cities in France but in all those in Europe as well', read the Brussels *Almanach des Négocians* in 1762.[32] Considering the supply of labour, however, reveals that the number of master tailors and journeymen was lower in France than in the Southern Netherlands. The overall share of male masters and journeymen in the garment industry in the Southern Netherlands appears to have been larger than in Paris or Lyon, although the differences should not be exaggerated. The Paris garment industry is known to have included *faux-ouvriers*: artisans who worked illegally in basements or attics or in districts outside the jurisdiction of the Paris craft guilds.[33] Nor should the balance in Paris and Lyon be assumed for all French centres: in Bretagne and Auvergne, for example, the monopoly of male tailors appears to have persisted.[34] In Vienna the actual number of tailors organized in guilds was very low as well in 1736: 457 masters or 2.8 per 1,000 inhabitants. Adding the *Dekretisten* (individuals declared free by the state), artisans employed by the Court and the military, and the moonlighters yields 1,646 artisans out of 160,000 inhabitants or 10.2 per 1,000 inhabitants.[35] This figure is virtually the same as the one for Berlin. The data from the different tables thus suggest that the situation in the Northern Netherlands is more likely to have been the exception: more seamstresses and fewer tailors were reported for this area than for the Southern Netherlands and most other European centres (except for a few French cities).

Why were the numbers of tailors lower in France and the Northern Netherlands? Theoretically, guilds may have been more difficult to join there. Higher fees for becoming a master might explain why fewer people became masters. This does not, however, appear to have been the case in the Dutch Republic. In both the Northern and the Southern Netherlands, aspiring master tailors were required to serve a two-year apprenticeship. Elsewhere, we compared the amount of money that aspiring masters had to pay the craft guild in ten cities in the Southern Netherlands, six cities in the Northern Netherlands, and a few French centres. This comparison revealed that the differences between North and South were not very great, and that obstacles to admission were definitely no higher in the Northern Netherlands. Admission criteria tended to be more rigid in French towns and cities. In addition to the requirement that aspiring masters in France pay an impressive sum following a three-year appren-

---

[31] Ehmer, 1988, p. 69.

[32] *Almanach des Négocians* (Brussels, 1762), 297. On Lyon, see Poni, 1998.

[33] Kaplan, 1988.

[34] Pellegrin, 1999, p. 762.

[35] Ehmer, 1998, p. 69.

ticeship, corporative relations in France were entirely different than they were in the Low Countries.[36] In 1660, it was proclaimed that no more than ten new master tailors would be admitted in Paris each year, and that each master might employ at most six journeymen.[37] This measure greatly curtailed the supply of Paris tailors. Since the garment market in Paris was undoubtedly proportionately larger than the export markets in towns in the Northern or Southern Netherlands, seamstresses would appear to have been more active in the garment industries in Paris and Lyon. A French dictionary from 1732 described a *tailleur de femme* as 'one who makes only the trunk of women's dresses and has seamstresses do the rest'.[38] The importance of cottage industries in putting-out networks in Paris has recently been highlighted.[39] Tailors in the French capital could thus not possibly have accommodated the rising demand without bending the rules. Their extensive subcontracting to seamstresses is understandable. The presence of an accessories export industry in Paris is believed to have expanded the labour market for seamstresses as well.

The greater rigidity of the French guilds made seamstresses indispensable. They often worked as subcontractors for master tailors, as the passage from the 1732 dictionary suggests. A few managed to become independent operators. Subcontracting women sometimes set in motion processes that were difficult to control. The economic and fiscal policy of the French state under Colbert and Louis XIV helps explain the more rigorous regulation of the corporative world, as well as the creation of several seamstresses' guilds in 1675. In 1673, one year after the Dutch War had started, Colbert ordered the incorporation of all economic sectors, with the sovereign receiving half the entry fees for new masters, thus raising precious revenue. This led to the creation of a seamstresses' guild in Paris in 1675, as well as in several other French towns. In still other towns, seamstresses could join the tailors' guilds.[40]

It has been noted earlier that corporative regulations in export industries were far more lenient in the Southern Netherlands than in France.[41] The same appears to have been the case for the garment industries in the Northern and Southern Netherlands: no town in these areas restricted the number of tailors to be admitted in a single year. No maximum number of journeymen was ever imposed in Antwerp, Ghent, Malines, or Louvain. In 1589 in Amsterdam and in 1680 in Brussels, however, masters were

---

36 Deceulaer and Panhuysen, 2000, pp. 90-1.

37 Franklin, 1987, p. 67; Roche, 1994, pp. 284-5.

38 Richelet, 1732, II.

39 Fairchilds, 1992, pp. 237-41.

40 Crowston, 2001, pp. 187-93. She signals autonomous seamstresses' guilds in Paris, Le Havre and Rouen. She found that seamstresses could join tailors' guilds in Abbeville, Laon, Caen, Coutances, Angers, Le Mans, Saint-Malo, Rennes, Langres, Nantes, Saintes, Clermont-Ferrand, Marseilles, and Arles: pp. 198-9. Coffin, 1994, p. 778 also mentions seamstresses' guilds in Chartres, Alencon, Blois, Orleans, Poitiers and Nancy.

41 Craeybeckx, 1962, p. 427.

prohibited from employing more than ten journeymen each,[42] although they were allowed to hire considerably more than in Paris. The more flexible relations in the Southern Netherlands enabled the guild-based garment industry to adapt to changing market situations and made for a more elastic supply. In some French towns and cities, external labour circumvented the more rigid rules and eventually became part of the corporative system in their own right.

3. Established and (partial) outsiders: men and women in the garment industry in North and South

The next question is how gender relations evolved in the garment industries of the two countries, and how they became institutionalized as a result of the changing market situation. Tailors' guilds in the Southern Netherlands were typically male occupational associations.[43] Fewer than a dozen women managed to become independent tailors. Most were successfully barred from joining the guild. The tailors' guilds did not necessarily object to women making clothes — wives and daughters were known to work in family businesses — but did not want women to become independent operators, which would have jeopardized the control men had over women's labour. Only in the Hainault town of Mons did women make a dent in the male monopoly of the master tailors. In Mons, the members of the tailors' guild included women by the start of the eighteenth century. Seamstresses, however, were considered to be inferior within the tailors' guild. They had the same financial responsibilities as guild members but were not invited to attend funeral ceremonies or celebrations of the patron saint. Hoping to escape from the iron grip of the master tailors, seamstresses requested permission to establish their own guild, as their counterparts had already done in the neighbouring French towns of Valenciennes and Rouen.[44] The central authorities dismissed the request of the seamstresses, arguing that no guild in the Southern Netherlands consisted exclusively of female members. An ordinance from 1741 subsequently stipulated that the seamstresses should become a subdivision within the tailors' guild. The measure from 1741 was never implemented: the master tailors refused to accept the seamstresses as members of their guild. The seamstresses, in turn, regarded the resolution from 1741 as cause to consider their organization an independent guild from that moment onward, with their own officials, guild aid, and patron saint. Since the organization of seamstresses lacked a formal privilege, question remains as to whether they were able to enforce a monopoly on sewing women's clothes. While some seamstresses were

---

[42] Quoted in A.R.A., GR OR, kartons, 435, 24 oktober 1780 and in GAA, GA 366, 466 (13 april 1589). See Panhuysen, 2000, p. 143.

[43] The following is based on Deceulaer, 2001.

[44] On 19 July 1663 a guild of the 'couturiers' had been established at Valenciennes, with a mainly female membership, who made clothes from non-woollen fabrics: Cappliez, 1893, pp. 235-6.

active in other towns in the Southern Netherlands, the few who attempted to become officially recognized within the tailors' guilds encountered fierce opposition.

The situation in the Northern Netherlands was more similar to the one in France, where separate seamstresses' guilds existed, and women were admitted as members of the tailors' guilds.[45] Like in France, the seamstresses here obtained corporative positions in the late seventeenth and early eighteenth centuries. Amsterdam was exceptional in this respect: seamstresses in this city organized their own guild back in 1579. Like the officials of the tailors' guild, the 'trial mistresses' or officials of the seamstresses' guild monitored compliance with the regulations of their trade independently. The subordination of the seamstresses to the authority of the tailors' guild was apparent only from their collective payment obligation: the woollen seamstresses' guild was required to pay one third of its revenues to the tailors' guild. This payment obligation of the woollen seamstresses' guild to the tailors was, however, often evaded. Corporative relationships between tailors and seamstresses were entirely different in nearby Haarlem. From the early eighteenth century, the seamstresses from this city operated as a subdivision of the tailors' guild. The trial mistresses of the woollen seamstresses were employed by the tailors' guild and in fact merely administered the trial for woollen seamstresses. In return for their obligation to pay dues to the tailors' guild, woollen seamstresses were entitled to financial support from the guild in the event of sickness, disability, or death and may therefore be regarded as members of the tailors' guild. They were second-class members, though, as these women were never entitled to any official input within the tailors' guild. Comparable arrangements existed in the cities of Gouda and Rotterdam in Holland.

Seamstresses in 's-Hertogenbosch and The Hague were granted complete freedom by the municipal authorities to practise their trade. In return, however, they were required to pay dues to the tailors' guild. They had to contribute six guilders a year, plus an additional fee for each apprentice they trained. Unlike their counterparts in Haarlem, these seamstresses had no rights at all within the guild. In this respect the seamstresses in 's-Hertogenbosch and The Hague are to be regarded as third-class members.

4. Culture, demographics, economy, or politics? Explaining the differences in gender relations

No straightforward explanation is available for local, regional, or even national differences in gender relations in the tailoring trades. The interpretation of the data in the previous section included reference to various cultural, economic, and institutional factors that affected the importance of women's labour in the tailoring trades. In this section we will review possible explanations for the differences between the Northern and the Southern Netherlands in gender relations in the tailoring trade, from cultural

[45] The following is based on Panhuysen, 2000, pp. 200-38.

aspects (mentality) to demographic (the surplus of women), economic (employment), and political-institutional (the political positions of craft guilds) ones.

Comparisons of the Northern and the Southern Netherlands have traditionally stressed cultural differences ('Calvinism' versus Counter Reformation Catholicism). Many overlook the fact that Calvinists were not the majority of the population in the Northern Netherlands. Max Weber has moreover noted that asceticism started to wane in the Northern Netherlands from the early seventeenth century.[46] The strong Catholic presence among the population of the Northern Netherlands is obviously significant as well. Stereotypes about the austere North and the hedonistic South nonetheless persist. Were people in the Catholic Southern Netherlands more interested in clothing than in the austere, Protestant North, and could the different levels of interest have affected the gender distribution of those employed in the industry? This explanation may seem plausible. Austerity and less rigid rules of etiquette certainly appear to have figured in the perceptions and self-awareness of people in the Northern Netherlands from the sixteenth century onward.[47] After the fall of Antwerp, many people in Holland grew irritated with the courtlier and more flamboyant mannerisms of migrants from the South. The first book of etiquette from the Northern Netherlands was published only in 1735.[48] The lifestyles of most regents in the Northern Netherlands during the eighteenth century were very different from those of the aristocracy in the Southern Netherlands, especially if we compare the elements associated with typically aristocratic leisure pursuits. In Gouda, for example, there was not a single fencing or dance teacher to be found. Balls and dances were far from popular among the local elites. Nor did the city have an opera hall or theatre. In the Dutch Republic, Carnival week masquerades were prohibited as a 'papal superstition'. Members of the elite in the Northern Netherlands were known for their placid, restrained, and bourgeois outlook on life.[49] In the Southern Netherlands, on the other hand, court activities thrived in Brussels after 1749. Every week the governor-general invited the social elite of the Southern Netherlands for refreshments, music, and card games. In addition, the governor, as well as the leading families of aristocrats, organized theatrical performances, hunting parties, balls, and evenings of card games. Fancy-dress parties and masked balls were especially popular.[50] These intensive interactions and festive events are sure to have boosted demand for garments considerably.

The question is whether these practices explain the lower number of tailors nearly everywhere in the Northern Netherlands. While the increase in social activities at the court in Brussels may very well have boosted local demand for garments, it is less likely to have affected the number of tailors in provincial towns such as Dendermonde or Aalst. The lifestyle of the Brussels elite was definitely not emulated throughout

---

46 Weber, 1964, p. 229.

47 Roodenburg, 1993, pp. 189-90.

48 Roodenburg, 1991, pp. 25, 28.

49 de Jongh, 1987, pp. 133-4, 177-8, 186, 220-1; Dekker and van de Pol, 1989, p. 18.

50 Van den Berg, 1985, pp. 145-8; Duerloo, 1996, p. 43; Verbrugge, 1996, p. 151.

the Southern Netherlands.[51] In addition, the Northern Netherlands had a court in The Hague, which experienced a similar heyday during the eighteenth century.[52] Other comparisons make the 'cultural' explanation less plausible. Did the high numbers of tailors in 's-Hertogenbosch or Zutphen indicate a very luxurious local lifestyle? The figures in Paris were rather low as well. In the international centre of eighteenth-century fashion, where the French aristocracy indulged in dizzying quantities of luxury items,[53] remarkably few tailors were listed.

Cultural factors may have influenced gender relations in the garment industry more indirectly as well. The different attitude on the part of the local authorities in the Northern Netherlands could have been attributable to a different perception of women's labour, based on the established tradition of economic independence among women in Holland. 'The wives of Holland buy and sell things at home, and use to saile to Hamburg and into England for exercise of traffique', wrote the Englishman Fyne Moryson after travelling through the United Netherlands at the end of the sixteenth century.[54] He also noticed that women in these regions were remarkably dominant, in both quantitative — 'the multitude of women is farre greater than of men, which I not only formerly heard of others, but my selfe observed to be true' — and in qualitative respects: 'I may boldly say, that the women of these parts are above alle truly taxed with this unnaturall dominering over their husbands.' English travellers returning from Holland often shared observations about the independence of Dutch women (who often managed their husband's business affairs during his absence or ran their own shops) and their allegedly domineering nature (women were said to be in control).[55] Attributing the difference in gender ratios in the garment industries in the Northern and Southern Netherlands to the independence of women in the North, however, would require demonstrating that those in the South were far more traditional. The many French and Italian visitors to the Southern Netherlands during the sixteenth and seventeenth centuries definitely had no such impression and were equally surprised at the extensive freedom they observed among women there.[56]

---

51 In eighteenth-century Antwerp, for example, the nobility consisted nearly of old merchant families, who had in most cases received their patents of nobility after 1650 or 1700. They were known for their rather Spartan lifestyles and spoke ill of what they regarded as the extravagance of the Brussels aristocracy, Degryse, 1985, pp. 137-8.

52 Groeneweg, 1991, pp. 69, 73, 75-6, 80.

53 Roche, 1994, pp. 188-93.

54 Jacobsen Jensen, 1918, pp. 272-3.

55 Van Strien, 1989, p. 158.

56 Such reports include Guicciardini, 1612, about Antwerp, as well as one from the French intendant de Bagnolz from 1697 about West Flanders, Ministry of Foreign Affairs, Paris, Mémoires et Documents France, 1568, Mémoire sur la Flandre Flamingante.

Another possible explanation for the ratios between tailors and seamstresses might be the demographic composition of the urban population, where women tended to outnumber men in pre-industrial Europe.[57] This surplus of women was proportionately greater, however, in cities and towns in eighteenth-century Holland. The natural balance between men and women was disrupted by the gender-based migration pattern, as research on the gender breakdown of migration flows to and from Amsterdam reveals.[58] While during the first half of the seventeenth century the burgeoning city of Amsterdam may even have had a surplus of men because of the massive influx of domestic and foreign male migrants, the ratios were reversed from the third quarter of the seventeenth century onward. When the Dutch economy stagnated, Amsterdam ceased to attract male fortune hunters. Around the same time, domestic migration surged on the part of women, especially from the eastern provinces. Known as the 'trek of maidservants' after the young girls from Overijssel and Gelderland that moved to the West in droves to try their luck as maidservants,[59] this trend added to the surplus of women in Amsterdam.

In addition to this deluge of young girls from the provinces, countless able-bodied young men went off to sea. Unlike the Southern Netherlands, the Dutch Republic was an important seafaring nation during the early modern period. In the seventeenth and eighteenth centuries, nearly one million men signed on with the United East India Company, of whom less than half ever returned to their home port. Casualties attributable to the 'Indian leak' were particularly high during the eighteenth century, when the Company's need for staff reached its peak.[60]

Because of the huge surplus of women, the Northern Netherlands had not only a large market for women's clothes but also an urban labour market inundated with unmarried, widowed, and even abandoned women in need of some means of subsistence. After domestic service, making and mending clothes was the most common female occupation. The larger share of the seamstresses in the Western towns, which were the

---

57 Sogner, 1994, p. 11.

58 van de Pol, 1994; van de Pol, 1996, pp. 106-13; van der Woude, 1980, pp. 148-56 and van der Woude, 1994.

59 Stokvis, 1987, p. 143.

60 Although the effects are difficult to compare for the period examined here, the nineteenth-century censuses generally reveal a surplus of women in the Netherlands and a surplus of men in Belgium. In Belgium, 10,000 more women than men were reported in 1846 (2,164,000 and 2,174,000), whereas there were 59,000 more women than men (1,499,000 and 1,558,000) in the Netherlands in 1849. In 1856, the surplus of men in Belgium was 14,000 (2,272,000 men and 2,258,000 women), while the Netherlands had a surplus of 51,000 women in 1859 (1,629,000 men and 1,680,000 women). In 1866 the surplus of men in Belgium reportedly increased to 18,000 (2,420,000 men and 2,408,000 women), whereas the surplus of women equalled 41,000 (1,764,000 men and 1,805,000 women) in the Netherlands in 1869. Considering these figures according to the age groups available on the labour market is more interesting: Belgium had systematically fewer women than men between ages 20 and 50 in 1846 and between 20 and 60 in 1856 and 1866. In the Netherlands,

most affected by the 'trek of maidservants' and the 'Indian leak', is unlikely to have been a coincidence.

In Antwerp, the gender ratios among the adult population may have been still more distorted than in Amsterdam.[61] Relative to the demographic composition of its population, this city had a high rate of seamstresses for the Southern Netherlands in 1796. In Ghent, however, where the surplus of women was among the lowest in the large cities of Flanders, seamstresses had a far smaller market share in 1796.[62]

Demographic discrepancies may be part of the reason for the differences in the supply of women's labour in the garment industry in large cities and small towns. Surpluses of women typically arose in towns and cities: gender ratios were more balanced among the rural adult population. This was attributable less to higher mortality rates among adult men in the cities than to migration by unmarried women and widows to the cities, the trek of maidservants from the East to the highly urbanized province of Holland. Unwed women faced far better subsistence prospects in the cities than in the countryside, where paid work for women was rare. In small towns, where the economies were more similar to the ones in the countryside, surpluses of women tended to be the lowest.[63] The figures for towns in the Southern Netherlands, such as Geraardsbergen or Oudenaarde, the town of Eibergen in Gelderland, and small German towns in the County of Mark, indicate relatively high numbers of tailors in places with few inhabitants (cf. tables 5.1 and 5.2).

Demographic factors, however, were not decisive: after all, a larger supply of female labour in the cities did not necessarily guarantee that they would find employment in the garment industry. In addition to the demographic composition of the urban population, alternative sources of income available to women therefore merit consideration as well.[64] Here, too, the Northern Netherlands differed from the Southern Netherlands.

After 1650, industrial cities in both the Northern and the Southern Netherlands declined because of the erosion of the domestic market and because of export problems. The textile industry nonetheless appears to have adapted to the economic changes more successfully in the Southern than in the Northern Netherlands.[65] During the eighteenth century, the textile industry was restructured to produce mixed fabrics. Women worked in various branches of the textile industry. In addition, lace-making expanded into a major export industry, providing thousands of women with work in

---

on the other hand, women clearly prevailed in all age groups, except for children and young adults under 20. Mitchel, 1975, pp. 19, 22, 30, 43.

61 van de Pol, 1996, p. 108.

62 Verbeemen, 1956, pp. 682-3, 686, 699-700 and table 5.3.

63 Faber, 1972, pp. 70-1; Noordam, 1986, p. 107; Paping, 1995, pp. 54, 194, and Verbeemen, 1956, pp. 691-4.

64 In the previous section we noted the differences in employment in the tailoring trades in the cities identified. Examples include the vast garment industry in national and international fashion centres, such as Paris, Lyon, and Brussels.

65 Lis and Soly, 2000.

many towns and cities in the Southern Netherlands. In Antwerp and Brussels, between 10,000 and 12,000 women — nearly 10 per cent of the total population — worked in the lace industry in 1738.[66] Their numbers increased in silk-weaving as well, whilst in the areas around Doornik and, to a lesser extent, Diest many women were knitting stockings.[67] Beguine courts and nuns' convents in the Southern Netherlands grew significantly as well in the late seventeenth century.[68] These alternatives were obviously not available to women in the Northern Netherlands.

The burgeoning lace and textile industries in the Southern Netherlands may have served as a buffer to absorb the flood of women looking for work from the second half of the seventeenth century onward. Precisely in this period, during which the labour market was under severe pressure as a result of the rising surplus of women, the textile industry was plummeting in Holland. Price competition from England and Liège had led cloth production to be transferred from the towns in Holland to the low wage areas in North Brabant.[69] Moreover, the Haarlem linen industry, which had been the mainstay of Holland's second major textile city since the end of the sixteenth century, declined during the second half of the seventeenth century, probably because of the inexpensive linens from Silesia, Gulik, Brabant, and Flanders. The heyday of the silk industry, a textile branch that began to thrive in the last quarter of the seventeenth century, especially in Amsterdam and Haarlem, was short-lived: protectionist measures from foreign markets brought an end to the prosperity of silk-weaving around 1740. While at the start of the eighteenth century the Haarlem silk industry employed about 10,000 men, women, and children, or approximately one third of the total population, about three quarters of these jobs had disappeared again by the mid-eighteenth century.[70] Women active in the textile industry in Holland therefore had to seek alternative employment. Outside the textile industry, women had few options for performing paid work. Maidservants' positions were the most common type of work for women during the early modern period. Most of those working as maidservants, who received low rates of pay and had little independence, were young, single women. Women were traditionally well-represented in retail as well. As maintaining supply levels in a shop required some capital, the women active here tended to be somewhat older. A great many women's occupations involved the clothing branch.[71] Many women in Holland found that working as washerwomen, knitters, or seamstresses were among their few opportunities for earning a living.

Catharina Lis and Hugo Soly have argued that the different trajectories of export industries in the Northern and Southern Netherlands are attributable in part to differ-

66 Thijs, 1987b, pp. 166-75, 180-2; Lis, 1986, p. 176. See the population figures in table 5.1.

67 Deceulaer, 2001.

68 Simons, 1991, p. 135.

69 de Vries and van der Woude, 1997, pp. 287-8.

70 Mulder, 1995, p. 56

71 van der Woude, 1987, pp. 173-202. Earle, 1989, pp. 328-53.

ences in political power of craft guilds.[72] Guilds did indeed have more administrative input in the Southern than in the Northern Netherlands. In towns and cities in Brabant, guild officials held key political offices until the end of the Ancien Régime. In Brussels, for example, the deans of the craft guilds served on the city council alongside the magistrate and the *Wijde Raad* (Broad Council, a board of former members of the magistrate and officials of the cloth guild, which was like a chamber of commerce). Proposals from the magistrate required a majority of votes from the three sections to be approved.[73] The influence of the Brussels guild deans extended beyond local politics. Indirectly, via the city's seat in the States of Brabant, they even became involved in provincial and national politics.[74] Prior to its incorporation in the Dutch Republic during the first half of the seventeenth century, the guilds in the present Dutch province of Brabant, formerly part of the Duchy of Brabant, figured within the political tradition of craft guilds in the Southern Netherlands as well. In 's-Hertogenbosch, guild deans formed the third section of the city council, serving alongside aldermen and jurors. After the city surrendered to the State troops in 1629, the guilds of 's-Hertogenbosch lost their role in local politics.[75] In the Northern Netherlands during the Dutch Republic, guilds had no political input whatsoever. In the province of Holland, guilds (except in Dordrecht) never even had any political rights. In the provinces of Utrecht and Zeeland, guilds lost any say in politics by the sixteenth century. Only in the province of Gelderland did guilds retain their political influence until well into the eighteenth century. Compared with the guilds in the Southern Netherlands, however, their power was limited: guilds in Gelderland had a say only in the appointment of the magistrate, and even then only via indirect elections. Members of the Zutphen magistrate, for example, were elected by a *college van gemeenslieden* (Common Council), a representation of citizens from the guilds and civic militias.[76]

Political influence might appear to be an important factor in this debate, since the share of seamstresses was so large precisely in the towns and cities in Holland. A more detailed comparative approach, however, reveals that the differences between men's and women's work in the garment industry in the Northern and Southern Netherlands were not — or were hardly — attributable to these different positions of political power. Within the Southern Netherlands, we would logically expect the share of women in the garment industry to be smallest in cities where craft guilds were politically influential, such as Antwerp or Brussels. These cities were the only ones in the Southern Netherlands, however, with substantial numbers of seamstresses. In Ghent, where the craft guilds had very little political say since 1540, there were very few

---

72 Lis and Soly, 1994c.

73 Van Honacker, 1994a, pp. 181-3.

74 Ibidem, p. 187. Lis and Soly, 1997c, p. 231. For a detailed survey of the guilds' political positions in Brabant and Mechelen, see Jacobs, 2000.

75 In 's-Hertogenbosch, guild deans formed the third section of the city council, which also comprised aldermen and jurors. Regarding the role in politics of the guild in 's-Hertogenbosch, see chapters 1 and 5 of van den Heuvel, 1946.

76 On the political influence of the Zutphen guilds, see Frijhoff, 1988.

seamstresses. The same held true for most cities and towns in the County of Flanders, where craft guilds were far less significant in politics than in the Duchy of Brabant. Any explanation focusing on the 'power positions' of craft guilds would obviously need to specify which craft guilds were more powerful than others. While this remains to be determined for the Southern Netherlands, various data indicate that craft guilds in the food industry (brewers, butchers, fishmongers) were very important, as were the mercers.[77] Tailors in the Southern Netherlands do not appear to have been among the most politically influential guilds.

The larger share of men in the garment industry of the 's-Hertogenbosch in the Northern Netherlands (see table 5.2) might relate to the remnants of the traditional social and political glory of craft guilds (until 1629), although the vast lace industry was probably a more important factor in this respect. Unlike neighbouring Dutch towns but like many other Brabant textile cities, 's-Hertogenbosch had major lace-making operations. This branch of industry rose rapidly from the mid-seventeenth century and thrived until well into the eighteenth century. In 1775, nearly 8 per cent of all heads of the household in 's-Hertogenbosch was employed in lace-making, which made the industry one of the largest in the city. The actual number of lace makers was probably far higher, as women who were married or who lived with their parents were not counted in this source.[78]

One possible impact of political structures was noticeable in the small Gelderland town of Zutphen. Here, each individual applicant to the seamstresses' guild was evaluated separately, culminating in a rigid quota of five seamstresses for the entire city in 1755. This modest erosion of the male monopoly on garment production in the mid-eighteenth century, when the political influence of the tailors' guild was declining, is unlikely to have been sheer coincidence. In 1747, the guilds had abandoned their political aspirations by waiving their right to appoint the magistrate to the *stadtholders*. Since the change does not appear to have fundamentally affected gender relations in the industry, the influence of political structures should not be overestimated for the garment industry.

Conclusion

The divergent trajectories in the garment industry in the Northern and Southern Netherlands aptly illustrate how the same economic challenge to the same sector in different regions could elicit entirely different institutional responses, which in turn could affect the way the market operated. Consumption of women's clothing rose every-

---

[77] Aerts, 1996, pp. 115-18; Swevers, 1999, pp. 70-83; Van Elsacker, 2000.

[78] Thanks are due to Maarten Prak for providing this information from his analysis of population records from 1775: GAHt, OA, C 106, Blokboeken 1775.

where in Western Europe from the late seventeenth century onward. In the Southern Netherlands, tailors remained largely in control of garment production, including women's wear, whereas woollen seamstresses started to enlarge their share of the market in the Northern Netherlands from the early eighteenth century. During this century, the number of male tailors per 1,000 inhabitants was therefore higher in the Southern than in the Northern Netherlands. Craft guilds in the industry in the South remained more exclusively male organizations, while in the North corporative membership forms for seamstresses were introduced.

The responses of the tailors' guilds and the seamstresses to economic challenges were clearly influenced by the demographic, economic, social, and cultural contexts of the cities and regions affected. Craft guilds did not have an infinite range of strategies at their disposal and were not free to pursue them in a voluntaristic manner. The measures they took to exclude women, force them to pay dues, or incorporate them depended on specific balances of power, which arose largely beyond their control.[79] On the other hand, once obtained, authorizations to produce clothes or official admissions as guild members could influence market relations in the industry.

Cities in the Northern Netherlands, especially those in the West, had a large surplus of women from the third quarter of the seventeenth century, as male immigration ceased, young men continued to perish at sea, and women kept arriving from the East of the country. Around this time, the urban textile industry in the Northern Netherlands entered a period of decline, and employment opportunities for women dwindled in this branch. This trend coincided with an increased demand for women's clothes, due to the larger share of women in the population, the gradual drop in textile prices (due to the increased use of cheap, lightweight materials), and a stronger awareness of fashions. The restructuring of institutional relationships on the labour market for men and women in many cities in the Northern Netherlands at the time is therefore far from coincidental. While the exact status of seamstresses with respect to tailors' guilds remained unclear throughout much of the seventeenth century, their position was redefined in the late seventeenth and early eighteenth centuries. Various systems were introduced in different cities, ranging from independent guilds for women, through second-class guild membership to dues-paying requirements or a maximum quota. The net result was institutional erosion of the monopoly of the male tailors virtually everywhere. This minor breach was to grow continuously over the course of the eighteenth and nineteenth centuries. Local authorities in the Northern Netherlands were not fiercely protective of guild monopolies, if the consequence was that many women would lose their means of subsistence. Prohibiting women from making clothes would have only increased the difficulties of single women in the Northern Netherlands.

The corporative status that Dutch seamstresses acquired in the late seventeenth or early eighteenth centuries presumably boosted the legitimacy of their products and consequently their market position. During the early modern period, when price

---

[79] 'We should be focusing on what the craft guilds and their members were *compelled* to do by market and institutional pressures, rather than on what they sometimes attempted to impose', Epstein, 1998, p. 705.

mechanisms were just beginning to emerge, guilds mediated between producers and consumers. Prospective members were required to complete their master trial successfully to be admitted to the guild. Guild membership thus guaranteed a minimum standard of quality, thereby boosting consumer confidence in the products of guild members.[80] Trust between producers and consumers was another major factor in the garment industry, as the prices of clothing were based less on wages than on the materials used, which were generally supplied by the customers.[81] Clients would most probably have preferred to entrust their valuable possessions to a proven professional able to use the fabric as efficiently as possible.

Large cities in the Southern Netherlands also had a substantial surplus of women. From the second half of the seventeenth century, however, the decline of the traditional textile industry was compensated by the expanding lace industry, where tens of thousands of women worked to keep body and soul together. In the course of the eighteenth century, moreover, the textile industry was successfully restructured to a low-wage industry that provided many women with work. Male tailors filled most of the increased demand for women's and other types of clothing in the Southern Netherlands. Seamstresses in the South were active primarily in Antwerp and Brussels, in non guild-based market sectors, such as accessories, household linens, fashion dealers, and so on. Excluding seamstresses in the Southern Netherlands from guild membership may have led consumers to question the quality of their products and at any rate did not boost confidence in them.

---

80 Gustafsson, 1991, p. 82.

81 Into the nineteenth century, the ratio of wages to fabric was about 3:1 or even 4:1. See van der Steur, 1991, p. 102.

Chapter 6

Religion and social structure: religious rituals in pre-industrial trade associations in the Low Countries

Alfons K.L. Thijs

From the late Middle Ages onward, many craft guilds had a religious orientation in addition to a social-economic one. Free associations of fellow tradesmen, such as guild brotherhoods and journeymen brotherhoods, even propagated religious worship as their chief mission. Did guild members partake in religious rituals and in some cases invest heavily in material religious infrastructure out of piety alone, or did their actions serve other purposes as well? This question, which has received little consideration so far, is the subject of this chapter. Lacking sufficient preliminary studies, this exercise has to be merely exploratory.

1. Religion in all types of associations

Medieval citizens deeply needed associations. As migrants from the countryside, many felt they had been wrenched from the comfort of familiar surroundings. Eager to escape their isolation as quickly as possible, they joined local networks. Their social integration efforts are part of the reason behind the success of religious brotherhoods established by lay people, formally dedicated to religious worship but often offering conviviality as well. The religious activities of these brotherhoods included setting up and maintaining an altar or even a chapel, as well as organizing religious celebrations, all intended to protect the spiritual welfare of the founders, members, and benefactors.[1]

Sometimes fellow tradesmen united in religious brotherhoods. These organizations differed from the craft guilds in that membership was not compulsory. Sometimes they encouraged people to join through social pressure. In the late thirteenth century, guild brotherhoods existed for at least four occupations in Bruges: curriers, hosiers, shoemakers, and the *pijnders* (transport workers) of the Sint-Jansbrug. Smiths formed religious associations in various towns in Flanders and Brabant in the

[1] Trio, 1993, pp. 340, 342-3.

thirteenth and especially the fourteenth centuries.[2] In Holland brotherhoods of fellow tradesmen arose from the fourteenth century, often preceding the establishment of craft guilds there.[3]

Craft guilds and religious craft brotherhoods often existed alongside one another and were in some cases affiliated. Some craft guilds arose from brotherhoods during the early modern period. The Antwerp retailers of woollen fabrics were approved by the magistrate as a craft guild after they set up an altar in the main church in 1492. They obtained official recognition by arguing that they needed such acknowledgement to maintain the altar, purchase ornaments, and hold religious services. The municipal authorities elevated the pre-corporative organizations of the dyers and the silk weavers to guilds for the same reason in 1521 and 1533, respectively.[4] Most Antwerp craft guilds, however, were economic organizations that enforced the guild regulations for brief or extended periods prior to setting up or sponsoring a religious division or altar. Although guilds had been officially recognized in Antwerp since the beginning of the fourteenth century, and 24 craft guilds joined Our Lady's procession in 1399, guild altars started to be constructed there only in the second half of the fifteenth century. The timing coincided with the heyday of religious congregations. Craft guilds joined the trend, as they realized that altars constructed voluntarily were proof of an organization's vitality and maturity.

The articles of association of craft guilds in Holland — at least the ones preceding the Dutch Revolt and the Reformation — might suggest that craft guilds in the North were dedicated less to social-economic causes and oriented more toward religious rituals than the ones in the Southern Netherlands were. This impression is deceptive, however. In Holland, where craft guilds arose later than in Flanders and Brabant, aspects of corporate organization were more likely to be regulated through municipal inspections than via guild regulations. Accordingly, a relatively large share of the articles of association of the guilds in Holland addressed non-economic affairs.

In 1566, the Iconoclasm that swept the Low Countries deeply affected religious sentiment, which by then had been waning for decades. This eruption of violence destroyed statues, paintings, and even entire altars. In addition to damaging the material infrastructure, it fostered doubt, upheaval, and dissent within the guilds. From the 1570s, the progressive rise of Protestantism eliminated virtually all religious features from the guild system. Shortly before and after 1580 several more guild altars were destroyed in yet another bout of iconoclasm instigated by Calvinist municipal authorities, often in conjunction with guild officials equally sympathetic to religious reform.

In the Southern Netherlands, following the return of Spanish rule in the mid-1580s, the Catholics recovered their authority. Master artisans were required to take an oath of loyalty to the Catholic Church. Corporatist religious rituals were restored. Guild

---

2 Wyffels, 1951, pp. 122-42.

3 Goudriaan, Hulshof, Lourens and Lucassen, 1996, pp. 12, 14.

4 On religious aspects of the guild system in Antwerp, see: Thijs, 1987b, pp. 192-4; Thijs, 1990, pp. 91-6, 117-22; Verleysen, 2001.

altars and chapels were rebuilt as well, often more elaborately than before. In the Northern Netherlands, however, where the Protestants were now largely in control, religious brotherhoods were abolished. Guild altars, as well as other altars, disappeared from the churches no longer used for Roman Catholic worship.

From the late Middle Ages onward, permanent religiously-affiliated organizations were established, whose memberships consisted exclusively of wage workers from a certain occupation and city. They are referred to as *knechtsgilden* in the literature from the Northern Netherlands,[5] whereas they appear as *knapenambachten* in Flemish sources, i.e. journeymen's guilds.[6] A list of occupationally based groups in Ghent from 1337 mentions an association of journeymen blue-dyers in addition to the list of master blue dyers. In the early fifteenth century in Gouda a guild of journeymen brewers joined the procession.[7] In fifteenth-century Ghent journeymen shoemakers and masons had brotherhoods. In Bruges, there were similar organizations of journeymen shoemakers,[8] masons, and mortar carriers, as well as of barge-hands and arms makers and in Antwerp of journeymen shoemakers and tailors. In 1463, journeymen weapon makers in Bruges were authorized by the board of Saint Salvator's Church to dedicate services at the Saint Leodegarius altar. In 1474, Groningen journeymen tailors reached an agreement with their masters concerning the 'wax money' (which replaced the original dues payable in wax) due from journeymen to their guild. In 1490, also in Groningen, journeymen bakers negotiated permission from the bakers' guild to collect money to burn candles in Saint Walburga's Church.[9] In 1502, the Malines city council, at the request of the journeymen and with the consent of the shoemakers' guild, published a decree about funding the services that journeymen shoemakers had arranged at the altar of the Holy Trinity in Saint Rumoldus' Church.[10]

The journeymen weavers' association already operating as Saint Rochus' guild in Amsterdam was authorized by the city council in 1563 to charge both journeymen weavers of woollens and linens a modest monthly fee to cover maintaining the religious services for the Saint Rochus altar at the Heilige Stede (Holy City) chapel. No later information is available because of the Calvinist takeover in Amsterdam in 1578.[11] In other centres in the Northern Netherlands, most journeymen guilds also faded once the Reformation prevailed. After all, one of their original objectives, which was to ensure spiritual welfare, had been eliminated. After the Reformation, material and moral support in the event of sickness and death became the chief objective of the journeymen guilds. This brought them within the scope of the *knechtsbossen*

---

5 Timmer, 1913.

6 Scholliers, 1956, p. 316.

7 The data about Gouda in this contribution are derived from: Goudriaan, Hulshof, Lourens and Lucassen, 1996.

8 Van Quathem, 1996, pp. 78-97.

9 Timmer, 1913, pp. 14-15.

10 Installé, 1989, p. 64.

11 Timmer, 1913, p. 184.

(journeymen boxes), which had existed for some time in several cities as sickness and funeral funds for wage workers.

Their customs of marching in processions, organizing religious services, and reaching collective agreements with craft guilds and municipal authorities proves that journeymen guilds were not illegal or secret societies. The authorities acknowledged or tolerated these organizations, because they helped enforce regulations and were concerned with the social welfare of their members. Employers and political rulers nevertheless experienced assemblies of exclusively wage workers in organizations of their own as a threat to social relations. This concern is apparent in part in the articles that the Middelburg authorities granted the society of journeymen tailors in 1502. The Middelburg authorities feared that the likelihood of 'conspiracy' would increase, if journeymen convened more frequently. Accordingly, they stipulated that journeymen might assemble only on the festival of their patron Saint Laurentius, on Corpus Christi and procession days, and at services commemorating a deceased fellow member.[12] It was feared that in such organizations economic group interests would prevail over moral religious objectives. In 1539 the authorities disbanded an unauthorized 'society' of 40 or 50 journeymen fullers in Bruges. The only stated purpose of this association, however, was an annual pilgrimage to the statue of Our Lady in nearby Meetkerke.[13]

These religiously inspired journeymen guilds never became very numerous. Most such organizations disappeared entirely in the course of the sixteenth century, in the South and the North alike. Their decline was understandable, since religious brotherhoods lost their appeal during the same period. As the Bruges journeymen fullers learned in 1539, the patronage had increasing difficulty tolerating workers who tried to pursue their own course amid rising social tensions.

Only at the end of the seventeenth century did occupationally-based religious associations of skilled wage workers resurface, albeit apparently in only a few cities in the Low Countries.[14] In 1686 in Antwerp the first new journeyman brotherhood was founded: the brotherhood for journeymen shoemakers. Similar journeymen organizations followed for journeymen silk weavers (1698), braid weavers (1722), bakers (1727), linen weavers (1730), tailors (1731), smiths (1737), wood retailers (1761), yarn twisters (before 1763), cobblers (before 1764), and diamond finishers (1778). These journeymen brotherhoods thus emerged both in export-oriented industries (e.g. silk weaving or diamond finishing) and in those serving local markets (e.g. baking and repairing shoes). During the eighteenth century in Louvain, confraternities existed for journeymen shoemakers, slaters, and carpenters. Each of these groups had its own patron saint. They were founded in keeping with the longstanding interest among craft guilds in their patron saint. While these journeymen brotherhoods lacked the financial

---

12 Timmer, 1913, pp. 187-8.

13 Thijs, 1994, pp. 232-6.

14 On these journeymen's organizations, see: Thijs, 1994, pp. 237-67.

resources to build and maintain their own chapel or altar, they tried to have their mass performed at the same house of prayer each year, making this hallowed area a part of their group identity.

The new journeymen organizations differed from the late medieval and sixteenth-century journeymen guilds. They restricted their activities to organizing religious celebrations and leisure activities, such as meals and balls. They left all technical and organizational aspects of their industry to the craft guild (to which their members belonged as journeymen). The social function made these movements particularly appealing. Many workers deeply needed a circle that would organize banquets, dances, or other secular festivities. They lacked the wealth to partake in the festivities of drama societies, marksmen associations, or other leisure associations of the upper classes.

These journeymen brotherhoods are not known to have had any organizational involvement in social conflicts. Few provided for needy members. This remained the responsibility of specialized boxes for the indigent and the infirm. Only a few of the Antwerp journeymen brotherhoods became mutual aid associations after many years. Among them were the journeymen shoemakers (1792) and the journeymen linen weavers (1812).

Several guild movements maintained a special box for the indigent and the infirm by the fifteenth century.[15] In the Northern Netherlands such boxes became more widespread following the Reformation. In Amsterdam after 1578, as ordered by the city council, several craft guilds set up boxes for the indigent, funding them with revenues previously used for the guild altar and religious celebrations.[16] The earliest mutual aid associations helped masters and journeymen alike. During the sixteenth century this solidarity eroded. Many mutual aid associations admitted masters only. Groups of skilled wage workers therefore set up special boxes for the infirm without any organizational ties to a guild during the seventeenth century. Especially during the economic depression at the start of the eighteenth century, these autonomous boxes for the infirm increased in number.[17] Most served both the deceased and the living by making decent burials possible for their members. In the Southern Netherlands these occasions coincided with mass, at which those managing poor boxes encouraged their members to worship the patron saint. Quite a few of these workers' mutual aid associations long survived the changes in regime from the end of the eighteenth century, albeit in some cases as 'combined' mutual aid associations, as financial need compelled them to admit masters as well. Only from the mid-nineteenth century did mutual aid associations in Belgium become more secularized and abandon Christian rituals as a result of the growing influence of the progressive-liberal bourgeoisie.[18]

---

15 On Flanders and Brabant, see: Huys, 1926.

16 de Ridder, 1994, pp. 108-9.

17 Posthumus, 1939, pp. 871-2.

18 Thijs, 1994, p. 251-67.

2. Legacy from the late Middle Ages: investing in religion

During the late Middle Ages, craft guilds, craft brotherhoods, and journeymen's guilds held a splendid mass in honour of their patron saint at least once a year (often in addition to regular weekly or even daily masses). They sought to please their saint, in the hope that he in turn would help and protect both the organization and its members.[19] Those present at the mass often listened to a eulogy of the saint. In many cases they received a print depicting the patron saint during the offering as a keepsake. After the service morality plays would be performed by some craft guilds, such as the surgeons' guilds of Middelburg and Veere.[20]

The festive service on the saint's day was followed by a 'gaily repast' (a *teerfeest* or annual dinner) for a select group. In some craft guilds only masters and their wives were invited to this event, while in others journeymen joined their masters. Those who where entitled to attend but did not participate were fined or charged the cost of a meal. Apprentices were not invited. In this manner the feast clearly reinforced the existing hierarchy and taught apprentices that they were not yet full-fledged members. In craft guilds with large memberships only the officials attended the joint banquets. Ordinary members (and in some cases apprentices as well), however, were allowed to collect food during the 'mass day' at the expense of the corporation upon presentation of a specially minted guild penny. Such meals often consisted of peas or rice pudding.

The rising tensions between masters and workers and the dichotomy between Catholics and Protestants sorely tried the spirit of solidarity during the sixteenth century. Nonetheless, celebrations continued, as everybody understood that eating, drinking, and making merry together were the best way to activate and reinforce the sense of solidarity and collective self-awareness within the organization. Organizers and participants alike used the festivity to highlight three important aspects of their group's — idealized — self-image: unity, internal hierarchy, and seclusion. They may not have been fully aware that their celebrations also helped them to pass on old customs and learn new ones. Traditions are so obvious that those practising them do not contemplate their deeper meaning. This 'self-evidence' conceals the festivity's quality of indoctrination and impact on attitudes and views among individuals and groups.

At first banquets were often served in the church itself. The repast was laid out in front of the altar.[21] Guild members regarded the altar as the actual domicile of their organization and in many cases stored their records there in addition to the ritual objects. General assemblies and elections of officials often took place at the guild altar. Some craft guilds recruited journeymen there as well. Over the course of the sixteenth

---

19 Many specific details about religious rituals in craft guilds of the Southern Netherlands are provided by Allossery, 1926, pp. 190-219. On the religious aspects of craft life in the Northern Netherlands, see Brouwer Ancher, 1895, p. 221-44; Bos, 1998, pp. 44-5.

20 van Andel, 1946, pp. 41-2.

21 Verschelde, 1863, p. 270.

century, however, the ecclesiastical hierarchy resisted all this. Combining profane customs with religious traditions became unacceptable, as the religious establishment had come to consider religion to be absolute and separate.

The day after the *teerfeest,* a requiem was held for the salvation of deceased members. This mass annually revived the bond of solidarity between the living and the dead. The prayers of the living were supposed to help release the deceased from purgatory as soon as possible. Affluent members bequeathed vast sums to pay priests for conducting series of masses. Most guild members, however, could not personally afford such luxuries or could pay for them only very rarely. Collective masses of the guild or fraternity were therefore of paramount importance to them. As a type of memorial, these occasions reminded the organization each year of its 'history': a 'possession' shared among all those concerned and enhancing group cohesion.

The mass in honour of the patron saint, the subsequent common meal, and the requiem mass were the highlights in the annual calender of each of these organizations. They confirmed the sense of solidarity among soul mates and reminded insiders and outsiders alike that the group was unique. Those concerned were very protective of these rituals, out of respect for their religious-magical aspects and especially because they guaranteed a continuity of social relations. In addition to the actual event, the preparations were also important for the group's cohesion. After all, a great many members worked closely together to plan and execute these occasions.

Mobilizing all or some of the members, dressed up to the nines, enabled corporations to make funerals solemn occasions. Corporations also provided a funeral escutcheon as well as a pall or shroud, featuring their insignia. On the day of the funeral of one of their members, several craft guilds had customarily delivered bread to the city's poor through bread tokens specially minted for this purpose, just as affluent families did at such events. These actions were considered important for the corporation's prestige. The gratitude of the family and friends of the deceased that these efforts elicited moreover reinforced group cohesion.

To ascertain whether all those supposed to participate were indeed present, corporations had their aids distribute attendance or identification badges in advance upon 'announcing' the death. These badges indicated the name of the holder and were to be returned to the guild's aid during the ceremony.

In a few cities craft guilds owned a common grave in the church: in Gouda, for example, this was the case for the shoemakers' and the basket and hamper makers' guilds in the fifteenth century. In Dordrecht such graves remained in use through the end of the nineteenth century.[22] Burial in the guild grave was usually restricted to officials, as a token of distinction with respect to the ordinary members. In Ghent the weavers were authorized in 1376 to arrange their own graveyard next to their chapel to bury their poor.[23]

---

22 Palmen, 1998, pp. 226-31.

23 Allossery, 1926, pp. 203, 214-15.

In the sixteenth century, in keeping with the established custom, some craft guilds would embark on a joint pilgrimage year after year to a pilgrimage site near their city. Until about 1511-1512, the Bruges fullers' guild (journeymen and masters alike) made annual pilgrimages to Our Lady in Meetkerke. The Bruges glove makers went on an annual trek to Oudenburg to bring a mantle to the statue of the Holy Virgin Mary there. The Bruges master coopers visited Our Lady in Ruiselede.[24]

These pilgrimages were more than mere expressions of devotion and had very worldly attributes. Presenting a mantle to the Holy Virgin in Oudenburg was, according to the late sixteenth-century author Zeghere van Male, merely a pretext for the Bruges glove makers to make merry. The joint pilgrimages that members of some craft guilds made greatly enhanced the sense of cohesion and identity of the participants thanks primarily to the drinking sprees that followed.

Each year the Bruges brewers travelled to Oudenburg to bear the reliquary of Saint Arnold in the procession. The Bruges journeymen coopers joined the circumambulation in Dudzele honouring Saint Leonard. Until 1527 the Antwerp mercers' guild (a corporation consisting largely of retailers) sent a large delegation, sometimes consisting of 125 members, to Merksem each year to carry the statue of Saint Ontcommer [Wilgefortis] in the procession. The Antwerp woodcutters had the privilege of carrying the reliquary of their patron Saint Gummarus in the procession in Lier, with accompanying torches.

Groups of craft guilds, craft brotherhoods, and some journeymen's guilds were especially likely to join processions and other religious parades organized by ecclesiastical and secular bodies in their home town. The different corporations were easy to recognize by the specific guild costumes (liveries) that their members wore on such occasions. Craft guilds were sometimes requested by the municipal authorities to perform a brief play or pantomime in the procession. According to their guild letter of 1486, the millers in Gouda displayed a working treadmill and Saint Victor, their patron saint. Sometimes only the officials marched in a parade. The deans of affluent craft guilds were particularly striking to behold. Wearing costly chains around their necks, armed with a decorated rod and bearing banners, signs, and torches, they commanded respect both as individuals and as representatives of an organization. Many ordinary members found participation tedious, and absenteeism became an increasingly serious problem in the course of the sixteenth century. This was attributable not only to the Reformation. In a city such as Gouda, which remained Catholic until the late sixteenth century, the municipal authorities issued decrees compelling guild members to participate. Whenever groups were assigned a special role in the parade, however, members would regard participating as a privilege and respond with greater enthusiasm. The shoemakers' guild in Ronse, for example, refused to surrender its exclusive right to carry the reliquary of Saint Hermes around the city.

The splendour of processions and religious celebrations was intended both to honour God and His saints and to enhance the local social prestige of the group and —

---

[24] Thijs, 1994, pp. 231-7.

indirectly — its members. Participants in processions marched in a specific sequence determined historically according to prestige, social status, and political influence. The great value that the corporations attributed to this reflection of the hierarchically structured urban society is apparent from the conflicts that consistently arose whenever a group tried to claim more glory than was its traditional due.

3. Changing times: The Northern Netherlands after the Dutch Revolt

When the Calvinists seized power around 1580, they largely eliminated the role of religion in the repertoire of associations in the Northern Netherlands. This was not the case in the Southern Netherlands, where Catholicism, due to the changing fortunes of war, started to prevail again from the 1580s.

The disappearance of guild altars from the houses of prayer and the definitive suspension of public Roman Catholic services (and therefore of religious celebrations of patron saints) in the Northern Netherlands did not mean that patron saints vanished from the collective memory of guild members there. Most corporations named after saints retained their name. Even without dedicated religious services, they continued to depict the old and trusted patron saint on their blazons, coffers, or other items of value. The rope makers' guild in Gouda had an oil painting made in 1663 featuring Saint Paul, the guild's patron saint prior to the Reformation. The 'box' of the same city's journeymen potters had a likeness of Saint Barbara painted on the side as late as 1667. After the painters and glass painters of Zwolle seceded from Saint Luke's guild in 1652, they placed their new organization under the patronage of Saint Bartholomew.[25] Into the first half of the eighteenth century, the butchers of 's-Hertogenbosch celebrated mass in honour of their patron Saint Nicholas, followed the next day by a requiem for deceased guild brothers.[26]

After the Reformation, the Amsterdam tailors refused to present their guild accounts on the usual date (the festival of Saint John the Baptist) anymore and switched to an arbitrary date (1 October) not dedicated to the previous patron saint.[27] Most corporations in the Northern Netherlands, however, continued to observe their traditional annual day of reckoning (and of festivities). In Dordrecht the hawkers' guild is known to have distributed bread to the city poor on 6 December, the day of its patron saint, St. Nicholas, until 1679.[28] Into the early nineteenth century in Amsterdam, the annual guild dues payable by members were known as the *jaarzang*, literally: annual song, a term reminiscent of the special celebratory songs customary at the masses of patron saints before the Dutch Revolt.[29]

---

25 Hoogewerff, 1947, pp. 69-70.

26 Prak, 1992, p. 71.

27 van Eeghen, 1965, p. 44.

28 Palmen, 1998, p. 228.

29 ter Gouw, 1866-1942, pp. 27-8.

In the 1630s Saint Luke's guild of Haarlem tried to reclaim its relic of Saint Luke, which was in the possession of individuals in Brussels. The officials informed the urban magistrate (truthfully or otherwise) that their demand for the return of the relic was not based on Catholic superstition. As good Haarlem citizens, they maintained, they simply could not tolerate unlawful transfer of traditional Haarlem property into the hands of unauthorized individuals.[30] Such events reveal the enormous value that many craft guilds associated with having their 'own' corporative patron saint, even in a setting where saint worship was frowned upon by Calvinist sentiment. This collective attachment to patron saints was attributable in part to the ongoing considerable Catholic membership of several corporations. Most Dutch craft guilds, at least in the western provinces of the Republic, admitted Catholics and Protestants alike, although they did not always allow Catholics to hold offices.

The second reason was the tremendous reluctance during the Ancien Régime to break with longstanding traditions. Customs handed down from one generation to the next legitimized group actions. When journeymen shoemakers in Groningen redrafted their 'roll' (the regulations of their organization) in 1606 and 1730, they acted as if public masses could still be read.[31] The regulations therefore continued to reflect the now pointless stipulations about Catholic celebrations. The journeymen shoemakers seemed to fear that blatant registration of a break with tradition would automatically jeopardize the legality of their organization as a whole.

Patron saints were so firmly embedded in the spirits of guild members because for centuries they had been crucial to the identity of the group entrusted to their protection.[32] These saints (nearly always the same ones for the same occupation) were regarded both by an ample share of the population and by the members themselves as specific and consequently as typical of the occupation concerned. Everybody knew, for example, that Saint Eligius was the patron saint of metal workers. By unanimously recognizing the same saint as their patron and propagating his name and likeness as the group's identifying symbol, members distinguished themselves collectively from their fellow citizens. Even non-denominational mutual aid associations founded in the second half of the nineteenth century needed a symbolic 'patron' for their social identity, albeit a profane historical figure by this time. As had been the case with saints, this hero (often a famous deceased fellow tradesman) was selected with the intention of having his prestige and fame rub off on the group that bore his name.

Even after the Dutch Revolt, most regulations of craft guilds in the Northern Netherlands and journeymen boxes stipulated mandatory attendance of funerals of deceased fellow members or their spouses.[33] After all, failure to provide a member with a 'decent' burial would tarnish the reputation of the corporation as a whole. The regulations therefore imposed fines on those not heeding the summons to appear

---

30 Hoogewerff, 1947, pp. 122-3.

31 Timmer, 1913, pp. 15-16.

32 On the significance of patron saints for group identity, see: Mory, 1981, and Mory, 1982.

33 Brouwer Ancher, 1895, pp. 244-9; Bos, 1998, p. 67.

dressed in mourning and join the other members to pay last respects to the deceased by accompanying the coffin covered with the pall and the guild insignia to the cemetery. Stripped of all religious significance (Protestants did not believe in purgatory), however, attendance at these funerals diminished progressively. Guild members often preferred paying the fine to 'wasting' valuable hours. As early as the seventeenth century, Amsterdam book printers and sellers could pay an annual waiver to purchase exemptions from funeral attendance.[34]

Especially during the eighteenth century, wealthy surviving relatives often refused to let the deceased be buried by his craft guild, because such interment was no longer considered to be dignified. Many guilds tolerated this deviation from tradition in return for a hefty payment.[35] Collective requiems to commemorate deceased guild members obviously ceased after the Reformation.

4. Corporative religion in the Southern Netherlands following the restoration of Catholic rule

Once Spanish rule was fully restored in the Southern Netherlands, the Catholic Church launched a major offensive, not only against Protestantism, but also against shortcomings within its own religious community. Leading Catholics, whether members of the clergy or lay people, made a concerted effort to institute reforms within the church. In 1565 the decrees of the Council of Trent (1545-1563) were published with a royal *imprimatur*. Only after the troubles ended, though, were they truly enforced. The Counter Reformation Church received major support from the secular rulers, who were convinced that having all their subjects practise one and the same faith would make their regime more stable.

Immediately after the expulsion of the Protestant rulers, municipal authorities officially ordered the craft guilds to rebuild the destroyed altars and to adorn them with the required ornaments and ritual items. They hoped, as did the clergy, that the corporations would provide cohesive support for Catholic worship. The guild boards, which had been purged of Calvinists as much as possible following instructions from the political authorities, did their best to comply with this order. Rebuilding the altars, however, did not happen overnight. Part of the reason was the guilds' tenuous financial situation during the years of economic upheaval that followed those of religious turmoil. Subsequent generations gradually gathered and rebuilt what they could the destruction left behind by the iconoclasts. Repairing the damage in a few short years was quite a challenge. Moreover, some members who had converted back to Catholicism merely for the sake of appearances refused to share the cost of the altars. The haste of the Antwerp silk-weavers' guild to rebuild their altar is at first sight remarkable. The reason was that the officials of this craft guild hoped the move would alleviate the suspicion on the part of the authorities toward the silk weavers. After all, prior

[34] van Eeghen, 1965, p. 114.

[35] Brouwer Ancher, 1895, pp. 244-9; van Eeghen, 1965, p. 36.

to the Spanish takeover, these guild members had predominantly supported Reform. In 1588, the deans invoked their efforts to restore the altar to prove that they were indeed 'loyal' Catholics.

Rarely did craft guilds build altars anymore without being urged or compelled to do so by clerical or secular authorities. This was very different from the practices during the heyday of religious community life in the fifteenth century. Groups volunteering to construct an altar were now sure to be motivated as much by material concerns. In 1597, the Antwerp tinsmiths asked the municipal authorities for permission to separate from the mercers' guild, promising that they would build their own altar. The Antwerp cloth dyers, whose corporation had been abolished by the city council in 1583, also promised they would maintain an altar if they were allowed to form a guild again.

Despite this lack of zeal on the part of most craft guilds to fund the material infrastructure for religious services, several corporations built extremely valuable and artistic altars during the Counter Reformation. They were motivated by a longing for respectability and the latent envy between the various corporations. Hoping that this competition would lead to ever more beautiful altars in the churches, the local clergy capitalized on this human shortcoming. In 1644, the priest at Saint George's Church in Antwerp asked the braid weavers' guild to renovate their altar in marble, as, he explained, craft guilds of similar importance had already done. The role of this Church-imposed competition in driving up the costs of constructing the altars is obvious.

Every priest wanted as many guild altars in his church as possible, as these altars enhanced the prestige, image, and of course revenues of his house of prayer. In 1603, when the Antwerp fishmongers wanted to transfer their altar from the cathedral to the Saint Walpurgis Church on the waterfront, the cathedral chapter denied their request. Likewise, the Antwerp silversmiths were prohibited from removing their altar from the main church in 1612, as were the dyers in 1613.

In some cases the quest for social prestige prevailed over piety. In 1625 the Antwerp carpenters' guild decided to have masses performed only on important Sundays (instead of on all Sundays and holidays). The members hoped that these cuts would enable them to purchase new ornaments for the guild altar. The same guild had an altarpiece painted in 1640: 'the wedding of the Holy Virgin and Saint Joseph', consisting largely of portraits of the board members and listing their names. This blatant mixture of piety and mortal vanity violated a regulation that the provincial synod in Malines had passed in 1607, stipulating that no likenesses of living individuals were to appear on the central panel of altarpieces. In 1628 affluent Antwerp silk weavers donated small copper pillars to seclude the guild chapel in Saint Jacob's Church. Was the gift a sign of piety? Perhaps, although some found it far more indicative of vanity. The herald at arms, who supervised compliance with heraldic regulations, imposed sanctions on several of these 'moderate' donors for applying blazons and helmet insignia on the pilasters, for which as non-aristocrats they lacked the authority.[36]

---

[36] Inscriptions funéraires et monumentales de la province d'Anvers. Arrondissement d'Anvers, vol. 2, 1863, pp. 245-7.

In the second half of the seventeenth century various craft guilds replaced simple structures from the late sixteenth and early seventeenth centuries with costly new-style portico altars. Once again, they were partly motivated by a quest for prestige. Guild members funded impressive constructions to demonstrate their financial means despite the dismal economic circumstances. On the verge of impoverishment and social degradation, they hoped such actions would earn them the respect of their fellow citizens. The well-known practice among the devout of spending more time and money on religion in periods of crisis must have influenced the spending habits of these craft guilds as well.

Like in the North, patron saints were obviously crucial in the identity of trade associations in the 'Catholic' South. Craft guilds only reluctantly obeyed the demand of the Counter Reformation clergy to feature a figure of Christ or a New Testament scene on the centre panels of new altars. The prints they produced for distribution during the offering at masses for their patron saint, or paper pennants to carry in the procession did not bear figures of Christ but (sometimes hagiographically questionable) depictions of their patron saint. This was also the case with the eighteenth-century religious prints of the journeymen brotherhoods. Guild members refused to allow the religious hierarchy, in its elitist quest for more internalized and less popular-devotional worship, to extend its controlling and steering influence to guild graphics. These engravings continued to manifest their attachment to their patron saint and the related legends.[37] Their popular-religious views received support from many lower-ranking and more pragmatic members of the clergy, keenly aware that ordinary believers were not ready for the arguments of erudite but unworldly theologians that saints were heroes to be emulated rather than patron saints that would solve problems and avert evil.

In the sixteenth century, pilgrimages caused an uproar both among Protestants and among 'righteous' Catholics, due to the turmoil that often coincided with them. Nonetheless, some corporations continued to venerate patron saints in this manner. From 1594, the Bruges coopers (presumably both masters and journeymen at the time) joined the procession honouring Saint Leonard of Dudzele. From 1624, they travelled to Ruislede, after the parish priest followed instructions from his bishop and invited them to march in the procession in honour of Our Lady of the Seven Sorrows, as the master coopers had once done. In 1631, at the urging of Archduchess Isabella, the brotherhood of Saint Guy was established for coachmen and valets of the court, which later came to include the coachmen of Brussels as well. Every year on the third day of Whit, hoping that Saint Guy would protect the horses from illness, members of this fraternity would attend a mass conducted at Saint Eligius and Saint Guy's chapel at the Zavel Church in Brussels, after which they marched in procession to Saint Peter and Saint Guy's Church in Anderlecht.[38] Until 1823, the Brussels meat carvers joined

---

37 On religious prints distributed by corporations, see: Thijs, 1993b, pp. 13-15, 90-5; Thijs, 1997.

38 Van den Berghe, 1938, p. 68.

the annual pilgrimage to Our Lady in Alsemberg. In 1780, their craft guild brought along an ingenious throne for the miraculous statue.[39]

The Episcopal order regarding Ruiselede and Isabella's involvement in the brotherhood of coachmen were part of the 're-Christening offensive' of the ecclesiastical and secular authorities, in which pilgrimages (dismissed by the Protestants as 'superstition') were an essential element.[40] All things considered, however, few occupationally based groups are known to have made pilgrimages together after the Dutch Revolt. The experience had become less enjoyable. Following the doctrinal renovation by Trent, the Catholic Church (as well as the secular governments) decided that devotion was incompatible with merrymaking. Gorging oneself in church after services, as the Bruges master coopers used to do in Ruiselede, was no longer acceptable.

In purging everything they regarded as profane from religious worship, however, the ecclesiastical authorities destroyed much of what had appealed to a great many masters and journeymen about the religion-based celebrations of the corporations. Many ordinary Catholics never grew accustomed to this more rigid form of religious worship. Even in 1777, the bishop of Antwerp complained that many regarded the feasts of patron saints as cause for spending the rest of the day, as well as the following night, imbibing excessively and engaging in 'lascivious' activities.[41] In Malines riotous guild members paraded the streets dressed up as their patron saint on such days. Parodying processions, others would march through town pulling a cart with a statue of the saint. As late as the nineteenth century, apprentices of shoemakers, smiths, and wood carvers continued to honour this tradition in Malines.[42]

The ecclesiastical hierarchy also believed that profane theatre could easily degenerate into a 'lascivious' experience. In the eighteenth century, however, it was unable to avert the rise in several Flemish cities and villages of amateur actor companies. Some of these local drama societies consisted of fellow tradesmen. Shoemakers appear to have been especially eager to stage performances (in Anzegem, Belle, Sint-Niklaas, and Tielt), although there were also societies of cobblers (Lier), butchers (Ghent), fishmongers (Ghent), smiths (Tongeren), and weavers (Etikhove and Ronse). Some drama groups comprised both masters and journeymen (e.g. in Anzegem in 1779), while others consisted exclusively of journeymen (Tielt in 1756). Most of the plays performed by shoemakers were about their patron saints Crispin and Crispinian.[43]

---

39 Devast, 1934, p. 25.

40 Thijs, 1996, pp. 273-81.

41 Wellens, 1784, p. 69.

42 Allossery, 1926, p. 200; Foncke, 1968, pp. 14-22.

43 Huyghebaert, 1998, pp. 368-70.

Conclusion: the functionality of religious rituals

After the Dutch Revolt, several craft guilds in the Southern Netherlands intervened more frequently against members shirking membership-related religious commitments. Many members no longer appeared at funeral ceremonies, stopped marching in processions, and even declined to attend masses honouring their patron saint. Such misdemeanours were subject to penalties, and municipal regulations regularly reminded guild members of their obligations. All for naught. In 1610, members of the Antwerp tailors' guild refused to pay the fines imposed. They argued that the relevant stipulations from 1456 had lapsed into disuse since the Calvinist regime. The rift in religious practices during the turmoil had indeed irreparably damaged the religious attributes of the guild system. This disinclination could even extend beyond individual members to include an entire corporation. In 1643, the smiths of Turnhout refused to attend a mass honouring their patron Saint Eligius on the grounds that they preferred to spend their day off indulging in worldly pleasures. They did, however, defy the clergy's prohibition by ringing the church bells to remind everybody that it was the festival of smiths.[44] This was how they rebelled against the authoritarian Counter Reformation Church that continuously infringed upon the guild system's recreational-religious and popular-devotional traditions.

This definitely did not mean that guild members in the Southern Netherlands had abandoned religion in the seventeenth century or merely paid lip service to religious worship in their private lives. Many joined all kinds of non-occupationally based religious brotherhoods. The Marian confraternities, founded by the Jesuits, for example, were far better equipped to offer spiritual guidance than corporations were.[45] Their efforts were supervised by specially trained fathers. Corporations, on the other hand, had to commission priests, who were responsible only for performing masses. The ecclesiastical hierarchy had moreover made the officially purely religious confraternities particularly attractive by liberally distributing indulgences in return for membership.

Little wonder, therefore, that guild members turned to these 'specialized' and 'pure' religious brotherhoods for spiritual relief. They rightly viewed their craft guilds as organizations intended primarily to handle material issues rather than spiritual ones. The secular clergy wanted believers to participate in the rituals of their own parish whenever possible. Accordingly, they made little effort to convince guild members to practise their faith in occupational organizations with a scope that extended beyond the parish framework.

The decline of religion in the craft guilds even in the Southern Netherlands, despite the political 'victory' of Catholicism there, was also the outcome of rising social tensions within many corporations. These tensions made it very difficult indeed for

[44] Van Autenboer, 1983, p. 557.

[45] Thijs, 1990, pp. 81-4; Châtellier, 1987.

these organizations to inspire religious devotion among their members.[46] They became increasingly sensitive to the financial cost associated with each of the religious rituals. Craft guilds in financial difficulties (usually as a result of squandering money) that had to dispose of some of their assets would usually sell religious objects first. In the eighteenth century, for example, some corporations sold their showpieces from processions.[47]

Considering the above, it would appear incomprehensible that journeymen continued to found religious brotherhoods in the late seventeenth and eighteenth centuries, and that the mutual aid associations of the journeymen had the time and money for religious celebrations. The explanation is in fact simple. Marginalized within craft guilds and aware that social advancement, especially in a time of economic decline, was out of the question, the workers sought comfort and compensation in religious practices that they themselves directed. 'Illustrious' religious ceremonies were moreover intended to provide them with a measure of social prestige. Coping with material shortages in their personal lives, the journeymen hoped their organizations would achieve an impact directly proportionate to the money that they invested collectively in their 'own' religious celebrations.

Purely religious confraternities, such as the Marian fraternitites, experienced a steady decline in membership from the 1680s onward. During that same period new journeymen brotherhoods dedicated to recreation and piety alike thrived. Since the Counter Reformation movement had abated in the mid-seventeenth century, confraternities obviously needed to offer more than religious celebrations to attract adherents.

In their desperate quest for respectability, journeymen, as skilled workers, manifested great piety to set themselves apart from the 'godless' lower ranks of the population. Yearning for prestige, they tried to copy the customs of more select religious organizations in their repertoire. Emulating the 'pure' religious brotherhoods, they meticulously kept 'yearbooks', in which they recorded the names of their board members in ornate script each year, often featuring artful illustrations. Like the other confraternities, journeymen brotherhoods honoured those celebrating their fiftieth anniversary as members with solemn masses and festive gatherings, where specially composed poems were often recited.

Compensating for their lack of social prestige through collective religious worship probably withheld these journeymen from engaging in more active social struggle. It can hardly have been a coincidence that the only group of skilled workers in Antwerp with a strong social resilience during the seventeenth and eighteenth centuries, i.e. the journeymen hat makers, never formed a religious brotherhood. As participants in a vast network of journeymen associations from their occupational field, journeymen hat makers coped with their sense of deprivation through profane means, such

---

46 Guild deans understood how delicate the balance within their organization often was. In songs and poems, featured at their best during the festivals of patron saints, they would emphasize (genuine or purported) good relations among members, as well as their own dedication.

47 Van Buyten, 1993, p. 354.

as strikes and other actions against their employers. Despite being men of faith, they relied on themselves and their organization to resolve social problems rather than on God and His saints and did not settle for a mere symbolic resistance to the progressive social decline.

The prominence of religious rituals in the collective repertoire of guild members from the Southern and — until the late sixteenth century — the Northern Netherlands is remarkable. This pattern was not exceptional and was widespread throughout the corporate world in the 'Catholic' areas. The perpetuation of this religious practice over the centuries was largely but not exclusively attributable to the strength of religious faith among the guild members concerned. The quest for a separate group identity and internal hierarchy and cohesion, as well as for a prestige within the urban community, also led those in privileged occupations to invest heavily in symbolic capital by establishing and maintaining altars and chapels and by organizing religious celebrations. At least as far as the craft guilds are concerned, regular pressure from the ecclesiastical and religious rituals since the end of the sixteenth century is known to have come into play as well. Conversely, the Calvinist prohibition on Catholic celebrations in public virtually eliminated religious rituals from the guild system in the Northern Netherlands by the end of the sixteenth century. The available data indicate that corporation members put up little resistance. Nonetheless, a substantial share of the population in the Northern Netherlands (and presumably of the artisans organized in guilds as well) is known to have defied the Calvinist regime and to have remained loyal to Catholicism.

Traditional customs are very difficult for authorities to eliminate. If repressed, these customs will adapt to the new circumstances and will become covert in the worst case. They will disappear only once they are no longer of use to those keeping the tradition. And indeed, investments in Catholic rituals lost all functional significance within corporatism in the Northern Netherlands — even for Roman Catholic artisans — once the Calvinists assumed power following the Dutch Revolt. They no longer generated prestige. Advocating 'papal pranks' would merely instigate division within the by then ideologically heterogeneous corporations and poison relations with the Calvinist authorities. Catholics soon turned out to have other facilities for spiritual guidance: they opened conventicles, for which they did not require craft guilds. The one element from the Catholic past of the craft guilds that persisted in the Northern Netherlands, with the consent of the Protestant members and in many cases until the disappearance of corporatism itself, was the reference to the patron saint in the name of the organization. The need for a symbolic figure embodying the group identity ultimately prevailed, even in the face of Calvinist abhorrence of Catholic 'superstitions'.

Chapter 7

A tradition of giving and receiving: mutual aid within the guild system

Sandra Bos

Introduction

In 1792 Martinus Schruijders, 'a former master tailor and resident burgher' of 's-Hertogenbosch, submitted a petition to the municipal authorities in which he asserted that nobody had contributed one penny a week to the guild box longer than he. The guild box was the fund from which the guild paid benefits to members no longer able to earn a living due to sickness or old age. Schruijders was one of these members: in addition to being very old, he was deaf, blind, and lame. He had been in this state for a long time, since the chart attached indicated that he had been collecting regular benefits from the guild since 1776. He had received over 500 guilders altogether. This sum, he complained, was over 300 guilders less than the amount to which he was entitled.[1] The shortfall was undoubtedly attributable to the longstanding financial difficulties of the tailors' box. Back in 1760, benefits for the elderly had been discontinued, from 1775 the ill were required to present a statement from a physician to be eligible for benefits, and in 1784 the benefits were reduced.[2] Schruijders' situation was an example of social benefits in the guild system. Guilds tried to maintain collective provisions for their members but constantly encountered the problems inherent in insuring small populations.

Mutual aid for and by the members has figured among the guilds' responsibilities from the outset.[3] In some provinces and towns this aid came to be regulated early on, in others it long remained informal. The 'insurance system' thus existed to varying degrees. As with all guild duties, however, mutual aid services varied widely among

1 's-Hertogenbosch municipal archive, Oud Archief, A 319: letters and reports, 5 September 1792.

2 's-Hertogenbosch municipal archive, Oud Archief, A 148: resolutions, 29 March 1775 (sheet 124r); A 311: letters and reports, 4 February 1784. Also see Prak, 1999, pp. 101-3.

3 The material concerning the Northern Netherlands in this study is derived from Bos, 1998. No current study on the Southern Netherlands is available, although the work and partial source publication by Huys, 1926, proved very useful.

guilds and cities and consequently differed between the Northern and Southern Netherlands. This diversity of mutual aid systems complicates comparing these two areas. In this chapter we shall nonetheless attempt a preliminary comparison of mutual aid services provided by guilds and journeymen's associations in the Northern and Southern Netherlands based on several local guild studies. This contribution revolves around the basic questions: what did the aid from guilds and journeymen's associations comprise, and how did it evolve? The chapter will also explore the differences within the insurance system of the early modern guild associations. What was the role of religion, municipal administration, and economic prosperity in the emergence of this system?

Sources are few and far between for the period in which the aid was informal and non-monetary. Support was issued primarily based on oral agreements, ad hoc collections, spontaneous generosity, and brotherly compassion. This complicates assessing the first forms of mutual aid. The establishment of separate guild-based boxes for the poor and sickness and burial funds — in the fourteenth and fifteenth centuries in the South and about a century later in the North — and the corresponding regulations and bookkeeping gave an increasingly clear impression of corporative relief services, until around 1820, when guild-based mutual funds ceased to exist in the Netherlands.

1. Guilds, guild brothers, and their self-help organizations

Guild brothers were artisans who supported themselves through manual labour. Sickness, invalidity, old age, and unemployment therefore meant loss of income and eventually poverty. This strong dependence on labour and the likelihood of one of these risks gave rise to social insecurity among this population group. During the guild era the risk of catching infectious diseases such as the plague, smallpox, or typhus was very high, occupational diseases and accidents were widespread, and seasonal unemployment was common in several branches of industry.[4] Unpredictable risks and lack of financial reserves prevented most artisans from arranging individual protection against loss of income. Guilds offered a solution. As collectives of fellow craftsmen, they provided their members, and in some cases the wives and children of their members as well with a social support network comprising help in kind or financial aid. This support made guild membership particularly attractive. Without the help of the guild and their relatives and neighbours, guild brothers, like most of their fellow townspeople, would have been at the mercy of public poor relief.

These circumstances figured from the outset in establishing what were known as boxes, the structures containing the social provisions of the guilds in all parts of the Low Countries. In 1581, for example, the Antwerp linen weavers intended to issue benefits to members who were 'elderly, infirm, or unable to work or earn a living due to illness or natural sickness or other serious shortcomings or unfortunate injuries or

[4] On occupational diseases, see e.g. Ramazzini, 1744; Dekker, 1992, pp. 112-47, 133; van Leeuwen, 2000.

had fallen on hard times due to circumstances beyond their control'. The individual concerned would first have to receive a visit from the poor relief masters, who would determine whether the need was serious enough to justify benefits.[5] Although many guilds had poor boxes like those of the Antwerp linen weavers, such provisions were certainly not universal.

Unfortunately, no systematic research is available on the Southern Netherlands that would enable us to assess the scope of the corporative social provisions. In Antwerp twenty guilds were known to have such arrangements, out of an approximate total of 65 guilds.[6] At any given point in time, roughly one third of the guilds in Antwerp would thus have had a poor box or similar provision. This situation is believed to have been typical for all cities in Brabant. In Flanders, however, occupational poor relief boxes were less commonplace.

We know more about this subject for the Northern Netherlands, at least for the period since the Reformation. As was already explained in chapter 2, about two thousand craft guilds existed in the Dutch Republic. Some provided no support benefits whatsoever. Members of these guilds relied on individual charity from their guild brothers and sisters and received aid from the poor relief board in the event of long-term indigence. Other guilds would have one of their members or the guild aid collect donations from members in cases of sickness or death. The monies collected provided emergency relief. Still other guilds had a box (possibly linked to the guild fund) from which they issued financial aid.[7] These guilds set aside certain fixed revenues to support their members, charged special box dues, and in some cases issued a separate box ordinance. Determining exactly how many guilds maintained boxes is difficult, as the different types of aid were not always easy to distinguish. Over 250 guilds in the Northern Netherlands are known to have had support funds. About seventy of these guilds organized wage-dependent municipal workers, such as peat and grain carriers. Approximately two hundred journeymen's boxes have been identified as well, including several in the textile industry (e.g. in Leiden) and over forty that belonged to sailors.[8] Additional research might reveal more. Provisionally, though, we may conclude that at least 10 and at most 15 per cent of the guilds in the Northern Netherlands offered their members some kind of regulated support. Large cities were an exception to this general pattern. In 1796, all but one of the Amsterdam guilds owned capital — one and a half million guilders altogether — and allocated the proceeds toward benefit payments. In other large cities in the Republic, this held true for about one quarter of the guilds at the end of the eighteenth century. The most advanced form of mutual insurance thus arose in the largest cities, which were in the West of the Dutch Republic.

---

5 Huys, 1926, (2) p. 102. Note that Huys' book comprises two separately numbered sections: (1) contains the text, (2) the documentation.

6 Huys, 1926, (2) pp. 3-142.

7 For literature about mutual aid, see van der Linden and Sluys, 1996; Bos, 1998; van Genabeek, 1999. See further the data files 'Gilden', 'Bussen' and 'Caisses' (IISH).

8 See the 'Bussen' and 'Caisses' data files (IISH).

2. Before the Reformation

Before the Reformation, and later mainly within small guilds, support benefits were taken for granted and therefore often not even mentioned in guild ordinances.[9] The informal nature of this early aid, often issued in kind, rendered written rules unnecessary. This aid might comprise bread and peat distributions, medical care, watches over someone who was seriously ill, funeral attendance, and pallbearer services. Some guilds nonetheless recorded the social obligations of members in the guild regulations. By 1302, the smiths' guild in 's-Hertogenbosch stipulated that if any of the smiths or a member's wife or children should pass away, all members 'would go to church with the body of the deceased and would be obliged to offer at the mass held for this person'.[10] Regarding indigent and infirm members, the 's-Hertogenbosch shoemakers' guild stipulated in 1448 that 'if any master of a guild falls upon hard times or becomes ill, … then that guild shall provide emergency aid, until he is able to earn his keep again'.[11] The occurrence of such stipulations in the Brabant city of 's-Hertogenbosch is no coincidence, since the southern districts were generally more advanced in this respect than those in the North. In the fourteenth and fifteenth centuries in Flanders and especially in Brabant, guilds started several poor relief boxes, often with elaborate regulations and designated officials (usually known as *armmeesters* or poor relief masters) entrusted with enforcement of the regulations. In the North, fixed dues and benefits were still rather unusual at the time, although the Dordrecht carpenters' guild determined by 1387 that each member was to contribute four pennies a week to support sick brothers. If this contribution proved insufficient, the guild would take up an additional collection.[12]

Two other aspects of the arrangement in Brabant and Flanders are significant in addition to the early regulations.[13] First, these regulations rarely distinguished between masters and journeymen. The benefits appear to have covered both groups. Separate journeymen's boxes did not emerge in the South until the seventeenth and eighteenth centuries.[14] Second, the boxes in the Southern Netherlands were very general. We quoted above from the regulations of the Antwerp linen weavers' box from 1581. The idea was for impoverished members to receive benefits, regardless of the cause. This practice was very common in Flanders and Brabant, and the identical box regulations of the Antwerp pin makers, hook makers, and needle makers (also in 1581) were no coincidence. Moreover, the Brussels surgeons started a box in 1748, for members 'so

---

9 Overvoorde, 1914, p. 366.

10 van den Heuvel, 1946, p. 260.

11 van den Heuvel, 1946, p. 257.

12 van Vollenhoven, 1923, p. 23.

13 Huys, 1926, (2) passim.

14 Huys, 1926, (2) pp. 28, 198, 203, 264, 337, 340, 341, 369; journeymen hatmakers were an exception in this respect, as they started their own box in Antwerp by the sixteenth century: Huys, 1926, (2) p. 113.

deeply affected by old age and ill fortune that they have fallen upon extreme poverty and misery … as well as those who fall ill'.[15]

Prior to the Reformation, guild benefits were religious arrangements in both the Southern and the Northern Netherlands. Sometimes these benefits were organized through special occupational religious brotherhoods, which were established from the thirteenth century onward. In addition to maintaining the guild altar, these brotherhoods helped poor guild brothers and other city paupers.[16] Some guilds in the Southern Netherlands, including the Bruges smiths' guild and the Brussels mercers' guild, set up hospices for needy members as well.[17] Most cities in the Northern Netherlands lacked occupational religious brotherhoods dedicated to relief work. Instead, such benefits were organized within the guild,[18] presumably because guilds were established later in the Northern than in the Southern Netherlands.[19] With the dramatic expansion of the guilds in the Northern Netherlands from the mid-sixteenth century onward, towns and cities in Holland already had a vast network of lay brotherhoods, hospitals and hospices, and other charitable institutions. The need for special guild brotherhoods dedicated to relief work was therefore less. In the North, such brotherhoods appear to have focused on religious duties.[20] Moreover, affluent artisans in the Northern Netherlands hardly ever presented their guild with the major donations necessary to fund charitable efforts. Were there no such solvent guild masters, or did they lack faith in how the guild would manage their donation? At any rate, few guild hospices or almshouses were established in the Northern Netherlands.[21]

In the guild system of the Northern Netherlands, relief work — especially after the Reformation, when the guilds had to abandon their church altars, requiems, and religious processions, and occupational religious brotherhoods were disbanded — was performed within a secularized guild culture. This distinction probably explains why the relief work of guilds in the Northern Netherlands had more in common with an insurance system, whereas in the South relief work continued to be arranged through religious charities.

---

[15] Huys, 1926, (2) p. 315.

[16] Huys, 1926, (1) pp. 27-40.

[17] Huys, 1926, (2) pp. 167, 237-8.

[18] van den Heuvel, 1946, pp. 258-9. In Utrecht, only six of the 21 guilds maintained a separate religious brotherhood, Overvoorde and Joosting, 1896-7.

[19] Regarding the periods when the guilds were established in the Northern Netherlands, see the contribution by De Munck, Lourens, and Lucassen in this volume; Bos, 1998, p. 34.

[20] Unger, 1930, pp. 4-5.

[21] Craandijk, 1904, pp. 14, 36; 1989, pp. 167-8; de Vos, 1913, pp. 59-62. For an exception to this rule, see Rommes and van der Spek, 2004.

3. After the Reformation

In the Northern Netherlands the Reformation brought an end to the religious role of the guild system. Mutual aid funds survived the changes, proving once again that benefits were not exclusively associated with the religious duties of the guilds but derived in equal measure from their secular artisanal culture. In this context, relief work enriched the collective identity of guilds and was part of their symbolic capital. Although Reformed city councils and churches tried to abandon pre-Reformation guild traditions, guilds in many places retained their patron saint, crypts, and drinking festivals.[22] In many cities in the Northern Netherlands, however, guilds adjusted their spending to the new religion and wishes of the authorities. Thanks to the strong economy and in some cases municipal financial support, mutual aid funds rapidly became more elaborate after the Reformation. Large cities in the West, especially Amsterdam, were at the vanguard of this trend.

The prohibition on religious services and church festivities changed the guilds' pattern of expenditure considerably. In 1572, the States of Holland determined that guild revenues, which in the past had been spent primarily on altar services, were to be allocated primarily 'toward common causes' and placed under the auspices of mayors and aldermen.[23] In Amsterdam the municipal authorities urged the guilds to stop squandering these monies on religious causes and other 'useless superstitions, drunkenness, and indecent carousing', and to spend them instead on benefits for their sick and needy brothers.[24] Following this decree, the Amsterdam Saint Joseph's guild (carpenters) stipulated that 'all pennies and penalties destined and allocated by the guild regulations to maintain religious and papal services and masses, and all others, shall be transferred to the box'.[25] Henceforth, this box was used to support needy guild brothers and sisters. Other guilds continued their traditional system of social care, funded from the common guild box or through spontaneous collections. Some did not establish a separate box for support benefits until years later. Ever increasing numbers of journeymen did so as well. Due in part to the religious changes and the increasing restrictions imposed on guilds, journeymen found themselves progressively excluded from the guild's social support network.[26] This situation led them to set up their own mutual aid funds, known as journeymen's boxes.

---

22 Among them were the 's-Hertogenbosch meat cutters' guild, which sponsored a mass on the day of its patron saint into the first half of the eighteenth century (Prak, 1992, p. 71), and the Utrecht hawkers' guild, which still spent money on candles and church wardens for the Buurkerk in 1798 (GAUtrecht SA III, Arch. Secr., No. 436: Minutes of provisional commissioners to the former guilds (22 Oct 1798 – 22 March 1803). In Dordrecht, some guilds retained their own chapel and crypts into the nineteenth century (Palmen, 1998). Also see Thijs' contribution to this volume.

23 Bruinvis, 1906, p. 3.

24 van Dillen, 1929-74.

25 Ordonnantien en willekeuren van het Jozephs-gilde binnen de stad Amsteldam (27-7-1579) (EHB 82 F 12).

26 Bos, 1998, pp. 177-9, 296-9. See also Wesoly, 1985, pp. 333-4.

Guild funds in the Southern Netherlands followed a different course. Prior to the Reformation, religious brotherhoods of master artisans and journeymen existed alongside the guilds, as did special associations for recreation and entertainment. The Counter Reformation restored the relationship between the Catholic Church and the guild associations. Guild altars were restored or redecorated for reasons of prestige, vanity, and devotion.[27] In addition to taking an interest in their altars, guilds in the Southern Netherlands remained involved with their patron saints, pilgrimages, and religious brotherhoods, although the Counter Reformation changed the outlook of master artisans on the Catholic Church and religious practices within the guild system. Journeymen were particularly active in forming religious brotherhoods from the seventeenth century, as well as religiously affiliated mutual aid associations. Looking for comfort and compensation for their marginalized status within the guild system, journeymen formed their own social associations. The role of religion in these associations continued to be taken for granted in this area at the time.

In both the Northern and the Southern Netherlands, journeymen thus felt the need to organize separately from the guild masters. They hoped that having their own association would make them less dependent on the guild and would foster solidarity among journeymen. Prior to the Reformation, journeymen associations were few and far between, especially in the Northern Netherlands. Their chief mission at the time was to worship together. As a consequence, these associations disappeared in the scuffle of religious changes. Most journeymen associations in the Northern Netherlands were established only in the first half of the eighteenth century, when nearly one third of the total of about two hundred journeymen's boxes were started.[28] The reasons for the rapid increase in these boxes include declining economic growth and progressive scale expansion in certain artisanal industries, increasing the need of journeymen for economic and social support. Most of those employed at these large companies had no hope of ever becoming masters and were resigned to spending their lives as journeymen. In cities with labour-intensive industries, such as Leiden (textile), Delft (ceramics), and Oudewater (rope), this group of permanently wage-dependent journeymen was largest. Most journeymen's boxes were formed in these towns and in some dated back further and were more numerous than the guild boxes. In Oudewater, for example, a small town with 2,700 inhabitants in 1670, a very elaborate journeyman rope twisters' box emerged at the large rope twisting plants (1730-<1916) and had over three hundred members in the nineteenth century.[29] No guild boxes ever existed in Oudewater.

---

27 Thijs, in this volume.

28 'Bussen' data file (IISH, 1998). Seven journeymen's boxes were founded before 1600; 46 between 1600 and 1650; 43 between 1651 and 1700; 61 between 1701 and 1750; 31 between 1751 and 1800; and eight after 1800. Cf. Lucassen, 1991, pp. 28-30.

29 Data file `Bussen' and `Caisses' (IISH); *Ziekenfondsen*, 1896, p. 116.

After the Reformation, journeymen's associations ceased to perform religious duties in the Northern Netherlands and became pure support boxes. They rarely served economic activities or funded strikes. Nor was socializing their primary objective. They hardly ever arranged joint celebrations or engaged in collective religious observance, according to the information from the regulations and ledgers.[30] The journeymen would probably not have received such permission from the local authorities, to the immense relief of their masters, who did not appreciate insurgent, well-organized journeymen's associations.

While the journeymen's brotherhoods in the Northern Netherlands tried to reinforce mutual ties primarily through the common support box, journeymen's associations in the Southern Netherlands engaged in collective religious worship and leisure pursuits. Among guilds in the Southern Netherlands, therefore, journeymen's associations long served to care for the dead rather than the living.[31] Only in the eighteenth century did material interests start to prevail over spiritual guidance. The change resulted in the transformation and establishment of special mutual aid associations for journeymen. In eighteenth-century Antwerp, for example, the first journeymen's mutual aid funds emerged alongside and from existing — religious — journeymen's brotherhoods 'to help one another in times of insufficient work, sickness, or other problems'.[32] In addition to serving as funds for poor relief, funerals, and sickness benefits, most journeymen's mutual aid funds were social associations and religious brotherhoods and sometimes even strike funds — the latter to the considerable irritation of the employers.[33]

4. Provisions

In the seventeenth century the guilds in the Northern Netherlands formalized their services, expanded their facilities, and adopted regulations concerning their role as insurance providers. Membership of these formalized mutual aid funds was compulsory, thus making all members responsible for the risk of each individual member. This system maximized distribution of risks within the confines of the guild. Compulsory membership also ensured a constant supply of new, young members in the fund and consequently revenues through admission fees and premiums. Another important feature of these mutual aid funds was their status as non-profit associations. All the money raised through dues, penalties, and interest was allocated toward mutual aid

---

30 Dekker, 1992, p. 116.

31 Thijs, 1994, p. 43.

32 The brotherhood of Antwerp journeyman shoemakers, established in 1686, formed a mutual aid fund only in 1792. Thijs argues that the presence of various religious journeymen's brotherhoods in Antwerp blocked the rise of journeymen's mutual aid funds. The Antwerp journeyman hat makers and cloth dressers, however, started a compulsory box for support benefits by 1608; Thijs, 1994, pp. 251-6, esp. 52.

33 Thijs, 1994, pp. 255-7.

after payment of operating expenses. Profit was not an objective. The social services comprised a broad, undifferentiated package. Unlike the specialized widows', funeral, and sickness funds that emerged during the eighteenth and nineteenth centuries and unlike the modern insurance system, guild and journeymen's boxes offered a comprehensive package. Premiums were not charged for specific risks. The format and composition of the services varied according to the guild and the fund and depended in part on the size of the guild membership. Guilds with few members tended to be highly cohesive and were less likely to need formal mutual aid arrangements than guilds with hundreds of members. Moreover, weekly revenues from dues were usually insufficient in small guilds to cover costly benefits over extended periods. The range of care also depended on the services that members needed, their financial resources, and the guild's assets. Guild brothers with few financial resources often needed sickness benefits more than their more affluent counterparts in the same predicament. Their wealthier counterparts had sufficient financial reserves or journeymen to continue their work and make ends meet, if they fell ill. Guilds with a lot of capital had the resources to provide costlier old-age and widows' benefits in addition to funeral and sickness benefits without charging their members for the entire cost. Proper bookkeeping was essential, although even in these cases the boxes remained vulnerable because of the small, uniform population insured. Many guild boxes were therefore ephemeral operations and folded relatively quickly. While guild boxes in the Netherlands usually covered carefully circumscribed risks, as will be explained below, the ones in the South addressed impoverishment in general, without specifying the cause. This complicated maintaining the fund, which appears to have been possible only by curtailing the number of benefit recipients.

5. Funeral aid in kind and money

Funeral arrangements were the oldest and most important service that guilds offered their members. Most early modern guilds extended this service beyond guild brothers to include the wives, widows, and sometimes even children of their members. Guild funerals were important events, due in part to their collective nature. They were also matters of prestige and standing for both the family of the deceased and for the guild. As a result, guild funerals were solemn ceremonies: processions of guild brothers, family members, and neighbours, preceded by the guild aid, would march from the home of the deceased to the grave. Guild members carried the coffin, draped with the pall and the guild's silver shields. In some cities guilds maintained crypts in one of the parish churches, while elsewhere deceased guild brothers and sisters were buried in the graveyard or later on the ramparts. Afterwards, guild brothers would gather at the home of the deceased or at the guildhall to eat or drink together.

All guild members were expected to attend the burial of a guild brother. Absences were penalized. Declining to bear the coffin was subject to a fine of a few pennies. In many guilds, the aid presented members with funeral tokens upon announcing a death. These tokens were to be returned at the funeral. Relatives generally paid the funeral costs before funeral benefits were introduced. Only if they could not afford these charges did the guild contribute. This changed in the eighteenth century, when some guilds in the Northern Netherlands started to offer funeral benefits. The service became monetarized concurrently with capital growth within the funds and a rising social need for funeral and life insurance. At first funeral benefits covered only (part of) the actual costs. By the end of the eighteenth century, however, the benefits amounted to forty to eighty guilders, leaving survivors with a bit extra as well.[34] Data from the Southern Netherlands suggest that the artisans there spent huge sums on funerals. Ghent tailors, for example, paid 84 guilders per funeral on average.[35] This was considerably more than the benefits the tailors' guild issued in the Northern Netherlands, although funeral benefits were very rare indeed among guilds in Flanders and Brabant.[36]

Guilds needed additional revenues to fund funeral benefits. Some funds raised the weekly dues during the weeks following a funeral. The Leiden box for journeyman chamois preparers, bleachers, and oil-tanners, for example, doubled the weekly dues during the three weeks following each funeral to cover the 12 guilders paid in funeral benefits 'for the Coffin or the like'.[37] Newcomers to other guilds paid additional dues known as dead man's money, to be distributed to the survivors after the member's death. The third financing method involved charging separate funeral dues, which were known as corpse fees. These dues ranged from one to four pennies and were levied for each funeral. The arrangement passed the cost of introducing and raising funeral benefits on to the guild brothers. Guilds with insufficient revenues to pay funeral benefits sometimes set up separate funeral or dead man's boxes for these payments.[38] Other guilds continued to provide their funeral aid exclusively in kind into the eighteenth century.

During the eighteenth century a remarkable increase occurred in the number of funeral regulations. Aside from stipulating the benefits, penalties for absenteeism, and the bearers, guild stipulations increasingly contained regulations about conduct and attire at funerals. Bearers were expected to wear mourning mantles with a jabot rented for the occasion, and the other guild brothers wore dark mantles. Smoking was prohibited in the house of mourning, and appearing at funerals with a pipe in one's mouth was subject to a fine of a few pennies.[39] The increase in the number of funeral regulations probably arose on the one hand from the desire to flaunt the guild's prestige and wealth and on the other hand from the diminishing interest among guild members

---

34 The money that remained after deducting the cost of the guild aid, the coffin, the beer, the rental of mantles, the pallbearers, and the pall went to the surviving relatives.

35 Deceulaer, 2001, p. 113.

36 Huys, 1926, (2).

37 GALeiden Bibl. LenO. 59986 pf (2-7-1705).

38 In 's-Hertogenbosch, for example, the ragmen's guild (1756), tanners' and shoemakers' guilds (1767), and the surgeons' guild (1780) started burial funds: Prak, 1992, p. 70.

39 See e.g. GALeiden Gerechtsdagboek 3B, 88 (2-3-1702).

in funeral ceremonies. Artisans, especially those belonging to large guilds, came to perceive the funerals of fellow members as onerous duties and interruptions of their work. Guilds tried to block individual initiatives to arrange funerals and uphold guild traditions by raising penalties for absenteeism and charging buyout fees for members whose relations preferred to organize their own funeral.[40]

The tradition of distributing bread to the city paupers at the funeral of a guild brother gradually disappeared in the Northern Netherlands but persisted in the Southern Netherlands.[41] This strengthens the suspicion that the guilds in the Northern Netherlands, especially in the towns in Holland, progressively drifted out of public life, restricted their sense of social responsibility to the wellbeing of their own members, and preferred mutual aid over public charity.

6. Sickness benefits

Sickness benefits were the most common provision after support in the event of a death. As sickness benefits were not a one-off payment the way funeral funds were and were moreover subject to fraud, guilds and mutual aid funds drafted various stipulations to organize and monitor their use. Sick brothers claiming benefits were required to notify their guild board or messenger. Before support benefits were approved for disbursement, a guild official would visit the applicant to determine whether this individual was indeed sick. In cases of doubt, a physician would be consulted. If his request was approved, the sick guild brother would receive benefits ranging from twenty to sixty pennies a week in the guilds of Holland and four to ten pennies in those in the Southern Netherlands. While they were collecting benefits, sick brothers were not to appear in public and certainly not at an inn or tavern, subject to being ordered to repay benefits received and having future benefits discontinued immediately. Sick members who were outside the city, and those who 'had become ill because of profligacy and drunkenness and from consorting with loose women or the like' were not eligible for benefits.[42] Nor were guild brothers ordinarily entitled to benefits during the first or in some cases even the first six years of membership, or if they fell behind in their dues payments.[43]

---

[40] In 1762, the Amsterdam Saint Joseph's guild raised the penalty for declining a guild funeral from 12 to 16 guiders to cover the cost of the increased number of members drawing benefits: GAAmsterdam 366, No. 1482-1483 (26-1-1720, 27-1-1762).

[41] Thijs, in this volume.

[42] van Dillen, 1929-74.

[43] The Amsterdam poultry merchants' guild stipulated that 'sick, old, and indigent male or female poultry merchants who have been members of the Guild for six years shall receive support (if desired) in the amount of twenty pennies a week': Noordkerk, Handvesten, 1270 (31-1-1721).

If guild brothers fell seriously ill, some guilds had their fellow members take turns watching over them without compensation. If the sick brother was afflicted with a 'Contagious or Pestilential disease', the obligation of holding watch did not apply.[44] Those suffering from extended and incurable illnesses were a heavy financial burden, forcing some boxes to discontinue benefits after a period, usually one year and six weeks. The sick then had to rely on family, neighbours, and poor relief.

In addition to sickness benefits, some boxes covered medical fees, including medicine and visits to the surgeon. The request from the Delft linen weavers' box to the hospital pharmacy for free medication reveals that these costs were considerable. With only six hundred guilders in its coffers, the box spent 360 guilders a year on medical costs. The hospital trustees refused to waive these charges, and the municipal authorities supported them.[45]

7. Old age benefits

Although many artisans were a long way off from retirement, the guild had to consider members who grew too old to support themselves. Elderly artisans had four options: live from investments, move in with family members, enter a hospice, or seek alms or mutual aid. Several guilds were concerned about the fate of their 'old mates' and issued old-age benefits. Eligibility for such benefits required satisfying an increasing number of conditions. Retirement age varied from fifty to sixty years, depending on the guild and the number of elderly benefit recipients. The Amsterdam hide merchants' and shoemakers' guild stipulated that guild brothers and sisters reaching the age of sixty or thereabouts and unable to support themselves due to bad eyesight, disability, or other causes were entitled to support benefits.[46] The Amsterdam Saint Joseph's guild issued benefits solely to elderly people 'reaching the age of 60 and having contributed to the box for six years, as well as those who were needy'.[47] Some guilds required 25 full years of loyal membership, which greatly curtailed the number of elderly members eligible for benefits.[48]

As the guilds experienced greater difficulty supporting their elderly members, pensions started to be increasingly need-based, and the number entitled to receive pensions was reduced. In some cases only the five or ten eldest guild members received benefits. Boxes that were unable to support their elderly (or incurably ill) members

---

44 See e.g. the ordinance of the Leiden journeyman chamois preparers, and bleachers', and oil-tanners (GALeiden Bibl. LenO 59986 pf (2-7-1705).

45 Oosterbaan, 1954, p. 290.

46 van Dillen, 1929-74.

47 GAAmsterdam, 5061, nr. 713, fol. 1.

48 The Amsterdam shoe repairers determined in 1634 that 'henceforth all disabled, infirm, and ailing Guild brothers, as well as those unable to work because of old age but otherwise

until their death would suspend benefits — which ranged from one to three guilders — after a while. Sometimes these members were paid a lump sum ranging from 12 to 25 guilders.[49] Some guilds in the Southern Netherlands provided their indigent elderly brothers with benefits as well. In Ghent, for example, former tailors received over 15 pennies a week, in addition to food donations.[50] Over time, the practice of donating food disappeared in cities in Holland.[51]

8. Widows' benefits

Since many women survived their husbands during the early modern period, and since these women rarely had adequate financial resources, guilds tried to protect guild widows from indigence. The first advice of the guilds was to remarry. The rising surplus of women in the early modern period, however, prevented most widows from pursuing this survival strategy. Most guilds therefore allowed widows to carry on their late husband's business, provided that they hire a master journeyman. In Utrecht, widows were allowed to carry on the business for a year and six weeks without paying the guild; after that period they would retain the full rights of a guild brother in return for paying half the regular dues.[52] This meant that 'if a guild brother died, and the guild wished to support his widow and paid her money from the box, [and the widow] became ill, she would receive the same amount from the box as other guild brothers'.[53] The Amsterdam cobblers decreed that widows carrying on their husband's business were to receive thirty pennies a year in sickness benefits and were obliged to 'contribute ten pennies a year to exempt them from attending church services to bury the dead'.[54] This meant that they bought off the attendance requirement. Widows who were unable or unwilling to continue their husband's business or incapable of making ends meet that way occasionally received separate widows' benefits. These benefits were a luxury that only the few guilds with adequate funds could afford to

---

healthy and having been Guild brothers for 25 years, shall draw no more than 20 pennies a week' (Noordkerk, Handvesten, 1417 (31-1-1634)).

49 The Delft coopers' box paid the incurably ill 25 guilders (GADelft, Arch. Heeren van de Weth, nr 2040 (3-11-1738); the voluntary box for journeyman tile makers in Rotterdam provided the elderly and incurably ill with a lump sum of 18 guilders: (GARotterdam, Keurboek V fol. 246 (26-1-1720)) the box for journeyman carpenters in Zwolle awarded its departing journeymen exit bonuses of 12 guilders (GAZwolle, AAZ01, 00276 (12-4-1772).

50 Old-age benefits issued by Ghent guilds (converted according to pennies a week): tailors 15; bakers 5.5; carpenters and woodcutters 12.5; brewers 13; masons and stonecutters 13; Deceulaer, 2001, pp. 551-2).

51 The exceptions included the Utrecht smiths' guild, which thanks to a bequest from 1603 distributed bread into the nineteenth century, primarily to indigent members: Bos, 1998, p. 145.

52 Hoogewerff, 1947, p. 102.

53 See the Amsterdam hide merchants' and shoemakers' guild: van Dillen, 1929-74.

54 Noordkerk, Handvesten, 1418 (24-7-1635).

offer. The petitions for raising dues and the conditions reveal that this costly provision often severely burdened the boxes. The Amsterdam inland bargemen's and seafarers' guild observed in 1750 that its box 'has been augmented so much by the thrifty and careful management of the elders that a distribution for widows has been proclaimed'. Implementing this measure, however, still meant raising the annual dues and admission fee.[55]

Widowhood alone was not enough to claim benefits in most guilds. As was the case with old-age benefits, years of membership, age, and need were standard selection criteria. To avert an excessive number of widows drawing benefits, some guilds limited the number that could receive them. The Amsterdam pilots' guild awarded benefits of thirty pennies a week to only the five eldest widows.[56] Guilds with insufficient funds for such added expenditures sometimes started separate boxes for widows. Membership of these widows' boxes was largely voluntary. Aging membership and extended benefits usually prevented these boxes from becoming long-term arrangements. Few widows of guild members actually benefited from the guild's support system; after the death of their husbands, most relied on support from family members and friends and alms.[57]

Financing

Expanding social services and introducing financial aid forced the guilds to adjust their pattern of revenues and expenditures. Problems arose in guilds where five to ten members fell ill for extended periods, or if the number of funerals rose sharply, for example as a result of an epidemic of the plague. In these situations the burden of so many needy members became intolerable, especially for members of small guilds. The guild would distribute the revenues among those in need, and the more sick members there were, the lower the individual benefits. Other guilds based the number of recipients on the amount in their coffers: a fuller guild box meant support for more guild brothers.

Hoping to improve the likelihood of benefits in the event of illness or disability, expand the provisions, and limit contributions from individual members, guilds in-

---

55 Annual dues were raised from 2.8 to 3 guilders, and members wishing to be eligible for widows' benefits paid 5 guilders. The admission fee for insiders increased from 10 guilders to 30 guilders and for outsiders from 40 guilders to 100 guilders: GAAmsterdam, 5028, nr 515 (7-11-1750).

56 The Amsterdam beer porters' guild requested that the maximum number of widows drawing benefits be reduced from 50 to 44, and that only widows above 45 be awarded benefits GAAmsterdam, 5028, nr 515 (22-1-1750) and nr 523, fol. 194-5.

57 In 1750 in Leiden, 26.5 per cent of the indigent at the Leiden Huiszittenhuis were widows without children and 12.2 per cent widows with children, whereas 5.7 per cent were men without children and 1.1 per cent men with children: Pot, 1994, p. 263. See also Schmidt, 2001.

creasingly sought additional sources of funding for their mutual aid. One approach was to set aside certain revenues for the needy. All Utrecht goldsmiths whose working hours exceeded the standard were required to donate two pennies a year 'for the needs of the indigent guild brothers and sisters at the Saint Eloy hospice'.[58] The second option was to collect special fixed dues to ensure a regular source of revenues and to keep members in distress from becoming dependent on the guild's other expenditures. In 1387 the Dordrecht carpenters' guild determined that each member was to contribute four pennies a week to support sick brothers.[59] These additional dues, earmarked to serve as mutual aid, made it possible to accumulate financial reserves during periods when few members died or fell ill. Moreover, fixed revenues made for fixed benefits; stipulations regarding the amount of the benefit and the conditions were henceforth established in writing, leading mutual aid to become progressively formalized.

To prevent benefits from being linked to the total revenues and expenditures of their guild, some guilds already disengaged their box for the infirm and the indigent from the guild box prior to the Reformation, creating two separate boxes, each one with its own revenues and expenditures. The Amsterdam masons' guild did this by 1527. Henceforth, sick and elderly masons who were members of the box received 12 pennies a week from admissions and annual fees collected specially for this purpose and supplemented by revenues from debenture bonds, leased properties, and special charges. Each year the masons' box received 13 guilders from 'the inspection of the stones'.[60] This early initiative of the Amsterdam masons was rather exceptional at the time but would be widely emulated after the Reformation (around 1580).

Social services, banquets and drinking sprees, processions, elegant guildhalls, and magnificent guild shields all cost money. Once spent, such money was gone, and since the assets of guilds and their members were rarely very large, careful choices needed to be made. This appears to have been the chief difference between the Northern and the Southern Netherlands. Most guilds in the Northern Netherlands opted for austerity: receiving money, saving, investing, and spending on social services. The ledgers reflect little spending on festivities and public manifestations. Exceptions obviously occurred, such as with the Leiden book printers, who in 1748 spent over two thirds of their income on 'eating a little fish with the ladies'.[61] They saved the rest for a festive repast at the end of the year. This guild of relatively affluent artisans neither saved nor invested nor provided support. In Amsterdam, on the other hand, guilds increased their capital by regularly raising admissions fees, weekly dues, and premiums, assessing charges, and investing in bonds and securities.[62] They spent part of their income on wages for the officials and the guild aid and miscellaneous items, such as guildhall

---

58 Overvoorde and Joosting, 1896-7, vol. 2, p. 406; vgl. Rommes and van der Spek, 2004, p. 40.

59 van Vollenhoven, 1923, p. 23.

60 van Dillen, 1929-74.

61 GALeiden, Arch. Gilden 94.

62 In 1798 the assets of the 45 Amsterdam guilds totalled nearly one and a half million guilders: Afschaffingsenquête, ARA wetg. col. 507 (1798).

repairs, a new guild cloth, paper, and drink. Benefits, however, were the largest expenditure. In some Amsterdam guilds benefits accounted for over 75 per cent of total expenditures. In other cities in the Northern Netherlands less was spent on support benefits.[63]

Trade associations in the Southern Netherlands set different priorities, as is apparent in part from their ledgers, which rarely reflect dues or investments in securities and bonds. Revenues consisted primarily of donations from affluent members and renting of properties. The Ghent tailors' guild, for example, supported six 'elderly men' from the rental income from six houses.[64] Any admission fees or weekly dues charged were usually too low to support a member. The Brussels ragmen, for example, paid only four pennies a year into their poor box.[65] The Amsterdam shipyard carpenters, on the other hand, paid over ten guilders toward their box each year, which in turn yielded considerably higher and more comprehensive benefits.[66] Sick Brussels ragmen received weekly support benefits of only six pennies. Amsterdam shipyard carpenters received fifty pennies sick pay or sixty pennies old-age pension a week.[67]

In addition to keeping benefits low, the poor boxes of guilds in Brabant and Flanders curtailed their spending by restricting the number of benefit recipients. Ghent tailors, for example, had their own hospice, which accommodated up to six needy members.[68] The poor box of the Brussels mercers' guild, which comprised nearly 300 artisans in 1738, supported 12 members in 1783. The guild provided incidental support as well, and such spending could obviously be adjusted to match the revenues.[69] Benefits were not a major expenditure among the guilds in the Southern Netherlands. Their ledgers do, however, reflect vast spending on meals, church altars, decoration of the guildhalls, and lawsuits. Such spending also reinforced internal cohesion between guild members; the same strategy was pursued by the boxes in the North as well. In addition, it enabled guilds in the Southern Netherlands to flaunt their prowess and wealth.

10. Diversity and distinction

Comparative research between the cities of Amsterdam, Utrecht, and Leiden in the Northern Netherlands reveals that the number of guilds in a city was hardly indicative of the number and type of guild and journeymen boxes and their range of services.[70]

---

63 Bos, 1998, pp. 169, 349-51.

64 Deceulaer, 2001, p. 550.

65 Deceulaer, 2001, p. 557.

66 Bos, 1998, p. 104.

67 Bos, 1998, pp. 98, 100.

68 Deceulaer, 2001, p. 364.

69 Huys, 1926, (2) p. 257; cf De Peuter, 1999, 373nt13.

70 Bos, 1998, pp. 251-8.

Amsterdam, the largest city of the Dutch Republic, had fifty guilds in 1750, nine fewer than Leiden, which was far smaller. While in Amsterdam virtually every guild had a compulsory guild box offering a broad range of services, Leiden had at most ten guild boxes. On the other hand, at least eighty voluntary mutual aid funds existed in Leiden between 1500 and 1800, primarily serving those active in the textile industry.[71] The discrepancies between the support system of the guilds in Amsterdam, Leiden, and Utrecht arose only in part from the differences in their respective population sizes. In the seventeenth and eighteenth centuries Amsterdam was by far the largest city in the Northern Netherlands, and one of the largest in Europe. As a result, many specialized guilds were formed, each with a large membership. In large cities with vast guilds, mutual cohesion was less than in small towns with small-scale guilds, which led guild brothers in the cities to formalize and institutionalize relief work sooner, to ensure that support benefits were available. Large population size also strengthened the foundations of the insurance arrangement. In smaller towns and guilds, support to members in need continued to be provided through traditional, informal aid systems. Few initiatives to establish funds got under way in these settings. The modest memberships of these guilds moreover complicated maintaining a solid system. Financial support for needy artisans was often left to the poor board here. In return for this aid, guilds contributed a share of their revenues to public poor relief.

The second factor determining the emergence and size of mutual aid funds was the affluence within a city and a guild. After all, members needed to have financial reserves to participate in a support fund. Costly services, such as old-age and widow's benefits, required a lot of capital as well. Since guild members were rarely able to raise such capital themselves, guilds tried to generate additional capital by investing in bonds and properties. The Amsterdam guilds clearly derived the greatest benefit from the economic prosperity of the Dutch Republic during the early modern period. Their investments in bonds increased their capital considerably. The interest was contributed to the support fund. Even a capital-rich guild with affluent members, however, could organize an effective support fund only if the guild received the necessary authorization and space from the city council. This depended largely on the attitude of the city council toward the guilds and the position of guilds in the city. This position was determined in part by the seniority of the guild system and the degree of organization among artisans.

In Amsterdam guilds soon started to organize mutual aid thanks to the tolerance of the city council. In Utrecht the strong political role of the guilds prior to 1528 placed them in a tight predicament and limited their room to manoeuvre in the seventeenth and eighteenth centuries.[72] The Utrecht city council, fearing a powerful, rebellious group of artisanal tradespeople, tried to curtail the authority of the local guilds. This

---

[71] Leiden had two boxes for masters, two combined ones (masters and journeymen), six boxes for city workers, and dozens of occupational boxes for journeymen and for textile workers and migrants: Bos, 1998, p. 206.

[72] From 1304 until Charles V seized power in 1528, the 21 Utrecht guilds were politically influential and indirectly elected the aldermen.

was part of the reason why in Utrecht the largely independent guild boxes became fully operational only in the eighteenth century. Finally, in Leiden, because of the negative stand of the city council and the weakness of the guilds, very few guild-based funds ever came into being, although the city did have the most sophisticated insurance system within the Republic. While in Amsterdam guild boxes were merely appendages of the guild funds, and the Utrecht boxes operated as semi-independent aid funds but were still related to the guilds because of their occupational base, most Leiden boxes were entirely separate from the guild system. They formed a different type of mutual aid, one that was most similar to the later insurance funds.

Deceulaer's research on the clothing industry in the Southern Netherlands has revealed similar differences between Ghent, Antwerp, and Brussels, with respect to the type and number of guild and journeymen's boxes.[73] A study of nine guilds in eighteenth-century Ghent has also indicated a broad range of mutual aid, from bread and meat distributions to rent subsidies, hospice care, and sickness and old-age benefits.[74] The Ghent tailors' guild mentioned above used its income from interest payments and rent collected on half a dozen houses to set up a foundation to support six indigent elderly tailors, providing them with about 15 pennies a week toward rent, firewood, stew, and allowance. Other guilds in Ghent paid their indigent guild brothers ten to twenty pennies a week as well.[75] Still, these arrangements were not actual boxes offering multiple services, premiums, and fixed benefits.

In Antwerp, however, tailors started a box that was compulsory, with an admissions fee and annual dues, and payments to members who were infirm or indigent. Other Antwerp guilds also emphasized mutual aid more prominent than the ones in Ghent did.[76] Antwerp was thus somewhat similar to the structure in the Northern Netherlands. Brussels was a hybrid case: Brussels tailors had a voluntary box, into which members paid modest annual dues. Membership was limited and the number of benefit recipients minimal. Sickness payments are believed to have gone to a small group of affluent members, while poor guild brothers had to settle for distributions of bread and meat. Here, mutual aid was primarily a type of charity.[77] These local variations are difficult to explain. Like in the Northern Netherlands, the differences were probably attributable to the size of the city and the guilds, affluence and financial and other choices of the guilds and their individual members, as well as to the position and influence of the guild system within the city.

---

[73] Deceulaer, 2001, pp. 549-59.

[74] Willem, 1995.

[75] Deceulaer, 2001, p. 551; Willem, 1995, pp. 142-45.

[76] Deceulaer, 2001, pp. 553-56.

[77] Deceulaer, 2001, pp. 556-57.

11. Conclusion

This chapter has reviewed the diversity of the guild and mutual support systems. Several agreements also existed between the guilds in the different cities and regions. The social responsibilities of guilds covered a broad range in both the Northern and the Southern Netherlands. Guilds in both regions tried, depending on the leeway the government gave them and the traditions and needs of the members, to establish an organization that extended beyond an economic trade association. Guild culture and professional honour were essential, as was internal cohesion. In this context, it is understandable that funerals were an important ritual everywhere as a token of respect for the deceased guild brother and a symbol of the guild's prestige, wealth, and internal cohesion. Manifestations of the symbolic capital of the guilds in the Southern Netherlands included their richly decorated guildhalls, their joint religious worship, and their social pursuits. Guilds in the North were well-known for their mutual aid funds.

Although mutual aid was part of the guild system virtually everywhere in Europe, it was not a permanent ingredient in corporative provisions anywhere. In the Northern Netherlands at most 15 per cent of the guilds had special funds for needy members. Such provisions undoubtedly enhanced mutual cohesion among the members and encouraged compliance with the collective code of conduct that guilds tried to impose on their members.[78] These incentives came in other forms as well, such as common repasts, religious experiences, or political rituals, to name but a few of the other activities of guilds. During the seventeenth and eighteenth centuries, guilds in the Northern Netherlands, especially those in Holland, nonetheless appear to have taken the vanguard in formalizing and institutionalizing mutual aid. In Amsterdam in particular, thanks in part to the strong economy and liberal environment in the seventeenth century, the system of mutual aid within the guilds was exceptionally well developed. In other cities in the West of the Dutch Republic, such as Rotterdam, The Hague, and Delft, such aid was very advanced as well. This institutionalized solidarity between fellow tradesmen was not new. Special guild boxes existed in Flanders by the fourteenth century, and an elaborate system of social services predated the Reformation in the German areas.

During the early modern period the Southern Netherlands, as well as the eastern provinces of the Republic in some respects, together with England and especially London, were a middle ground between the sophisticated support system among the guilds in the Northern Netherlands and the German areas and the total lack of guild-based mutual funds in the Catholic regions in the South, i.e. France, Italy, and Spain. Here, religious brotherhoods, in some cases in conjunction with the guilds, provided much-needed social and financial assistance in times of poverty and sickness during the seventeenth and eighteenth centuries. In the Northern Netherlands mutual aid, organized in formal boxes, replaced religion as a cohesive force and manifestation of collective identity of the craftsmen sooner than in the Southern regions. During

---

[78] Compare Olson, 1965 and Panhuysen, 2000, pp. 17-26.

the eighteenth century in the Southern Netherlands, as well as elsewhere in Europe, efforts to form mutual aid funds, within guilds or outside, increased progressively. Government involvement in social security and the establishment of trade unions continued to further this trend.

Chapter 8

Corporative capital and social representation in the Southern and Northern Netherlands, 1500-1800

Johan Dambruyne

1. Introduction

The renewed international interest in craft guilds has led to new findings and interesting insights in several fields. Not all aspects of guilds, however, have received equal consideration from historians in recent years. Some areas have been largely neglected. The issue referred to here as 'corporative capital' is a case in point. Very little is known at this time about patterns of ownership and investment among craft guilds and related corporative representation strategies.[1] One of the main reasons for the dearth of studies on forms of corporative capital is that good sources are lacking. The number of inventories of guild property is not very high. This is because such archives were assembled only very sporadically and mainly under exceptional circumstances, such as confiscation, reorganization, or suspension of the organization concerned. These inventories of assets and estates are nonetheless interesting, because they reflect the guild's material wealth at a certain point in time. One of the disadvantages is that the vast chronological range, across which most of the remaining inventories of guilds were compiled, complicates comparative analysis. There were, however, a few times when collective inventories were made up in the Southern and Northern Netherlands. We refer to the confiscation of corporative gold and silver in 1578,[2] as well as the seizure of the possessions of the guilds at the end of the eighteenth century in the Southern Netherlands (1795) and the Northern Netherlands (1798). The written records from the confiscation of 1578 are incomplete and concern only one aspect of the material wealth of the guilds.[3] As for the confiscation of the possessions of guilds

---

1 This essay deals only with craft guilds. Although several statements on the subject of capital undoubtedly apply to civic militias as well, these guilds are not addressed here.

2 The confiscation was part of the quest of the central government for new means of payment. In addition to the craft guilds, monasteries, convents, churches, hospitals, civic militias, brotherhoods, cities, and other institutions had to surrender their gold and silver.

3 The inventories remaining include one for Bruges in the Southern Netherlands and one for Utrecht in the Northern Netherlands. These inventories were published in Schouteet, 1968,

in the Southern Netherlands of 1795, the problem is that the central confiscation file is not preserved in the Belgian archives.[4] For the Northern Netherlands, the situation is clearer: the central file is at the Nationaal Archief in The Hague; it has been catalogued by the International Institute of Social History (Amsterdam).[5]

A second kind of source which provides information about the possessions of corporative associations are the guild accounts. They were compiled far more frequently (often annually) than property inventories. Many accounts remain for both the Southern and the Northern Netherlands for the seventeenth and eighteenth centuries. These sources have various advantages: they enable us to examine corporative capital from a more dynamic perspective (evolution over time) and they provide a more complete and more accurate impression of the material wealth of the guilds.[6] On the other hand, research of corporative property structures on the basis of accounts is undoubtedly more labour intensive and more difficult than when property inventories are used, which may be part of the reason why this source material is rarely used for such research. The best approach is provided by a combination of the two sources.

The main question in this chapter is: did corporative capital in the Northern Netherlands differ from corporative capital in the Southern Netherlands? If so, how did this discrepancy come about? Given the lack of case studies, this essay is not intended to generate definitive statements about analogies or differences between the guilds of the Southern and the Northern Netherlands with respect to patrimony, capital accumulation, material culture, and symbolic capital. As the available data concern only a select number of regions and cities in the South and the North, such an ambitious approach is not feasible at this time. Our objective is therefore more modest. Especially regarding the issue of corporative capital, we will formulate only a few tentative hypotheses as a foundation for elaboration. We will deal consecutively with the importance of guildhalls, guild interiors, guild chapels and altars, and public manifestations among guilds in the Southern and Northern Netherlands. Before launching a comparative study, however, some theoretical observations are in order.

---

pp. 217-46 and Muller Fz., 1879, pp. 284-337. In 1572 the States of Holland had already launched a similar initiative to fund the Dutch Revolt, ordering guilds, convents, and other religious institutions to surrender the silver and gold objects they did not need for religious services.

4 Hugo Soly has suggested that the confiscation registers may be at the Archives Nationales in Paris. This source has yet to be explored. Moreover, the documents contained in the different municipal archives concerning public sales of movable and immovable guild properties (1798) have been virtually overlooked thus far.

5 Nationaal Archief in The Hague, Wetgevende Colleges, 507. Piet Lourens and Jan Lucassen have included this source in the IISH guilds database. This does not mean, however, that replies have been submitted or preserved for all guilds that still existed in the Netherlands in 1798.

6 Accounts reflect the value of goods more often than property inventories do. Moreover, the value indicated is usually the purchase price, which is obviously a more objective criterion than the proceeds of confiscated goods sold through public auctions.

This essay is indebted to the reflections of Pierre Bourdieu regarding capital. During the 1980s, this renowned French sociologist made several inspiring and original theoretical observations on this subject.[7] Bourdieu regards capital as accumulated labour (in both materialized and embodied forms) that individual actors or groups acquire. He notes that capital is to be interpreted as a very broad concept that can take on different shapes. He identifies three fundamental forms: economic, cultural, and social capital. Economic capital is materialistic, can be converted directly into cash, and may be institutionalized through property rights. Social and cultural capital are to be viewed as transformed, concealed manifestations of economic capital. They are material and immaterial forms of capital; they function as symbolic capital.[8] Cultural capital relates to education, science, and art.[9]

Bourdieu defines social capital as all existing or potential resources that derive from ownership of a more or less institutionalized, sustainable network of relations of mutual familiarity and acknowledgement, or from membership of a group that supports each of its members through the collective capital.[10] Less abstractly, social capital therefore relates to group membership and investment in this group's social prestige. Such investments thus do not yield a direct personal financial gain but aim to enhance or at least consolidate the social standing of the group's members. Investments in social relations and reputations are of a highly diverse nature. They may involve distributing business gifts, rendering services, organizing drinking sprees and banquets, participating in municipal festivities and parades, attending religious services and funerals, constructing buildings, purchasing or renting chapels, wearing uniforms and insignia, purchasing all kinds of objects, and so on. Such investments need to be perceived in the context of representation strategies of social groups.[11] They contribute to displaying and activating internal and external group identity.[12]

Bourdieu has rightly noted that explaining the structure and operation of social mechanisms requires considering capital in all its manifestations. This statement is in our view equally applicable to the world of guilds. All guilds needed economic capital. After all, the many functions (economic, social, religious, political, military, and

---

7 Bourdieu, 1983, pp. 183-198. An English translation of the original German essay appears in Richardson, 1986, pp. 241-58.

8 Symbolic capital denotes any type of capital whatsoever, provided that it is represented, i.e. perceived in symbolic terms, and regarded as a subject of recognition or misunderstanding. On this concept, see Bourdieu, 1978, pp. 13-19.

9 The popular term 'human capital' relates to cultural capital. On this subject, see the reference work of Becker, 1964.

10 In addition to the publications reported in footnote 7, see Bourdieu, 1980, pp. 2-3.

11 The 'representation' concept has become firmly embedded in historical literature in recent years. See e.g. Ankersmit, 1990, and Chartier, 1989, pp. 1505-20. For an application of the representation theory to late medieval society, see the collection of essays edited by Blockmans and Janse, 1999.

12 The conspicuous consumption theory in Veblen, 1899, relates closely to social and symbolic capital.

cultural) which corporations held in urban society rendered financial resources indispensable.[13] Moreover, these tasks were often not strictly private but had a semi-public or even public character. To survive and function properly, guilds needed adequate and regular sources of income. Admission fees from new members and membership dues from established masters were an important source of income for most guilds. Often, however, these annual amounts were insufficient. Moreover, total returns were highly uncertain, because the number of dues-paying members could fluctuate strongly from year to year. Many guilds started to look for additional sources of income soon after they were established. Cash surpluses, gifts, and legacies were invested in immovable and movable property. Rents on properties, leases, and interests generated additional revenues. This way, the guild finances obtained a more solid basis.

Economic capital was a matter of major concern for all guilds, as their solvency largely determined their actions. But guilds were also interested in continuously producing and reproducing cultural and social capital as well. Guilds organized their own schooling. Training, knowledge transfer, education, and social advancement took place within the guild structures. The corporative world thus invested in cultural capital on a large scale. Several studies have demonstrated that guild members were very concerned about the image of their organization. With this in mind, guild boards subjected their members to all kinds of social and deontological rules of conduct and religious obligations.[14] Their objective was to stress and promote actual or ostensible mutual solidarity, social homogeneity, group identity, and cohesion among members. After all, they had to defend their reputation. Professional honour and concern for quality played an important role in this respect. To confirm the self-image and the image as it was perceived by others, guilds were involved with image-building and they devoted much time and care to public relations. Symbolic capital and social communication were therefore essential parts of the guilds' investment strategy.

2. Guildhalls

From the late Middle Ages onwards, many guilds in the Southern Netherlands endeavoured to obtain their own guildhall. In the course of the fifteenth century, most corporations acquired such premises, which they needed for practical reasons. Having their own hall enabled guild members to convene board meetings and plenary assemblies discreetly and without interruptions and to store guild privileges and other important documents in a safe place. In addition to serving as a meeting place and a repository for archives, guildhalls had a symbolic and a social function: on the one hand they

---

13 This multiplicity of functions distinguished guilds from other private associations in cities, such as civic militias, brotherhoods, chambers of rhetoric, neighbourhood associations…

14 These rules and obligations were not always observed, however, as is apparent from the participation requirement (attending plenary meetings, funeral ceremonies of guild brothers, guild masses, banquets, and processions). Frequent complaints about the high rate of absenteeism suggest that true corporative solidarity and cohesion did not apply in practice.

Figure 8.1 *'Het vleeshuis', guildhall of the Antwerp butchers, first half of the sixteenth century*
© Johan Dambruyne

symbolized and materialized a guild's official recognition, while on the other hand they were a status symbol and proof of corporative power. Like the homes of burghers, guildhalls reflected the guilds' financial means and social prestige and are to be considered as expressions of 'conspicuous consumption'.[15] Corporative associations competed with each other to procure the largest and most elegant building. In cities in the Southern Netherlands, most guilds owned or rented a guildhall. The proportion that owned a guildhall in the small towns is not clear, but in large and medium-sized towns, the majority of corporations did. Nearly three quarters of the 58 official Ghent guilds, for example, owned their hall in 1540.[16] Only the least solvent guilds continued to meet in churches, convents, inns, or at the homes of board members. Throughout the early modern period, ownership of a guildhall was not a constant. Some guilds lost their premises over time, often due to financial problems, but acquired another guildhall later on. Deeply in debt, guilds sometimes regarded selling their guildhall as the only option.[17] In addition to purchasing, rebuilding, and renovating properties, guilds had new halls built until well into the eighteenth century.[18] Old halls were replaced by new ones upon becoming dilapidated or old, or if they were destroyed. In 1695, for example, many guildhalls burned to the ground when the French troops of Louis XIV bombarded Brussels.[19] However, the Brussels guildhalls were rebuilt virtually overnight.[20] Although guildhalls in the Southern Netherlands tended to be built in a very traditional style — Gothic architecture prevailed until the end of the seventeenth century — some guilds, such as the fishmongers in Malines, preferred more fashionable and progressive architectural styles.[21]

Many corporations spared no expense on their guildhall. In 1707 the Brussels brewers informed the city council that their new house had cost 40,000 Brabant

15 On the importance of buildings as expressions of 'conspicuous consumption', see Burke, 1988, pp. 163-84.

16 Dambruyne, 1997, p. 155.

17 In some cases dire financial need led guildhalls to be sold at a serious loss. In 1506, for example, the Ghent furriers' guild sold its house on the Onderstraat for less than half of what the guild board had paid for the building in 1484. City Archives of Ghent, series 301, nr. 58, f. 8r; no. 69, f 91r.

18 In 1767-1768, for example, the Bruges coopers built an entirely new guildhall on the site of their former premises. Esther, 1986, p. 27.The united guild of Bruges carpenters and joiners built new premises as well in 1764-1765. Ryckaert, 1975, p. 40.

19 Culot, Hennaut, Demanet and Mierop, 1992. In Antwerp, for example, the guildhalls of the coopers, the bargees, and the fishmongers went up in smoke during the Spanish Fury of 4 November 1576. Dilis, 1926, pp. 264-5; Prims, 1935b, p. 330, 360.

20 A rather detailed review of the Brussels guildhalls appears in Jacobs, 1994, pp. 95-114.

21 Between 1530 and 1535 the fishmongers' guild in Malines built their magnificent, renaissance-style guildhall 'De Grote Zalm'. The façade may well feature the first application in our districts of the classical ordinance with the three colonnades superimposed. Van Uytven, 1991, p. 143.

guilders.[22] Although most other guildhalls cost less than the brewers', building a new guildhall or purchasing an existing one usually entailed considerable costs.[23] Lacking the necessary funds, most guilds borrowed large sums of money, incurring major debts.[24] The façades of most guildhalls looked very different from the average urban house. Unlike most of the burghers' residences, most guildhalls were made of brick by the sixteenth and seventeenth centuries. Some of the more expensive guildhalls had natural stone façades (sand-lime brick or bluestone), which enhanced their prestige.[25] Many guildhalls were also remarkably large buildings. They were wider, taller, and deeper than private residences. Some had turrets, such as the Antwerp Vleeshuis (the butchers' guildhall, figure 8.1). Another difference was their richly decorated façade, which featured guild symbols. Many façades were adorned with statues, bas-reliefs, medallions and cartouches. Images of patron saints, guild blazons and mottos, and sculptures referring to their occupation (e.g. tools) were the most frequent. As a tribute and to highlight good relations with the various authorities, certain guild façades featured the coats of arms of the city, or the ruler and his device.[26] Many of these sculptures were polychrome. Some decorations remain attractive to this day, such as the six life-size statues of Morisco dancers on the pinnacles of the Ghent masons' house or the majestic bronze equestrian statue of Governor Charles of Lorraine adorning the gable of the Brussels brewers' house.

Most guilds let parts of their guildhall. Many corporations used only one level, a few rooms, or only a single room in their premises.[27] The cellar areas were usually let as well. Various rental leases reveal that some guilds rarely used their hall at all.[28] The guilds that restricted their activities to one or a few rooms were not necessarily the smaller or less affluent ones. This reinforces the idea that many corporations regarded

---

22 Culot, Hennaut, Demanet and Mierop, 1992, p. 216.

23 The guildhall built by the Bruges coopers, for example, cost over 10,500 guilders.

24 In 1768, the Bruges coopers borrowed 9,600 guilders to pay for their guildhall.

25 The façades of the Ghent masons' and bargees' houses were made of sandstone and those of the Antwerp coopers' house, the Bruges carpenters' house, the Bruges coopers' house, and the Ghent smiths' house of bluestone.

26 The coat of arms of Emperor Charles V (a shield with an eagle and two pillars) and his motto 'Plus Oultre', as well as two Saint Andrew's crosses and the Burgundy coat of arms adorned the guildhall of the Ghent bargees from 1530. The same decoration appeared on the masons' guildhall (1528). The building named 'Huis der hertogen van Brabant' on the Grote Markt in Brussels, which accommodated six guildhalls, features busts of Dukes and Duchesses of Brabant.

27 Regarding the Brussels guildhalls, see the general survey from 1795: City Archives of Brussels, ancient archieves, file 723A.

28 A rental lease from 1550 for the guildhall of the Bruges masons stipulates that the tenant was to make the first floor, the dining room, the kitchen, the gallery, and the garden available to the guild for only three days a year. The dining room was also to be vacated on the days the accounts were drafted. City Archieves of Bruges, clerks of the Vierschaar, register no. 639, protocols of clerk Jan van Overyle, p. 587.

their guildhall primarily as a status symbol. Still, some guilds used their entire guildhall, either because they needed a lot of space, or because they feared that letting part of it would erode their prestige.

Another common characteristic of many guildhalls in the Southern Netherlands was their topographical location. Virtually all guildhalls were in the administrative and economic centre of the city. In 1540, about 90 per cent of all the guildhalls in Ghent were inside the old city centre known as the *Kuip van Gent*.[29] Guildhalls were remarkably concentrated around or in the immediate proximity to public market squares and other sites serving a specific economic purpose, such as the harbour. Several guildhalls were situated in close proximity to the industrial or commercial activities in which these guilds engaged.[30] The prevalence of guildhalls on certain streets is equally remarkable. Six guilds (brewers, sawyers, coopers, furriers, second hand dealers, and joiners) had their premises on the Onderstraat in Ghent.[31] There were four guilds (bakers, masons, shoemakers, and carpenters) on the Steenstraat in Bruges.[32] The Grote Markt in Antwerp was the site of the halls of the coopers, mercers, cloth dressers, cloth shearers, tanners, shoemakers, tailors, and the masters of Saint Luke's guild.[33] Corporative concentration was best exemplified by the Grote Markt in Brussels, however, where no less than sixteen guilds occupied stately edifices (figure 8.2).[34]

Guildhalls and burghers' residences differed not only in visual appearance, but also in terms of their value on the urban real estate market. The average rental and sales prices of guildhalls were considerably higher than those of an average private residence.[35] Yet, research on guildhalls in Ghent has revealed that the values of these premises varied considerably. The most expensive guildhall, that of the grocers (priced at 2,375 guilders), was worth 16 times as much as the one owned by the belt makers in

---

29 Dambruyne, 1997, p. 157.

30 Surrounding or in immediate proximity to the Ghent Vrijdagmarkt, where textiles, clothes, furniture, leather goods, household items, and all kinds of tools were sold, were the guildhalls of the mercers, second hand dealers, shoemakers, wood turners, cartwrights, and coopers.

31 Dambruyne, 1997, p. 158.

32 Vandewalle, 1985, p. 12.

33 In the immediate surroundings of the Grote Markt were also the guildhalls of the bargees, fishmongers, braid weavers (all on Gildekamerstraat), and furriers (on Maanstraatje). Bouwen, 1990, pp. 28-32, 58-69.

34 The locations of the different guildhalls are indicated on the map in Culot, Hennaut, Demanet and Mierop, 1992, pp. 196-7.

35 In 1540, for example, 58 per cent of the guildhalls in Ghent had a monetary value equivalent to at least 2,000 summer's day wages of a skilled worker. This was the case for only 3.7 per cent of the private residences sold on the property market between 1493 and 1503. Dambruyne, 1997, p.160. And while in Antwerp the rents for small and medium-sized burghers' residences ranged from 48 to 150 guilders between 1577 and 1586, the rent was 200 guilders for the Antwerp bargees' house and 300 guilders for the coopers' house. Tijs, 1993, p. 154.

Figure 8.2 *Guildhalls on the Brussels Grote Markt, after 1695*
© Johan Dambruyne

1540.[36] As is the case in many other fields, studies of property values confirm that the guild world was rigidly hierarchical, and that economic and political power and social prestige had material consequences as well.

The central government was well aware that corporations in the Netherlands cared deeply about their guildhalls. In towns where the guilds blocked the process of centralization, the government did not hesitate to eliminate guildhalls from the cityscape or to standardize their appearance. In all cases the intention was the same: to erode corporative power and identity. Following the Ghent uprising of 1539-1540, Emperor Charles V had all guildhalls in that city seized and sold at public auctions. In Brussels, after the bombardment of 1695, Governor Maximilian Emmanuel II of Bavaria wanted to turn the Grote Markt into a space that glorified the authority of the central state. Architect Willem de Bruyn was commissioned to join individual houses under common uniform façades, of which the structure and iconography were intended to simulate a royal residence and exude the symbolic presence of the governor general. According to designs that have been preserved, each block of houses was to be adorned with many symbols of central power, such as sculptures, crowned globes, a statue of Hercules, royal coats of arms, and so on. This plan was fiercely opposed by the Brussels guilds, however, because it eroded their corporative individuality.[37] In the end, only six guildhalls were united behind a common façade.

In addition to their guildhall, some corporations in the Southern Netherlands owned a hospice in the city. Unlike the hospices owned by municipal authorities or private citizens, however, the ones run by the guilds were not intended for the indigent and the invalid. Recent case studies reveal that most served as old age homes for well-to-do masters.[38] Corporative hospices had little to do with charity, as those without property did not stand a chance at being admitted. Those taking up residence there, known as *proveniers* (boarders), were required to leave all their possessions to the hospice. If the guild had its own chapel, these hospices would be adjacent; otherwise, they would be part of the guildhall. Corporations that owned a hospice tended to be very affluent guilds with a large membership or considerable political power. It was no coincidence that in Antwerp the three chief guilds (bargees, cloth dressers, and mercers) each owned a hospice.[39] Like guildhalls, corporative homes for the elderly served in part to highlight the association's social prestige. A minority of guilds ran hospices.[40] This select group of guilds was thus materially and visually distinct from the others.

---

36 Dambruyne, 1997, p. 159.

37 Culot, Hennaut, Demaret and Mierop, 1992, pp. 154, 187, 192.

38 See e.g. Eeraerts, 1997.

39 The smiths, tanners, and furriers acquired hospices in the fifteenth century as well, although the tanners sold their heavily indebted hospice again in 1724. Prims, 1947, pp. 290-1, 294 and Prims, 1939a, pp. 308-9.

40 In Ghent seven guilds (cloth weavers, fullers, bargees, tailors, tick weavers, smiths, and brewers) owned hospices. Dambruyne, 1997, p. 161. In Bruges the same held true for the weavers, smiths, bargees, tailors, bakers, and goldsmiths. Schouteet, 1975, p. 25.

In the Northern Netherlands, guilds were less visible in the urban landscape than they were in the South. There were no impressive corporative sites there, such as the Grote Markt in Brussels and Antwerp and the Graslei in Ghent. Far fewer guilds had their own guildhalls in the Northern Netherlands than in the South during the early modern period. In 1798, only 99 guilds out of the 592 (in 69 towns) for which data are available owned one or several buildings.[41] These data indicate that at most 17 per cent owned a guildhall. The actual share was probably even lower, since not every corporation used its premises as a guildhall. In only 26 of the 69 cities examined (i.e. 38 per cent of the total), did guilds actually own a hall, or an equivalent. In 1798, rates of guildhall ownership were highest in Maastricht (58 per cent), Alkmaar (56 per cent), and Amsterdam (50 per cent). Next came Hoorn (42 per cent), Enkhuizen (41 per cent), Bergen op Zoom (40 per cent), Arnhem (38 per cent), Haarlem (32 per cent), Nijmegen (21 per cent), and Dordrecht (18 per cent). Six of these ten towns were in the province of Holland, two in Gelderland, and one each in Limburg and North-Brabant. The data from 1798 also reveal that certain occupational groups were more likely than others to own a guildhall. Bargees and bakers owned one in nine cities, carpenters in seven, coopers and shoemakers in six, and mercers, goldsmiths, and fishmongers in five. Fragmentary data from the sixteenth and seventeenth centuries suggest that the number of guildhalls was no higher than at the end of the eighteenth century.[42] On the contrary, fewer corporations are believed to have owned guildhalls at the time. During the Dutch Republic most corporations had a guild room at public buildings (meat halls, cloth halls, city gates, city towers, city weighing houses, convents, hospitals, beguinages) and inns. Prior to the Reformation, many guilds met in churches.[43] The guild altar was considered the actual domicile of the corporation. Some guilds purchased a guildhall during the early modern period[44] or built one.[45]

Guildhalls in the North were also less striking than the ones in the South. In the North they were rarely impressive, or richly decorated and were less likely to be concentrated in the city centre. The value of these premises also proves that guilds in the Northern Netherlands invested less in guildhalls. Unlike in the South, the sales and rental prices of guild halls were rarely higher than those of average burghers' residences.[46] The same holds true for corporative hospices — usually referred to as

---

41 Based on the IISH guilds database.

42 Amsterdam, Haarlem, The Hague, Zwolle, Arnhem, and 's-Hertogenbosch were the main focus.

43 Goudriaan, 1996, p. 23; Graswinckel, 1933, pp. 93-121.

44 The bakers of Haarlem, for example, purchased a building in 1784. Nationaal Archief in The Hague, Wetgevende Colleges, 507. That same year the Zwolle bargees acquired a guildhall as well; they had previously convened at 'De Keiser' tavern. City Archives of Zwolle, AAZ 0, nr. 323

45 In 1644, for example, the Haarlem mercers' guild built a guildhall. Bot, 1996, p. 13.

46 Lesger, 1986.

hofjes in the North: they existed but were not nearly as widespread as in the Southern Netherlands.[47]

3. Guild interiors

What did the interiors of guildhalls in the Southern Netherlands look like? Were they lavishly decorated, and which objects were the most prominent? Reviews of guild interiors should reflect a chronological distinction between the sixteenth and eighteenth centuries, with the seventeenth century as a transition period. Most objects in guildhalls were furnishings and other household items. The household effects of guilds were rarely very valuable,[48] although their value varied considerably depending on the guild.[49] Guilds with large memberships tended to own costlier furnishings than those with fewer souls. In addition, the value of the household effects was directly proportional to that of the guildhall. The most valuable furnishings appeared in the more expensive guildhalls. Conversely, corporations without guildhalls logically did not have furniture or other household items either. The average furnishings of corporative associations did not compare in monetary value or number to those of the social elite and the middle class.[50] Overall, the total value of the household items corresponded with their number, i.e. costlier guildhall furnishings tended to include a far higher quantity of objects than less valuable ones. Some guilds had dozens of furniture items, while others owned only a few. Wooden benches, seats, tables, trunks, and office furniture were the most common items. Office furniture (writing desks and storage devices) was extremely common in guildhalls because of the administrative function of such premises. Considering the role of guildhalls as meeting venues, the presence of seats and tables is obvious. Since trunks were the most common storage devices until well into the seventeenth century, cabinets did not become widespread in guildhalls until the eighteenth century. The records of guilds were usually kept in specially designed trunks. Most guilds spent little on lighting or heating devices, such as chandeliers, candle holders, hearth plates, fire racks, tongs, and bellows.

During the sixteenth and the first half of the seventeenth centuries, few guilds in the Southern Netherlands were interested in decorative objects. A minority of

---

47 Bos, 1998, p. 45. Saint Eligius' hospice of the Utrecht smiths' guild housed eight proveniers. Ritter, 1987, pp. 100-5.

48 The median value of the household effects seized from the Ghent guilds amounted to the equivalent of 32 day's pay of a skilled wage worker in the construction industry in 1540, the arithmetic average of the equivalent of 56 day wages. Dambruyne, 1998, p. 5.

49 The household effects of the Ghent wine cask gaugers, for example, were worth 75 times as much as those of the plasterers in 1540.

50 See e.g.: 'Inventaire du mobilier de la corporation des tanneurs de Bruges', in *Le Beffroi: arts, héraldique, archéologie* vol 2, 1864-1865, pp. 264-74. This 1479 inventory makes abundantly clear that most objects pertained to the chapel rather than to the guildhall.

corporations owned one or more paintings, which tended above all to feature religious scenes. Several paintings depicted the Last Judgement, probably due to the law practised by the guilds. Many aldermen's courtrooms are known to have been adorned with paintings of the same topic.[51] These paintings illustrated the dispensation of justice. In the course of the seventeenth century the number of paintings increased, in part because many old altarpieces were transferred from chapels and churches to the guildhalls. Unlike halls of civic militias, guild chambers contained very few portraits of board members. Among the few exceptions were six portraits of former deans in the guild chamber of the Malines' wheelbarrow porters. By the end of the eighteenth century the Antwerp butchers had a portrait gallery featuring fifteen former deans. Antwerp's Saint Luke's guild had many portraits of former deans as well.[52] In the second half of the seventeenth century the first group portraits of board members began to appear in guild chambers in the Southern Netherlands.[53] The reason that far more group portraits were painted for guild altars than for guildhalls was probably that this type of decoration yielded greater social benefits when placed in a public space. More expensive decorations, such as sculptures and tapestries, are rarely found in guildhalls. Many guilds owned drinking utensils, such as pitchers, mugs, and dishes, but were far less likely to have cooking and eating utensils. This suggests that guild meals were not always taken at the guildhall, or that masters brought their own utensils and cooking implements from home.

The most valuable guild objects were undoubtedly the ones made of precious metals. They exuded the most prestige. Nearly all precious metal guild objects were made of silver. Gold objects were exceedingly rare. Most corporations owned a few pieces of silver, which cost them far more than their furniture and other household effects. While the wealthiest guilds generally had the most expensive silver objects, exceptions occurred. Profane silver guild objects consisted primarily of drinking and eating implements (pitchers, mugs, dishes, plates and utensils) and guild insignia and seals. Within the guild world, much communication was done through symbols.[54] Guild insignia were an important aspect of visual culture during the early modern period.[55] At public ceremonies, meetings, and processions, members of the guild board wore their guild insignia. Guilds valued such distinguishing badges as ways to set themselves apart from the other corporations, and because they were visible to all the townspeople

---

[51] de Ridder, 1989.

[52] Schoeffer, 1996, p. 368; Prims, 1935a, p. 388. A few guilds had portraits painted of their chaplains (e.g. the Antwerp mercers).

[53] The group portraits that remain include those of the Bruges tailors, bargees, and smiths (Bruges, Groeningemuseum) and the Malines tailors (Malines, Hof van Busleyden). During the fifteenth century and the early decades of the sixteenth century, board members generally had their likenesses immortalized together with their guild's patron saint on miniatures, as manifested by the miniatures remaining in the guild registers of the Ghent tanners, brewers, woodcutters, and carpenters (City Archives of Ghent).

[54] Farr, 1988, pp. 153-4.

[55] On wearing insignia, see Koldeweij, 1999, pp. 307-28.

during public parades and festivities. Usually the guild aid had a special silver plate as well (often a shield worn on his chest).[56] The weight, size, workmanship, and cost of such insignia varied widely. These emblems generally featured the guild's coat of arms, patron saint, or other symbols (such as miniature anchors for the bargees, or miniature hats for the hatmakers). Board members and the guild aid wore their insignia on a silk ribbon or on a chain around their neck, on their chest, or had it affixed to their hat. Many guilds also owned a silver mould of their seal.

The interiors of guildhalls in the Southern Netherlands appear to have been transformed during the course of the early modern period. A gradual change in attitude became apparent after the mid-seventeenth century. The costly baroque gilt leather interior placed in the council chamber of the Antwerp brewers' guildhall in 1664 exemplified this trend. Another early example is the magnificent stucco ceiling ornamentation in the conference room of the Ghent brewers' guildhall from 1679.[57] In addition to the symbols of the brewers' guild, the de la Faille coat of arms, and a medallion featuring the brewers' tools, four other medallions depicting the Labours of Hercules appear on the ceiling. Only in the eighteenth century, however, did guild interiors generally become more lavish. The well-preserved guild chamber of the Bruges tailors' guild, for example, had an elaborate classicist interior. The wall grisaille above the entrance door makes clear that this room was decorated in 1779. The walls and ceiling feature elegant stucco. All four walls are rhythmically separated by grooved pilasters with Corinthian capitals. The ceiling features an octagonal painting, with an elaborate ornamental border. The guild commissioned the renowned Bruges painter Jan Beerblock to do the fancy paintings on the ceiling and the heraldic doorframe. In the centre hangs a beautiful crystal chandelier. The entrance to the chamber has a marble frame adorned with the Bruges coat of arms, as well as coats of arms of the several sections of this guild. The interior is also decorated with a Louis XVI black marble mantelpiece. In 1779 the tailors spent 4,102 guilders on remodelling and furnishing their house, decorating the new guild chamber, and building a new Louis XVI wooden stairway.[58] This example from Bruges aptly illustrates the guilds' desire for bourgeois grandeur during the eighteenth century.

From the final quarter of the seventeenth century, guilds started to purchase noticeably more expensive furniture, more silver, and other luxury items. One such item is the wall fountain featuring sea gods that belonged to the Brussels fishermen. The guild ordered this sculpture group from Gabriël Grupello in 1675 to use as a wine cooler in the conference room. During the eighteenth century guild interiors appear

---

[56] See e.g. the beautiful silver insignia of Namur's millers, porters, mercers, potters, butchers, bakers, bargees and joiners depicted in Toussaint, 1998, pp. 10, 23, 30, 57, 93, 108, 153, 165.

[57] The stucco is by Jan Christiaen Hansche. The commission came not from the guild itself but from the nobleman Pieter de la Faille, the administrative supervisor of the corporation at the time: Van Vaeck, 1997, pp. 51-2.

[58] This amount does not include finishing the staircase. The total cost of the staircase, which was completed in 1787, exceeded 1,427 guilders. Esther, 1991, p. 27.

to have been furnished more elaborately than during the sixteenth century, although exceptions occurred. In some cases financial troubles necessitated the sale of part of the guild property. Around the mid-eighteenth century, the Antwerp coopers' guild, for example, faced massive debts and saw no other option but to sell its silverware, raising 1,110 guilders in the process.[59] The more elegant furnishings of the guild interiors in the Southern Netherlands during the eighteenth century may not have been a specifically guild-related phenomenon, and probably arose from changes in consumer tastes during the early modern period.[60]

Guilds in the Northern Netherlands appear to have compared poorly with their counterparts in the Southern Netherlands in material culture as well, with the gap widening during the eighteenth century. The confiscation list from 1798 offers the most comprehensive account for the North and reveals that among the 592 registered guilds, only 90 (i.e. 15 per cent) of the corporations examined owned furniture. The items occurring most frequently on the list are tables, chairs, and trunks (for storing records and instruments for administering the masterpiece). Guild furnishings were the most common in the larger cities. In the city of Groningen at the end of the eighteenth century over 90 per cent of all guilds owned household goods, compared with 61 per cent in Alkmaar, 27 per cent in Amsterdam, and 15 per cent in Rotterdam. Calculating the value of the household goods for Groningen reveals that the furniture of the 37 guilds represented a combined capital of 919 guilders, averaging 25 guilders for each guild. As in the South, considerable differences existed between guilds in Groningen. The furniture of the guild with the largest number of items, for example, was worth 94 times the value of the household goods of the guild with the smallest number of items. Bakers, goldsmiths, and tailors owned the most valuable household goods, assessed at 142, 104, and 71 guilders, respectively.

Nor could the silver collections of the guilds in the Northern Netherlands hold a candle to those of their counterparts in the Southern Netherlands. In 1798 only one quarter of the guilds (152 out of 592) owned silver objects. The low rate is partly because guilds ceased to own silver ritual items (except for pall ornaments) from the 1570s.[61] Aside from these guild emblems that adorned the pall, mugs, spoons, forks, knives, and guild aid symbols were the most common silver items. Some guilds owned silver salt tubs, pepper pots, platters, goblets, scissors, and servant boxes as well. Silver cutlery was the most prevalent among guilds in Groningen (95 per cent of all guilds), Veere (64 per cent), Arnhem (63 per cent), Goes (54 per cent), The Hague (50 per cent), Leeuwarden (50 per cent), Utrecht (36 per cent), Nijmegen (36 per cent), Amsterdam (33 per cent), Delft (27 per cent), and Rotterdam (26 per cent). In 1798 the silver cutlery of the 39 Groningen corporations represented a combined capital of 8,945 guilders, averaging 229 guilders for each guild. Vast discrepancies

---

[59] There were two wine pitchers, three salt tubs, three pepper pots, three mustard jars, six drinking vessels, 24 forks and spoons, a large octagonal dish, and two jugs: Dilis, 1926, pp. 277-8.

[60] Brewer and Porter, 1993. See also, McKendrick, Brewer and Plumb, 1982.

[61] van den Bergh-Hoogterp and Dubbe, 1997, pp. 47-52.

existed between the guilds in Groningen: the monetary value of the guild possessing the highest number of silver objects was 701 times that of the guild with the fewest such items. Bargees ranked first (3,821 guilders), followed by a wide margin by the mercers (516 guilders), tailors (505 guilders), and bakers (501 guilders). The value of the silver owned by the Groningen guilds was nearly tenfold that of their furniture.

Unlike civic militias, very few craft guilds in Holland and the other provinces spent their money on group portraits. The dignified Amsterdam surgeons appear to have been exceptional in this respect. Hanging on the walls of their chambers were paintings of former board members from 1679, 1684, 1699, 1706, 1731, and 1732, as well as many paintings of anatomy lessons (1603, 1619, 1626, 1632, 1656, 1679, 1683, 1728, and 1758).[62] The collection included two world-renowned canvases by Rembrandt: the 'Anatomy Lecture of Dr. Nicolaes Tulp' from 1632 and the one of 'Dr. Joan Deijman' from 1656. Compared with other corporations, however, the Amsterdam surgeons' guild was an exclusive group of affluent citizens.[63]

4. Guild chapels and guild altars

In the Southern Netherlands the presence of guilds was palpable in areas of worship throughout the early modern period as well. Religion has always been essential in corporative circles. Not only did all guilds honour a patron saint,[64] but most also owned an altar or chapel in one of the parish or convent churches from the fifteenth century onward and frequently organized masses honouring their patron saint and commemorating their deceased guild brothers. Guild members hoped that such acts of piety would ensure their spiritual salvation.[65] In some cities (e.g. Ghent and Bruges),[66] guilds had a full chapel in the church, whereas guilds in other centres (e.g. Antwerp) merely had an altar. Because of the large number of candidates (craft guilds, civic militias, chambers of rhetoric, brotherhoods, neighbourhood associations), the demand for chapels usually exceeded the supply, forcing several associations to share a chapel in the choir or nave. In many churches altars were even placed against pillars along the nave. Some corporations maintained common altars to reduce costs. The huge

---

62 Kurpershoek, 1994, p. 89.

63 According to standards of the Northern Netherlands, the admission fee of the Amsterdam surgeons' guild was very high (more than the annual wages of a guildsman at the end of the eighteenth century), and setting up an independent practice required substantial start-up capital as well. Lourens and Lucassen, 1996, p. 15.

64 Patron saints were constituent to the group identity of guild members. Their personalities highlighted the 'virtue' of their trade. Guild members therefore tended to select a genuine or alleged former fellow tradesman as their patron saint. Thijs, 1994, p. 239. A list of the different corporative patron saints in the Southern Netherlands appears in Heirwegh and Van Belle, 1991.

65 Black, 1989, pp. 104, 270-71.

66 Eighty-six per cent of all guilds in Ghent had their own chapel. Dambruyne, 1997, p. 161.

demand enabled church boards to charge high prices. Guilds were often required to pay part of the cost of constructing or finishing the chapel. Despite these major investments, no guild could be sure of retaining its chapel or altar over the long term. Church boards might eventually assign the dedicated space to a different guild or private association.[67]

While religious motives were undoubtedly important for investing in a space of prayer, other factors came into play as well. Owning a chapel or altar afforded guilds with an additional means to legitimize their existence. Moreover, collective worship continued and reinforced solidarity among members. Some guilds used their chapel for board meetings as well. Last but not least, chapels and altars were ideal for corporations to flaunt their social prestige. A splendid altar was a token of prestige for affluent and less affluent corporations alike. As churches were heavily frequented public venues, guild chapels and altars drew crowds of viewers. Investing in religious buildings tied in perfectly with the representation strategies of the guilds. This reveals why guilds took such pains to obtain spaces of prayer.

In large and medium-sized cities, some churches contained noticeably more guild altars than others.[68] This concentration arose first of all from the location of the guildhalls. Since these tended to be in the city centre, most guild altars were in centrally situated parish and convent churches.[69] While guilds regularly moved to a different chapel during the early modern period, they almost always remained loyal to their church.[70]

Several affluent guilds built their own chapel within their guildhall or hospice.[71] These chapels usually consisted of a single nave and were topped with a roof turret. Like the guildhalls, their façades were adorned with guild iconography (a statue of the patron saint, coats of arms, and other guild emblems). Several guilds could even afford two chapels: one connected to their guildhall or hospice and another in a parish or mendicant order church to enhance the guild's prestige. All these corpora-

---

[67] In 1628, the priest and the church wardens of Saint Jacob's Church in Antwerp repeatedly urged the sawyers' guild to arrange illustrious religious services on all Sundays and holidays, instead of only on major holidays; otherwise, they would consider transferring the chapel to the wealthier satin workers' guild. City Archives of Antwerp, Privilegekamer 726 (rekestboek 1627-1628), f. 185r.

[68] There were about twenty guild altars in Antwerp's Cathedral of Our Lady. Marinus, 1993, p. 58. In Malines, many guilds had their altar in Saint Romuald's Cathedral.

[69] In some cities the church where the guild had its altar correlated with the political power of the corporative associations. Among over twenty guilds with altars in Antwerp's cathedral, only five did not serve on the municipal Broad Council. Verleysen, 2000, pp. 62-3.

[70] The Bruges tailors were exceptions. In 1600 they moved their altar from Saint Christopher's Chapel on the Markt to Saint Saviour Cathedral: Van Houtryve, 1975, p. 71.

[71] In Bruges the weavers, smiths, painters-saddle makers, musicians, bargees, and brokers each had their own chapel. Schouteet, 1975, p. 22. In Malines the smiths (until the early seventeenth century) and the tanners did. After all, Malines was an important production centre of leather. Schoeffer, 1996, vol. 3, pp. 12-13, 28.

tions were widely respected within the urban community.[72] In our view, these guilds invested greater efforts in arranging their altars in their church than in arranging the ones in their own chapel because of the higher public visibility of the chapels in the parish churches.[73] Guilds were extremely sensitive to loss of prestige, as manifested by the vehement resistance on the part of several important Antwerp guilds to the use of their exclusive chapels as Sunday school classrooms in the early seventeenth century.[74] Since the children taught there were of humble social origins, the guilds were concerned about their reputation.

In addition to competing with each other to obtain the finest, most spacious, and most centrally situated chapels,[75] guilds vied in their ornamentation. Most chapels had a marble, bronze, cast-iron, or wooden enclosure and lavishly decorated altars and wooden seats, as well as other ornaments. Many guilds owned ritual silver for celebrating masses at their altar, especially communion cups, ampullae, patens, crucifixes, and ciboriums. Fewer owned silver statuettes of patron saints and reliquaries. In addition to precious metal objects, many guilds owned chasubles,[76] altar gowns, antependiums, metal candelabra, holy-water fonts, and printed missals. Most ritual objects featured the guild emblem. The finery displayed at religious celebrations highlighted the prestige of the guilds.[77] Organ music and choirs made the most important masses (e.g. on the patron saint's day) especially festive. Chapels and altars were cleaned and beautifully decorated for these occasions.

Altars were the main eye-catchers of the ritual guild furnishings. Many of the altarpieces were of a high artistic value, and considerable sums were spent on them. In the late 1670s, for example, the new altar of the Antwerp coopers cost over 8,000 guilders.[78] Not only in large cities, but also in small towns guilds spent huge sums on their altars.[79] These investments weighed heavily on the guilds' budget. The Iconoclasm

---

72 In Antwerp, the following six important guilds had two chapels: mercers, smiths, cloth dressers, furriers, bargees, and tanners.Verleysen, 2000, p. 63. In Ghent, the bargees, smiths, tick weavers, and butchers had two chapels: Dambruyne, 1997, p. 162.

73 This is apparent in part from the common practice of placing discarded paintings and the church's old ritual objects in the chapel or guild room: Verleysen, 2000, p. 63.

74 Poffe, 1895, p. 47.

75 In Gouda the guild hierarchy in processions was in fact determined by the location of the altar in Saint John's Church. Guilds with altars near the presbytery marched with two torches and the others with only one: Goudriaan, 1996, p. 35.

76 In 1520, the Antwerp mercers had a new chasuble made. They commissioned the famous German painter Albrecht Dürer, who was in their city at the time, to depict their patron Saint Nicholas and other figures.

77 Popular worship tends to emphasize ritual over actual religious substance: van Dülmen, 1986, p. 19.

78 Prims, 1938b, p. 300.

79 After purchasing Saint John's chapel from the linen weavers in 1713, the Aalst guild of shopkeepers, for example, installed a new altar made of Genoese marble valued at 4,000 guilders. Extensive data concerning the equipment and maintenance of the guild chapels and altars in Aalst appear in Van Nuffel, 1911, pp. 41-88.

of 1566 caused indescribable damage to corporative altars. Following the Catholic Reconciliation (1584-1585), guilds in the Southern Netherlands were obliged by the central government and the municipal authorities to rebuild their altars. Although the heyday for new altars was undeniably in the late sixteenth and early seventeenth centuries, guilds continued to renovate their altars until well into the eighteenth century.[80]

Affluent guilds commissioned paintings from renowned artists. Rogier van der Weyden, Quinten Metsys, Barend van Orley, Pieter Bruegel the Elder, Pieter Pourbus, Michiel Coxcie, Maarten de Vos, Frans and Ambrosius Francken, Otto van Veen, Pieter Paul Rubens, and countless other great artists produced magnificent altar scenes for guilds.[81] The contracts that remain reveal that the guilds instructed the painters as to the materials to be used and the size and price of the painting. Other guilds obtained magnificent altarpieces as donations (usually from affluent members).[82] During the fifteenth and sixteenth centuries, most corporations purchased scenes of their patron saint (especially of their saint's death as a martyr). Depictions of their patron saint at the altar obviously enabled the guilds to emphasize their corporation's identity to outsiders. Other guilds used biblical scenes relating to their own occupational activities.[83]

---

80 In honour of its anniversary, Saint Luke's guild in Antwerp built a new altar in 1753. The previous one was from 1602. Prims, 1939b, pp. 379-81; Peeters, (forthcoming).

81 In 1508, the Antwerp joiners ordered a triptych ('The Lamentation') from Quinten Metsys (now in the Royal Museum of Fine Arts of Antwerp). Metsys also painted the altarpiece 'Descent from the Cross' for the Antwerp coopers. Prims, 1938b, pp. 296, 300. The court painter Barend van Orley executed a triptych for the altar that the Brussels carpenters and masons shared at the Sablon Chapel. Jacobs, 1994, p. 99. Pieter Bruegel the Elder is known to have assisted with the altarpiece of the Malines glove makers. Monballieu, 1964, pp. 92-110. After 1585 in Antwerp, the Francken family, Maarten de Vos, and Otto van Veen executed many paintings for guilds and other associations. See Peeters, 2000, volume 1, chapter 3; A. Zweite, 1980; Muller Hofstede, 1957. The Antwerp mercers ordered an altarpiece from Maarten de Vos in 1586 and another scene from Otto van Veen in 1607 (priced at 2,700 guilders). Prims, 1938c, p. 333. In 1618, the Malines fishmongers ordered the well-known painting 'The Miraculous Draught of Fishes' from Pieter Paul Rubens. The guild paid 1,600 guilders for the work of art. Schoeffer, 1996, pp. 167-8.

82 In 1480, for example, the wealthy Bruges tanner and alderman Pieter Bultync donated Hans Memling's painting 'Seven Blessings of the Virgin' into the chapel of the tanners' guild. The magnificent panel is now at the Alte Pinakothek in Munich.

83 In 1576, for example, the Bruges fishmongers ordered a painting from Pieter Pourbus depicting 'The Miraculous Draught of Fishes', now at the Royal Museums of Fine Arts of Belgium, Brussels. Van Houtryve, 1975, pp. 71-2. In 1598, Ambrosius Francken painted 'Multiplication of the Loaves' for the Antwerp bakers and 'Marriage at Cana' for the wine innkeepers. Peeters, 2000; Prims, 1939, pp. 303-4. Rogier van der Weyden is believed to have painted the panel 'Saint Luke drawing the Virgin' for the chapel of the Brussels Saint Luke's guild at the Church of Saint Gudule in Brussels. The original of this theme is in Boston, at the Museum of Fine Arts, although many copies exist. De Vos, 1999, pp. 200-6. In 1602, Maarten de Vos produced a scene of a similar subject for Antwerp's Saint Luke's guild. Prims, 1939, p. 379; Peeters (forthcoming).

Board members had images of themselves painted on some altarpieces on the wings or even on the centre panels.[84]

The sixteenth-century triptych 'De Vier Gekroonden' (the Four Crowned) of the homonymous Brussels guild, now at the Broodhuis Museum in Brussels, exemplifies how guild altarpieces demonstrated the guild's identity. The legend of the four patron saints appears on the centrepiece, while tradesmen at work are depicted on the side panels. The right panel features masons and slaters building a house, while the left one depicts the stonecutters and sculptors at work. On the foreground of the side panels four guild deans kneel before their instruments. The altarpiece 'Wedding of Mary and Joseph' of the Antwerp carpenters of 1640 reveals members of the guild board on the centre panel.[85] Fifteen former and current board members appear on the painting as witnesses to the marriage. The priest performing the ceremony is the guild's chaplain. Painter Pieter van Lint has engraved the names of those depicted on two stone columns. The officials appear in formal attire, wearing black gowns with white lace collars. These portraits are to be perceived as both a means of self-representation, and as an advertisement of the social prestige of the parties depicted.[86]

From the end of the sixteenth century, religious censorship and regulations became visible in altarpieces.[87] The rise of Jansenism reinforced this trend. The Counter Reformation Church issued rigid directives and scrupulously monitored them. From the seventeenth century onwards, for example, at least the centre panel of the altar triptychs was required to feature a scene of Christ or a subject from the New Testament. Both the traditional scenes of patron saints and the guild altars that served mainly as tributes to the board members were challenged. Ecclesiastical authorities regarded portraits on altarpieces as blatant secularization of saints. Accordingly, the third provincial synod of Malines stipulated in 1607 that live persons were no longer to be depicted on the centre panels of triptychs. The altarpiece of the Antwerp carpenters was therefore harshly criticized by the clergy in the 1640s; and was replaced within a few years with a new painting, which no longer featured the members of the guild board.[88]

---

84 See e.g. the altarpieces of the Antwerp wine innkeepers (Maarten de Vos), schoolteachers and soap boilers (Frans Francken), and smiths (Ambrosius Francken). Peeters, 2000, volume 3, cat. no. F9, pp. 21-7; cat. no. A3, pp. 5-8; Vandamme, 1988, pp. 146, 148. The altarpiece of the Antwerp peat carriers' guild features the deans, the elders, and the chaplain on the predella.

85 Prims, 1935a.

86 Burke, 1987.

87 Although formulated during the Council of Trent (1545-1563), the decrees on art (the use of the image in the Catholic doctrine) were only followed only from the end of the sixteenth century onwards. Baudoin, 1986, p. 107.

88 Prims, 1938a, p. 287.

The triumph of the Catholic Counter Reformation in the Southern Netherlands coincided with a religious investment drive on the part of the guilds. This did not necessarily signify a more sincere or intense sense of devotion on the part of guild members. There are no indications that rebuilding the altars and chapels and reinstating religious services meant that corporative religiosity was reawakening.[89] The intention of these investments appears to have been secular rather than religious. The religious customs, especially rebuilding the altars, apparently served primarily to legitimize and confirm the social position of the guilds in the community.[90] The economic decline and the major shifts in the corporative world at the end of the sixteenth century necessitated reaffirming old prerogatives and consequently increased concern about external display. The Antwerp carpenters' guild was a case in point. In 1625, the guild decided to reduce the frequency of religious services from all Sundays and holidays to the most important holidays only. The purpose of this measure was to have more money to spend on the guild altar.[91]

Until the Dutch Revolt, the guild policy in the Northern Netherlands of maintaining a presence of guilds in religious spaces was virtually identical to that in the Southern Netherlands. Until the 1570s, most guilds owned an altar in a parish church.[92] Guilds in the North also adorned altars with beautiful retables and triptychs and commissioned works from renowned painters. In 1532, for example, Haarlem's Saint Luke's guild had Maarten van Heemskerk execute a painting of its patron saint, while in 1546 the Haarlem cloth dressers' guild ordered a triptych from the same renowned artist.[93] As in the South, several important guilds owned an exclusive chapel at their guildhall or hospice.[94] From the end of the sixteenth century, though, the North pursued a progressively different course from the South. While in the Southern Netherlands the Dutch Revolt meant only a temporary hiatus in corporative investments in religious buildings, the change in the Northern Netherlands was irreversible. From the 1570s, guild altars and the accompanying statues of saints, altarpieces, chasubles, and other paraphernalia were permanently banned from the churches, together with the Catholic services.[95] Under the Dutch Republic, the government encouraged the guilds to become involved in social causes. Allocating the guild's financial resources toward support for needy members was deemed worthier than spending on religious causes. Most guilds allowed other users to take over their chapel.[96] Only the burial rituals

---

[89] Thijs, 1990.

[90] This is very clear from F. Verleysen's case study of Antwerp: Verleysen, 2001, pp. 153-74.

[91] Thijs, 1987a, p. 103.

[92] In Gouda, for example, all but one of the guilds had an altar in Saint John's Church: Goudriaan, 1996, p. 24.

[93] van der Ree-Scholtens 1995, p. 89; Allan, 1874-1888, vol. 1, p. 212.

[94] In Gouda the bargees, fishmongers, and porters each had their own chapel.

[95] Lourens and Lucassen, 1996, p. 14.

[96] Palmen, 1998, p. 229.

were continued under the Republic. In several cities, guilds maintained crypts. In Dordrecht and Utrecht, half the guilds still had a crypt at one of the parish churches in 1798.[97] These tombs featured guild insignia and were thus forms of social representation. Neither the appearance of, nor the investments in these humble tombs, however, could hold a candle to the magnificent guild altars in the Southern Netherlands. In the eighteenth century, the average grave in Dordrecht's Grote Kerk (Great Church) cost 68 guilders, while a typical tombstone cost 11 guilders.[98] This was a pittance compared to the amounts that guilds in the Southern Netherlands spent on their altars. In the South, the Counter Reformation offered new opportunities for guilds to exhibit their social prestige, whereas in the North, Protestantism rigidly curtailed demonstrative capital in religious spaces.

5. Public manifestations

Within the world of guilds there was a permanent urge for social recognition and respectability. In addition to building striking corporative edifices as an expression of their constant quest for social appreciation and affirmation, they participated in all kinds of public manifestations. Public rituals were highly symbolic events for guilds. After all, festivals were channels for socio-professional groups to exchange all kinds of information, opinions, feelings, and acts. Guild turnout was always high in both public events for religious causes (processions, royal baptisms, weddings, and funerals) and profane festivities (royal entries, royal visits, heraldic parades, and so on). Guild members were far more than passive observers at these occasions. Processions, because of their high frequency, were perfect opportunities for corporative associations to appear in public. Solemn processions marched through town on the most important religious holidays. Occasionally, processions were also organized by the central government and the city magistrate to obtain peace, to invoke familial and political good fortune of the sovereign, to protect the Catholic faith, or to request Divine protection from infectious diseases and other disasters. Within the guild world of the Southern Netherlands, these parades served a religious, political, and social purpose. Collective participation in processions legitimized and affirmed the position of guilds in urban society and nurtured solidarity among fellow tradesmen. The most important and most universal procession was indisputably that of Corpus Christi.[99] This procession took place in all cities in Europe on Sacrament day. Highly symbolic, it invoked

---

97 In Haarlem the shoemakers and brewers were the only guilds that still had a crypt in 1798. In Gouda the shoemakers and the basket and hamper makers owned one or more graveyards since the fifteenth century.

98 Prices ranged from 30 to 264 guilders, depending on the location and size of the grave. Palmen, 1998, p. 230.

99 James, 1983, pp. 3-13; Zemon Davis, 1981, pp. 64-6, 68. In addition to the Corpus Christi procession, nearly every city had one or several processions more magnificent than the

Figure 8.3 *Polychromed procession torch of the Ghent masons' guild, 1747*
© Johan Dambruyne

physical metaphors. The body of Christ was related to the 'social body', emphasizing the unity of the urban community and at the same time acknowledging that this body comprised several 'limbs'. The sequence of the Corpus Christi procession was rigidly hierarchical. All guilds cared deeply about the place they were assigned in processions and other parades.[100] In addition to conveying the social position of the guilds in the urban community, the sequence reflected the corporative hierarchy. Since the prestige and honour of the participating groups was at stake, infringements on the traditional order were often cause for heated quarrels and discussions. In various cities only the privileged guilds had a fixed place in the processions. In Antwerp, for example, this privilege was restricted to the 25 or so guilds represented on the city's Broad Council. Such rituals thus divided the guilds according to those who were participants and those who were excluded. Guilds marching in front tended to be the most socially prestigious and those at the rear the least. In some cities the reverse arrangement applied. In Ghent and Antwerp the parade was led by the bargees, who in both cities: (1) had high social prestige, (2) were major economic forces, and (3) wielded great political power and influence. In some cities the sequence depended on the seniority of the guild. Accordingly, smiths marched at the front of the procession in Malines.[101] While in many cities the sequence remained unchanged for centuries, it was revised in Namur, for example, at the end of the Ancien Régime. From 1779 proof of seniority was the sole determining factor.[102] Various other elements besides sequence determined the social prestige of the guilds. The number of procession torches a corporation was authorized to carry was equally indicative in many cases. In several cities the positions of the guilds correlated directly with the prestige of their urban properties. In Ghent, for example, all guilds that ran hospices marched in the first third of the Corpus Christi procession, while all corporations with their own chapel were at the head of the parade as well.

Compared with other types of social capital, participation in processions rarely required major corporative investments. This was because the recurring annual expenditures tended to be minimal and were often limited to purchasing candles, torches, and wax. Major expenses, such as new procession torches, pennants, and silver guild insignia, were sporadic, see figure 8.3.[103] These objects would last dozens of years. Special processions were a different matter and imposed a heavy financial burden on guilds. In honour of the seventh centennial anniversary of Saint Macharius, one of Ghent's patron saints, for example, the municipal authorities asked each guild to

others. In Brussels it was the Sablon procession, in Bruges the Holy Blood procession, in Gouda the Saint John's procession, and in Antwerp the processions on Holy Trinity Day and Ascension Day.

[100] Burrage and Corry, 1981, pp. 375-93; Muir, 1981.

[101] Schoeffer, 1996, vol. 3, p. 2.

[102] Jacobs, 1997, p. 259.

[103] In the financial year 1617-1618 the Antwerp mercers' guild invested over 430 guilders, or 13 per cent of its total expenditures, in new procession torches. Verleysen, 2000, p. 95.

design a magnificent float in 1767. The triumphal carriage shared by the mercers' and roofers' guilds cost a total of 1,267 guilders.[104] Lacking the necessary cash, the roofers had to borrow money to pay their share.

Some guilds in the Southern Netherlands organized annual pilgrimages to places of worship near the city.[105] The Bruges brewers and glove makers, for example, made an annual journey to the Oudenburg pilgrimage site, while the Bruges coopers travelled in groups to the Saint Leonard procession in Dudzele or the procession of Our Lady in Ruislede. The Antwerp mercers' guild sent a large delegation to Merksem each year. These pilgrimages served to impress the public. To this end, the Bruges fullers had trumpet players accompany them on their journey to Meetkerke, and the Bruges coopers made their way to Ruislede by horse and cart rather than on foot.

Guilds in the Southern Netherlands also capitalized on joyous entries and other major public ceremonies revolving around their ruler to appear before their fellow citizens.[106] In honour of royal visits monumental triumphal arches, colonnades, and outdoor theatres were built, countless candles, torches, flambeaux, and pitch vats were lit, and city gates, public buildings, and guildhalls were decorated with carpets, pennants, and banners. Processions were held and all kinds of live performances organized, such as plays, musical recitals, and tableaux vivants. During the sixteenth century, guilds were deeply involved in these events and provided large financial contributions to the festive decorations.[107] These were perfect opportunities for corporations to make an impression and to display their social prestige. In the seventeenth century the central government reduced the role of its subjects and consequently of the guilds as well during joyous entries of new governors to that of passive onlookers, thereby discouraging corporations from making financial contributions.[108] In 1635 the Antwerp guilds deemed the expenditures for the joyous entry of Cardinal Infante Don Fernando to be excessive. They vehemently resisted the magistrate's proposal to cover the costs by extending the term of the additional beer duties.[109] After the mid-seventeenth century, the solemn entries gradually lost their splendour.

Funerals of guild members were also public events. All members were expected to attend the ceremony, and the guild pall would be draped over the coffin. The devotional prints of the guilds were also regarded as investments in social capital. These graphics were a relatively cheap medium, as most were small, inexpensive devotional prints. Many guilds in the Southern Netherlands issued such prints until the end of

---

[104] Dambruyne, 1992, p. 128.

[105] Thijs, 2000, pp. 120, 127.

[106] In sixteenth-century Ghent, regular parades and tournaments on the waterfront with a high turnout from craft guilds, civic militias, neighbourhood associations, and other societies were organized in honour of royal visits.

[107] Of the eleven tableaux vivants designed in Bruges for the joyous entry of Charles V in 1515, for example, two were commissioned by the magistrate, one by the burghers, and the other eight by the guilds. Soly, 1984a, p. 346.

[108] Soly, 1984b, pp. 605-36.

[109] Soly, 1984a, p. 359.

the Ancien Régime. They were distributed primarily during the oblation of the annual mass held in recognition of the patron saint and depicted him or her, usually surrounded by symbols or tools of the trade. Corporative devotional prints served several purposes. In addition to their religious, moralizing, and educational role, they were presented as business gifts and had a communicative value.[110]

Until the Dutch Revolt, processions were also prime opportunities for guilds in the Northern Netherlands to assert their social and hierarchical presence. From the final quarter of the sixteenth century, however, processions ceased in the Dutch Republic, thereby eliminating an important means of communication.[111] Guilds continued to march in secular processions and parades, but such appearances were sporadic.[112] The large military cavalcades that replaced the processions were the exclusive purview of the civic militias.[113] Funerals of guild brothers became the only occasions for guilds to appear before their fellow townspeople as a social entity. All guild members were required to attend the funeral service in special attire. The funeral procession departed from the residence of the deceased in hierarchic sequence. The bier was followed by the board members. Next came the ordinary masters. The bier, which was carried by guild brothers, was covered by the guild's pall, from which silver coats of arms were usually suspended. Although such funeral processions were visually impressive, they did not compare to the striking parades of the civic militias or the glorious Counter Reformation processions in the Southern Netherlands.

6. Conclusions

This chapter is in fact rather premature, as systematic research on the various types of capital of guilds during the early modern period has not yet been forthcoming about the Southern or the Northern Netherlands. Some provisional conclusions may nonetheless be reached. During the early modern period, guilds clearly invested not only in economic capital but also in social and cultural capital. Social capital was a substantial element of the corporative investment and representation strategies.

As was the case in economic, social, and political affairs, guilds were far from homogeneous with respect to their material wealth. Research on corporative capital has revealed striking differences.[114] Some guilds owned an impressive patrimony, whereas others had virtually no possessions whatsoever. Level of affluence was obviously a major factor determining the operations of guilds. Corporations with a broad financial base were far more able to defend their privileges and rights than those

[110] Thijs, 1993b, pp. 13, 74, 79-81. See also Van der Stock, 1998.

[111] Magry, 1993, pp. 174-96.

[112] Snoep, 1975.

[113] Knevel, 1994, pp. 271-88.

[114] In Ghent, for example, six guilds owned over half the total corporative patrimony. Dambruyne, 1997, p. 188.

lacking financial resources, which usually encountered serious financial problems in the event of legal disputes. The present lack of in-depth studies about the different occupational associations precludes a general model explaining why some guilds owned considerably more goods and invested more in certain types of capital than others did. It has become clear, however, that the huge diversity within the guild world with respect to capital accumulation and capital investment was attributable to not one but several factors, including financial situation, economic position, membership size, personal wealth of the masters, donations and bequests, political power, social prestige, and corporative involvement of the members. The respective ranks of the guilds in the material hierarchy appear moreover to have corresponded largely with their positions in political, social, and economic hierarchies, although the correlation between wealth, social prestige, political power, and economic status was not absolute.

The investment strategies of the guilds in the Low Countries focused essentially on economic and social capital. Every guild invested in economic capital to perpetuate the multiform functions of their institution. After all, productive investments were necessary to fuel the corporative social security system. The financial and practical benefits of interests and bonds (long-term loans to private persons and public institutions), outweighed the advantages of urban and rural real estate. Investment patterns among guilds in the Northern Netherlands nonetheless appear to have differed considerably from those of corporations in the Southern Netherlands during the seventeenth and eighteenth centuries. From the last quarter of the sixteenth century, investment of corporative capital generally differed between the North and the South. Guilds in the Southern Netherlands focused on social capital, whereas those in the Northern Netherlands were predominantly interested in economic capital.

The tremendous value that guilds in the Southern Netherlands attributed to social capital and conspicuous consumption is inextricably linked with the prominence of these corporations in urban life and with the rigidly hierarchical structure of corporations, which in turn led to internal emulation. Investing in social capital was a rational decision in the Southern Netherlands, given the awareness among the guilds there that social positions faced perpetual challenges. Highly prestigious guilds therefore flaunted their superiority constantly, while those that were less widely respected aimed to enhance their social status. On their quest for optimal social exposure, guilds in the Southern Netherlands used channels made available by profane and religious circles alike. Financial resources were indispensable to exhibit corporative group identity. Rather than serving as evidence of corporative protectionism, as the older literature suggests, the more rigid admission criteria that numerous guilds imposed on new masters during the seventeenth and eighteenth centuries seem, in our view, to have arisen from the irresistible urge for social exposure on the part of the guilds.[115] The primary purpose of most guildhalls as symbols of prestige is demonstrated beyond question by the fact that most of these buildings were let, with the guilds in fact using only one or a few of the rooms.

---

[115] While admission fees and membership dues were raised in the North as well, these increases were far more likely to arise from expansions to the corporative social security system: van Genabeek, 1994, p. 78.

During the sixteenth and seventeenth centuries most guilds in the Southern Netherlands attributed noticeably greater value to the exterior of their guildhall than to its interior. Public spaces of guildhalls were carefully distinguished from areas intended for private use. The main reason in our view concerned the representation strategies of guilds, i.e. the way that guilds presented themselves in public. Guilds found investments in social capital worthwhile and profitable only if they were perceptible to their fellow citizens. Purchasing or building a guildhall was highly conducive to this effect. Guildhalls differed greatly from average residences by virtue of their stone façades, their size, their ornamentation featuring guild symbols, and their higher value. Guilds regarded their properties as material foundations of their social importance and prestige. Unlike occasional processions or parades, guildhalls reminded the townspeople perpetually of the guilds' presence and value to urban prosperity. This was why corporations made sure that their houses were centrally located in the city. The same investment strategy is apparent from the guild chapels, guild altars, and hospices. Like guildhalls, chapels and altars were highly worthwhile investments, both because they were long-term arrangements, and because churches were heavily frequented venues. The wealthiest guilds, however, did not settle for their own house and a chapel or altar in one of the parish or convent churches. Instead, they would build an exclusive chapel next to their guildhall or hospice to set themselves apart.

Until well into the seventeenth century, the furnishings of the guildhalls were very Spartan. Nearly all guilds invested only in what was absolutely necessary, purchasing very basic household items, such as tables, seats, storage devices, and drinking vessels. Guildhall interiors did not exude opulence and abundance and were in most cases rather bare. They did not compare to the interiors of the social elite and the middle classes, which tended to contain more numerous, more varied, and more expensive furnishings and other household items. This difference was attributable in part to the more limited range of functions of guildhalls with respect to the uses of private residences, as well as to the tendency of most guilds to use only a small section of their guildhall. On the other hand, corporations had little incentive to invest heavily in furniture and household accessories, as such investments generated no social return or added value. After all, the objects placed in the guild interior were concealed from public view and thus not visible to the other citizens. This also explains why guilds spent liberally on silver insignia, procession torches, pennants, ritual silver objects, and chasubles. Processions and masses were opportunities for citizens to admire these objects in all their glory. Some guildhalls were nonetheless more elaborately furnished than others. The most economically affluent guilds tended to own more numerous and costlier objects than the poorer corporations did. Ornamental and luxury items were found almost exclusively among large, affluent guilds. In the eighteenth century, several guild interiors were transformed. Guild chambers were equipped with more comfortable furnishings. Aesthetic aspects were taken more seriously, and the number of accessories increased. This trend was not limited to corporations, however, but figured in the interior decoration of private residences as well and was closely related to what came to be known as the 'consumer revolution'.

Corporative capital made guilds more powerful. In cities where guilds acquired excessive political power, however, as they did in Ghent, the central government readily curtailed the impact of corporative capital. Following the revolt of the Ghent guilds in 1539-1540, Emperor Charles V and his advisors devised a strategy of subjugation aimed at eroding corporative identity and solidarity.[116] The strategy targeted the economic and social capital of the guilds in Ghent in particular: all houses, household items, interests, banners, arms, munitions, military tents, records, and other immovable and movable possessions of the corporations were confiscated. Ritualized collective manifestations in which the guilds figured prominently, such as the renowned Auweet (culminating in the parade of guild masters bearing arms and wearing suits of armour and waving banners in mid-Lent) and the frequently tumultuous pilgrimage to Sint Lievens-Houtem were prohibited. The central government and municipal authorities kept a close watch over guild funds from that point onward to prevent the guilds of Ghent from quickly rising up out of their ashes.

In the Northern Netherlands guilds invested far less in social capital than they did in the Southern Netherlands. This difference was already perceptible in the fifteenth and sixteenth centuries but became still more pronounced in the course of the next two centuries. Peter Burke's observation that conspicuous consumption was far less widespread in the Dutch Republic than in Italy thus appears to hold true for guilds in the Northern Netherlands as well.[117] Compared with the South, only a minority of corporations owned their guildhall. Nor did guildhalls in the North have the impressive appearance and prestige that those in the Southern Netherlands did. While corporative hospices existed in the Dutch Republic, they were far less widespread than in the South. And, unlike in the South, guilds here lost their altars and chapels from the last quarter of the sixteenth century and ceased to march in processions. This change may appear odd at first, since we know from the publications of Piet Lourens and Jan Lucassen that the number of guilds rose spectacularly during the Dutch Republic.[118] Still, this corporative expansion did not increase investments in social capital. What were the reasons? In our view, they were threefold. First, the corporative system in the Northern Netherlands appears to have been far less multiform than in the Southern Netherlands.[119] During the Dutch Republic corporative functions changed but did not increase. While purely economic concerns prevailed during the seventeenth century, social security considerations progressively gained ground during the eighteenth century.[120] Municipal authorities compelled the guilds to invest primarily in expanding their social benefit fund, i.e. in productive capital.[121] As a result, little money remained

---

116 Dambruyne, 1999, p. 120. A more detailed argument appears in Dambruyne, 2002, pp. 169-72.

117 Burke, 1992, p. 69.

118 Lourens and Lucassen, 1994, pp. 34-62.

119 Lis and Soly, 1997b, p. 23.

120 Lourens and Lucassen, 1997a, p. 59.

121 See the synthesis study by Bos, 1998, and the case study by de Ridder, 1994, p. 108. During the eighteenth century, most guilds extended their financial support beyond the sick to

for social representation. The second factor was the minimal power of guilds in the Dutch Republic. Since guilds, except in a few cases, had no formal political power in towns in the Northern Netherlands, they felt less of a need to demonstrate their social prestige to their fellow citizens.[122] Finally, guilds operated within a specific religious context. While the Catholic Counter Reformation in the South encouraged corporations there to invest in social capital, Protestantism provided no such incentive in the North. On the contrary, Protestant religion greatly curtailed the range of corporative communication media. Guild altars and guild processions disappeared from urban society, making the most visible traces of the late medieval guilds vanish from the cityscape. Perhaps guilds in the Northern Netherlands invested less in social capital than their counterparts in the South not so much for lack of sincere corporative interest in such types of capital as because of the specific duties, prohibitions, and restrictions imposed on them by the state and the church in the Dutch Republic.

include aid to elderly people and widows and thus had to become far more active in fund-raising.

122 Prak, 2000, pp. 71-83.

Conclusion

Jan Lucassen and Maarten Prak

Recent guild historiography has been more successful at destroying old images of the corporate system than in perceiving a new one. As we saw in the introduction, in the past twenty years craft guilds were not necessarily opposed to economic modernization. New scholarship has alerted us to the fact that craft guilds were much more than a 'conspiracy against the public' (to use Adam Smith's phrase) to protect sectional economic interests. They produced a rich cultural life and participated in politics. Craft guilds helped build and sustain social identities. What may be even more noteworthy, the new historiography has destroyed the image of guilds as stationary, unchanging, and unchangeable institutions of the Old Society. Much like the other elements of their society, craft guilds had to deal with high rates of mobility and massive changes in the course of the half millennium of their existence. They were — who would deny it? — impressively flexible in their adaptation to these changes, and at times even helped bring them about.

The craft guilds in the Low Countries were no exception to this pattern. As in other European countries, they varied greatly.[1] In many respects the findings presented in this book confirm what had already been established for other regions and countries — sometimes with new types of (quantitative) evidence. First, craft guilds in the Low Countries were perfectly compatible with economic modernization.[2] Initially Flanders, later Brabant, and then Holland were among the most advanced regions of Europe economically during the late Middle Ages and early modern periods. All three areas also had a corporate system,[3] and this system developed significantly during periods of economic expansion: in Flanders during the thirteenth and fourteenth centuries, in Brabant during the fifteenth and sixteenth centuries, and in Holland during the seventeenth century. Second (an element often underrated in the new historiography), guilds in all parts of the Low Countries were strongly linked to political structures. In many ways, one might argue, their history was determined as much by their political as by their economic role. If we want to understand the corporate system, it may well behove us to start with the political aspect of that system.

---

1 As a result, every sentence in this conclusion might be qualified with a handful of exceptions; for reasons of clarity we have refrained from doing so. For those exceptions the reader is referred to the individual chapters of this book.

2 As defined in de Vries and van der Woude, 1997.

3 The word 'system' is used here to identify a coherent set of social ideas and practices.

Although the many varieties make a general definition that fits all cases impossible to formulate, the great majority of craft guilds were societies of private individuals united by a common trade, or set of trades, which they exercised in a specific town under a government licence. Their regulations generally gave them exclusive right to the independent exercise of their trade and forced anyone intending to exercise the trade to join the guild first. Guild privileges also helped to establish the industrial dominance of the towns over the countryside. During the Middle Ages, guilds might receive their privileges from regional princes, but as time went on they built up an exclusive relationship with local authorities, at least in the Low Countries.

These political relationships were of three types. In the southern parts of the Low Countries, guild revolutions in 1302 and shortly afterwards established guilds as partners in the local government. This gave entrepreneurs in these towns privileged access to the corridors of power. In the economically underdeveloped western areas of the Northern Netherlands, this type of development was very rare outside the few very old towns such as Dordrecht and Utrecht. When the economies of the North became more dynamic, local authorities ensured that the guilds were excluded from formal representation. Instead, merchant elites continued to hold power. Although guilds were not able to gain political representation in the eastern areas either (except for the oldest towns of Groningen and Liège), indirectly their members were involved in official politics through wards or similar forms of middle class representations.

The importance of the local context is exemplified in the quantitative development of the corporate system in the Low Countries. The number of guilds, as well as the increase and decline in these numbers, was determined primarily by local population growth, or the lack of it. While all towns in the Low Countries (except for the very smallest, and very few of the villages) actually had guilds, the size and variety of the system was different from town to town. Expansion occurred when the town as a whole grew and the groups of artisans (and shopkeepers) became sufficiently numerous to establish, and maintain, their own organizations. This explains why the corporate system in the South expanded in the Middle Ages, and why a similar expansion occurred in the North during the seventeenth century. Although access to the guilds in the Low Countries was relatively easy compared to other parts of Europe, some notable variations can be observed among the regions in the area. In the West of the northern Netherlands, access was very easy: there were no formal obstacles, and entry rates were modest. In the eastern provinces of the Dutch Republic rates were higher, and only Calvinists could become members. In the southern provinces guild membership was much more expensive than it was in the North, and only Catholics were admitted.

Gendered patterns of inclusion and exclusion display a similar structure. In the western areas of the Dutch Republic guilds were relatively accessible to women, even though they remained second-class members in most guilds. In the eastern areas it was more difficult for women to be admitted to guilds, but in the Southern Netherlands it was almost impossible. This was not necessarily the result of an express policy of exclusion by the guilds, although it certainly played a role. It was the political balance of power that helped determine the outcome: to the extent that merchants dominated local governments it was much more difficult to exclude women from the crafts, while in towns with strong representative institutions it was much easier to do so.

Many, arguably most, guild members produced for and sold on the local market. The products they made fed, housed, and clothed their neighbours and other fellow citizens. Others, however, were involved in supplying more distant markets. For too long historians have been obsessed with whether (and how) guilds and capitalism were compatible. The situation in the Low Countries clearly shows that they were. Nonetheless, various patterns of guild-government relationships led to different patterns of local economic development. In the Southern Netherlands guild participation in local government gave industrial interests pride of place in the determination of local economic policies. The guilds became socially polarized, and subcontracting was rampant. In the Northern Netherlands, especially in the West, guild industrial interests usually remained subordinate to the dominant trade interests. Ironically, curtailment of the guilds' economic development generally seems to have made them less internally polarized.

As local organizations, the guilds were closely linked to the overall institutional structures of local societies. Local citizenship was a prerequisite everywhere to enter a guild. And guilds were involved in local fire-fighting, local defence, and also in local churches. During the Middle Ages' guilds maintained their own altars, participated in annual processions, and generally added to the community's public life. The Reformation was to change that to some extent, temporarily in the South during the second half of the sixteenth century, and more permanently in the North. Although Calvinism became the public religion in the Dutch Republic and caused the removal of guild altars from churches, Dutch guilds retained a remarkable number of pre-Reformation religious customs after 1600. Patron saints remained a significant point of reference, guild burials continued, and some guilds also continued to maintain their own graves in local churches, where members could be buried with their guild brothers and sisters. In the South the guilds participated in the authorities' Counter Reformation project of re-Christianization.

The religious affiliation of the guilds was not only important to the church, but was also a significant element in the structure of guild social solidarity. As relatively small societies, towns and guilds were plagued by free-riders. An overwhelming concern of the guilds everywhere in Europe was infringement by non-members on the guild's collective monopoly. To counter such threats it was necessary to be vigilant and maintain a permanent watch over the conditions of production in the workshops of members and non-members alike. The members may have been as likely to break the rules when it was in their private interest as were the non-members. Both to ensure that members followed the rules and to recruit their help in apprehending illegal producers (as well as rural producers, peddlers, and others), it was necessary to create a bond of solidarity among the 'insiders', i.e. the members of the guild.[4] Religious rituals had always been an important aspect of that, but as time went on the emphasis shifted

[4] See also Gary Richardson, 'Craft Guilds and Christianity in Late-Medieval England: A Rational-Choice Analysis', unpublished paper.

towards more material benefits. In the Dutch provinces this was fairly straightforward, as former contributions to the church were channelled to social relief benefits after the Reformation of the 1580s. Such social relief schemes were most developed in the West, where the authorities may have been less fearful of the influence of substantial guild coffers and where the need to tie guild members to the social status quo may have been greater because they did not have political representation. In the South the formal system of guild benefits remained less developed.

Representational strategies may have been aimed at the guild membership as much as at society as a whole. In any event, local society was the stage where the guilds chose to play their role. In the Southern Netherlands the guilds displayed their wealth and power in their richly decorated houses, which were highly visible in the most prominent locations. The fact that these premises were largely leased to other users underscores the value the guilds attached to their property. In comparison, Dutch guilds were only able to mobilize limited resources to express their dignity, and many did not even bother to do so. Given their limited political role, there was no obvious reason for such display.

Despite all the disparities, guilds in the Low Countries played a highly significant role, not only in the lives of their own members, but also in shaping the societies they were part of. Those societies were primarily local. They did have strong economic ties with the outside world, but weak political ones. The way guilds were embedded in the wider world partially explains both their longevity and continued importance in the urban societies of the Low Countries. Yet these societies were not all the same. The development of the corporate system in the Low Countries suggests three distinct patterns, exemplified in the three regions we have distinguished. In the Southern Netherlands towns were ruled by (uneasy) coalitions of patricians and representatives of the guilds. The urban economies in this area were dominated by export industries, which were generally incorporated. Guilds thus exercised significant political and economic power. The guilds in the Southern Netherlands required high entrance fees, banned women from their ranks, were religiously active, and displayed a high degree of social polarization.

Craft guilds in the western parts of the Dutch Republic were almost the exact opposite. The towns in Holland were ruled by merchant oligarchies, and the guilds had no political power at all. The export industries in these towns occupied a special place — whether that was within or outside the corporate system is still an issue.[5] These guilds were easy to enter, and no questions were asked about religious affiliation (as long as the applicant was not Jewish). Although firm data are lacking, it is quite possible that social polarization was limited. The eastern part of the Dutch Republic was in some respects midway between the North and South. Guilds were indirectly represented in urban governments, but the export industries were of little significance. Guilds insisted on proper religious affiliations, but otherwise access was easier than in

[5] Davids, 1996; Lourens and Lucassen, 1998.

the Southern Netherlands, and more difficult than it was in the West. Women's access to the trades was more restricted than in the West, but less than in the South. Thus, our investigations distinguish three 'guild regions' (or *Zunftlandschaften*, as they are called in German). To what extent do these three patterns reflect the situation in other parts of Europe?

One way to proceed is to look at other *Zunftlandschaften*, or guild regions. In the German areas bordering on the Low Countries four types, or models, of guild society interrelationships can be distinguished in the eighteenth century. In the Imperial Cities, which had so much autonomy that they were almost city-states, guilds participated in local government, although government was dominated by the merchants. Industries tended to seek refuge in the countryside. In the Prussian territories rural industries were even more predominant, as guild control gave way to state legislation, along with loss of political autonomy for the towns. In the principality of Berg, where the iron industry was very important, guilds were politically and economically marginal; merchants were in charge. In the prince-bishoprics' guilds remained politically influential, but the economy was primarily oriented towards the region itself. In the latter areas the guilds' religious orientation was reinforced by the Counter Reformation.[6] The situation in the Imperial Cities was closest to the western provinces of the Dutch Republic, while that of the prince-bishoprics at first was much like the eastern provinces of the Dutch Republic, where we find a similar constellation of regional economic orientation, guild participation in politics, and an emphasis on the religious aspects of the corporate system. But on closer inspection substantial differences become apparent. The Westphalian guilds charged far higher rates to new masters, they insisted on their members leading an 'honest life' and proving their middle class roots by owning their own homes. These requirements were rare in the corporate system of the Low Countries.[7]

Such differences between the Low Countries and other regions show that the Low Countries cannot be a model for the whole of Europe. The characteristics that made Dutch society stand out in Europe inevitably shaped its corporate system. Thus, for instance, the dominance of the towns and the absence of countervailing powers with enough authority to check the urban guilds resulted in an almost total absence of rural guilds in the Low Countries. In other parts of Europe, rural guilds were more common.[8] But it would be an error to see such highly developed rural guilds as proof of economic backwardness, and contrast them to the Low Countries' (and English) situations, portrayed as models of modern liberal economies.[9] If the present book has clarified anything, it is surely that the Low Countries were not liberated from the

6 Reininghaus, 2002.

7 See also Lourens and Lucassen, 2000.

8 Reininghaus, 1990, p. 62; Reith, 2002, 47-9; Ehmer, 2002, pp. 101, 103; but see also Mastboom, 1994.

9 Ogilvie, 1997, ch. 11; see also Pfister (forthcoming).

'shackles' of corporatism, and that corporatism was not necessarily a negative factor in economic development.

Rather than seek isolated points of comparison, it may be more fruitful to explore patterns of similarity and dissimilarity. Thus, our investigations suggest that the political, economic, and socio-cultural characteristics of the corporate system were interrelated in very specific ways. Viewed from this perspective, several generalizations can be made about the European situation as a whole. One striking similarity that seems to apply almost everywhere — Great Britain is the main exception — is the chronology of guild development. One of the remarkable results of our investigations showed that guilds became more numerous after the Middle Ages rather than less so. The Golden Age of corporatism was not the fourteenth and fifteenth centuries, but rather the seventeenth and eighteenth. The same can be observed in other parts of Europe.[10] In Austria, for instance, the number of surviving guild regulations increases so dramatically in the seventeenth century that it must be more than just the coincidental result of archival preservation.[11]

Another aspect where the pattern of the Low Countries may be representative of trends elsewhere in Europe is the gender balance in the guilds. Women were admitted to guilds and incorporated trades in inverse relation to the political power of the guilds. It is therefore no surprise to find women entering the English clothing trades in the later seventeenth century, when guild privileges came under siege and ready-made clothes were starting to replace tailored clothing in English towns.[12] In German 'home towns', on the other hand, women were barred from the incorporated trades until the end of the eighteenth century, especially in towns where guilds were politically entrenched.[13]

As far as the guilds and the economy go, our investigations also suggest a European-wide pattern. In the Spanish (later Austrian) Netherlands, because of the strong institutional positions of the guilds, the industrial entrepreneurs could remain in control of the export trades. In the southern towns subcontracting networks allowed for a dynamic system of industrial production for export markets within a corporate context. In German towns, such as Dortmund, Braunschweig, and Augsburg, a similar constellation provided the fertile background to industrial expansion for some time. In the Northern Netherlands, on the other hand, the weaker political position of the guilds allowed merchant capital to become more influential in industry. In the eighteenth century that merchant capital abandoned many Dutch industries. Reduced guild influence led to a similar undermining of industrial vitality in commercial cities outside the Low Countries.[14]

Such connections show that guild political power was as important in the rest of Europe as it was in the Netherlands. Clearly, the sample from the Low Countries does

[10] Ehmer, 1998, pp. 36-7; Haupt, 2002b, p. 19.

[11] Ehmer, p. 91.

[12] Lemire, 1997, ch. 2.

[13] E.g. Roper, 1989, pp. 40-8

[14] This is discussed in greater detail in Lis and Soly, (forthcoming).

not cover the full European range of possibilities. The role of the towns diminished the potential for development of centralized institutions in the Low Countries. In other countries different systems of government prevailed. In England, for example, early development of a national state significantly weakened the autonomy of the towns and guilds. Guilds were subject to national regulation, most famously in the Statute of Artificers of 1563 that regulated the training of apprentices.[15] In France guild privileges were nullified by the crown and then sold again to the trade for hard cash.[16] In German territorial states' guilds became instruments in a policy of 'national' (i.e. Prussian and Bavarian) integration, both of the economy and the political system.[17] As in the Low Countries, urban autonomy and the development of guilds were closely interrelated. Perhaps an extreme but enlightening example is the city of Vienna, which lost its autonomy in 1526, at the same time that artisans were explicitly barred from membership in the town council; the councillors were henceforth to be recruited from among the 'resident citizens, who are not tradesmen'.[18] A year later all guilds in Austria were formally abolished, although the reason for this was to allow the government to bring the guild regulations of the various towns and trades in line.[19] But this project was a significant step towards the creation of a nationally — as opposed to a locally — consolidated society. Likewise, the marginalization of urban autonomy and guild privileges in the Italian territorial states, such as Lombardy, Tuscany, and the Kingdom of Naples, especially during the eighteenth century, points to the close connection between urban autonomy and the development of corporatism, as does the absence of such policies in the city-states of Italy, where guilds remained independent.[20]

In 1787 Lombardy was the first country in Europe not only to abolish the guilds — France had already attempted that in 1776 — but to persist in that policy.[21] The abolition of the guilds around 1800 shows the significance of the political dimension in guild history, a dimension that has been repeatedly overlooked or played down in the historiography of the craft guilds. The tendency to disregard the political dimension dates back to the abolition itself, when it was claimed that the step was necessary to free the economy of its medieval 'shackles'.[22] We can now observe, however, that the process was in fact driven as much by a political as an economic dynamic. In much of Europe the corporate system was far from moribund; it was actually thriving.[23] It is true that in the country of the Industrial Revolution the guilds had lost ground when

15 Crossick and Haupt, 1995, p. 24.

16 Kaplan, 1986, pp. 211-14.

17 Reith, 2002, p. 45.

18 Ehmer, 2002, p. 112.

19 Ibid., p. 114.

20 Frigo, 2002b, pp. 199, 208-10.

21 Haupt, 2002b, p. 36. The Dutch province of Friesland also temporarily abolished the guilds in the mid-eighteenth century, but then quickly revived them.

22 For early critics of guilds in the Dutch Republic, see Davids, 2001.

23 See the contributions collected in Haupt, 2002a.

they tried to control the urban economy.[24] But on the continent the first country to industrialize was Belgium, where guilds had been extremely important. The abolition of the guilds in France (1791), the Low Countries (1798), Venice (1807), and the Rhine provinces in Germany was a direct result of the French Revolution, which did not set out to reform the economy so much as to change the political system. It was only in the course of the nineteenth century that the economic arguments against guilds gained strength. Both the political and the economic reforms, however, were directed against an Old Regime that valued local over national institutions. Seen from that perspective, the entire history of the abolition of the guilds is also the history of the triumph of nationhood as the guiding principle in organizing 'modern' society. Guild-like organizations, notably for doctors, notaries, and similar professions demonstrated that even in the nineteenth century the corporate concept retained some of its attraction, albeit in national organizations. As local institutions, however, craft guilds proved incompatible with this particular form of modernity.

24 But even for England that picture needs to be revised: see Berlin (forthcoming).

Bibliography

A note on surnames: in Belgium, prefixes such as De and Van are an integral part of a person's surname, spelled with a capital D or V, and included in the alphabetical order. In the Netherlands, on the other hand, they are spelled with lower case letters and not considered for the alphabetical order. We have applied both systems in this bibliography. Surnames with a prefix spelled De and Van should be found under D and V respectively in this bibliography, whereas for instance de Bruin and van der Woude are to be found under B and W respectively.

Absolon, M. (1994), *Prosopografische benadering van timmerlieden en schrijnwerkers te Brugge in de achttiende eeuw. Een analyse met behulp van de historische informatiekunde*, unpublished MA-thesis, Vrije Universiteit Brussel.

Aerts, E. (1996), *Het bier van Lier. De economische ontwikkeling van de bierindustrie in een middelgrote Brabantse stad (eind 14de – begin 19de eeuw)*, Brussel.

Allan, F. (1874-1888), *Geschiedenis en beschrijving van Haarlem, van de vroegste tijden tot op onzen dagen*, Vol. 1, Haarlem.

Allossery, P. (1926), *Het gildeleven in vroeger eeuwen*, Brugge.

Andel, M.A. van (1946), *Chirurgijns, vrije meesters, beunhazen en kwakzalvers. De chirurgijnsgilden en de practijk der heelkunde (1400-1800)*, Amsterdam.

Ankersmit, F. (1990), *De navel van de geschiedenis. Over interpretatie, representatie en historische realiteit*, Groningen.

Arnade, P. (1996), *Realms of Ritual: Burgundian Ceremony and Civic Life in Late Medieval Ghent*, Ithaca/London.

Arrighi, G. (1994), *The Long Twentieth Century: Money, Power and the Origins of Our Times,* London/New York.

Aten, D. (1999), 'Amsterdamse gilden en regenten contra de Zaanse nijverheid, 1600-1800', in C. Lesger and L. Noordegraaf (eds), *Ondernemers en bestuurders. Economie en politiek in de Noordelijke Nederlanden in de late Middeleeuwen en vroegmoderne tijd*, Amsterdam, pp. 61-76.

Augustyn, B. (2000), 'Staten van Brabant', in R. Van Uytven, C. Bruneel, H. Coppens and B. Augustyn (eds), *De gewestelijke en lokale overheidsinstellingen in Brabant en Mechelen tot 1795*, Brussels, pp. 97-132.

Autenboer, E. van (1983), 'Volkskunde', in H. De Kok and E. van Autenboer (ed.), *Turnhout. Groei van een stad*, Turnhout.

Bainbridge, V.R. (1996), *Gilds in the Medieval Countryside. Social and Religious Change in Cambridgeshire, c 1350-1558*, Woodbridge.

Bairoch, P. (1994), 'La Belgique dans le commerce international, 1830-1930', in P. Klep and E. Van Cauwenbergh (eds), *Entrepreneurship and the Transformation of the Economy (10th–20th Centuries). Essays in Honour of Herman Van der Wee*, Leuven, pp. 627-51.

Barbour, V. (1950), *Capitalism in Amsterdam in the Seventeenth Century*, Baltimore.

Barry, J. (1994), 'Introduction', in J. Barry and C. Brooks (eds), *The Middling Sort of People: Culture, Society, and Politics in England, 1550-1800*, London, pp. 1-27.

Baudouin, F. (1972), 'Altars and Altarpieces before 1620', in J.R. Martin (ed.), *Rubens before 1620*, Princeton, pp. 45-91.

Baudouin, F. (1986), '1585, een belangrijke datum voor de geschiedenis der beeldende kunsten te Antwerpen', in F. De Nave (ed.), *Antwerpen en de scheiding der Nederlanden (17 augustus 1585)*, Antwerpen.

Becker, G.S. (1964), *Human Capital*, New York.

Berg, M. and H. Clifford (eds) (1999), *Consumers and Luxury: Consumer Culture in Europe, 1650-1850,* Manchester/New York.

Bergh-Hoogterp, L.E. van den and B. Dubbe (1997), *Edele en onedele metalen. De verzamelingen van het Centraal Museum Utrecht*, Vol. 4, Utrecht.

Bergsma, W. (1995), 'Church, state and people', in K. Davids and J. Lucassen (eds), *A miracle mirrored. The Dutch Republic in a European Perspective*, Cambridge, pp. 196-228.

Berkenvelder, F.C. (1989), 'De gilden te Zwolle tot 1600', *Overijsselse Historische Bijdragen*, 104, pp. 7-34.

Berlin, M. (forthcoming), 'Guilds in Decline? London Livery Companies and the Rise of a Liberal Economy', in: S.R. Epstein, M. Prak (eds), *The guilds, technology and the economy*, Cambridge.

Bigwood, G. (1900), *Les impôts généraux dans les Pays-Bas autrichiens. Etude historique de législation financière*, Leuven.

Bischof, F. (1926), *Der Anteil der Gilden am Stadtregiment in den westfälischen Städten*, Warendorf.

Black, A. (1984), *Guilds and Civil Society in European Political Thought from the Twelfth Century to the Present*, London.

Black, C.F. (1989), *Italian Confraternities in the Sixteenth Century*, Cambridge/New York.

Blockmans, W.P. (1978), *De volksvertegenwoordiging in Vlaanderen in de overgang van Middeleeuwen naar Nieuwe Tijden (1384-1506)*, Verhandelingen van de Koninklijke Vlaamse Academie voor Wetenschappen, Letteren en Schone Kunsten van België, Klasse der Letteren, vol. 90, Brussels.

Blockmans, W.P. (1983), 'Vers une société urbanisée', in E. Witte (ed.), *Histoire de Flandre, des origines à nos jours*, Brussel.

Blockmans, W.P. (ed.) (1985), *1477. Het algemene en de gewestelijke privilegiën van Maria van Bourgondië*, Standen en Landen, vol. 80, Heule/Kortrijk.

Blockmans, W.P. (1987), 'Mobiliteit in stadsbesturen 1400-1550', in D.E.H. de Boer and J.W. Marsilje (eds), *De Nederlanden in de late Middeleeuwen*, Utrecht, pp. 236-60.

Blockmans, W.P. (1998), 'Alternatives to Monarchical Centralisation: The Great Tradition of Revolt in Flanders and Brabant', in H.G. Koeningsberger (ed.), *Republiken und Republikanismus im Europa der Frühen Neuzeit*, Schriften des Historischen Kollegs, vol. 36, Munich, pp. 145-54.

Blockmans, W.P. (1999), 'Regionale Vielfalt im Zunftwesen in den Niederlanden vom 13. bis zum 16. Jahrhundert', in K. Schulz (ed.), *Handwerk in Europa. Vom Spätmittelalter bis zur Frühen Neuzeit*, Schriften des Historischen Kollegs, vol. 41, Munich, pp. 51-63.

Blockmans, W.P., and A. Janse (eds) (1999), *Showing Status. Representation of Social Positions in the Late Middle Ages*, Turnhout.

Blok, P.J. (1894), 'Raad en gilden te Groningen omstreeks 1525', *Opstellen aangeboden aan Robert Fruin bij zijn aftreden als hoogleraar aan de Rijksuniversiteit Leiden*, Den Haag, pp. 39-74.

Blomme, J. and H. Van der Wee (1994), 'The Belgian Economy in a Long-Term Historical Perspective: Economic Development in Flanders and Brabant, 1500-1812', in A. Maddison and H. Van der Wee (eds), *Economic Growth and Structural Change, Comparative Ap-*

proaches over the Long Run, Proceedings of the Eleventh International Economic History Congress, Session B13, Milan.

Blondé, B. (1987), *De sociale structuren en economische dynamiek van 's-Hertogenbosch 1500-1550*, Bijdragen tot de geschiedenis van het Zuiden van Nederland, vol. 74, Tilburg.

Blondé, B. (1999), *Het Brabantse stedelijke netwerk: een economie met verschillende snelheden.Ongelijkheden in de opbouw en ontwikkeling van het Brabantse stedelijke netwerk (ca. 1750-ca. 1790)*, Verhandelingen van de Koninklijke Vlaamse Academie van België voor Wetenschappen en Kunsten. Klasse der Letteren, Jaargang 61, no. 166, Brussel.

Bok, M.J. (1994), *Vraag en aanbod op de Nederlandse kunstmarkt, 1580-1780*, Utrecht.

Boer, D.E.H. de (1978), *Graaf en grafiek. Sociale en economische ontwikkelingen in het middeleeuwse 'Noord-Holland' tussen ca. 1345 en ca. 1415*, Leiden.

Boer, M.G. de (1893), *De woelingen in Stad en Lande in het midden der zeventiende eeuw*, Groningen.

Boone, M. (1990), *Gent en de Bourgondische hertogen ca. 1384 - ca. 1453. Een sociaal-politieke studie van een staatvormingsproces*, Verhandelingen van de Koninklijke Academie van Wetenschappen, Letteren en Schone Kunsten van België, Klasse der Letteren, vol. 133, Brussel.

Boone, M. (1994a), 'Les métiers dans les villes flamandes au bas Moyen Age (XIVe-XVIe siècles): images normatives, réalités socio-politiques et économiques', in P. Lambrechts and J.P. Sosson (eds), *Les métiers au Moyen Age. Aspects économiques et sociaux*, Louvain-la-Neuve, pp. 1-21.

Boone, M. (1994b), 'Städtische Selbstverwaltungsorgane vom 14. bis 16. Jahrhundert. Verfassungsnorm und Verwaltungswirklichkeit im spätmittelalterlichen flämischen Raum am Beispiel Gent', in W. Ehbrecht (ed.), *Verwaltung und Politik in Städten Mitteleuropas*, Cologne/Weimar/Vienna, pp. 20-46.

Boone, M. (2002), 'Een verstedelijkte samenleving onder spanning. Het graafschap Vlaanderen omstreeks 1302', in R.C. Van Caenegem (ed.), *1302: Feiten en mythen van de Guldensporenslag*, Antwerp, pp. 26-77.

Boone, M. and M. Prak, (1995), 'Rulers, patricians and burghers: the Great and Little Traditions of urban revolt in the Low Countries', in K. Davids and J. Lucassen (eds), *A Miracle Mirrored. The Dutch Republic in a European Perspective*, Cambridge, pp. 99-134.

Bos, P.G. (1904), *Het Groningsche gild- en stapelrecht tot de Reductie in 1594*, Groningen.

Bos, S. (1998), '*Uyt liefde tot malcander*'. *Onderlinge hulpverlening binnen de Noord-Nederlandse gilden in internationaal perspectief (1570-1820)*, Amsterdam.

Bosch, J.W. (1962), 'Le statut de la femme dans les anciens pays-bas septentrionaux', *La femme, Recueils de la société Jean Bodin pour l'histoire comparative des institutions 2*, Brussel.

Bossenga, G. (1991), *The politics of privilege. Old Regime and revolution in Lille*, Cambridge.

Bot, M. (1996), *Het Haarlemsche koopmansgilde. De strijd tegen de ventjagerij in de zeventiende en achttiende eeuw en de uiteindelijke afschaffing van dit gilde,* unpublished MA-thesis, Vrije Universiteit Amsterdam.

Boumans, R. (1965), *Het Antwerps stadsbestuur voor en tijdens de Franse overheersing. Bijdrage tot de ontwikkelingsgeschiedenis van de stedelijke bestuursinstellingen in de Zuidelijke Nederlanden*, Brugge.

Bourdieu, P. (1978), 'Capital symbolique et classes sociales', *L'Arc*, 72, pp. 13-19.

Bourdieu, P. (1980), 'Le capital social: notes provisoires', *Actes de la recherche en sciences sociales*, 31, pp. 2-3.

Bourdieu, P. (1983), 'Ökonomisches Kapital, kulturelles Kapital, soziales Kapital', in R. Kreckel (ed.), *Soziale Ungleichheiten (Soziale Welt*, Sonderheft 2), Göttingen, pp. 183-98.

Bouwen (1990) *door de eeuwen heen. Inventaris van het cultuurbezit in België. Architectuur, deel 3na: Stad Antwerpen*, Turnhout.

Braekman, W.L. (1998), 'Gelegenheidsliederen op het feest van het Brugse chirurgijnsgilde (midden 18de eeuw)', *Biekorf*, 98, pp. 362-7.

Brake, W.P. te (1989), *Regents and Rebels. The Revolutionary World of an Eighteenth Century Dutch City*, Oxford.

Brans, P.H (1957), 'Les collèges médicaux dans les Pays-Bas Méridionaux', *Janus. Revue Internationale de l'Histoire des Sciences, de la Médecine, de la Pharmacie et de la Technique*, 46.

Brewer, J., and R. Porter (eds) (1992), *Consumption and the World of Goods*, London/New York

Briels, J. (1985), *Zuid-Nederlanders in de Republiek, 1572-1630. Een demografische en cultuurhistorische studie*, Sint-Niklaas.

Brouwer Ancher, A.J.M. (1895), *De gilden*, Den Haag, 1895.

Brouwers, D. (1910), 'Les tours des merciers de Walcourt et de Ciney', *Annales de la Société archéologique de Namur*, 29, pp. 57-72.

Bruinvis, C.N. (1906), *Alkmaarsche bedrijfs- en ambachtsgilden; hun bestaan, vernietiging en nalatenshap*, Haarlem.

Brulez, W. (1970), 'The Balance of Trade of the Netherlands in the Middle of the 16th Century', *Acta Historiae Neerlandicae*, 4, pp. 20-48.

Bruneel, C., and L. Delporte (1997), 'Approche socio-professionnelle de la population bruxelloise en 1783', *Revue du Nord*, 79, pp. 463-94.

Bruneel, C. L. Delporte and B. Petitjean (1996), *Le dénombrement général de la population des Pays-Bas Autrichiens en 1784: édition critique*, Brussel.

Buchner, Th. (2004), *Möglichkeiten von Zunft. Wiener und Amsterdamer Zünfte im Vergleich (17.-18. Jahrhundert)*, Forschungen und Beiträge zur Wiener Stadtgeschichte vol. 43, Vienna.

Burke, P. (1987), *Historical Anthropology in Early Modern Italy. Essays on Perception and Communication*, Cambridge.

Burke, P. (1988), 'Schitterende façades: demonstratieve consumptie in het zeventiende-eeuwse Italië', in P. Burke, *Stadscultuur in Italië tussen Renaissance en Barok*, Amsterdam, pp. 163-84.

Burke, P. (1992), *History and Social Theory*, Cambridge.

Burrage, M.D., and D. Corry (1981), 'At sixes and sevens: occupational status in the City of London from the fourteenth to the seventeenth century', *American Sociological Review*, 46, pp. 375-93.

Bussels, M. (1960), 'De goede ambachten en de vaardige ambachtslieden van het oude Hasselt', *De Tijdspiegel*, 15, pp. 89-97.

Caroloregium (1966) *Valde Concelebratur, MDCLXVI-MCMLXVI. Bilan de trois siècles d'histoire locale*, Charleroi.

Cerutti, S. (1988), 'Du corps au métier: la corporation des tailleurs à Turin entre XVIIe et XVIIIe siècle', *Annales ESC*, 43, p. 323-52.

Cerutti, S. (1990), *La ville et les métiers. Naissance d'un langage corporatif (Turin, 17e-18e siècles)*, Paris.

Chartier, R. (1989), 'Le monde comme représentation', *Annales ESC*, 44, pp. 1505-20.

Châtellier, L. (1987), *l'Europe des dévots*, Paris (translated as *The Europe of the devout*, Cambridge 1989).

Coffin, J.G. (1994), 'Gender and the Guild Order. The Garment Trades in Eighteenth-century Paris', *Journal of Economic History*, 54, pp. 768-93.

Coffin, J.G. (1996), *The Politics of Women's Work. The Paris Garment Trades, 1750-1915*, Princeton.

Cohen, J.S. (1996), 'Institutions and Economic Analysis', in T.G. Rawski et al. (eds), *Economics and the Historian*, Berkeley, pp. 60-84.

Coornaert, E. (1930a), *Un centre industriel d'autrefois. La draperie sayetterie d'Hondschoote (XIVe-XVIIIe siècles)*, Paris.

Coornaert, E. (1930b), *Une industrie urbaine du XIVe au XVIIe siècle: l'industrie de la laine à Bergues-Saint-Winoc*, Paris.

Coornaert, E. (1950), 'Draperies rurales, draperies urbaines. L'évolution de l'industrie flamande au Moyen Age et au XVIe siècle', *Revue Belge de Philologie et d'Histoire*, 28, pp. 59-96.

Coornaert, E. (1968), *Les corporations en France avant 1789*, Paris.

Coppejans-Desmedt, H. (1971), 'De enquête van 1784 over het ambachtswezen in de Oostenrijkse Nederlanden. Bijdrage tot een kritisch onderzoek', *Archief- en bibliotheekwezen in België*, 42, pp. 34-47.

Coppejans-Desmedt, H. (1989), 'Aspecten van de industriële politiek in de Oostenrijkse Nederlanden', in H. Houtman-Desmedt (ed.), *Overheid en economie. Economische aspecten van de overheidspolitiek in en met betrekking tot de Oostenrijkse Nederlanden. Handelingen van het Colloquium te Antwerpen, 27 februari 1988,* Antwerp.

Craandijk, J. (1904), *De Haarlemsche hofjes*, Haarlem.

Craeybeckx, J. (1957), 'De handarbeiders. De 17de en de 18de eeuw', *Flandria Nostra*, Antwerpen, pp. 281-328.

Craeybeckx, J. (1962), 'Les industries d'exportation dans les villes flamandes au XVIIe siècle, particulièrement à Gand et à Bruges', *Studi in onore di Amintore Fanfani*, vol. 4, Milan, pp. 413-68.

Craeybeckx, J. (1976), 'L'industrie de la laine dans les anciens Pays-Bas méridionaux de la fin du XVIe au début du XVIIIe siècle', in Spallanzani (ed.), *Produzione, commercio e consumo dei panni di lana. Atti della "seconda settimana di studio" (10-16 aprile 1970): Istituto Internazionale di Storia Economica "F. Datini" Prato*, Florence, pp. 21-43.

Crahay, R. (ed.) (1982), *La tolérance civile. Colloque international organisé à l'Université de Mons du 2 au 4 septembre 1981 à l'occasion du deuxième centenaire de l'Edit de Joseph II*, Etudes sur le XVIIIe siècle, Vol. Hors Série no. 1, Brussel.

Crossick, G. (1996), 'Formation ou invention des "classes moyennes"? Une analyse comparée: Belgique-France-Grande Bretagne', *Revue Belge d'Histoire Contemporaine*, 26, pp. 105-38.

Crossick, G. (ed.) (1997), *The Artisan and the European Town*, 1500-1900, Aldershot.

Crossick, G., and H.G. Haupt (1995), *The Petite Bourgeoisie in Europe 1780-1914*, London.

Crowston, C.H. (2001), *Fabricating Women. The Seamstresses of Old Regime France, 1675-1791*, Durham/London.

Culot, M., E. Hennaut, M. Demanet and C. Mierop (1992), *Le bombardement de Bruxelles par Louis XIV et la reconstruction qui s'en suivit 1695-1700*, Brussel.

Cuvelier, J. (1935), *Les institutions de la ville de Louvain au Moyen Age*, Brussel.

Cuvelier, J. (1940), 'Documents concernant la réforme de la bienfaisance à Louvain au XVIe siècle', *Bulletin de la Commission Royale d'Histoire de Belgique*, 105.

Daems, K. (1988), *Vrouwenarbeid te Antwerpen in de achttiende eeuw*, unpublished MA-Thesis, Universiteit Gent.

Dambruyne, J. (1992), 'Het werkkader van de bouwsector: de ambachtsgilden', in J. Dambruyne, G. Bral, A. Rambaut and D. Laporte, *Een stad in opbouw. Gent van 1540 tot de wereldtentoonstelling van 1913*, Tielt, pp. 101-43.

Dambruyne, J. (1994), 'De Gentse bouwvakambachten in sociaal-economisch perspectief, 1540-1795', in C. Lis and H. Soly (eds), *Werken volgens de regels: ambachten in Brabant en Vlaanderen, 1500-1800*, Brussels pp. 51-100.

Dambruyne, J. (1997), 'Rijkdom, materiële cultuur en sociaal aanzien. De bezitspatronen en investeringsstrategieën van de Gentse ambachten omstreeks 1540', in C. Lis and H. Soly (eds), *Werelden van verschil: ambachtsilden in de Lage Landen*, Brussels, pp. 151-211.

Dambruyne, J. (1998a), 'Guilds, Social Mobility and Status in Sixteenth-Century Ghent', *International Review of Social History*, 43, pp. 31-78.

Dambruyne, J. (1998b), 'Pracht noch praal. De Gentse ambachtsgilden en hun materiële cultuur tijdens de eerste helft van de 16de eeuw', *Oost-Vlaamse Zanten. Tijdschrift voor volkscultuur in Vlaanderen*, 73, pp. 2-29.

Dambruyne, J. (1999), 'Identité urbaine et culture politique à Gand sous le règne de Charles-Quint', in H. Soly en J. Van De Wiele (eds), *Carolus. Charles-Quint, 1500-1558*, Gent.

Dambruyne, J. (2000), *Aspiraties van corporatieve middengroepen. Een onderzoek naar sociaal-economische en politiek-institutionele patronen en interacties in het 16de-eeuwse Gent*, unpublished PhD-thesis, Universiteit Gent.

Dambruyne, J. (2001), *Mensen en centen. Het 16de-eeuwse Gent in demografisch en economisch perspectief*, Verhandelingen der Maatschappij voor Geschiedenis en Oudheidkunde te Gent, vol. 26, Gent.

Dambruyne, J. (2002), *Corporatieve middengroepen. Aspiraties, relaties en transformaties in de 16de-eeuwse Gentse ambachtswereld*, Verhandelingen der Maatschappij voor Geschiedenis en Oudheidkunde te Gent, vol. 28, Gent.

Davids, C.A. (1995), *De macht der gewoonte? Economische ontwikkeling en institutionele context in Nederland op de lange termijn*, Amsterdam.

Davids, K. (1996), 'Neringen, hallen en gilden. Kapitalisten, kleine ondernemers en de stedelijke overheid in de tijd van de Republiek', in C.A. Davids, W. Fritschy and L.A. van der Valk (eds), *Kapitaal, ondernemerschap en beleid. Studies over economie en politiek in Nederland, Europa en Azië van 1500 tot heden*, Amsterdam, pp. 95-119.

Davids, K. (2001), 'From De La Court to Vreede. Regulation and Self-Regulation in Dutch Economic Discourse from c. 1600 to the Napoleonic Era', *Journal of European Economic History*, 30, pp. 245-89.

Davids, K. (unpublished paper), 'Guilds, guildsmen and technological innovation in early modern Europe: the case of the Dutch Republic'.

Davids, K., and J. Lucassen, (eds) (1995), *A Miracle Mirrored. The Dutch Republic in a European Perspective*, Cambridge.

Davids, K., and L. Noordegraaf (eds) (1994), *The Dutch Economy in the Golden Age: Nine Essays*, Amsterdam.

De Belder, J. (1974), *Elementen van sociale identificatie van de Antwerpse bevolking op het einde van de XVIIIde eeuw. Een kwantitatieve studie*, 2 vols, unpublished PhD-thesis, Universiteit Gent.

De Belder, J. (1976), 'Beroep of bezit als criterium voor de sociale doorsnede. Een aanzet tot de uniformisering van reconstructiemethoden', *Tijdschrift voor Sociale Geschiedenis*, 6, pp. 258-79.

De Munck B. (2003), 'Vaardigheid in de praktijk. De toegevoegde waarde van ambachtsgilden (16de-18de eeuw)', in B. De Munck and D. Dendooven, *Al doende leert men. Leertijd en ambacht in het Ancien Régime*, Catalogue of the exhibition at the Stedelijk Onderwijsmuseum in Ieper, Bruges, pp. 40-8.

De Munck, B. (2001), 'Medische praktijken. Conflicten rond competentie in de Antwerpse medische sector, 17de en 18de eeuw', *Tijdschrift voor Sociale Geschiedenis*, 27, pp. 459-84.

De Munck, B. (2002), *Leerpraktijken. Economische en sociaal-culturele aspecten van beroepsopleidingen in Antwerpse ambachtsgilden, 16de-18de eeuw*, unpublished PhD-thesis, Vrije Universiteit Brussel.

De Peuter, R. (1979), 'De economische ontwikkeling', in J. Stengers (ed.), *Brussel: groei van een hoofdstad*, Antwerp, pp. 116-29.

De Peuter, R. (1988), 'Industrial Development and De-Industrialization in Pre-Modern Towns: Brussels from the Sixteenth to the Eighteenth Century', in H. van der Wee (ed.), *The rise and decline of urban industries in Italy and the Low Countries (late middle ages — early modern times)*, Leuven, pp. 213-40.

De Peuter, R. (1999), *Brussel in de achttiende eeuw. Sociaal-economische structuren en ontwikkelingen in een regionale hoofdstad*, Brussel.

De Ridder, J. (1989), *Gerechtigheidstaferelen voor schepenhuizen in de Zuidelijke Nederlanden in de 14de, 15de en 16de eeuw*, Brussel.

De Schryver, R. (1965), *Jan van Brouchoven, graaf van Bergeyck (1644-1725). Een halve eeuw staatkunde in de Spaanse Nederlanden en in Europa*, Brussel.

De Vos, D. (1999), *Rogier van der Weyden, het volledige oeuvre*, Antwerpen.

Decavele, J. (1984), '"Genève" van Vlaanderen', in J. Decavele (ed.), *Het eind van een rebelse droom. Opstellen over het calvinistisch bewind te Gent (1577-1584) en de terugkeer van de stad onder de gehoorzaamheid van de koning van Spanje (17 september 1584)*, Gent.

Decavele, J., and P. Van Peteghem (1989), 'Ghent "absolutely" broken', in J. Decavele (ed.), *Ghent. In Defence of a Rebellious City,* Antwerp, pp. 107-13.

Deceulaer, H. (1994), 'Conflicten en conflictregeling in de Antwerpse ambachtswereld (1585-1796). Een verkenning van de juridische en sociaal-politieke aspecten op het lokale terrein', in C. Lis and H. Soly (eds), *Werken volgens de regels: ambachten in Brabant en Vlaanderen, 1500-1800*, Brussel, pp. 137-77.

Deceulaer, H. (1996), 'Guilds and Litigation: Conflict Settlement in Antwerp (1585-1796)', in M. Boone and M. Prak (eds), *Individual, Corporate and Judicial Status in European cities (late middle ages and early modern period)*, Leuven/Apeldoorn, pp. 171-208.

Deceulaer, H. (1998), 'Zuid-Nederlandse ondernemers voor en na 1585: het geval van de Antwerpse huikmakers', *Belgisch Tijdschrift voor Filologie en Geschiedenis*, 76, pp. 403-17.

Deceulaer, H. (2000), 'Entrepreneurs in the Guilds: Ready-to-wear Clothing and Subcontracting in Late Sixteenth and early Seventeenth-Century Antwerp', *Textile History*, 31, pp. 133-49.

Deceulaer, H. (2001), *Pluriforme patronen en een verschillende snit. Sociaal-economische, institutionele en culturele transformaties in de kledingsector in Antwerpen, Brussel en Gent, 1585-1800,* Amsterdam.

Deceulaer, H., and B. Panhuysen (2000), 'Schneider oder Näherinnen? Ein geschlechtbezogener Vergleich der Bekleidungshandwerke in den Nördlichen und Südlichen Niederlanden während der Frühen Neuzeit', in W. Reininghaus (ed.), *Zunftlandschaften in Deutschland und den Niederlanden im Vergleich*, Münster, pp. 85-106.

Declercq, (1979), 'Gilden en ambachten te Ronse', *Annalen van de Geschied- en Oudheidkundige Kring van Ronse*, pp. 17-35.

Degryse, K. (1974), 'Sociale ongelijkwaardigheid te Antwerpen in 1747', *Bijdragen tot de Geschiedenis*, 57, pp. 136-45.

Degryse, K. (1985), 'De Antwerpse adel in de 18de eeuw', in J. Verbesselt et al., *De adel in het Hertogdom Brabant*, pp. 133-41.

Dekker, R. (1990), 'Labour Conflicts and Working-Class Culture in Early Modern Holland', *International Review of Social History*, 35, pp. 377-420.

Dekker, R. (1992), 'Handwerkslieden en arbeiders in Holland van de zestiende tot de achttiende eeuw: identiteit, cultuur en protest', in P. Te Boekhorst, P. Burke and W. Frijhoff (eds), *Cultuur en maatschappij in Nederland, 1500-1800. Een historisch-antropologisch perspectief*, Heerlen, pp. 109-47.

Dekker, R., and L. van de Pol (1989), *Vrouwen in mannenkleren. De geschiedenis van de vrouwelijke travestie*, Amsterdam.

Deneweth, C. (1987), *Vrouwenarbeid te Brugge in de achttiende eeuw*, unpublished MA-thesis, Universiteit Gent.

Denolf, J. (1981), *Brugge 1748. Een socio-demografische schets van een stedelijke samenleving rond het midden van de 18e eeuw*, unpublished MA-thesis, Universiteit Gent.

Denolf, J. (1983), 'Socio-professionele structuren binnen de Brugse samenleving rond het midden van de achttiende eeuw', in J. de Belder, W. Prevenier, C. Vandenbroeke (eds), *Sociale mobiliteit en sociale structuren in Vlaanderen en Brabant*, Gent pp. 79-117

Derville, A. (1972), 'Les draperies flamandes et artésiennes vers 1250-1350. Quelques considérations critiques et problématiques', *Revue du Nord*, 54.

Des Marez, G. (1901), 'Le compagnonnage des chapeliers bruxellois (1576-1909)', *Annuaire-Bulletin de la Société pour le Progrès des Etudes Philologiques et Historiques*, pp. 44-6.

Des Marez, G. (1904), *L'organisation du travail à Bruxelles au XVe siècle*, Brussel.

Des Marez, G. (1909), 'Le compagnonnage des chapeliers bruxellois (1576-1909)', *Annales de la Société d'Archéologie de Bruxelles*, Vol. 23, pp. 137-243.

Des Marez, G. (1911), 'Mutualités et compagnonnages à Bruxelles au XVe siècle', *Jaarboek van het Congres van het Oudheid- en Geschiedkundig Verbond van België*, 22, pp. 209-13.

Despretz Van De Casteele, S. (1965), 'Het protectionisme in de Zuidelijke Nederlanden gedurende de tweede helft der 17e eeuw', *Tijdschrift voor Geschiedenis*, 78, pp. 294-317.

Deter, G. (1990), *Rechtsgeschichte des Westfälischen Handwerks im 18. Jahrhundert: das Recht der Meister*, Münster.

Devast, V. (1934) *O.L. Vrouw van Alsemberg: Geschiedenis — kunstschatten — Mariavereering*, Brasschaat.

Dickschen, S. (1995), *De Antwerpse ambachten tegen de dorpsneringen. De koninklijke ordonnantie van 1685*, unpublished MA-thesis, Vrije Universiteit Brussel.

Dievoet, G. Van (2000), 'De Blijde Inkomst. De geschreven grondwet van Brabant', in R. Van Uytven, C. Bruneel, H. Copppens and B. Augustyn (eds), *De gewestelijke en lokale overheidsinstellingen in Brabant en Mechelen tot 1795*, Brussel, pp. 19-31.

Dilis, E. (1926), 'Het huis, de kamer en het altaar van het voormalig Antwerpsch kuipersambacht', *Bijdragen tot de Geschiedenis*, 17, pp. 263-89.

Dillen, J.G. van (1940), 'De economische positie en betekenis der joden in de Republiek en in de Nederlandse koloniale wereld', in I.H. Brugmans and A. Frank (eds), *Geschiedenis der Joden in Nederland*, Vol. 1, Amsterdam, pp. 561-616.

Dillen, J.G. van, (1929-1974) *Bronnen tot de geschiedenis van het bedrijfsleven en het gildewezen van Amsterdam*, 3 vols, 's-Gravenhage.

Dixhoorn, A. van (1997), *Voorstanden van de vrije wetten. Burgerbewegingen in Arnhem 1703 tot 1707: een studie naar de participatie van burgers in de stedelijke politieke cultuur aan het begin van de achttiende eeuw*, unpublished MA-thesis, Universiteit Utrecht.

Dixhoorn, A. van (1999), '"Voorstanden van de vrije wetten". Burgerbewegingen in Arnhem en de Republiek tussen 1702 en 1707', *Tijdschrift voor sociale geschiedenis*, 25, pp. 25-54.

Dorren, G. (1998), *Het soet vergaren. Haarlems buurtleven in de zeventiende eeuw*, Haarlem.

Duco, D.H. (1981), 'De kleipijp in de zeventiende-eeuwse Nederlanden', in P. Davey (ed.), *The Archaeology of the Clay Tobacco Pipe*, Vol. 5, *Europe*, 2, Part 2, Oxford.

Duerloo, L. (1996), 'Arenberg en Habsburg', *De blinde hertog. Louis Engelbert van Arenberg & zijn tijd, 1750-1820*, Brussel.

Dülmen, R. van (1986), 'Volksfrömmigkeit und konfessionelles Christentum im 16. und 17. Jahrhundert', in W. Schieder (ed.), *Volksreligiosität in der modernen Sozialgeschichte*, Göttingen, pp. 14-31.

Dumolyn, J. (1997), *De Brugse opstand van 1436-1438*, Standen en landen, vol. 101, Kortrijk/Heule.

Dumont, B. (1994), *Aux origines des communes. Les communautés villageoises dans les Pays de Dalhem et de Limbourg, XVIe-XVIIIe siècle: genèse, structures, evolution*, Brussel.

DuPlessis, R.S. (1997) *Transitions to Capitalism in Early Modern Europe,* Cambridge.

DuPlessis, R., and M.C. Howell (1982), 'Reconstructing the Early Modern Urban Economy: the cases of Leiden and Lille', *Past and Present*, no. 94, pp. 49-84.

Duvosquel, J.M., and A. Dierkens (eds) (1991), *Villes et campagnes au Moyen Âge. Mélanges Georges Despy*, Liège.

Earle, P. (1989), 'The Female Labour Market in London in the late 17th and early 18th century', *Economic history review*, 2nd ser., 42, pp. 328-53.

Eck, A. (1931), 'A propos des draps d'Ypres à Novgorod', *Revue Belge d'Histoire et de Philologie*, 10.

Eeghen, I.H. van (1965, 1974[2], 1989), *De gilden, theorie en praktijk*, Bussum.

Eeraerts, J. (1997), *Het weversgodshuis te Gent in de 16de en 17de eeuw. Een prosopografische studie*, unpublished MA-thesis, Universiteit Gent.

Eerenbeemt, H.F.J.M. van den (1955), *'s Hertogenbosch in de Bataafse en Franse tijd, 1794-1814. Bijdrage tot de kennis van de sociaal-economische structuur*, Nijmegen.

Eggertsson, T. (1990), *Economic Behaviour and Institutions*, Cambridge.

Egmond, F. (1994), 'Erezaken: rond een echtelijk conflict in het zestiende-eeuwse Haarlem', *Tijdschrift voor Geschiedenis*, 107, pp. 7-22.

Ehmer, J. (1998), 'Traditionelles Denken und neue Fragestellungen zur Geschichte von Handwerk und Zunft', in F. Lenger (ed.), *Handwerk, Hausindustrie und die historische Schule der Nationalökonomie. Wissenschafts-und gewerbegeschichtliche Perspektiven*, Bielefeld, pp. 19-77.

Ehmer, J. (2002), 'Zünfte in Österreich in der frühen Neuzeit', in H.G. Haupt (ed.), *Das Ende der Zünfte*, pp. 87-126.

Elias, J.E. (1923), *Geschiedenis van het Amsterdamsche regentenpatriciaat*, Den Haag.

Elias, J.E. (1963), *De vroedschap van Amsterdam, 1578-1795*, 2 vols, Amsterdam.

Elte, S. (1930), 'Interdict en gildenwoelingen te Zwolle in het begin der vijftiende eeuw', *Tijdschrift voor geschiedenis*, 45, pp. 374-89.

Epstein, S.A. (1991), *Wage Labor and Guilds in Medieval Europe*, Chapel Hill/London.

Epstein, S.R. (1998), 'Craft Guilds, Apprenticeship, and Technological Change in Preindustrial Europe', *Journal of Economic History*, 58, pp. 684-713.

Espinas, G. (1923), *La draperie dans la Flandre française au Moyen Age*, Paris.

Esther, J.P. (1986), 'De analyse van een 18de-eeuwse arduinen gevel: het ambachtshuis van de kuipers in de Vlamingstraat in Brugge', *Monumenten & Landschappen*, 5, pp. 27-39.

Esther, J.P. (1991), 'De ambachtskamer van de kleermakers in Brugge', *Monumenten & Landschappen*, extra nummer, open monumentendag, pp. 26-27.

Everaert, L. (1975), *Histoire de la ville de Hal d'après les documents originaux*, Brussel.

Faber, J.A. (1972), *Drie eeuwen Friesland. Economische en sociale ontwikkelingen van 1500 tot 1800*, Wageningen.

Fairchilds, C. (1992), 'The production and marketing of populuxe goods in eighteenth-century Paris', in J. Brewer and R. Porter (eds), *Consumption and the World of Goods*, London, pp. 228-48.

Farr, J. (1988), *Hands of Honor. Artisans and Their World in Dijon, 1550-1650*, Ithaca/ London.

Farr, J.R. (1997), 'On the Shop Floor: Guilds, Artisans, and the European Market Economy, 1350-1750', *Journal of Early Modern History*, 1, pp. 24-54.

Farr, J.R. (2000), *Artisans in Europe, 1300-1914*, Cambridge.

Favresse, L. (1961), *Etudes sur les métiers bruxellois au Moyen Age*, Brussel.

Felix, D.A. (1919), *Het oproer te Utrecht in 1610*, Utrecht.

Foncke, R. (1968), 'De verering van Sint-Elooi in Vlaanderen en inzonderheid te Mechelen', *Verslagen en mededelingen van de Kon. Vlaamse Academie voor Taal- en Letterkunde*.

Formsma, W.J. et al. (1976), *Historie van Groningen. Stad en Land*, Groningen.

Franklin, A. (1987), *Dictionnaire historique des arts, métiers et professions exercés à Paris depuis le XIIIe siècle*, Marseille.

Frigo, D. (2002), 'Die italienische Zünfte am Ende des Ancien Régimes: Stand, Probleme und Perspektiven des Forschung', in H.G. Haupt (ed.), *Das Ende der Zünfte*, pp. 197-214.

Frijhoff, W. (1988), 'Geschiedenis als strijdbijl. Burgerij, gemeenslieden en magistraat in Zutphen (vijftiende tot achttiende eeuw)', in B. Looper, J.C. Riemens (eds), *Geschiedenis in Zutphen. Over geschiedschrijving, geschiedbeoefening en historisch besef*, Zutphen, pp. 40-55.

Füglister, H. (1981), *Handwerksregiment: Untersuchungen und Matrialen zur sozialen und politischen Struktur der Stadt Basel in der ersten Hälfte des 16. Jahrhunderts*, Basler Beiträge zur Geschichtswissenschaft, vol. 143, Basel.

Fujii, Y. (1990), 'Draperies urbaines et draperies rurales dans les Pays-Bas méridionaux au bas Moyen Age', *Journal of Medieval History*, 16, pp. 77-97.

Fuks-Mansfeld, R.G. (1989), *De Sefardim in Amsterdam tot 1795. Aspecten van een joodse minderheid in een Hollandse stad*, Hilversum.

Gabriëls, A.J.C.M. (1985), 'Patrizier und Regenten: städtische Eliten in den nördlichen Niederlanden 1500-1850', in H. Schilling and H. Diederiks (eds), *Bürgerliche Eliten in den Niederlanden und in Nordwestdeutschland*, Städteforschung, vol. A/23, Cologne/Vienna, pp. 37-64.

Gabriëls, A.J.C.M. (1990), *De heren als dienaren en de dienaar als heer. Het stadshouderlijk stelsel in de tweede helft van de achttiende eeuw*, Hollandse Historische Reeks, vol. 14, 's-Gravenhage.

Garden, M. (1970), *Lyon et le Lyonnais au XVIIIe siècl*e, Paris.

Gelder, H.E. van, and M. Hoc (1960), *Les monnaies des Pays-Bas bourguignons et espagnols*, Amsterdam.

Genabeek, J. van (1994) 'De afschaffing van de gilden en de voortzetting van hun functies', *NEHA-Jaarboek voor economische, bedrijfs- en techniekgeschiedenis*, vol. 57, pp. 63-90.

Genabeek, J. van (1999), *Met vereende kracht risico's verzacht. De plaats van onderlinge hulp binnen de negentiende-eeuwse particuliere regelingen van sociale zekerheid*, Amsterdam.

Gérard, E. (1935), *Histoire de la ville de Dinant*, Namur.

Geyl, P. (1971), 'Democratische tendenties in 1672', in P. Geyl, *Pennestrijd over staat en historie*, Groningen, pp. 72-129.

Gillissen, J. (1962), 'Le statut de la femme dans l'ancien droit belge', *La femme, Recueils de la société Jean Bodin pour l'histoire comparative des institutions 2*, Brussels, pp. 255-321.

Gilté, S. (1996), *Het Brugse bakkersambacht in de Nieuwe Tijden*, unpublished MA-thesis, Universiteit Gent.

Goedleven, E. (1993), *De Grote Markt van Brussel, centrum van vijf eeuwen geschiedenis*, Tielt.

Goetstouwers, J.B. (1908), *Les métiers de Namur sous l'Ancien Régime*, Louvain/Paris.

Goris, J.A. and G. Marlier (eds) (1970), *Le journal de voyage d'Albert Dürer dans les anciens Pays-Bas, 1520-1521*, Brussel.

Goudriaan, K. (1996), 'Gilden en broederschappen in de middeleeuwen', in K. Goudriaan, M. Hulshof, P. Lourens and J. Lucassen (eds), *De gilden in Gouda*, Gouda/Zwolle, pp. 21-63.

Goudriaan, K., Hulshof, M., Lourens , P. and Lucassen, J. (1996), *De Gilden in Gouda*, Gouda/Zwolle.

Gouw, J. ter (1866,1942) *De gilden, een bijdrage tot de geschiedenis van het volksleven*, 's-Gravenhage.

Graswinckel, D.P.M. (1933), 'Ontstaan en ontwikkeling van de gilden te Arnhem', *Arnhem, zeven eeuwen stad*, Arnhem, pp. 93-121.

Grayson, J.C. (1980), 'The Civic Militia in the County of Holland 1560-81: Politics and Public Order in the Dutch Revolt', *Bijdragen en Mededelingen betreffende de Geschiedenis der Nederlanden*, 95, pp. 35-63.

Greup-Roldanus, S.C.R. (1936), *Geschiedenis der Haarlemmer blekerijen*, 's-Gravenhage.

Groeneweg, I. (1991), 'Enkele aspecten van mode en kleedgedrag in Nederland naar aanleiding van de brieven van de familie van Hogendorp uit de late 18de eeuw', *Textielhistorische Bijdragen*, 31, pp. 69-80.

Groot, A. de (1939), 'De Arnhemsche ambachtsgilden in de 17de en 18de eeuw', *Bijdragen en Mededeelingen Gelre*, 42, pp. 79-119.

Guibal, C.J. (1934), *Democratie en oligarchie in Friesland tijdens de Republiek*, Assen.

Guicciardini, L. (1612), *Beschrijvinge van alle de Nederlanden andersints ghenoemt Neder-Duytschlandt, overgeset in de Nederduytsche spraeke door Cornelium Kilianum*, Amsterdam.

Guignet, P. (1990), *Le pouvoir dans la ville au XVIIIe siècle. Pratiques politiques, notabilité et éthique sociale de part et d'autre de la frontière franco-belge*, Paris.

Gurp, G. van (2004), *Brabantse stoffen op de wereldmarkt. Proto-industrialisering in de Meijerij van 's-Hertogenbosch 1620-1820*, Bijdragen tot de geschiedenis van het Zuiden van Nederland, Tilburg.

Gustafsson, B. (1991), 'The Rise and Economic Behaviour of Medieval Craft Guilds', in B. Gustafsson (ed.), *Power and Economic Institutions. Reinterpretations in Economic History*, Aldershot/Brookfield, pp. 69-106.

Hafter, D.M. (2001), 'Women in the underground business of eighteenth-century Lyon', *Enterprise and Society*, 2, pp. 1-40.

Hansotte, G. (1950), 'Naissance et dévelopement des métiers liégeois (XIIIe et XIVe siècles)', *Bulletin de la Société d'Art et d'Histoire du Diocèse de Liège*, 36, pp. 1-34.

Hansotte, G. (1987), *Les institutions politiques et judiciaires de la Principauté de Liège aux Temps Modernes*, Brussels.

Hart, M. 't (1997), 'The Merits of a Financial revolution: Public Finance, 1550-1700', in M. 't Hart, J. Jonker and J.L. van Zanden (eds), *A Financial History of The Netherlands*, Cambridge, pp. 11-36'.

Harte, N.B. (1991), 'The Economics of Clothing in the Late Seventeenth Century', *Textile History*, 22, pp. 277-96.

Hartkamp-Jonxis, E. (1989), 'Katoendrukkerijen in de Noordelijke Nederlanden, 1678-1820', in *Katoendruk in Nederland*, Tilburg, pp. 15-30.

Hasquin, H. (1971), *Une mutation. Le 'Pays de Charleroi' aux XVIIe et XVIIIe siècles. Aux origines de la Révolution industrielle en Belgique*, Brussel.

Haupt, H.G. (ed.) (2002a), *Das Ende der Zünfte: ein europäischer Vergleich*, Göttingen.
Haupt, H.G. (2002b), 'Neue Wege zur Geschichte der Zünfte in Europa', in H.G. Haupt (ed.), *Das Ende der Zünfte*, pp. 9-38.
Heirwegh, J.J. (1981), *Les corporations dans les Pays-Bas autrichiens, 1738-1784*, unpublished PhD-thesis, Université Libre de Bruxelles.
Heirwegh, J.J. (1983), 'Artisanat et industrie à Mons au XVIIIe siècle', in J.M. Cauchies and J.M. Duvosquel (eds), *Recueil d'Etudes d'Histoire hainuyère Offertes à Monsieur A. Arnould*, vol. 1, Mons, pp. 291-317.
Heirwegh, J.J. (1989), 'Les corporations dans les Pays-Bas autrichiens', in G. Gayot and J.P. Hirsch (eds), *La Révolution française et le développement du capitalisme. Actes du Colloque de Lille, 19-21 novembre 1987,* Lille, special issue of *Revue du Nord*, pp. 365-8.
Heirwegh, J.J. and Belle, J.L. Van (1991), *Les saints patrons des métiers en Belgique*, Brussel.
Hélin, E. (1963), 'La démographie de Liège au XVIIe et XVIIIe siècles', *Verhandelingen Koninklijke Academie van België, Klasse der Letteren*, LVI, 4, appendix 1.
Helsen, J., Moermans, W., Severijns, P. and Vandeplas, E. (1988), *2000 jaar Tongeren. 15 voor Chr. tot 1985*, Hasselt.
Henderikx, P.A. (2001), 'Het ontstaan en de vroegste ontwikkeling van Zierikzee tot circa 1300', in P.A. Henderikx, *Land, water en bewoning. Waterstaats- en nederzettingsgeschiedenis in de Zeeuwse en Hollandse delta in de Middeleeuwen*, Hilversum, pp. 81-103.
Heuvel, N.H.L. van den (1946), *De ambachtsgilden van 's-Hertogenbosch voor 1629. Rechtsbronnen van het bedrijfsleven en het gildewezen*, Utrecht.
Hewak, M. and S. Hugue (eds) (1993), *Albert Dürer: Journal de voyage aux Pays-Bas pendant les années 1520 et 1521*, Paris.
Historiens (1991) *et populations. Liber amicorum Étienne Hélin*, Louvain-la-Neuve.
Hodgson, G.M. (1988), *Economics and Institutions. A Manifesto for a Modern Institutional Economics*, Oxford.
Holbach, R. (1994), 'Frühformen von Verlag und Großbetrieb in der gewerblichen Produktion (13.-16. Jahrhundert)', *Vierteljahrschrift für Sozial- und Wirtschaftsgeschichte, Beiheft 110*, Stuttgart.
Hoogewerff, G.J. (1947), *De geschiedenis van de St. Lucasgilden in Nederland*, Amsterdam.
Hufton, O. (1998), *The Prospect before Her. A History of Women in Western Europe. Volume One 1500-1800*, London.
Huisman, F.G. (1992), *Stadsbelang en standsbesef. Gezondheidszorg en medisch beroep in Groningen 1500-1730*, Rotterdam.
Huisman, F. (1993), 'Gevestigden en buitenstaanders op de medische markt. De marginalisering van reizende meesters in achttiende-eeuws Groningen', in W. de Blécourt, W. Frijhoff and M. Gijswijt-Hofstra (eds), *Grenzen van genezing. Gezondheid, ziekte en genezen in Nederland, zestiende tot begin twintigste eeuw*, Hilversum, pp. 115-55.
Huisman, M. (1902), *La Belgique commerciale sous l'empereur Charles VI*, Brussels.
Hulshof, M. (1997), 'De Goudse ambachtsgilden', in K. Goudriaan, M. Hulshof, P. Lourens and J. Lucassen (eds), *De gilden in Gouda*, Gouda/ Zwolle, pp. 87-148.
Huyghebaert, J. (1998), 'Schoenmakers spelen de martelie van St.-Crispijn', *Biekorf*, 98.
Huys, E. (1926), *Duizend jaar mutualiteit bij de Vlaamsche gilden*, Kortrijk.
Installé, H. (1982), *Patriciërs en ambachtslui in het stadsbestuur te Mechelen onder Maria-Theresia. De sociale status van Burgemeesters en Schepenen (1740-1780)*, Mechelen.
Installé, H. (1989), *Inventaris van het fonds der lederverwerkende ambachten op het Stadsarchief te Mechelen*, Mechelen.
Isenmann, E. (1988) *Die deutsche Stadt im Spätmittelalter, 1250-1500. Stadtgestalt, Recht, Stadtregiment, Kirche, Gesellschaft, Wirtschaft*, Stuttgart.

Israel, J. (1979), 'The Holland Towns and the Dutch-Spanish Conflict, 1621-'48', *Bijdragen en Mededelingen betreffende de Geschiedenis der Nederlanden,* 94, pp. 41-69.

Israel, J. (1990), *Dutch Primacy in World Trade, 1585-1740*, Oxford.

Israel, J. (1995a), *The Dutch Republic: Its Rise, Greatness and Fall, 1477-1806*, Oxford.

Israel, J. (1995b), 'De Republiek der Verenigde Nederlanden tot omstreeks 1750. Demografie en economische activiteit' in J.C.H. Blom, R.G. Fuks-Mansfeld and I. Schöffer (eds), *Geschiedenis van de Joden in Nederland*, Amsterdam.

Jacobs, M. (1986), *Justitie en politie in 's-Hertogenbosch voor 1629*, Brabantse Rechtshistorische Reeks, vol. 1, Assen.

Jacobs, M. (1997), 'Oude structuren en verse vis. Representaties van corporaties te Nieuwpoort in de tweede helft van de achttiende eeuw', in C. Lis and H. Soly (eds), *Werelden van verschil. Ambachtsgilden in de Lage Landen*, Brussel, pp. 243-92.

Jacobs, M. (2000), 'De ambachten in Brabant en Mechelen (12de eeuw-1795)', in R. Van Uytven, C. Bruneel, H. Coppens and B. Augustyn (eds), *De gewestelijke en lokale overheidsinstellingen in Brabant en Mechelen tot 1795*, vol. 2, Brussel, pp. 558-624.

Jacobs, M. and M. Vanbellinghen, (1999), *Ambachten in de Zuidelijke Nederlanden (voor 1795). Een bijdrage tot de samenstelling van een bibliografische lijst van studies verschenen in de 19de en 20ste eeuw*, Brussel.

Jacobs, R. (1994), *Brussel, de geschiedenis in de stad*, Brugge.

Jacobsen Jensen, J.N. (1918), 'Moryson's reis door en zijn karakteristiek van de Nederlanden', *Bijdragen en mededeelingen van het historisch genootschap,* 39, pp. 214-305.

Jaegher, M. de (1973), *Sociaal-economische structuren te Oudenaarde in de XIVe en XVe eeuw*, unpublished MA-thesis, Universiteit Gent.

James, M. (1983), 'Ritual, Drama and Social Body in the Late Medieval English Town', *Past and Present*, no. 98, pp. 3-29.

Jansen, H.P.H. (1976), *Hollands voorsprong*, Leiden.

Jansen, H.P.H. (1983), 'Een economisch contrast in de Nederlanden: Noord en Zuid in de twaalfde eeuw', *Bijdragen en Mededelingen betreffende de Geschiedenis der Nederlanden*, 98, pp. 59-70.

Jongh, J.J. de (1985), *Met goed fatsoen. De elite in een Hollandse stad, Gouda, 1700-1790*, Amsterdam.

Jongh, J.J. de (1987), *Een deftig bestaan. Het dagelijks leven van regenten in de 17de en 18de eeuw*, Utrecht.

Jongste, J.A.F. de (1984), *Onrust aan het Spaarne: Haarlem in de jaren 1747-1751*, 's-Gravenhage.

Juratic, S. and N. Pellegrin (1994), 'Femmes, villes et travail en France dans la deuxième moitié du XVIIIe siècle', *Histoire Economie Société*, 13, pp. 477-500.

Kalveen, C.A. van (1972), 'De Gildenbeweging van april 1525 en haar voorgeschiedenis', *Jaarboek Oud-Utrecht*, pp. 93-114.

Kalveen, C.A. van (1974), *Het bestuur van bisschop en Staten van Utrecht in het Sticht en Oversticht, 1483-1520*, Utrecht.

Kalveen, C.A. van (1979), 'Bijdrage tot de geschiedenis van de Gildenbewegingen te Utrecht, mei-augustus 1525', *Jaarboek Oud-Utrecht*, pp. 54-86.

Kaplan, B.J. (1995), *Calvinists and Libertines. Confession and Community in Utrecht, 1578-1620*, Oxford.

Kaplan, S.L. (1979), 'Réflexions sur la police du monde du travail, 1700-1815', *Revue historique*, 103, pp. 17-77.

Kaplan, S.L. (1986), 'Social classification and representation in the corporate world of eighteenth-century France: Turgot's "Carnival"', in S.L. Kaplan and C.J. Koepp (eds), *Work in France. Representation, organization, and practice*, Ithaca/London, pp. 176-228.

Kaplan, S.L. (1988), 'Les corporations, les "faux-ouvriers" et le faubourg Saint-Antoine au XVIIIe siècle', *Annales ESC*, 43, pp. 453-78.

Kaplan, S.L. (1996), *Le meilleur pain du monde. Les boulangers de Paris au XVIIIe siècle*, Paris.

Kaplan, S.L. (2001), *La fin des corporations*, Paris.

Kaplan, Y. (1995), 'De Joden in de Republiek tot omstreeks 1750. Religieus, cultureel en sociaal leven', in J.C.H. Blom, R.G. Fuks-Mansfeld and I. Schöffer (eds), *Geschiedenis van de Joden in Nederland*, Amsterdam.

Kaptein, H. (1998), *De Hollandse textielnijverheid, 1350-1600. Conjunctuur en continuïteit*, Hilversum.

Klein, P.W. (1989), 'De Nederlandse handelspolitiek in de tijd van het mercantilisme: een nieuwe kijk op een oude kwestie?', *Tijdschrift voor Geschiedenis*, 102, pp. 189-219.

Klep, P.M.M. (1981), *Bevolking en arbeid in transformatie. Een onderzoek in Brabant, 1700-1900,* Nijmegen.

Kloek, E. (1994), 'Introduction', in E. Kloek, N. Teeuwen and M. Huisman (eds), *Women of the Golden Age. An International Debate on Women in Seventeenth-century Holland, England and Italy*, Hilversum, pp. 9-18.

Knevel, P. (1994), *Burgers in het geweer. De schutterijen van Holland, 1550-1700,* Hollandse Studiën, vol. 32, Hilversum.

Kockelbergh, I., E. Vleeschdrager and J. Walgrave (1992), *The Brilliant Story of Antwerp Diamonds*, Antwerp.

Koldeweij, J.(1999), 'The Wearing of Significative Badges, Religious and Secular: The Social Meaning of a Behavioural Pattern', in W.P. Blockmans and A. Janse (eds), *Showing Status representation of social positions in the Late Middle Ages*, Turnhout, pp. 307-28.

Kooijmans, L. (1985), *Onder regenten. De elite in een Hollandse stad: Hoorn 1700-1780*, Dieren.

Kriedte, P., H. Medick and J. Schlumbohm (1977), *Industrialisierung vor der Industrialisierung. Gewerbliche Warenproduktion auf dem Land in der Formationsperiode des Kapitalismus*, Göttingen.

Kupper, J.L. (1991), 'Le village devenu une cité', in J. Stiennon (ed.), *Histoire de Liège*, Toulouse, pp. 54-64.

Kurpershoek, E. (1994), *De Waag op de Nieuwmarkt*, Amsterdam.

Lambrechts, P. (1994), 'L'historiographie des métiers dans les principautés des anciens Pays-Bas: acquis et perspectives de recherches', in J.P Sosson (ed.), *Les métiers au Moyen Age. Aspects économiques et sociaux*, Louvain-la-Neuve, pp. 143-55.

Leeuwen, M. van (2000), *De rijke Republiek: gilden, assuradeurs en armenzorg, 1500-1800*, Zoeken naar zekerheid, vol. 1, 's-Gravenhage/Amsterdam.

Lemire, B. (1997), *Dress, Culture and Commerce. The English Clothing Trade Before the Factory, 1660-1800*, London/New York.

Lenders, P. (1990), *Gent, een stad tussen traditie en verlichting (1750-1787): een institutionele benadering*, Standen en Landen, vol. 92, Kortrijk/Heule.

Lesger, C. (1986), *Huur en conjunctuur. De woningmarkt in Amsterdam, 1550-1850*, Amsterdam.

Lesger, C., and L. Noordegraaf (1999), 'Inleiding', in C. Lesger and L. Noordegraaf (eds.), *Ondernemers en bestuurders. Economie en politiek in de Noordelijke Nederlanden in de late Middeleeuwen en vroegmoderne tijd*, Amsterdam, pp. 11-60.

Linden, M.M. van der and J. Sluijs (1996), *Onderlinge hulpfondsen: historische en ethnografishe essays,* Amsterdam.

Lindert, P.H. (1998), 'Poor Relief before the Welfare State: Britain versus the Continent, 1770-1889', *European Review of Economic History*, Vol. 2, pp. 101-40.

Lis, C. (1986), *Social Change and the Labouring Poor: Antwerp, 1770-1860*, New Haven/London.

Lis, C. and Soly, H. (1987), *Een groot bedrijf in een kleine stad: de firma De Heyder & Co. te Lier, 1757-1834*, Lier.

Lis, C. and Soly, H. (1990), 'Restructuring the Urban Textile Industries in Brabant and Flanders during the Second Half of the Eighteenth Century', in E. Aerts and J. Munro (eds), *Textiles of the Low Countries in European Economic History, Proceedings of the Tenth International Economic History Congress*, Session B15, Leuven, pp. 105-13.

Lis, C. and Soly, H. (1994a), 'An Irresistible Phalanx: Journeymen Associations in Western Europe, 1300-1800', in C. Lis, J. Lucassen and H. Soly (eds), *Before the Unions. Wage Earners and Collective Action in Europe, 1300-1850*, Cambridge, *International Review of Social History*, Supplement 2, pp. 11-52.

Lis, C. and Soly, H. (1994b), 'Entrepreneurs, corporations et autorités publiques au Brabant et en Flandre à la fin de l'Ancien Régime', *Revue du Nord*, 76, pp. 725-44.

Lis, C. and Soly, H. (1994c), 'Corporatisme, onderaanneming en loonarbeid. Flexibilisering en deregulering van de arbeidsmarkt in Westeuropese steden (veertiende tot achttiende eeuw)', *Tijdschrift voor Sociale Geschiedenis*, 20, pp. 365-90.

Lis, C. and Soly, H. (1994d), 'De macht van "vrije arbeiders": collectieve acties van hoedenmakersgezellen in de Zuidelijke Nederlanden (zestiende-negentiende eeuw)', in C. Lis and H. Soly (eds), *Werken volgens de regels. Ambachten in Brabant en Vlaanderen, 1500-1800*, Brussel, pp. 15-50.

Lis, C. and Soly, H. (1997a), 'Städtische Industrialisierungswege in Brabant und Flandern: De Heyder & Co. in Lier (1750 bis 1815)', in D. Ebeling and W. Mager (eds), *Protoindustrie in der Region. Europäische Gewerbelandschaften vom 16. bis zum 19. Jahrhundert*, Bielefeld, pp. 297-319.

Lis, C. and Soly, H. (1997b), 'Ambachtsgilden in vergelijkend perspectief: de Noordelijke en Zuidelijke Nederlanden, 15de-18de eeuw', in C. Lis and H. Soly (eds), *Werelden van verschil. Ambachtsgilden in de Lage Landen*, Brussel, pp. 11-42.

Lis C. and Soly, H. (1997c), 'Different Paths of Development: Capitalism in the Northern and Southern Netherlands during the Late Middle Ages and the Early Modern Period', *Review*, 20, pp. 228-38.

Lis, C. and Soly, H. (2000), 'Exportgewerbe, Zünfte und kapitalistische Entwicklungen in den Nördlichen end Südlichen Niederlanden im späten Mittelalter und der Frühen Neuzeit', in W. Reininghaus (ed.), *Zunftlandschaften in Deutschland und den Niederlanden im Vergleich*, Münster, pp. 45-70.

Lis, C. and Soly, H. (2002), 'Die Zünfte in den Österreichischen Niederlanden', in H.G. Haupt (ed.), *Das Ende der Zünfte*, pp. 155-80.

Lis, C. and Soly, H. (forthcoming), 'Subcontracting in Guild-based Export trades, Thirteenth-Eighteenth Centuries', in S.R. Epstein and M. Prak (eds), *The guilds, technology and the economy*, Cambridge.

Lis, C. and Vanthemsche, G. (1995), 'Sociale zekerheid in historisch perspectief', in M. Despontin and M. Jegers (eds), *De sociale zekerheid verzekerd? Referaten van het 22ste Vlaams Wetenschappelijk Economisch Congres*, Brussel, pp. 37-43.

Lootens, H. (1971), *Brood en broodzetting te Brugge van de XVe tot de XIXe eeuw*, unpublished MA-thesis, Universiteit Gent.

Louant, A. (1935), 'Les nations de Bruxelles et les Etats de Brabant de 1556-57', *Bulletin de la Commission Royale d'Histoire* 99, pp. 223-50.

Lourens, P., and J. Lucassen (1994), 'Ambachtsgilden in Nederland: een eerste inventarisatie', *NEHA-Jaarboek voor Economische-, Bedrijfs- en Techniekgeschiedenis*, 57, pp. 34-62.

Lourens, P., and J. Lucassen (1996), 'Ambachtsgilden in Nederland, een beknopt overzicht', in K. Goudriaan et al., *De gilden in Gouda*, Zwolle, pp. 9-20.

Lourens, P., and J. Lucassen (1997a), 'De oprichting en ontwikkeling van ambachtsgilden in Nederland (13de-19de eeuw)', in C. Lis and H. Soly (eds), *Werelden van verschil. Ambachtsgilden in de Lage Landen*, pp. 43-78.

Lourens, P., and J. Lucassen (1997b), *Inwoneraantallen in Nederlandse steden, ca 1300-ca 1800*, Amsterdam.

Lourens, P., and J. Lucassen (1998), 'Ambachtsgilden binnen een handelskapitalistische stad: aanzetten voor een analyse van Amsterdam ca. 1700', *NEHA-Jaarboek voor economische, bedrijfs- en techniekgeschiedenis*, 61, pp. 121-62.

Lourens, P., and J. Lucassen (2000), '"Zunftlandschaften" in den Niederlanden und im benachbarten Deutschland', in W. Reininghaus (ed.), *Zunftlandschaften in Deutschland und den Niederlanden im Vergleich*, Münster, pp. 11-44.

Lucassen, J. (1991), *Jan, Jan Salie en diens kinderen. Vergelijkend onderzoek naar continuïteit en discontinuïteit in de ontwikkeling van arbeidsverhoudingen*, Amsterdam.

Lucassen, J. (1992), 'Het Welvaren van Leiden (1659-1662): de wording van een economische theorie over gilden en ondernemerschap', in B. de Vries et al. (eds), *De Kracht der Zwakken. Studies over arbeid en arbeidersbeweging in het verleden*, Amsterdam, pp. 13-49.

Lucassen, J. (1994), 'Joodse Nederlanders, 1796-1940: een proces van omgekeerde minderheidsvorming', in H. Berg, T. Wijsenbeek and E. Fischer (eds), *Venter, fabriqueur, fabrikant. Joodse ondernemers en ondernemingen in Nederland, 1796-1940*, Amsterdam, pp. 32-47.

Lucassen, J. (2001), 'Mobilization of labour in early modern Europe', in M. Prak (ed.), *Early Modern Capitalism. Economic and social change in Europe, 1400-1800*, London/New York, pp. 161-74.

Lucassen, J., and M. Prak, (1998), 'Guilds and Society in the Dutch Republic 16th-18th Centuries', in S.R. Epstein, H.G. Haupt, C. Poni and H. Soly (eds), *Guilds, Economy and Society, Proceedings of the Twelfth International Economic History congress*, Session B1, Sevilla, pp. 63-77.

Maarschalkerweerd, P. (1997), 'De steden', in C. Dekker et al. (eds), *Geschiedenis van de provincie Utrecht*, vol. 1, Utrecht.

Mackenney, R. (1987), *Tradesmen and Traders: The World of the Guilds in Venice and Europe, c.1250-c.1650*, London/Sydney.

Maddens, N. (1989), 'Het Kortrijkse antwoord op de regeringsenquête van 1784 naar de neringen', *Actief in archief. Huldeboek Hilda Coppejans-Desmedt*, Antwerp, pp. 101-14.

Magry, P.J. (1993), 'Processie versus stille omgang. Het probleem van de openbare godsdienstoefening buiten gebouwen en besloten plaatsen in Holland', *Holland, regionaal-historisch tijdschrift*, 25, pp. 174-96.

Marinus, M.J. (1993), 'Instellingen en mensen in de Onze-Lieve-Vrouwekerk. De bisschoppen en hun kathedraal', in W. Aerts (ed.), *De Onze-Lieve-Vrouwekerk van Antwerpen*, Antwerpen.

Marnef, G. (1987), *Het calvinistisch bewind te Mechelen 1580-1585*, Standen en Landen, vol. 87, Kortrijk/Heule.

Marnef, G. (1996), *Antwerp in the age of reformation*; *underground Protestantism in a commercial metropolis, 1550-1577*, Baltimore.

Märtins, R. (1976), *Wertorientierungen und wirtschaftliches Erfolgsstreben mittelalterlicher Großkaufleute. Das Beispiel Gent im 13. Jahrhundert*, Cologne/Vienna.

Mastboom, J.M. (1994), 'Guild or Union? A Case Study of Rural Dutch Weavers, 1682-1750', *International Review of Social History*, 39, pp. 57-75.

Mathieu, J. (1946), *Histoire sociale de l'industrie textile de Verviers*, Verviers.

McKendrick, N., J. Brewer and J.H. Plumb (eds) (1982), *The Birth of a Consumer Society. The Commercialisation of Eighteenth-Century England*, London.

Meij, P.J. (1975), 'Gelderland 1492-1543', in P.J. Meij et al. (eds), *Geschiedenis van Gelderland 1492-1795*, Zutphen, pp. 13-78.

Mendels, F.F. (1972), 'Proto-Industrialization: The First Phase of the Industrialization Process', *Journal of Economic History*, 32, pp. 241-61.

Mendels, F.F. (1984), 'Des industries rurales à la protoindustrialisation: historique d'un changement de perspective', *Annales ESC*, 39, pp. 977-1008.

Mertens, J. (1995), *Handel en wandel van de Teuten in de Duitse gewesten*, Lommel.

Mitchel, B.R. (1975), *European Historical Statistics, 1750-1970*, London.

Monballieu, P. (1964), 'Bruegel en het altaar van de Mechelse handschoenmakers (1551)', *Handelingen van de Koninklijke Kring voor Oudheidkunde, Letteren en Kunst van Mechelen*, 68, pp. 92-110.

Mooij, C. de (1998), *Geloof kan bergen verzetten. Reformatie en katholieke herleving te Bergen op Zoom 1577-1795*, Hilversum.

Morsa, D. (1987), 'Les petites villes dans le principauté de Liège à la fin du XVIIIe siècle. Premières approches', *Histoire & Mesure*, 2, pp. 73-92.

Mory, P. (1981), 'Les fêtes patronales à Tournai et dans le Tournaisis du 18e siècle à aujourd'hui. Essai d'analyse de leurs fonctions et de leurs significations', *Mémoires de la Société royale d'histoire et d'archéologie de Tournai*, 2, pp. 119-61.

Mory, P. (1982), 'Les fêtes patronales à Tournai et dans le Tournaisis du 18e siècle à aujourd'hui. Essai d'analyse de leurs fonctions et de leurs significations', *Mémoires de la Société royale d'histoire et d'archéologie de Tournai,* 3, pp. 103-140.

Mozzarelli, C. (1988), *Economia e corporazioni: il governo degli interessi nella storia dell'Italia dal medioevo all'età contemporanea*, Milan.

Mud, R. (1995), 'Gilden in Leeuwarden in de 18de eeuw', lecture, Amsterdam, International Institute of Social History.

Muir, E. (1981), *Civic ritual in renaissance Venice,* Princeton.

Mulder, F. (1995), 'De Haarlemse textielnijverheid in de periode 1575-1800', in H. Rombouts (ed.), *Haarlem ging op wollen zolen. Opkomst, bloei en ondergang van de textielnijverheid aan het Spaarne*, Schoorl, pp. 55-109.

Muller, S.Fz. (1879), 'Inventaris van het goud- en zilverwerk der Utrechtse geestelijke gestichten in 1578', *Archief voor de geschiedenis van het aartsbisdom Utrecht*, 7, pp. 284-337.

Muller Hofstede, J. (1957), `Zum Wercke Otto van Veen 1590-1600', *Bulletin Koninklijke Musea voor Schone Kunsten van België*, 3-4, pp. 127-74.

Munro, J.H. (1994), *Textiles, Towns and Trade: Essays in the Economic History of Late Medieval England and the Low Countries*, Aldershot.

Munro, J.H. (1999), 'The Symbiosis of Town and Textiles', *Journal of Early Modern History*, 3.

Naujoks, E. (1985), *Kaiser Karl V. und die Zunftverfassung. Ausgewählte Aktenstücke zu den Verfassungsänderungen in den oberdeutschen Reichsstädten (1547-1556)*, Stuttgard.

Nicholas, D. (1992), *Medieval Flanders,* London/New York.

Nierop, H.F.K. van (1997), 'Popular Participation in Politics in the Dutch Republic', in P. Blickle (ed.), *Resistance, Representation and Community,* Cambridge, pp. 272-90.

Nierop, L. van (1930), 'De zijdenijverheid van Amsterdam historisch geschetst', *Tijdschrift voor Geschiedenis*, 45, p. 18-40, 151-72.

Nieuwenhuis, T. (1995), *Vroedmeesters, vroedvrouwen en verloskunde in Amsterdam 1746-1805*, Amsterdam.

Noordam, D.J. (1986), *Leven in Maasland. Een hoog-ontwikkelde plattelandssamenleving in de achttiende en het begin van de negentiende eeuw*, Hilversum.

North. D.C. (1981), *Structure and Change in Economic History*, New York/London.

North, D.C. (1990), *Institutions, Institutional Change and Economic Performance*, Cambridge.

North, D.C. (1991), 'Institutions', *Journal of Economic Perspectives*, 5, pp. 97-112.

Nováky, G. (1997), 'On Trade, Production and Relations of Production. The Sugar Refineries of Seventeenth-Century Amsterdam', *Tijdschrift voor Sociale Geschiedenis*, 23, pp. 459-89.

Nusteling, H.P.H. (1985), *Welvaart en werkgelegenheid in Amsterdam 1540-1860. Een relaas over demografie, economie en sociale politiek van een wereldstad*, Amsterdam/ Dieren.

Odink, H. (1965), 'Het kleermakersgilde te Eibergen', *Kroniek en volksmond van de Gelderse Achterhoek*, Alkmaar, p. 308-17.

Oexle, G. (1982), 'Die mittelalterliche Zunft als Forschungsproblem. Ein Beitrag zur Wissenschaftsgeschichte der Moderne', *Blätter für Deutsche Landesgeschichte*, 118, pp. 1-44.

Oexle, G.O. (1989), `Die Kaufmannsgilde von Tiel', in: H. Jankuhn and E. Ebel (eds), *Untersuchungen zu Handel und Verkehr der vor- und frühneuzeitlichen Zeit in Mittel- und Nordeuropa*, vol. 4: *Organisationsformen der Kaufmannsvereinigungen in der Spätantike und im frühen Mittelalter*, Göttingen, pp. 173-96.

Ogilvie, S. (1997), *State Corporatism and Proto-industry: The Württemberg Black Forest, 1580-1797*, Cambridge.

Oldewelt, W.F.H. (ed.) (1945), *Kohier van de Personeele Quotisatie te Amsterdam over het jaar 1742*, 2 vols, Amsterdam.

Oldewelt, W.H.F. (1952), 'De beroepsstructuur van de bevolking der Hollandse stemhebbende steden volgens de kohieren van de familiegelden van 1674, 1715 en 1742; vervolg: de personele quotisatie van 1742', *Economisch Historisch Jaarboek*, 25, pp. 167-248.

Olson, M. (1965), *The logic of collective action. Public goods and the theory of groups*, Cambridge.

Olson, M. (1982), *The Rise and Decline of Nations: Economic Growth, Stagflation, and Social Rigidities*, New Haven/London.

Oosterbaan, D.P. (1954), *Zeven eeuwen geschiedenis van het Oude en Nieuwe Gasthuis te Delft*, Delft.

Orléan A. (ed.) (1994), *Analyse économique des conventions*, Paris.

Overvoorde, J.C. (1914), 'De Leidsche ambachtsbroederschappen', *Rechtshistorische Studiën aangeboden aan prof. S.J. Fockema Andrea*, Haarlem, pp. 334-75.

Overvoorde, J.C. and J.G.C. Joosting, (eds) (1896-97), *De gilden van Utrecht tot 1528. Verzameling van rechtsbronnen*, 2 vols, 's-Gravenhage.

Païs-Minne, E. (1952), 'Weldadigheidsinstellingen en sociale toestanden te Antwerpen in de XVIIIde eeuw', in *Antwerpen in de XVIIIde eeuw,* Antwerpen, pp. 179-83.

Païs-Minne, E. (1975), 'Weldadigheidsinstellingen en ondersteunden', in *Antwerpen in de XVIde eeuw,* Antwerpen.

Palmen, E. (1998), 'De gilden en hun sociale betekenis', in W. Frijhoff, H. Nusteling and M. Spies (eds), *Geschiedenis van Dordrecht van 1572 tot 1813*, Dordrecht/Hilversum, pp. 221-33.

Panhuysen, B. (2000), *Maatwerk: Kleermakers, naaisters, oudkleerkopers en de gilden, 1500-1800*, Amsterdam.

Paping, R.F.J. (1995), '*Voor een handvol stuivers.' Werken, verdienen en besteden: de levenstandaard van boeren, arbeiders en middenstanders op de Groninger klei, 1770-1860*, Groningen.

Peeters, N. (2000), *Tussen continuïteit en vernieuwing. De bijdrage van Frans en Ambrosius Francken I, en de jonge generatie Francken, tot de historieschilderkunst te Antwerpen, ca. 1570-1620*, unpublished PhD-thesis, Vrije Universiteit Brussel.

Peeters, N. (forthcoming), `A corporate image? Decoration for the Saint Luke's altarpiece for the Cathedral of Our Lady in Antwerp (1589-1602)', in *Florilegium: huldeboek voor Prof. Dr. C. Van de Velde*, Brussel.

Pellegrin, N. (1999), 'Les vertus de 'l'ouvrage'. Recherches sur la féminisation des travaux d'aiguille (XVIe-XVIIe siècles)', *Revue d'Histoire Moderne et Contemporaine*, 46, pp. 747-69.

Pethegem, P. (1988), 'La notion de ville impériale aux Pays Bas. Quelques réflections sur Deventer en tant que «ville impériale»', in P.L. Nève, O. Moorman van Kappen (eds), *Conservare Jura*, Deventer, pp. 115-37.

Petit, P. (1975), 'De ambachten te Ieper in de vijftiende eeuw, naar A. Vandenpeereboom', *Gidsenkring*, 13, p. 18.

Pfister, U. (forthcoming) 'Craft guilds, the theory of the firm, and early modern proto-industry', in S.R. Epstein, M. Prak (eds), *The guilds, technology and the economy.*

Piergiovanni, P.M. (1993), 'Technological Typologies and Economic Organisation of Silk Workers in Italy, from the XIVth to the XVIIIth Centuries', *Journal of European Economic History*, 22, pp. 544-60.

Pietersma, A., et al. (red.) (2000), *`Een paradijs vol weelde': geschiedenis van de stad Utrecht*, Utrecht.

Pirenne, H. (1909-22), *Histoire de Belgique*, 4 vols, Brussels

Pirenne, H. (1910), *Les anciennes démocraties des Pays-Bas,* Paris.

Pirenne, H. (1930), 'Draps d'Ypres à Novgorod au commencement du XIIe siècle', *Revue Belge d'Histoire et de Philologie,* 9.

Poelwijk, A. (1999), 'Wet- en regelgeving in de Amsterdamse zeepnijverheid, ca. 1500-1630', in C. Lesger en L. Noordegraaf (eds), *Ondernemers en bestuurders. Economie en politiek in de Noordelijke Nederlanden in de late Middeleeuwen en vroegmoderne tijd*, Amsterdam, pp. 417-31.

Poffe, E. (1895), *De gilde der Antwerpsche schoolmeesters van bij haar ontstaan tot aan hare afschaffing*, Antwerpen.

Pol, L. van de (1994), 'The Lure of the Big City. Female Migration to Amsterdam', in E. Kloek, N. Teeuwen and M. Huisman (eds), *Women of the Golden Age. An International Debate on Women in Seventeenth-century Holland, England and Italy*, Hilversum, pp. 73-81.

Pol, L. van de (1996), *Het Amsterdams hoerdom. Prostitutie in de zeventiende en achttiende eeuw*, Amsterdam.

Pollard, S. (1991), 'Regional Markets and National Development', in M. Berg (ed.), *Markets and Manufacture in Early Industrial Europe*, London/New York, pp. 29-56.

Pols, J.F. (1996), 'Arnhemse regenten in de achttiende eeuw', *Bijdragen en Mededelingen Gelre,* 87, pp. 85-116.

Poncelet, E. (1900), *Les bons métiers de la cité de Liège*, Liège.

Poni, C. (1991), 'Local Market Rules and Practices. Three Guilds in the Same Line of Production', in S. Woolf (ed.), *Domestic Strategies: Work and Family in France and Italy, 1600-1800*, Cambridge, pp. 69-101.

Poni, C. (1998), ' Mode et innovation. Les stratégies des marchands en soie de Lyon au XVIIe et XVIIIe siècle', *Revue d'Histoire Moderne et Contemporaine*, 45, pp. 589-625.

Ponsot, P. (1987), 'Tissus et vêtements: marchands et clients en Bourgogne du Sud: XVIIe et XVIIIe siècles', in *112e Congrès national des Sociétés Savantes*, Lyon, pp. 63-75.

Posthumus, N.W. (1908-39), *De Geschiedenis van de Leidsche lakenindustrie*, 3 vols, The Hague.

Posthumus, N.W. (1926), 'De industriële concurrentie tusschen Noord- en Zuid-Nederlandsche nijverheidscentra in de XVIIe en XVIIIe eeuw', *Mélanges d'histoire offerts à Henri Pirenne,* Brussels.

Pot, G.P.M. (1994), *Arm Leiden: levensstandaard, bedeling en bedeelden, 1750-1854*, Hollandse Studien, vol. 31, Hilversum.

Prak, M. (1988), 'Sociale geschiedschrijving van Nederlands Ancien Régime', *Tijdschrift voor Sociale Geschiedenis*, 14, pp. 133-59.

Prak, M. (1992), 'Een verzekerd bestaan. Ambachtslieden, winkeliers en hun gilden in Den Bosch (ca. 1775)', in B. de Vries et al (eds), *De kracht der zwakken*, Amsterdam, pp. 49-79.

Prak, M. (1994a), 'Ambachtsgilden vroeger en nu', *NEHA-Jaarboek voor economische, bedrijfs- en techniekgeschiedenis*, 57, pp. 10-33.

Prak, M. (1994b), 'Verfassungsnorm und Verfassungsrealität in den niederländischen Städten des späten 17. und 18. Jahrhunderts. Die Oligarchie in Amsterdam, Rotterdam, Deventer und Zutphen 1672/75-1795', in W. Ehbrecht (ed.), *Verwaltung und Politik. Beiträge zu Verfassungsnorm und Verfassungswirklichkeit in altständische Zeit*, Städteforschung, vol. A/34, Cologne/ Vienna, pp. 55-83.

Prak, M. (1995), 'Cittadini, abitanti e forestieri: Una classificazione della popolazione di Amsterdam nella prima età moderna', *Quaderni Storici,* no 89, pp. 331-57.

Prak, M. (1996), 'Individual, Corporatism and Society: The Rhetoric of Dutch Guilds (18th Century)', in M. Boone and M. Prak (eds), *Individual, Corporate and Judicial Status in European Cities (Late Midle Ages and Early Modern Period)*, Leuven/Apeldoorn, pp. 255-79.

Prak, M. (1999), *Republikeinse veelheid, democratisch enkelvoud. Sociale verandering in het Revolutietijdvak: 's-Hertogenbosch, 1770-1820*, Nijmegen.

Prak, M. (2000), 'Politik, Kultur und politische Kultur: die Zünfte in den Nördlichen Niederlanden', in W. Reininghaus (ed.), *Zunftlandschaften in Deutschland und den Niederlanden im Vergleich*, Münster, pp. 71-83.

Prak, M. (2002), 'The politics of intolerance: citizenship and religion in the Dutch Republic (17th-18th C.)', in R. Po-chia Hsia and H.F.K. van Nierop (eds), *Calvinism and Religious Toleration in the Dutch Golden Age*, Cambridge, pp. 159-75.

Prak, M. (2003), 'Guilds and the development of the art market during the Dutch Golden Age', *Simiolus*, 30, pp. 236-51.

Prevenier, W. (1975), 'Bevolkingscijfers en professionele structuren der bevolking van Gent en Brugge in de 14de eeuw', in *Album Charles Verlinden*, Gent, pp. 269-303.

Prevenier, W. (1983), 'La démographie des villes du comté de Flandre aux XIIIe et XIVe siècles. Etat de la question. Essay d'interprétation', *Revue du Nord*, 65, pp. 255-75.

Prevenier, W. (1986), 'Henri Pirenne et les villes des anciens Pays-Bas au bas Moyen Age', in *La fortune historiographique des thèses d'Henri Pirenne. Actes du Colloque organisé à l'occasion du cinquantenaire de la mort de l'historien belge par l'Institut des Hautes Etudes de Belgique*, Archives et Bibliothèques de Belgique, special issue 28, Brussel.

Prevenier, W. and Boone, M. (1993), 'De sociale geschiedenis van de steden in de Zuidelijke Nederlanden en het prinsbisdom Luik van de 13de tot de 19de eeuw: nieuwe tendensen', *Het Tijdschrift van het Gemeentekrediet*, 47, pp. 25-42.

Price, J.L (1994), *Holland and the Dutch Republic. The Politics of Particularism*, Oxford.

Prims, F. (1935a), 'Oud-Antwerpsche portretten', *Antwerpiensia*, 9, p. 388.

Prims, F. (1935b), 'Het huis der vier Winden', *Antwerpiensia,* 9, pp. 324-31.

Prims, F. (1938a), 'Het Antwerpsch altarenvraagstuk', *Antwerpiensia*, 12, p. 287.

Prims, F. (1938b), 'De schilderijen van het kuipersaltaar', *Antwerpiensia*, 12, pp. 296-301.

Prims, F. (1938c), 'Het altaar van de meerseniers', *Antwerpiensia*, 12, pp. 328-33.

Prims, F. (1939a), 'Het altaar van de bontworkers', *Antwerpiensia*, 13, pp. 308-14.

Prims, F. (1939b), `Het altaar der Sint Lucasgilde', *Antwerpiensa*, 13, pp. 376-83.

Prims, F. (1942), *Geschiedenis van Antwerpen.* VIII: *Met Spanje (1555-1715).* 2[de] boek: *De economische orde*, Antwerpen.

Prims, F. (1947), 'De Huidevetterskapel', *Antwerpiensia*, 18, pp. 290-3.

Quathem, K. Van (1996), 'Het broederschap van de schoenmakersknechten of 'elsenaars' te Brugge', *Handelingen Genootschap voor geschiedenis,* 133, pp. 78-97.

Ramazzini, B. (1744), *Historisch natuur- en geneeskundige verhandeling van de ziekten der konstenaars, ambagtslieden en handwerkers. Mitsgaders der geletterde, waarbij gevoegt is de onderhouding der gesondheid van de nonnen die in kloosters leven*, Leiden.

Ree-Scholtens, G.F. van der (ed.) (1995), *Deugd boven geweld. Een geschiedenis van Haarlem, 1245-1995*, Hilversum.

Reininghaus, W. (1990), *Gewerbe in der frühen Neuzeit*, Munich.

Reininghaus, W. (1995), *Die Stadt Iserlohn und ihre Kaufleute (1700-1815)*, Dortmund.

Reinighaus, W. (2000a), 'Zünfte und Regionen. "Zunftlandschaften" als Forschungsproblem', in W. Reininghaus (ed.), *Zunftlandschaften in Deutschland und den Niederlanden im Vergleich*, Münster, pp. 3-9.

Reininghaus, W. (2000b), 'Stadt und Handwerk. Eine Einführung in Forschungsprobleme und Forschungsfragen', in K.H. Kaufhold and W. Reininghaus (eds), *Stadt und Handwerk in Mittelalter und früher Neuzeit*, Cologne, pp. 1-19.

Reininghaus, W. (2002), 'Zünfte und Zunftpolitik in Westfalen und im Rheinland am Ende des Alten Reiches', in H.G. Haupt (ed.), *Das Ende der Zünfte: ein europäischer Vergleich*, Göttingen, pp. 72-85.

Reith, R. (2002), 'Zünfte im Süden des Alten Reiches: Politische, wirtschaftliche und soziale Aspekte', in H.G. Haupt (ed.), *Das Ende der Zünfte: ein europäischer Vergleich*, Göttingen, pp. 39-70.

Richardson, G. (unpublished paper), 'Craft Guilds and Christianity in Late-Medieval England: A Rational-Choice Analysis'.

Richardson, J.G. (1986), *Handbook of Theory and Research for the Sociology of Education*, New York.

Richelet, P. (1732), *Dictionnaire de la langue française, ancienne et moderne, augmenté de plusieurs additions d'histoire, de grammaire, de critique, de jurisprudence et d'une liste alphabetique des auteurs et des livres citez dans ce Dictionnaire*, vol. 2, Amsterdam.

Ridder, M. de (1994), 'De ondersteuningsfondsen van de Amsterdamse gilden in de achttiende eeuw', *NEHA-jaarboek voor economische, bedrijfs- en techniekgeschiedenis*, 57, pp. 107-21.

Rijckeghem, J. Van (1988), 'Eenvoud en raffinement. Kleding en sieraden te Gent', *Oost-Vlaamse Zanten*, 63, pp. 33-50.

Ritter, G. (1987), *Het Utrechtse smedengilde. Metaalbewerkers in Utrecht in de 17e en 18e eeuw*, unpublished MA-thesis, Universiteit Utrecht.

Roche, D. (1989), *La culture des apparences. Une histoire du vêtement (XVIIe-XVIIIe siècles)*, Paris.

Roche, D. (1994), *The Culture of Clothing: Dress and Fashion in the Ancien Regime*, Cambridge.

Rommes, R., and J. van der Spek (2004), *Met hand en hart. Zeven eeuwen smedengilde en St. Eloyengasthuis in Utrecht, 1304-2004*, Utrecht.

Roodenburg, H. (1991), 'Over korsetten, lichaamshouding en gebaren. Een cultuurhistorische verkenning van de "nieuwe fatsoenen" tussen ruwweg 1580 en 1630', *Textielhistorische Bijdragen*, 31, pp. 20-39.

Roodenburg, H. (1992), 'Naar een etnografie van de vroegmoderne stad: de *gebuyrten* in Leiden en Den Haag', in P. Te Boekhorst, P. Burke and W. Frijhoff (eds), *Cultuur en maatschappij in Nederland, 1500-1850*, pp. 219-43.

Roodenburg, H. (1993), 'De "hand van vriendschap". Over het handen schudden en andere gebaren in de Republiek der Zeven Verenigde Provinciën', in J. Bremmer en H. Roodenburg (eds), *Gebaren en lichaamshouding van de oudheid tot heden*, Nijmegen, pp. 171-211.

Roper, L. (1989), *The Holy Household: Women and Morals in Reformation Augsburg*, Oxford.

Rosser, G. (1997), 'Crafts, guilds and the negotiation of work in the medieval town', *Past and Present,* no.154, pp. 3-31.

Ryckaert, M. (1975), 'Ambachtshuizen te Brugge. De huizen van de timmerlieden, de metselaars, de tegeldekkers en de kapel van de smeden', in W.P. Dezutter en M. Goetinck, *Tentoonstelling op en om de bouwwerf. Ambachtswezen — oud gereedschap*, Brugge, pp. 37-57.

Safley, T.M. (1997), *Charity and Economy in the Orphanages of Early Modern Augsburg*, New Jersey.

Sas, N.C.F. van (1987), 'Politiek als leerproces: het patriottisme in Utrecht, 1783-1787', *Jaarboek Oud-Utrecht*, pp. 9-42.

Schaïk, R. van (1989), 'Zutphens geschiedenis: van de elfde tot het einde van de zestiende eeuw', in W.Th.M. Frijhoff et al. (eds), *Geschiedenis van Zutphen*, Zutphen, pp. 48-80.

Schama, S. (1977), *Patriots and Liberators. Revolution in the Netherlands 1780-1813*, New York.

Schilling, H. (1975), 'Aufstandsbewegungen in der stadbürgerlichen Gesellschaft des Alten Reiches. Die Vorgeschichte des Münsteraner Täuferreiches, 1525-1534', in H.U. Wehler (ed.), *Der deutsche Bauernkrieg 1524-1526*, Göttingen, pp. 193-238.

Schilling, H. (1980), 'Calvinistische Presbyterien in Städten der Frühen Neuzeit — eine kirchliche Alternativform zur bürgerlichen Repräsentation? (Mit eine quantifizierenden Untersuchung zur holländischen Stadt Leiden), in W. Ehbrecht (ed.), *Städtischen Führungsgruppen und Gemeinde in der werdenden Neuzeit*, Städteforschung, vol. A/9, Cologne/Vienna, pp. 385-444.

Schimmelpenninck van der Oye, C.O.A. (1971), 'Het optreden der gemeenslieden te Zutphen, 1538-1543, naar de memorie van Johan van Voorthuisen', *Bijdragen en mededelingen Gelre,* 65, pp. 39-83.

Schlugleit, D. (1935), *Geschiedenis van het Antwerpsche diamantslijpersambacht, 1582-1797*, Antwerpen.

Schmidt, A. (2001), *Overleven na de dood. Weduwen in Leiden in de Gouden eeuw*, Amsterdam.

Schoeffer, J. (1996), *Historische aanteekeningen rakende de kerken, de kloosters, de ambachten en andere stichten der stad Mechelen*, vol. 3, Brussel.

Scholliers, E. (1956), 'Vrije en onvrije arbeiders voornamelijk te Antwerpen in de 16e eeuw', *Bijdragen voor de geschiedenis der Nederlanden*, 11, p. 285-322.

Schoonjans, E. (1996), *De Gentse ambachten van de timmerlieden, de houtbrekers en de schrijnwerkers, 1700-1795*, unpublished MA-thesis, Universiteit Gent.

Schotel, P. (1998), 'Strijd om de macht', in W. Frijhoff, H. Nusteling, M. Spies (ed.), *Geschiedenis van Dordrecht van 1572 tot 1813*, Hilversum, pp. 15-37.

Schoute-Bosma, C.W.S. (1944), *De gilden te Utrecht van 1600-1650*, unpublished MA-thesis, Universiteit Utrecht.

Schouteet, (1968), 'Inventaris van het goud- en zilverwerk in april 1578 te Brugge opgeëist', *Handelingen van het Genootschap voor Geschiedenis gesticht onder de benaming Société d'émulation te Brugge*, 105, pp. 217-46.

Schouteet, (1975), 'Ambachten te Brugge onder het ancien régime' in W.P. Dezutter en M. Goetinck, *Tentoonstelling op en om de bouwwerf. Ambachtswezen — oud gereedschap*, Brugge, pp. 37-57.

Schulz, H. (1993), *Das ehrbare Handwerk. Zunftleben im alten Berlin zur Zeit des Absolutismus*, Weimar.

Schulz, K. (1994), 'Die politische Zunft. Eine die spätmittelalterliche Stadt prägende Institution?', in W. Ehbrecht (ed.), *Verwaltung und Politik. Beiträge zu Verfassungsnorm und Verfassungswirklichkeit in altständische Zeit*, Städteforschung, vol. A/34, Cologne/Vienna, pp. 1-20.

Schuttelaars, A. (1998), *Heren van de raad. De bestuurlijke elite van 's-Hertogenbosch in de stedelijke samenleving 1500-1580*, Nijmegen.

Schuurman, A., J. de Vries and A. van der Woude (eds) (1997), *Aards geluk. De Nederlanders en hun spullen, 1550-1850*, Amsterdam.

Shammas, C. (1994), 'The Decline of Textile Prices in England and British America prior to Industrialisation', *Economic History Review*, 48, pp. 484-98.

Simon-Muscheid, K. (1998), 'Frauenarbeit und Männerehre. Der Geschlechterdiskurs im Handwerk', in K. Simon-Muscheid (ed.), *Was nützt die Schusterin dem Schmied? Frauen und Handwerk vor der Industrialisierung*, Frankfurt/New York, pp. 13-34.

Simons, W. (1991), 'Een zeker bestaan: De Zuid-Nederlandse begijnen en de Frauenfrage, 13de — 18de eeuw', *Tijdschrift voor Sociale Geschiedenis*, 17, pp. 125-46.

Smekens, F. (1950), 'De Antwerpse antwoorden op de Oostenrijkse ambachtsenquête van 1784', *Annales de la Fédération achéologique et historique de Belgique*, 1, pp. 227-36.

Smit, W.J. (1928), *De katoendrukkerij in Nederland tot 1813*, Rotterdam.

Sneller, Z.W. (1930), 'De tijkweverij te Rotterdam en te Schiedam in de eerste helft der 17e eeuw', *Tijdschrift voor Geschiedenis*, 45, pp. 237-66.

Snoep, D.P. (1975), *Praal en propaganda. Triumfalia in de Noordelijke Nederlanden in de 16de en 17de eeuw*, Alphen aan den Rijn.

Sogner, S. (1994), 'Introduction', in A. Fauve-Chamoux and S. Sogner (eds), *Socio-economic Consequemces of Sex-ratios in Historical Perspective, 1500-1900, Proceedings 11th International Economic History Congres*, Milan.

Soly, H. (1968), 'De brouwerijenonderneming van Gilbert van Schoonbeke, 1552-1562', *Belgisch Tijdschrift voor Filologie en Geschiedenis*, 46, pp. 337-92, 1166-1204.

Soly, H. (1970), 'Fortificaties, belastingen en corruptie te Antwerpen in het midden der 16de eeuw', *Bijdragen tot de Geschiedenis*, 53, pp. 197-205.

Soly, H. (1975), 'Nijverheid en kapitalisme te Antwerpen in de 16e eeuw', *Album Charles Verlinden ter gelegenheid van zijn dertigjarig professoraat*, Gent, pp. 331-52.

Soly, H. (1976), 'De bouw van de Antwerpse citadel (1567-1573). Economische en sociale aspecten', *Belgisch Tijdschrift voor Militaire Geschiedenis*, 21, pp. 549-78.

Soly, H. (1977), *Urbanisme en kapitalisme te Antwerpen in de 16de eeuw. De stedebouwkundige en industriële ondernemingen van Gilbert van Schoonbeke*, Brussels.

Soly, H. (1984a), 'Plechtige intochten in de steden van de Zuidelijke Nederlanden tijdens de overgang van Middeleeuwen naar Nieuwe Tijd: communicatie, propaganda, spektakel', *Tijdschrift voor Geschiedenis*, 97, pp. 341-60.

Soly, H. (1984b), 'Openbare feesten in Brabantse en Vlaamse steden, 16de-18de eeuw', *Het openbaar initiatief van de gemeenten in België, historische grondslagen (Ancien Régime)*, Brussel, pp. 605-36.

Soly, H. (ed.) (2000), *Karel V, 1500-1558. De keizer en zijn tijd*, Antwerpen.

Soly, H., and A.K.L. Thijs (1979), 'Nijverheid in de Zuidelijke Nederlanden, 1490-1585', *Algemene Geschiedenis der Nederlanden,* 6, Haarlem/Bussum, pp. 27-57.

Sonenscher, M. (1986), 'Journeymen's Migrations and Workshop Organisation in Eighteenth-Century France', in S.L. Kaplan and C. Koep (eds), *Work in France. Representations, Meaning, Organisation and Practice*, Ithaca, pp. 74-96.

Sonenscher, M. (1989) *Work and Wages: Natural Law, Politics and the Eighteenth-Century French Trades*, Cambridge.

Sortor, M. (1993), 'Saint-Omer and Its Textile Trades in the Late Middle Ages: A Contribution to the Proto-industrialization Debate', *American Historical Review*, 98, pp. 1475-99.

Sosson, J.P. (1962), 'L'artisanat bruxellois du métal: hiérarchie sociale, salaires et puissance économique (1360-1500)', *Cahiers Bruxellois*, vol. 7, pp. 225-58.

Sosson, J.P. (1966), 'La structure sociale de la corporation médiévale. L'exemple des tonneliers de Bruges de 1350 à 1500', *Revue Belge de Philologie et d'Histoire*, 44, pp. 457-78.

Sosson, J.P. (1977), *Les travaux publics de la ville de Bruges, XIVe-XVe siècles. Les matériaux. Les homes,* Brussel.

Sosson, J.P. (1984), 'Die Körperschaften in den Niederlanden und Nordfrankreich: neue Forschungsperspektiven', in K.N. Friedland (ed.), *Gilde und Korporation in den nordeuropäischen Städten des späten Mittelalters*, Cologne/Vienna, pp. 79-90.

Sosson, J.P. (1990), 'Les métiers: norme et réalité. L'exemple des anciens Pays-Bas méridionaux aux XIVe et XVe siècles', in J. Hamesse and C. Muraille-Samaran (eds), *Le travail au Moyen Age. Une approche interdisciplinaire*, Louvain-la-Neuve, pp. 339-48.

Spaans, J. (1989), *Haarlem na de Reformatie. Stedelijke cultuur en kerkelijk leven, 1577-1620*, Den Haag.

Spanninga, H. (1999), 'Om de vrije magistraatsbestelling. Machtsverhoudingen en politiek in Leeuwarden', in R. Kunst (ed.), *Leeuwarden 750-2000: Hoofdstad van Friesland*, Franeker, pp. 131-44.

Speck, W. (1995), 'Britain and the Dutch Republic', in K. Davids and J. Lucassen (eds), *A miracle mirrored. The Dutch Republic in European Perspective*, Cambridge, pp. 173-95.

Sprenkel, J.W.B. van der (1923), *Geschiedenis van het bisdom Utrecht van 1281 tot 1305*, Utrecht.

Stabel, P. (1995), *De kleine stad in Vlaanderen. Bevolkingsdynamiek en economische fluctuaties van de kleine en secundaire stedelijke centra in het Gentse kwartier (14de-16de eeuw)*, Brussel.

Stabel, P. (1997a), 'Ambachten en textielondernemers in kleine Vlaamse steden tijdens de overgang van Middeleeuwen naar Nieuwe Tijd', in C. Lis and H. Soly (eds), *Werelden van verschil. Ambachtsgilden in de Lage Landen*, Brussel, pp. 79-98.

Stabel, P. (1997b), 'Dmeeste, oirboirlixste ende proffitelixste let ende neringhe. Een kwantitatieve benadering van de lakenproductie in het laatmiddeleeuwse en vroegmoderne Vlaanderen', *Handelingen der Maatschappij voor Geschiedenis en Oudheidkunde te Gent*, 51, pp. 113-55.

Steur, A.G. van der (1991), 'Van kleermaker tot confectiewinkel. Veranderingen in de aanschaf van herenbovenkleding in ons land', *Textiel-Historische Bijdragen,* 31, pp. 99-113.

Stokvis, P.R.D. (1987), *De wording van modern Den Haag. De stad en haar bevolking van de Franse tijd tot de Eerste wereldoorlog*, Zwolle.

Streng, J.C. (1997), *'Stemme in staat'. De bestuurlijke elite in de stadsrepubliek Zwolle 1579-1795*, Hilversum.

Strien, C.D. van (1989), *British Travellers in Holland during the Stuart period,* Amsterdam.

Swevers, M. (1999), *Brouwers en politiek in Leuven tijdens de 17de eeuw*, unpublished MA-thesis, Vrije Universiteit Brussel.

Thijs, A.K.L. (1968), 'De Antwerpse zijdeverver Roelant Stappaert', *De Vlaamse Stam*, 4, pp. 235-41.

Thijs, A.K.L. (1969), *De zijdenijverheid te Antwerpen in de zeventiende eeuw*, Brussel.

Thijs, A.K.L. (1970), 'Schets van de ontwikkeling der katoendrukkerij te Antwerpen (1753-1813)', *Bijdragen tot de Geschiedenis*, 53, pp. 157-90.

Thijs, A.K.L. (1987a), 'De Contrareformatie en het economisch transformatieproces te Antwerpen na 1585', *Bijdragen tot de Geschiedenis*, 70, pp. 97-125.

Thijs, A.K.L. (1987b), *Van 'werkwinkel' tot 'fabriek'. De textielnijverheid te Antwerpen (einde 15de - begin 19de eeuw)*, Brussel.

Thijs, A.K.L. (1988), 'Structural changes in the Antwerp industry from the fifteenth to the eighteenth century', in H. Van der Wee (ed.), *The rise and decline of urban industries in Italy and the Low Countries (late middle ages — early modern times)*, Leuven.

Thijs, A.K.L. (1989), 'De nijverheid', *Antwerpen in de XVIIde eeuw*, Antwerpen, pp. 131-51.

Thijs, A.K.L. (1990), *Van Geuzenstad tot contrareformatorisch bolwerk. Maatschappelijke betekenis van de kerk in contrareformatorisch Antwerpen*, Antwerpen/Turnhout.

Thijs, A.K.L. (1993a), 'Antwerp's Luxury Industries: the Pursuit of Profit and Artistic Sensitivity' in J. Van der Stock (ed.), *Antwerp: Story of a Metropolis, 16th-17th Century*, Antwerp, pp. 105-13.

Thijs, A.K.L. (1993b), *Antwerpen, internationaal uitgeverscentrum van devotieprenten 17de-18de eeuw*, Leuven.

Thijs, A.K.L. (1994), 'Religieuze rituelen in het emancipatieproces van Vlaamse en Brabantse handwerksgezellen zestiende-negentiende eeuw', in C. Lis and H. Soly (eds), *Werken volgens de regels: ambachten in Brabant en Vlaanderen, 1500-180*, Brussel, pp. 231-82.

Thijs, A.K.L. (1996), 'Over bedevaarten in Vlaanderen: van stichtelijke propaganda naar wetenschappelijke interesse', *Volkskunde*, 97.

Thijs, A.K.L. (1997), 'Communicatie via religieuze drukgrafiek in het preïndustriële corporatisme (Brabant en Vlaanderen)', in C. Lis and H. Soly (eds), *Werelden van verschil: ambachtsilden in de Lage Landen,* Brussels, pp. 213-41.

Thijs, A.K.L. (2000), 'Private en openbare feesten: communicatie, educatie en omgaan met macht (Vlaanderen en Brabant, 16de-midden 19de eeuw)', *Volkskunde*, 101.

Thoen, E. (1988), *Landbouweconomie en bevolking in Vlaanderen gedurende de late Middeleeuwen en het begin van de Moderne Tijden. Testregio: de kasselrijen van Oudenaarde en Aalst, eind 13de — eerste helft 16de eeuw*, Gent.

Tijs, R. (1993), *Tot Cieraet deser Stadt. Bouwtrant en bouwbeleid te Antwerpen van de middeleeuwen tot heden*, Antwerpen.

Timmer, E.M.A. (1913), *Knechtsgilden en knechtsbossen in Nederland. Arbeidersverzekering in vroeger tijden,* Haarlem.

Tollebeek, J. (2002), 'De cultus van 1302: twee eeuwen herinneringen', in R. C. Van Caenegem (ed.), *1302: Feiten en myhen van de Guldensporenslag*, Antwerpen, pp. 194-239.

Tollebeek, J. and Verschaffel, T. (2002), 'Helden en herdenkers. De geschiedenis van een romantische mythe en een nationaal symbool', in P. Trio, D. Heirbaut and D. Van den Auweele (eds), *Omtrent 1302,* Leuven, pp. 183-205.

Toussaint, J. (ed.) (1998), *Corporations de métiers à Namur au XVIIIe siècle*, Namur.

Trio, P. (1993), *Volksreligie als spiegel van een stedelijke samenleving. De broederschappen te Gent in de late Middeleeuwen*, Leuven.

Trompetter, C. (1993), 'Ontmoedigend overheidsbeleid als stimulans voor ondernemerschap. De tariefherziening van 1725 en het ontstaan van de bombazijnnijverheid in Twente', *Textielhistorische Bijdragen,* 33, pp. 43-54.

Trompetter, C. (1997*), Agriculture, Proto-Industry and Mennonite Entrepreneurship. A History of the Textile Industries in Twente, 1600-1815*, Amsterdam.

Truick, J.E.A.L. (1960), *Gelre en Habsburg 1492-1528*, Arnhem.

Unger, R.W. (1978), *Dutch Shipbuilding before 1800: ships and guilds*, Assen.

Unger, R.W. (1995), 'The Scale of Dutch Brewing, 1350-1600', *Research in Economic History*, 15, pp. 261-92.

Unger, R.W. (2001), *A History of Brewing in Holland, 900-1900*, Leiden.

Unger, W.S. (1923), *Bronnen tot de geschiedenis van Middelburg in den landsheerlijken tijd*, vol. 1, Rijksgeschiedkundige Publicatiën, vol. 54, Den Haag.

Unger, W.S. (1930), *Archief der gemeente Middelburg: de archieven der gilden en beurzen*, Middelburg.

Vaczy, P. (1960), 'La transformation de la technique et de l'organisation de l'industrie textile en Flandre aux XIe-XIIIe siècles', *Studia Historica Academiae Scientiarium Hungaricae*, 48, pp. 3-26.

Van Buyten, L. (1985), *De Leuvense stadsfinanciën onder het Oostenrijks Regiem (1713-1794)*, 2 vols., Leuven.

Van Buyten, L. (1989), *Leuven Anno 1789*, Leuven,

Van Buyten, L. (1993), 'Aspecten van de feestcultuur in Brabant en de Zuidelijke Nederlanden van ca. 1500 tot ca. 1800', *De Brabantse folklore en geschiedenis*, no. 280.

Van de Velde, A. (1909), *De ambachten van de timmerlieden en de schrijnwerkers te Brugge, hun wetten, hun geschillen en hun gewrochten*, Gent.

Van den Berg, M. (1985), 'De adel in de 18[de] eeuw: een leissure-class?' in J. Verbesselt et al., *De adel in het hertogdom Brabant*, Brussels, pp. 143-83.

Van den Berghe, G. (1938), *Anderlecht door de eeuwen heen*, Brussel.

Van den Berghe, Y. (1972), *Jacobijnen en Traditionalisten. De reacties van de Bruggelingen in de Revolutietijd (1780-1794)*, Pro-Civitate Historische Uitgaven vol. 32, Brussel.

Van den Broeck, A. (1993), '"Marchands de tout, faiseurs de rien": Het Lierse meerseniersambacht tijdens de tweede helft van de 18de eeuw', *Lira Elegans*, 3, pp. 51-83.

Van der Eycken, M. (1980), *Geschiedenis van Diest*, Diest.

Van der Stock, J. (1998), *Printing Images in Antwerp: The Introduction of Printmaking in a City, Fifteenth Century to 1585*, Rotterdam.

Van der Wee, H. (1988), 'Industrial Dynamics and the Process of Urbanization and De-Urbanization in the Low Countries from the Late Middle Ages to the Eighteenth Century: A Synthesis', in H. Van der Wee (ed.), *The Rise and Decline of Urban Industries in Italy and the Low Countries (Late Middle Ages – Early Modern Times),* Louvain, pp. 307-81.

Van der Wee, H. (1995), 'Continuïteit en discontinuïteit in de economische ontwikkeling van Nederland, 1500-1815', *Tijdschrift voor Sociale Geschiedenis*, 21, pp. 273-80.

Van der Wee, H. (1999), 'Was the Dutch Economy during its Golden Age really Modern?', *European Review*, 7.

Van Elsacker, B. (2000), 'Secretelijck opgegeten of ongeruste geesten? De politieke participatie van het bestuur van het Antwerpse meerseniersambacht in de zeventiende eeuw', *Tijdschrift voor Sociale Geschiedenis*, 26, pp. 129-63.

Van Honacker, K. (1990a), 'Reorganisatie in Brussel of de strijd om de privileges. Het conflict tussen de ambachten en de aartshertogen van 1619', *Bijdragen tot de Geschiedenis*, 73, pp. 299-312.

Van Honacker, K. (1990b), 'Stedelijke oproeren voor en tijdens de Brabantse omwenteling', in J. Craeybeckx and F. Scheelings (eds), *De Franse Revolutie en Vlaanderen. De Oostenrijkse Nederlanden tussen oud en nieuw*, Brussel, pp. 187-200.

Van Honacker, K. (1992), 'Citizens and politics in the Duchy of Brabant: political opportunity and political culture in Brussels, Antwerp and Leuven in the seventeenth century', in W. Thomas (ed.), *Rebelión y Resistencia en el Mundo Hispánico del Siglo XVII*, Leuven, pp. 41-52.

Van Honacker, K. (1994a), 'De politieke cultuur van de Brusselse ambachten in de achttiende eeuw: conservatisme, corporatisme of opportunisme?', in C. Lis and H. Soly (eds), *Werken volgens de regels: ambachten in Brabant en Vlaanderen, 1500-1800*, Brussel pp. 179-228.

Van Honacker, K. (1994b), *Lokaal verzet en oproer in de 17de en 18de eeuw. Collectieve acties tegen het centraal gezag in Brussel, Antwerpen en Leuven*, Kortrijk/Heule.

Van Honacker, K. (1996), 'Alliances et conflits dans la société bruxelloise au 18e siècle: maîtres artisans, doyens des métiers et autorités urbaines', in M. Boone and M. Prak (eds), *Individual, Corporate and Judicial Status in European Cities (Late Middle Ages and Early Modern Period)*, Leuven/Apeldoorn, pp. 209-24.

Van Honacker, K. (2000), 'Résistance locale et émeutes dans les chefs-villes brabançonnes aux XVIIe et XVIIIe siècles', *Revue d'Histoire Moderne et Contemporaine*, 47, pp. 37-68.

Van Houtryve, (1975), *De vishandel en het visambacht te Brugge*, Brugge.

Van Houtte, H. (1920), *Histoire économique de la Belgique à la fin de l'Ancien Régi*me, Gent.

Van Houtte, J.A. (1964), *Economische en sociale geschiedenis van de Lage Landen*, Zeist.

Van Laerhoven, J. (1971), 'De kanthandel te Antwerpen in de 18de eeuw: de firma Van Lidth de Jeude', *Bijdragen tot de Geschiedenis*, 54, pp. 173-90.

Van Nuffel, P. (1911), *Alostum Religiosum. Beelden en schetsen uit den besloten tijd*, Aalst.

Van Roey, J. (1963), *De sociale structuren en de godsdienstige gezindheid van de Antwerpse bevolking op de vooravond van de Reconciliatie met Farnese 17 augustus 1585*, unpublished PhD-thesis, Universiteit Gent.

Van Roey, J. (1968), 'De correlatie tussen het sociale beroepsmilieu en de godsdienstkeuze te Antwerpen op het einde van de 16de eeuw', *Bronnen voor de religieuze geschiedenis van België. Middeleeuwen en Moderne Tijden. Bibliothèque de la revue d'Histoire Ecclésiastique*, vol. 47, pp. 239-57.

Van Rompuy, P. (1991), *Inleiding tot de economie*, Leuven.

Van Uytven, R. (1962), 'Plutokratie in de "oude democratieën der Nederlanden". Cijfers en beschouwingen omtrent de korporatieve organisatie en de sociale structuur der gemeenten in de late Middeleeuwen', *Handelingen van de Koninklijke Zuidnederlandse Maatschappij voor Taal- en Letterkunde en Geschiedenis*, 16, pp. 373-409.

Van Uytven, R. (1975), 'Die ländliche Industrie während des Spätmittelalters in den südlichen Niederlanden', in H. Kellenbenz (ed.), *Agrarisches Nebengewerbe und Formen der Reagrarisierung im Spätmittelalter und 19./20. Jahrhundert*, Stuttgart, pp. 57-76.

Van Uytven, R. (1976), 'La draperie brabançonne et malinoise du XIIe au XVIIe siècle: grandeur éphémère et décadence', in M. Spallanzani (ed.), *Produzione, commercio e consumo dei panni di lana. Atti della "seconda settimana di studio" (10-16 aprile 1970): Istituto Internazionale di Storia Economica "F. Datini" Prato*, Florence, pp. 85-97.

Van Uytven, R. (1978), 'Les bourgeois dans les villes brabançonnes au XIIIe siècle', in A. Dierkens (ed.), *Bourgeois et littérature bourgeoise dans les anciens Pays-Bas au XIIIe siècle*, Brussel.

Van Uytven, R. (1980a) *Leuven. "De beste stad van Brabant". Deel I: De geschiedenis van het stadsgewest Leuven tot omstreeks 1600*, Leuven.

Van Uytven, R. (1980b), 'Sociale groepen, juridische en politieke structuren', in R. Van Uytven (ed.), *Leuven: de beste stad van Brabant*, Leuven.

Van Uytven, R. (1982), 'Stadsgeschiedenis in het Noorden en het Zuiden', in P.J. Blok et al. (eds), *Algemene geschiedenis der Nederlanden*, vol. 2, Bussum, pp. 188-253.

Van Uytven, R. (ed.) (1991), *De geschiedenis van Mechelen. Van heerlijkheid tot stadsgewest*, Tielt.

Van Vaeck, M. (1997), 'Beelden van omhoog. Hansches 17de-eeuwse plafonddecoraties in stucwerk in de kastelen van Horst, Modave en Beaulieu en in het Gentse Brouwershuis', *Monumenten & Landschappen*, 16.

Van Werveke, H. (1942), 'Ambachten en erfelijkheid', *Mededeelingen van de Koninklijke Vlaamsche Academie voor wetenschappen, Letteren en Schoone Kunsten van België, Klasse der Letteren, en der Moreele en Staatkundige Wetenschappen*, 4, pp. 5-26.

Van Werveke, H. (1943), 'De medezeggenschap van de knapen (gezellen) in de middeleeuwsche ambachten', *Mededeelingen van de Koninklijke Vlaamse Academie voor Wetenschappen, Letteren en Schoone Kunsten van België, Klasse der Letteren*, 5.

Van Werveke, H. (1947), *Gent. Schets van een sociale geschiedenis*, Gent.

Van Werveke, H. (1951), 'Introduction historique', in G. De Poerck (ed.), *La draperie médiévale en Flandre et en Artois. Technique et terminologie*, Brugge, pp. 7-25.

Vandamme, E. (ed.) (1988), *Catalogus schilderkunst oude meesters. Koninklijk Museum voor Schone Kunsten Antwerpen, departement oude meesters*, Antwerpen.

Vandewalle, A. (1985), 'De Brugse schoenmakers en timmerlieden in het ambachtswezen (13de-19de eeuw)', in A. Vandewalle and D. Marechal (eds), *De Brugse schoenmakers en timmerlieden. De ambachten en hun huizen, 14de-20ste eeuw*, Brugge, pp. 5-14.

Vandewalle, A. (1999), 'De Brugse stadsmagistraat en de deelname van de ambachten aan het bestuur, 14de-15de eeuw', in W. Prevenier en B. Augustyn (eds), *De Vlaamse instellingen tijdens het Ancien Régime: recent onderzoek in nieuw perspectief*, Brussel, pp. 27-40.

Vastesaeger, S. (1998), *Vrouwen in ambachten in Brussel in de achttiende eeuw*, unpublished MA-thesis Vrije Universiteit Brussel.

Veblen, T. (1899), *Theory of the Leisure Class*, New York.

Verbeemen, J. (1955), 'Steden der Antwerpse Kempen in 1755. Hun demografische en economische toestand', *Oudheid en Kunst*, 38, pp. 145-63.

Verbeemen, J. (1956), 'De werking van economische factoren op de stedelijke demografie der XVIIe en der XVIIIe eeuw in de Zuidelijke Nederlanden', *Belgisch Tijdschrift voor Filologie en Geschiedenis*, 34, pp. 680-700.

Verbeemen, J. (1956), 'De Mechelse economie rond 1740', *Tijdschrift voor Geschiedenis en Folklore*, 19, pp. 79-86.

Verbrugge, A. (1996), 'De garderobe', *De blinde hertog. Louis Engelbert van Arenberg & zijn tijd, 1750-1820*, Brussels, pp. 151-9.

Verhavert, J. (1940), *Het ambachtswezen te Leuven tot circa 1500*, Leuven.

Verhulst, A. (1972), 'La laine indigène dans les anciens Pays-Bas entre le XIIe et le XVIIe siècle. Mise en oeuvre industrielle, production et commerce', *Revue Historique*, 96, pp. 281-322.

Verhulst, A. (1990), *Précis d'histoire rurale de la Belgique*, Brussel.

Verhulst, A. (1999), *The Rise of Cities in North-West Europe*, Cambridge.

Verkerk, C.L. (1992), *Coulissen van de macht. Een sociaal-institutionele studie betreffende de samenstelling van het bestuur van Arnhem in de middeleeuwen en een bijdrage tot de studie van stedelijke elitevorming*, Hilversum.

Verleysen, F. (2000), *Ambachten en Contrareformatie. Godsdienstige aspecten van de corporatieve wereld na de val van Antwerpen (1585-1633)*, unpublished MA-thesis, Universiteit Gent.

Verleysen, F. (2001), 'Pretense Confrerieën? Devotie als communicatie in de Antwerpse corporatieve wereld na 1585', *Tijdschrift voor Sociale Geschiedenis*, 27, pp. 153-74.

Vermaut, J. (1974), *De textielnijverheid in Brugge en op het platteland in westelijk Vlaanderen voor 1800. Konjunktuurverloop, organisatie en sociale verhoudingen*, unpublished PhD-thesis, Universiteit Gent.

Vermaut, J. (1988), 'Structural Transformation in a Textile Centre: Bruges from the Sixteenth to the Nineteenth Century', in H. Van der Wee (ed.), *The Rise and Decline of Urban Industries in Italy and the Low Countries (Late Middle Ages — Early Modern Times)*, Leuven, pp. 187-205.

Vermeersch, V. (1988), 'Gilden en Ambachten', *Museumpromenade*, 2, Bruges, pp. 23-33.

Verschelde, K. (1863), *De kathedrale van Sint Salvator te Brugge*, Brugge.

Vijlbrief, I. (1950), *Van anti-aristocratie tot democratie. Een bijdrage tot de politieke en sociale geschiedenis der stad Utrecht*, Amsterdam.

Vogel, J. (1986), 'De zijdelintindustrie te Haarlem, 1663-1780', *Jaarboek voor Geschiedenis van Bedrijf en Techniek*, 3, pp. 76-91.

Vollenhoven, A. van (1923), *Ambachten en neringen in Dordrecht*, 's-Gravenhage.

Vos, P.D. de, (1913), *De voormalige kloosters en liefdadige instellingen te Zierikzee*, Zierikzee.

Vries, B. de, J. Lucassen, P. Lourens and H. Nijboer (2003), 'Het economische leven: spectaculair succes en diep verval', in S. Groenveld (ed.), *Leiden. De Geschiedenis van een Hollandse stad*, vol. 2, 1574-1795, Leiden, pp. 84-107.

Vries, J. de (1984), *European Urbanisation, 1500-1800*, London.

Vries, J. de, and A. van der Woude (1997), *The First Modern Economy. Success, Failure, and Perseverance of the Dutch Economy, 1500-1815*, Cambridge.

Warnkoenig, L.A. and Gheldof, A. (1851), 'Histoire de la Flandre et de ses institutions civiles et politique jusqu'à l'année 1305', *Histoire constitutionelle et administrative de la ville de Bruges et du pays du Franc, jusqu'au XIVe siècle*, vol. 4, Brussel.

Weber, M. (1961), *General Economic History*, translated by Frank H. Knight, New York.

Weber, M. (1964), *L'ethique protestante et l'esprit du capitalisme*, Paris.

Wellens, J.T.J. (1784), *Algemeyne verzaemelinge van de werken*, Antwerpen.

Wertheim-Gijse Weenink, A.H. (1984), 'Een kwarteeuw burgerverzet in de beide Nederlanden (1698-1719). Voorspel van de "democratische revoluties"', *Bijdragen en Mededelingen betreffende de Geschiedenis der Nederlanden*, 99, pp. 408-34.

Wesoly, K. (1985), *Lehrlinge und Handwerksgesellen am Mittelrhein. Ihre soziale Lage und ihre Organisation von 14. bis ins 17. Jahrhundert*, Frankfurt/Main.

Wijnne, H.A. (1865), *Handel en ontwikkeling van stad en provincie Groningen, geschiedkundig beschouwd*, Groningen.

Wijsenbeek, T. (1987a), 'Van pristeersters en posituées. Beroepen van vrouwen in Delft en Den Haag tijdens de achttiende eeuw', *Jaarboek voor vrouwengeschiedenis*, 8, pp. 173-202.

Wijsenbeek, T. (1987b), *Achter de gevels van Delft, Bezit en bestaan van rijk en arme in een periode van achteruitgang (1700-1800)*, Hilversum.

Willem, C. (1995), *Ambachtelijke zekerheid. Sociale voorzieningen bij negen ambachten in het achttiende-eeuwse Gent*, unpublished MA-thesis, Universiteit Gent.

Wiskerke, C. (1938), *De afschaffing der gilden in Nederland*, Amsterdam.

Woude, A.M. van der (1980), 'Demografische ontwikkeling van de Noordelijke Nederlanden 1500-1800', in D.P. Blok (ed.), *Algemene Geschiedenis der Nederlanden*, vol. 5, Haarlem, pp. 102-68.

Woude, A.M. van der (1994), 'Sex Ratio and Female Labour Participation in the Dutch Republic', in A. Fauve-Chamoux and S. Sogner (eds), *Socio-economic consequences of sex-ratios in historical perspective, 1500-1900 Proceedings of the 11th International Economic History Congress*, Milan.

Wyffels, C. (1951), *De oorsprong der ambachten in Vlaanderen en Brabant*, Verhandelingen van de Koninklijk Vlaamse Academie voor Wetenschappen, Letteren en Schone Kunsten van België, Klasse der Letteren, vol. 13, Brussel.

Xhayet, G. (1994), 'Le rôle politique des métiers liégeois à la fin du Moyen Age' in J.P. Sosson (ed.), *Les métiers au Moyen Age. Aspects économiques et sociaux*, Louvain-la-Neuve, pp. 361-78.

Yntema, R.J. (1994), 'Tot welvaren der brouwers. Gilden en brouwersorganisaties in de 17de en 18de eeuw', in R.E. Kistemaker and V.T. vn Vilsteren (eds), *Bier. Geschiedenis van een volksdrank*, Amsterdam, pp. 118-31.

Yntema, R.J. (1995), 'Entrepreneurship and Technological Change in Holland's Brewing Industry, 1500-1580', in C. Lesger and L. Noordegraaf (eds), *Entrepreneurs and entrepreneurship in Early Modern Times. Merchants and Industrialists within the Orbit of the Dutch Staple Market*, 's-Gravenhage, pp. 185-201.

Zanden, J.L. van (1985), 'Kosten van levensonderhoud en loonvorming in Holland en Oost-Nederland, 1600-1850. De voorbeelden van Kampen en Alkmaar', *Tijdschrift voor Sociale Geschiedenis*, 11, pp. 309-23.

Zanden, J.L van (1993a), 'Holland en de Zuidelijke Nederlanden in de periode 1500-1750: divergerende ontwikkelingen of voortgaande economische integratie?, in E. Aerts et al. (eds), *Studia Historica Oeconomica. Liber Amicorum Herman van der Wee*, Leuven, pp. 357-67.

Zanden, J.L. van (1993b), *The Rise and Decline of Holland's Economy: Merchant Capitalism and the Labour Market*, Manchester, New York.

Zeiler, F.D. (1994), '"Men segt, dat hier so een gilde is…". Semi- en buitenstedelijke gilden in Noordwest-Overijssel in de zeventiende en achttiende eeuw', *NEHA-Jaarboek voor economische, bedrijfs- en techniekgeschiedenis*, 57, pp. 91-106.

Zelck, F. (1988), 'De Staten van Brabant op het einde van het ancien régime: hun invloed op de besluitvorming op sociaal-economisch gebied (1770-1794)' in J. Craeybeckx and F. Daelemans (eds), *Bijdragen tot de Geschiedenis van Vlaanderen en Brabant. Sociaal en Economisch*, vol. 3, Brussel.

Zemon Davis, N. (1981), 'The Sacred and the Body Social in Sixteenth-Century Lyon', *Past and Present*, no. 90, pp. 40-70.

Ziekenfondsen (1896) *in Nederland: rapport uitgebracht door eene commissie van onderzoek*, Amsterdam.

Zweite, A. (1980), *Marten de Vos als Maler*, Berlin.

Index of industries and professions

Index of geographical names